DATE DUE

Creativity and Its Discontents

Creativity and Its Discontents

China's Creative Industries and
Intellectual Property Rights Offenses

Laikwan Pang

Duke University Press
Durham and London 2012

© 2012 Duke University Press
All rights reserved
Printed in the United States of America
on acid-free paper ∞
Typeset in Minion and Hypatia Sans
by Tseng Information Systems, Inc.

Library of Congress Cataloging-in-Publication Data
appear on the last printed page of this book.

Duke University Press gratefully acknowledges
the support of the Chiang Ching-Kuo Foundation
for International Scholarly Exchange, which provided
funds toward the production of this book.

Contents

Acknowledgments

It took me a long time to come up with a page of acknowledgments for my first book. But the list of people I feel obliged to thank grows as my research broadens, and I realize that the older I get, the more people I am indebted to. This is a good feeling.

Several scholars have read parts of the manuscript in different stages and offered me their valuable comments and criticisms. They include Sandra Luft, Arif Dirlik, Helen Grace, Stefano Harney, Francis Ching-Wah Yip, Winnie Wong, and the anonymous reviewers at *positions*, *Social Text*, *Theory, Culture and Society*, and Hong Kong University Press. My love and gratitude goes particularly to Sandra, who first introduced me to the world of theories and taught me that doing scholarship is ultimately a leap of faith. I did not know how much I was indebted to her teaching until I began this project, and her lessons will continue to enrich my scholarly attempts in the years to come. Among others, Jane Gaines, Michael Dutton, Lisa Rofel, Meaghan Morris, and Rey Chow have genuinely believed in my endeavor, giving me the needed courage to embark on this almost directionless academic journey. I also want to thank those artists, curators, and filmmakers, including Leung Mee Ping, Li Xianting, Li Feixue, Wang Yan, Zhang Tingjun, and a number of young film directors in Hong Kong whose identities I would like to keep anonymous, who have generously shared with me their works, future ambitions, and current frustrations. Their real-life experiences as creative agents are essential for me to understand the ways creativity is practiced and embedded in their social conditions.

Earlier versions of chapters of this book were presented in invited lectures at Hong Kong Baptist University, National Taiwan University, Vanderbilt University, New York University, Columbia University, University of Washington, and Lancaster University. Here I must thank Emilie Yueh-yu Yeh, Tsung-yi Michelle Huang, Ling Hon Lam, Zhen Zhang, Rebecca Karl, Weihong Bao,

Yomi Braester, and Adrian MacKenzie for their kind invitations. I also thank Chris Berry, Nitin Govil, Olivia Khoo, and Sean Metzger for inviting me to conferences in London, New Delhi, and Sydney, which gave me the fuel I needed to continue the project. I am grateful for all the questions and comments from participants in these and other events where I presented parts of this manuscript. I particularly want to thank those participants in the *boundary 2* Hong Kong conference in 2006 who have shown their support and endorsed this research when it was still in its formative stage. The anonymous reviewers of Duke University Press have generously shared with me their scholarship and expertise, pointing out the weaknesses and bias of my previous draft and reminding me what else needed to be read. All the mistakes still contained in this version, of course, are mine.

A good part of the manuscript was written during my sabbatical at New York University, and I would like to thank NYU's Department of East Asian Studies for hosting my stay, and specifically Rebecca Karl for her belief in my work and her unyielding friendship. Among others, Angela Zito, Zhen Zhang, Magnus Fiskesjö, Qian Zhu, Lorraine Wong, Jane Gaines, and Weihong Bao kindly welcomed my family as theirs. I thank Reynolds Smith, Ken Wissoker, and other colleagues of Duke University Press for bringing this manuscript to print, and I sincerely appreciate the careful and constructive copy-editing of Dawn Ollila and Fiona Ng. Wu Zhi, Cui Yanli, Leung Mee Ping, Dominique Chiu, Adele Wong, Zhang Weiping, and the Cai Studio helped me with some of the figures in the book. Jeannie Simms and Fiona Ng never stop giving me the illusion that my work is important. They are dear to me.

Some of the research carried out for this book was made possible by the generous support of the Hong Kong Research Grant Council and the Chinese University of Hong Kong. My research also benefited from the contributions of my research assistants at various stages; they include Amy Li, Olive Cheung, Zhou Weiwei, Yeung Yang, and Joseph Li. The colleagues and students at the Chinese University of Hong Kong, my home institute, support my work, accept my weaknesses, and nourish my intellectual and emotional growth. Angela Wong continues to be my dearest friend and sister, who never reserves her love and care for people around her. I am indebted to Helen Grace for the many intelligent insights she has shared with me, which directly inform my studies. I would particularly like to take this chance to salute my research students. They inspire me to learn, to respect, and to be gentle. I also thank them for trusting me as a friend and allowing me to be a part, however small, of their lives. I am proud of every one of them, and humbly hope for the vice versa.

I live under the shelter made up of the affection and tolerance of Kwai-cheung Lo, my husband, as well as the cheerfulness of my sons, Haven and Hayden. My academic career would not be possible without their understanding, compassion, and support. As I know I will never be able to pay back what they have given me, let me be reminded how fortunate I am to be a part of this family.

This research began where my earlier book on movie piracy ended, when I realized how ignorant I was about the related fields and how important intellectual property rights are to the understanding of today's global capitalism. But I had no idea where I was heading, knowing how extensive the scope of this research could be, which also excites me exceedingly. Those who know my work are familiar with my interdisciplinary approach, which does not reflect any grand academic mission but simply my impulsive tendency to venture into areas with which I am not familiar. To quote Joshua Goldstein's sympathetic review on my previous book, "The importance of Pang's book lies not in her theorizations of Chinese modern subjectivities but, rather, in her daring to leave her comfort zone (film studies) to tackle the intertextual. . . . As such, Pang is both blessed and cursed" ("The Distorting Mirror," 519). I am sure this book is even more cursed than my earlier one in this regard, and in the pages to come specialists might find lots of academic holes and too many inadequate conclusions reached without full scholarly justification. But I also hope that readers will find my academic journey as recorded in this book a delightful one that deserves your company. Needless to say, I thank all readers who have found my work worthy of reading.

The earlier versions of chapters 3, 4, 7, and 8 appeared in the following publications, respectively: "The Labor Factor in the Creative Economy: A Marxist Reading," *Social Text* 99 (Summer 2009), 55–76; "Depoliticization through Cultural Policy and Intellectual Property Rights: The Case of Lijiang in China," *positions*, forthcoming; "The Transgression of Sharing and Copying: Pirating Japanese Animation in China," in *Cultural Studies and Cultural Industries in Northeast Asia: What a Difference a Region Makes*, ed. Chris Berry, Jonathan D. Mackintosh, and Nicola Liscutin (Hong Kong: Hong Kong University Press, 2009), 119–34; and "'China Who Makes and Fakes': A Semiotics of the Counterfeit," *Theory, Culture and Society* 25, no. 6 (2008), 115–38. A small part of chapter 5 appeared in *Futures of Chinese Cinema: Technologies and Temporalities in Chinese Screen Cultures*, ed. Sean Metzger and Olivia Khoo (Bristol: Intellect Books, 2008). I thank these publications for granting me the rights to publish updated versions of these essays.

Introduction

A global innovation and design consultancy firm based in Palo Alto, IDEO, has been ranked in the top twenty-five most innovative companies by *Business Week*; most impressive, it does consulting work for all the other twenty-four companies on the list.[1] The company designed Apple's first mouse and the Palm V PDA, and it also engages in many nonprofit activities, such as developing a social marketing campaign for Acumen Fund to spread awareness in India and Kenya about the importance of safe drinking water.[2] Like almost all global firms, IDEO is also trying to expand its business in China, which, however, is reportedly not faring well. As IDEO's chairman David Kelley says, "There will be one day when the China market becomes ready for us."[3] Obviously there is something incongruent between the practices of this allegedly "most innovative" global firm and China's own situation.

A recent issue of IDEO's online journal is devoted to China's *shanzhai* culture, citing several examples of how creativity is practiced in China. "Shanzhai," a concept I discuss in chapter 9, is a popular Chinese term referring to copycat designs of brand-name products, which often introduce something new to cater to the specific needs of potential niche clients. For example, one man customized his new QQ, the cheap Chinese version of the economical GM Sparkle, with a Mercedes emblem, so that he can brag to his fellow villagers that he is a successful businessman. Another delivered his history lectures on the Internet, where they have been watched more than half a million times, after the national television station CCTV declined his proposal for a series because he is not a professor. The authors of the article that offers these examples comment that it is such *shanzhai* grassroots humor that will attract many Chinese consumers, "people who work hard, whose lives are improving, and who are optimistic about the future."[4] Though admiring the grassroots creativity found in China, IDEO has not been able to enter that market. Asked to comment on the new China market, IDEO's Asia Pacific CEO Li Ruizhe states, "There are 1.3 billion people in China. We don't see them as ordinary masses, but each one of them is an entrepreneur, 1.3 billion entrepreneurs. We are seeing consumers modifying their newly acquired items to make them fit one's need. I am really happy to see a new open design culture developing in China, and everyone can design."[5] The enigma is how this elite global innovation firm can continue to charge an astronomical service fee if everybody can innovate like them. Trying to understand the ways creativity is conceptualized and practiced in contemporary China within a global context is a main goal of this book.

As IDEO continues to expand across nations, across sectors, and across classes, it is clear that innovation has become the ubiquitous object of desire globally. But IDEO's sincere attempt, though in vain, to come to terms with China's shanzhai culture, which made the country "unready" for IDEO, demonstrates the company's understanding of creativity: everyone can create, yet only a very small group of global elites, with expensive research, can do it well. Our economic globalization is composed not only of the legacies of Microsoft and the iPhone, but also an increasing demand for creativity that can attract attention to ever new services and commodities, be they profit-making or charity. But how to understand and "own" creativity continues to be a mystery. Creativity and economy are now so intertwined that no social sector or operation can survive without absorbing both organically into their overall profile and undertaking. Worse, this rhetoric of creativity has infiltrated not only the public sector and the commercial world, but it has impacted people's self-management and identity. The more powerful creativity has become, the more it escapes definition.

This fetishization of creativity is not a new phenomenon, but its intensification is particularly observable in the past ten or twenty years, not only in the design and advertising industries but also in production and management of all sorts. Accordingly a wide range of related business phenomena have appeared, and they aim to provide new workplace environments emphasizing the cultivation of creativity and to teach individuals how to be creative.[6] Nowadays even the service industry is characterized by constant innovation; new ideas and methods are demanded not only to cater to the ever evolving market environment but also to counteract copying by competitors.[7] Creativity is now required from educators, performers, managers, engineers, and service providers of all kinds. This invasive spread of desire for creativity is generally understood as a result of the rise of the creative economy.

Like many scholars of creative industries, John Howkins defines the creative economy as constituted by various industries that produce intellectual property rights (IPR) products.[8] The creative economy and IPR are in fact twin concepts, in the sense that the creative economy is made up of the transactions of products that qualify for IPR protections,[9] and the notion of "creativity" in this economy is embodied in some kind of exchangeable IPR goods or services. In the logic of the creative economy, creativity is not conceptualized as the generation and communication of symbolic meanings, because meanings cannot be easily quantified and exchanged; instead creativity is reified as intellectual property which the rights holders own and can benefit from. The term "creative economy" is sometimes used interchangeably with other, related terms, such as new economy, digital economy, experience economy, knowledge economy, and information economy, which I will not differentiate here.[10] But it is worth pointing out that the developed world is said to be evolving from a knowledge economy to a creative economy, suggesting the superiority of the latter to the former.[11] However, in spite of the increasingly wide circulation of the concept, other than the actual effects of IPR, the definition of the creative economy and creativity remains obscure.

Howkins suggests Bob Geldof, the famous Irish singer and songwriter, as a representative figure of this new culture. Howkins describes how Geldof is most creative when he is most depressed, and he quotes Geldof's hazy language to define creativity: "Depression is a state of tiredness where the foreconscious clashes constantly with the subconscious. It is at this woozy moment, that unconnected or seemingly unconnected moment, when you leap across the synapses."[12] Fetishizing and mystifying such moments of trance and abstraction, Howkins concludes his study of Geldof, not surprisingly, with a discussion of how much money Geldof has made, although Howkins points only to the returns from the Live Aid concerts instead of profits made directly from his albums, most likely to maintain the overall humanistic aura of the creative economy discourse in his book. In the business of popular music, what matters is as much inspiration as the selling of the output of such magical and fetishized moments; while profit is the ultimate goal, this goal can be realized only by the mystification of creativity. More precisely, the creative economy operates under the dual mechanisms of managing and confusing creativity, a concept which must remain unclear to facilitate its valorization.

Generally speaking, the term "creative economy" appears in two different domains. In policy discourse creative economy is almost entirely defined by the support of creative industries, whereas in the business world creativity is understood and rendered not only as products but more pluralistically as management skills, marketing strategies, and company image. Academically, different disciplines chart and reflect on these developments in the policy and the business domains, and a unique strain of creative industries scholarship has been developing vigorously in the past few years. Two main approaches have been developed in this scholarship. The first approach embraces the creative economy as an advanced socioeconomic development that should be supported or guided by proper policy; the creative economy discussed in these studies is often based on products produced by creative industries. This strain of scholarship, in other words, is closely related to policy studies and is intended to criticize and supplement existing policy or to drive new policy-making.[13] While the previous cultural industries approach focused more on the industries' ideologically autonomous status rather than their economic values,[14] the creative industries scholarship tends to emphasize the fortification of industrial structure, product diversity, and reception democracy. The creative economy itself is often understood as a natural stage of economic development, one which countries and people should strive to attain.[15] It is the work not of a single genius but of a network of people with related skills; it requires new skills and rhetoric and it is transnational.[16] Scholars in this strain tend to celebrate risk taking, start-up entrepreneurialism, increasingly diversified niche marketing, and the pluralization of styles, whose unstable nature feeds precisely on the fussy concepts of creativity.

The second main approach to the creative economy takes a more critical stance, focusing specifically on the workers involved. Some critics argue that the creative economy provides a new, congenial environment for workers who are motivated not only by salary but also by passion;[17] however, others are increasingly wary of the exploitation involved. There are new employment patterns in the new creative economy that allow management to obscure labor exploitation under the guise of flexible work hours and freelance employment and that put workers' career stability, job prospects, and fringe benefits in jeopardy.[18] While many in the new generation of workers identify with this new workplace freedom, workers are also responsible for their own career development and security; during layoffs, therefore, people are quickly disillusioned with workplace democracy.[19] It is also argued that in the creative economy production and consumption merge, and those participating increasingly organize and understand their lives according to late capitalist logic. There is a particular "club culture" lifestyle associated with this new class of creative workers, which is at heart extremely discriminatory and alienating.[20] Many scholars remind us of the enduring value of Marxist analysis in understanding this current stage of economic development.[21] Other critical scholars take non-Marxist positions: some focus on exploring how government initiatives can provide a better working environment for these new cultural workers; others promote the democratization of creativity to discourage the monopolization of creative discourse.[22] In general, this strain of scholarship is motivated not so much by the desire to advance the new economy but by the economy's effects of hegemony and exploitation; these scholars believe there is a need to articulate a new counter-rhetoric to expose and fight against this new social structure, whose neoliberal outlook hides new, more severe forms of exploitation.

These approaches articulate opposite appraisals of the new structure: the creative economy provides a bright future toward which people should strive, or the creative economy promotes new class conflicts and abuses that make the world even more unfair. I identify more closely with the second approach and share much of the critical wariness of the propensity for class exploitation in the creative economy. But I find scholars' emphasis on society and the resultant avoidance of the exploration of creativity as a concept and a practice running the risk of complicity with the logic of the creative economy, which depends heavily on the abstract quality of creativity. It is my aim in this book to demystify and deconstruct such fetishization of creativity. I argue that creativity features two mutually conditioning dimensions: it is a result of social praxis that demands labor, and it is also a form of textuality that proliferates on its own. As a form of social praxis, creativity needs people, but not in the sense of lone individuals; rather, creative acts involve a community, with people influencing, observing, and copying each other (discussed in chapter 2). As a form of textuality, creativity should be understood as both construction and destruction; it operates on its own and resembles how cultures and history evolve (discussed in chapters 1 and 3). The two seemingly conflicting understandings of creativity in fact mutually legitimate and confine each other. I believe that a careful analysis of the dynamics between these two forces not only helps us understand the operation of the current creative economy, but also offers us a critical position to envision an alternative reading of creativity beyond the creative economy model.

On the one hand, creativity is democratized and instrumentalized, as when people believe that problem solving requires creative input, and such kinds of creativity can be cultivated in specific ways.[23] Human beings' creative faculty is now understood as universal: everyone can be an artist, and everything can be a product of art, although what makes an art or a design "cool" is mostly arbitrary. This understanding has conjured a new type of quasi-democracy, which is based not on political participation but on free access to creativity;

although everybody can be creative and everybody can consume creative products according to their individual tastes, such abilities must be cultivated. In the past decade, there has been an unprecedented urge for education reform all over the world, shifting pedagogical emphases from the transmission of collective knowledge to the cultivation of individual creative abilities in order to produce subjects who are competitive in the new creative economy.[24] There are many books, self-help kits, and educational programs that claim to help cultivate the creative thinking skills of individuals. Creativity is also pursued as a global means of persuasion and manipulation; those products that are most "creative" are also the ones most successful in persuading the intended consumer, so creativity must be coupled with extensive market research and product testing.

However, this type of new education and management—which aspires to replace, if only partly, traditional disciplinary knowledge with the cultivation of abstract transformative ability—is also highly volatile. We all know that it is very difficult to teach creativity. The lessons of those who claim to teach creativity in schools often only reflect their anger toward the existing framework of compliance, as well as their own desire to escape from or to resist the constraints and frustrations of daily academic life.[25] Creativity continues to be unreachable. The unpredictable and uncontrollable dimension of artistic creativity is held dear by the current post-Fordist consumerism. Although consumers are increasingly seen as discretely informed subjects, their taste is conditioned by the creativity embodied in the commodities they buy. Creativity is often understood as freedom; its emancipation is associated with the rules it breaks, the boundaries it crosses, and the new terrain it opens up. The abstract empowerment brought with the new products that claim to contain such creativity lures people into incessant consumption. Creativity is a highly kinetic concept, implying unlimited potentiality and unknown prospects, and therefore perfect for propelling the continual development of capitalism.

I do not disagree with either of the two common understandings of industrial creativity and artistic creativity, but I urge readers to confront the two contradictory definitions, which both construct and deconstruct the creative economy, at the same time. To launch a productive critique against the creative economy, we need to oppose its instrumentalist tendency, and it is important to emphasize the textual dimension of creativity, in the sense that creativity, like writing, is an open structure based on differences. Emphasizing the essential linkage between creativity and textuality, we can counter the desire for control of the capitalist machine, which closes off the meaning of creativity in order to objectify, manage, engineer, and circulate discrete creative products. At the same time, we should still hold on to creativity's public and social dimension in order to keep it from being mystified by some kind of naturalism, and to rediscover the labor dimension of the creative economy. We tend to understand artistic creativity as a form of radical subjectivism, therefore neglecting other modes of creativity, "such as the creativity sparked by dialogue and collaboration, or the creativity inherent in popular traditions."[26] Rearticulating the communal dimension of creativity, we can avoid fetishizing its subjective and private dimension. In general, it is important to come to terms with both the active and the passive status of creativity (creativity as a subject that runs and as an object being run). Precisely due to its Janus-faced nature, creativity can fuel or topple the creative economy. The creative economy has no teleological direction, and it favors the development of infinite niche markets, reinforcing the myth of ultra-individualism. But the creative economy also demands an industrial structure to organize, incorporate, and produce creativity. In this new set of social conditions, we find the seemingly easy but indeed contested coexistence between the postmodern proliferation of styles and the instrumental exercise of discipline. Precisely because of such internal contradictions, the creative economy also has a propensity to resist itself. The first part of the book (chapters 1 to 3) is dedicated to exploring these dynamics.

The Case of China

Parallel to the dual—spontaneous and industrial—dimensions of creativity, I would argue that there is a natural affinity between creating and copying, in spite of our privileging of the former over the latter. The second part of the book (chapters 4 through 9) examines actual situations of creating and copying in China, in terms of both the burgeoning development of the creative industries and its discontents, specifically IPR offenses. These piracy and counterfeiting activities, I believe, most pertinently reveal the artistic and collective dynamic of creativity that is beyond IPR's logic. China provides many interesting case studies that allow an intimate exploration of the prevalence and the demise of the creative economy,[27] but my focus on China does not amount to an assumption of unity in contemporary Chinese culture—quite the contrary. The country's chaotic capitalization experiences are germane to the development of the creative economy and also render its problems visible.

As Michael Keane aptly explains, there is nationwide enthusiasm about the transition from "Made in China" to "Created in China."[28] The People's Republic of China central and provincial governments at all levels have shown keen interest in the notion of creativity, from supporting creative industries in order to "upgrade" the economy, to pursuing regional or city branding to provide positive images and cultural capital.[29] Up until now the country's economic miracle has been based largely on its cheap labor, and a vast majority of its people will continue to stay poor in this "world factory" economy. Sweatshops can drive the development of the national economy only to a degree, and there is always competition from other developing countries, which may have even lower labor costs. In fact there is already a decline in foreign investments in the Chinese manufacturing sector, and transnational manufacturers are quick to move their factories at any sign of business risk.[30] Between 2007 and 2008, although the utilized foreign direct investment (FDI) in China in actual money terms continued to rise, the number of projects dropped substantially, by 27.3 percent.[31] The government must find ways to lessen the national economy's heavy reliance on labor-intensive manufacturing based on FDI; the development of local creative industries is an extremely attractive alternative. Creative industries involve lower investment costs, high profit yields, and few environmental problems. An economy based on innovation is also seen as an effective means to escape the global dominance of the developed world. If *gaige kaifang* 改革開放 (reform and open) was the dominant policy principle of the PRC government in the 1980s and 1990s, the recent Hu Jintao government has shifted its attention to *gaige chuangxin* 改革創新 (reform and innovation), emphasizing the importance of innovation and the production of the new.[32]

In the West the discourse of creative industry began with policymakers trying to pool resources for two major cultural sectors, each with specific industrial demands. The established media conglomerates, which already enjoy their market share and privileges, press for the protection of their existing interests, while the smaller enterprises and individual artists and designers, who are generally considered the more vigorous components of the creative economy, actively demand government's special cultivation, often in hope of offsetting the existing monopoly enjoyed by established media and cultural industries. In the case of China, because the government is still the key rule setter, its creative economy arises from the intense overlap of interests between the private sectors and the state. While many creative practitioners sincerely believe in the cultural value of their work, there are also many opportunistic investors and officials who simply want to hop on the fast train for a quick profit. The liberal and fleeting nature of the creative economy has a special affinity with present-day China, where we are seeing the pursuit of the creative economy not only in rich urban areas but all over the country.

The development of proper policy protections is a legitimate demand for many creative workers who simply try to make a living from their work, but the field of culture has also become a happy hunting ground for officials and businessmen alike, who take advantage of unstable policy and resultant gray areas. In today's China we have seen the odd but happy marriage between real estate and the fine arts, the complete dematerialization of architecture and even road systems that are conceptualized entirely as images, and the simultaneous salutation and trivialization of IPR concepts. Politicians and capitalists find themselves working together intimately in the construction of the creative economy, where both money and image can be produced by the manipulation of culture.

In spite of this national privileging of innovation, many critics still characterize the development of China's creative economy and creative industries as slow. It is widely argued that the level of China's state control over cultural industries is still too high—and its marketization level is still too low—for the current creative industries model to succeed there.[33] The development of creative industries is considered dependent upon a socioeconomic environment allowing small enterprises and freelance producers to work independently and creatively. This is certainly true, but creative industries developing from the bottom up and demanding a liberal cultural environment to survive might be only one aspect of the whole picture. The more dispersed the modes of cultural production in creative industries are encouraged and fed upon, the more they need new mechanisms to facilitate control.[34] As I mentioned, the creative industries rely heavily on the IPR regime and need committed support from powerful global institutions, like the World Trade Organization (WTO), in order to prevail. The PRC government might still fear liberalization, but it also actively adapts to the global IPR environment to realize the infrastructure of the creative economy (see chapter 4). The number of IPR litigations has risen rapidly, for example, in Shanghai's courts. In 2008 they accepted 1,757 IPR-related cases and resolved 1,634; this was 43.1 and 33.2 percent, respectively, higher than in the previous year. More than 15 percent of cases involve overseas parties, mostly from the United States, Britain, Japan, and Germany.[35] The recent agreement between Disney and Shanghai to build the world's sixth Disney theme park in the city is also based partly on the city's determination to correct its lax IPR protections. All this reveals less about the actual IPR infringement situation in China than the country's willingness to embrace international rules.

Recently innovation has been hailed not only as the driver of the national economy but as the source of cultural pride, conflating political, aesthetic, and economic values. Two mainland scholars claim, "The products produced by industries associated with creativity are the highest civilization achievements of a nation or a region."[36] It is here we see the intersection of such divergent discourses as soft power, nationalism, and neoliberal capitalism. Simply, soft power and cultural nationalism exploit culture for political ends, while the creative economy extracts economic values from culture. Although they seem to operate in and for different arenas, the discourses heavily influence each other.

The notion of soft power was first introduced by Joseph Nye describing an American power asset: the United States has the ability to get others to want what it wants, and this soft power, he argues, arises from America's values and its attractive culture.[37] Attracted by Nye's arguments and U.S. diplomatic power in general, many governments, including the PRC, began to invest in developing their own soft power in the past ten years. Some states tap into the already prominent transnational cultural traffic to improve the image of their country, such as South Korea's capitalization of the recent Korean cultural wave in Asia; others hold on to or engineer selected cultural institutions to promote a sense of cultural superiority, as shown in the many Confucius institutes planted by the PRC all over the world.[38] While soft power is primarily a diplomatic concept describing a nation's external influences, nationalism refers to the internal identification of the people with the nation, which guarantees the totality of the state's geographic and ideological sovereignty. But increasingly nationalism relies on soft power to promote people's sense of belonging domestically or in the diaspora, as seen in the magical effects of the recent spectacular Opening Ceremony of the Beijing Olympics on Chinese people all over the world. Chinese nationalism can be fueled when the Chinese people feel that they are respected and esteemed internationally, both in terms of their cultural supremacy and the wealth the country is accruing. Culture and economy, internal identification and external influences, all impinge on each other.

In her studies of China's advertising culture, Jing Wang compares Saatchi and Saatchi's vision of branding China and Joshua Cooper Ramo's "The Beijing Consensus," both of which stress the incorporation of innovation as a national attribute of China. Wang recommends that the commercial and political discourses learn from each other to make way for synergies, in order to "succeed in destigmatizing the name of China and turning it into a hot ticket on the international market place."[39] However attractive such ideas are to different sectors in China, we should not remain uncritical of the forged relationships among concepts such as innovation, branding, and national strength. Here the discourses of soft power and nationalism are facilitated by economic success, and it is increasingly impossible to separate the interests of transnational firms like Saatchi and Saatchi from those of the Beijing government. The notions of innovation and creativity are co-opted into a story about perpetual competitiveness with the West, materialized spectacularly, for example, in bold architectural and urban designs.[40] These grand architectures contribute to China's soft power and nationalism, even though they are also signs of the late capitalist order that dematerialize dwelling and the everyday life.

Arif Dirlik has criticized the fact that embedded in the celebration of national innovation is the fetishization of innovation, which has gained a life of its own, free from contamination by social and political goals.[41] Pertinent as it is, we also need to analyze the politicization of the idea of innovation. We must understand the heavy negotiations behind it: innovation is safe as long as it is understood as politically neutral technological development; it becomes dangerous when it promotes radical changes. This intricacy is revealed in the concept of national cultural security (國家文化安全 *guojia wenhua anquan*). The concept was first announced by President Hu Jintao in August 2003, when the Political Bureau of the Communist Party held its regular collective study, this time specifically on the topic of cultural industries.[42] In his speech accompanying the workshop, which focused primarily on the economic values of culture, Hu emphasized culture's political dimensions: "We need to raise the flag of Socialist culture high. We cannot just copy cultural concepts [from the West], neither can we simply mimic their development models. We are determined to prevent fraudulent and regressive cultural ideas from corrupting the mind of our people, in order to guarantee our national cultural security and social stability."[43] The notion of "cultural security" was thus officially endorsed by the Fourth Plenary Session of the Sixteenth Central Committee of the Communist Party of China as one of the four national securities, along with political security, economic security, and information security.[44]

The notion is most elaborately followed up in a book written by the leading mainland creative industries scholar, Hu Huilin. In spite of his criticism of the government's bureaucratization and heavy management style, which suffocate the development of culture, Hu Huilin's real target is American culture: U.S. soft power is potentially dangerous to China, so China must promote its own, continually producing new cultural products for the Chinese markets. Hu argues that the U.S. is using its cultural imperialist power to transform people's value systems and indirectly interfere with other countries' sovereignty. In order to safeguard the cultural security of the country against the new cultural imperialism, China must construct a "national cultural security management system," composed of a set of "objective indicators" which can help the government monitor and provide early warning of foreign cultural invasions.[45]

This notion of national cultural security helps us further understand and expound on Dirlik's criticism of the depoliticization tendency of the innovation discourse. National cultural security is clearly a political notion, but it does not repoliticize the creative economy in a way that challenges late capitalism. Advocating both protectionism for fending off foreign culture and the exportation of China's cultural content, the ultimate political agenda of the innovation discourse is to support cultural nationalism and enhance China's own soft power, while disempowering the people from thinking against the state. The development of the creative industries is advantageous only when it encourages the consumption of China's national culture by Chinese people and foreigners, promoting both soft power and nationalism, but not in the direction of cultural liberalization. It is in this contrived vein that we see a conflation of cultural, economic, and political strengths. This is not a concern unique to China, but it reflects a core issue of the creative economy: creative products are not politically naïve, and their flows have grave ideological effects.

The Chinese media care far less about how many foreign women are wearing Chinese-made lingerie than how many visitors and global TV viewers found a new and innovative Olympics hosted in China. Global events like this could provide employment and foreign tourist money, but more important, they can boost national pride and perhaps mitigate people's political discontent. The cultural and political importance of an Oscar, which China still desperately craves, is far greater than the number of shoes produced in Chinese factories, although the economic impact of the latter clearly exceeds that of the former. In China, no matter how economic development alienates its people, it is always justified by the promise of a better culture. As Lisa Rofel demonstrates, cosmopolitan culture has lately been idealized as an end result of China's capitalism, allowing Chinese people to become global citizens.[46] Economic exploitation is legitimized by a desire for better cultural experiences, human relationships, and national image—all in the name of culture.

With the advent of the creative economy, cultural nationalism now has a new face, which no longer celebrates just high art and traditional practices as the essence of a national culture, but increasingly promotes the constantly changing popular culture (such as K-pop), prominent brand names (such as

Nokia), and the hosting of major international events (such as the Olympics) that galvanize cultural pride, although (and because) these cultures and events are also deeply transnational. Patriotism is no longer characterized solely by strong emotions, self-sacrifice, or collective homogeneity; it is now imbued with the lightness of leisure and entertainment, attesting to powerful yet largely invisible economic forces. A major manifestation of Chinese nationalism currently is the people's obsession with new Chinese blockbuster films, which in the past few years have enjoyed higher domestic box office receipts than Hollywood films.[47] The high national and international popularity of Zhang Yimou's commercial films is greeted with equally fierce criticism, and participation in such waves of critical discourse has almost become a national pastime.[48] Production and reception are now leveled, so that every viewer and consumer can be a cultural critic of the national product, and the political discourses of soft power and nationalism actively participate in and benefit from these leisure activities to interpellate the desired and desiring subjects.

With its "democratic" promises, the creative economy seems to empower everybody as creative, critical, and independent, but at the same time it also more effectively subjects people to the ideological, because choices and self-reflection help sustain the illusion that the subject can rationally inhabit the system.[49] The creative economy, which democratizes the production, reception, and criticism of cultural products, empowers common Chinese people to participate in collective "China-making" through their own individual rationality and their renewed relationships with ever new products. Such nationalism is maintained by the subject's own illusion that he or she is conscious of and in control of his or her relationship with national products, making people even more comfortable identifying with their country and culture.

The collective obsession with creativity currently manifesting in China can also be seen as a result of nationalist anxiety. Underlying this creativity craze is an equally heavy sense of lowliness, as many Chinese people are quick to condemn traditional culture as well as official ideology's inability to promote creativity; thus it is believed that the Chinese tendency is copying rather than innovating. It is also here that we find a strange echo between the international IPR condemnation of China's rampant piracy and China's own creative surge. China has always been seen as the opposite of creative. Before, a common Western assumption of China was the Confucian tendency toward compliance, suppressing both individuality and creativity.[50] Now, with the rise of China's capitalist power, it is all too common for Western countries to accuse

China of disrespect for IPR; such accusations are often façades hiding more complex political and economic conflicts and negotiations. Central to this current phase of the creativity deficiency theory is no longer China's Confucian tradition but its incarnation of disruptive creativity, so that the kind of mimicry performed in China might eventually destroy the "true" creativity embodied in the Western business world. Clayton Christensen, the author of the bestseller *The Innovator's Dilemma*, argues that currently Chinese and Indian firms are undermining established companies by offering "disruptive" innovation: while firms invest heavily in trying to deliver what a small elite group of consumers wants, upstarts—particularly those in China and India, which have their own large domestic markets—offer inferior technologies and products at much lower prices, pushing incumbents into ever smaller niches.[51] In other words, China is not creative, but it is mimetic, and its copying only disrupts and destroys creativity (see chapter 8).

Most Chinese people do not disagree with international IPR-related condemnation, and the state is driven to build a strong IPR environment. Some economics researchers assert that a strong IPR environment would ultimately bring wealth to the country because IPR legislation and effective enforcement encourage multinational firms to transfer technology internationally, as the parent firm can be assured that local firms will not use the patented components of its technology without its consent.[52] However, many Chinese buy into the IPR values not because of concrete material gains, but because the symbolic links forged between IPR and knowledge and creativity, which are currently the most powerful modernity indicators, demonstrate how sophisticated the country and the people have, or have failed to, become.[53] The more IPR offenses are practiced, the less advanced the people are, and many Chinese people believe that the proliferation of piracy and counterfeiting demonstrates their low civil standards in general. Modernity continues to function as a structure of desire,[54] and China, like many other non-Western countries, tries very hard to take the lead in this new wave of competition for modernity, in which creativity has now replaced science and technology as the object of desire and the symbolic benchmark of progress. Competition is crucial, and there is increasing research attention in China to how various national or city cultural policies benefit competitiveness.[55] Although the notion of national creativity is beyond common sense, the Chinese government and many others around the world are working hard to cultivate creativity as a national asset. Creativity, in creative economic logic, serves both the interests of a specific national government and the operation of global economic flows.

Understanding the situation of China according to a simple global development scale might risk endorsing a reductionist globalization discourse, and we need to point out that there is a specific history of China, itself very disjointed, that was made to confront the creative economy in the 1990s. It is true that the Chinese culture tends not to dichotomize creativity and copying. Copyright and creative industries scholars such as William Alford and Michael Keane have carefully delineated their understandings of the ways traditional China cultivated knowledge and innovation, which I do not need to repeat here.[56] I would only like to stress that a cyclical system of thinking based on repetitions also tolerates and indeed welcomes change and creativity. Wang Hui has demonstrated that while the history of Chinese thought is characterized by the institutionalization of dominant ideologies, it is also full of spaces for innovation, in the sense that new thoughts constantly arise to challenge the status quo. Wang's studies demonstrate that it is these constant intellectual inventions and interventions that propel the history of Chinese thought and activate the culture's creativity out of a seemingly conservative holism.[57]

I believe it is vital to avoid reiterating that traditional Chinese culture has or has not its own history of creativity, which can surely be detected in all cultures, for such claims often run the risk of cultural essentialism, suppressing too many exceptions for a clean delineation. Instead I think we can demonstrate that there was a dominant value system, which is not natural but cultural, that shaped a hegemonic ideological landscape determining how knowledge and culture should be viewed. Michael Puett has provided solid and pertinent scholarship in this regard. Puett argues that the idea that "human culture is simply a part of the natural world, and that true sages never created anything but simply replicated patterns in the natural world" is not a simple Western cultural stereotype of China, but arose and became dominant in China itself. In his careful studies of ancient Chinese texts, Puett demonstrates that a vigorous debate among thinkers spanning several centuries regarding the relationship between culture and nature was settled in the Han dynasty. Since then the Chinese literati have always been taught that the sages' creation of material culture is the proper and moral completion of the process begun by Heaven, so there was no radical rupture of changes that the concept of innovation is based upon.[58] It is undeniable that in general Chinese thinking favors continuity instead of radical rupture or newness, and copying has always been a highly respected act in traditional Chinese culture,[59] but this cultural inertia was a historical construction, not just born with the culture.

A collectivist understanding of culture was not only a product of the Confucian saga, but was also reinforced and modified by China's recent socialist experiences. Between 1949 and Deng Xiaoping's Open Door Policy, the government outlawed private property, tangible and intellectual. It was forbidden to privatize culture, and creativity was not considered an individual asset but something meant to serve collective national well-being (see chapter 4). Some Chinese critics have argued that current Chinese efforts to protect property rights are an act of depoliticization, because the concept of property rights ignores the historical conditions of socialism—which cherished collective ownership—and smoothly transfers property from the people to the new bourgeois and the transnational capitalists, bypassing vigorous political debate.[60] Normalizing intangible materials like creativity and ideas into private property produces an even more devastating effect, because IPR concepts both depoliticize the socialist tradition and disturb the public nature of culture as understood traditionally.

Generally speaking, we can say that IPR's fear of copying, and the creative economy's cherishing of the permanent ownership of ideas and innovations, are alienating to China in relation to both its Confucian past and its socialist legacy.[61] The Chinese people have experienced radical ideological shifts in the past century, from the sudden embrace of Western modernity in the late nineteenth century, to the cult of austerity officially sponsored by the Chinese Communist Party (CCP) in the 1950s to the 1970s, and now to the proliferation of hedonist consumerism promoted by global media.[62] What is lost in this creative economy is not only the traditional Chinese and socialist sense of cultural sharing, but also a political sensitivity to culture. The CCP had a most acute understanding of the political dimension of culture, and in the Cultural Revolution Mao Zedong and his colleagues were committed to (however problematically) exposing and manipulating the aggressive and pervasive dimensions of culture in order to conceptualize and reach for a better world. Residues of such political understanding of culture linger, but they are not utilized for self-reflection or for opening a new ethical path; most of them are channeled to the nationalist or soft power discourse to fight against the part-imaginary, part-real enemy of globalization. Offering strong support to the creative economy, the PRC continues to have direct centralized control over the cultural scene in spite of the current rapid marketization of culture. These policies are not meant to counter neoliberalism but to maintain the country's—and the Party's—political stability. Any political understanding of culture has been quickly absorbed into the nationalist discourse and made a tool for the legitimization of state control against the aggression of "other" cultures, and late capitalism continues to be sheltered as long as the agenda of national empowerment is not deterred.

Politicizing Creativity

As I will show in chapters 4 to 9, I believe that only by exploring carefully the unique yet universal Chinese experience can we understand how the global creative economy discourse interacts with China's own situation, and can critically respond to related situations. This book is as much about repoliticizing China as repoliticizing creativity. In this sense, the particularities of China, of its IPR issues, constantly interact with and challenge the universalities of global events. Let us return to the global creative economy discourse to explore its global evasiveness.

The already immanent creative economy can be viewed as a result of a few social phenomena. First, there is the development of new media, not only digital media content but also new working environments and the wide range of products and life patterns engendered by the digital age. The copying of and access to cultural commodities have become ever easier. There is also the further reinforcement of commodity society, expanding the range of emotions and experiences to be commodified. It has been argued that advanced Western countries have a surplus of productivity; one solution is to increase consumption in developing countries, and another is to develop new spheres of consumption in developed countries, leading to the expansion of knowledge-related and leisure activities.[63] At the same time, the market economy is being adopted globally, and the business world has shifted a large number of investments to idea-related sectors (such as R&D and advertising) in order to reach a wider but also increasingly diversified market, leading to the intensification of the global circulation of transient trends and fashions. These phenomena conjoin and engender a new environment of production, distribution, and consumption, feeding intangible materials to this new phase of capitalism.[64]

Contrary to the common perception of the decreasing importance of the nation-state under globalization, state governments move ever more quickly to support, and thus enter into, the creative economy in order to meet these business demands. Related to the creative economy is Australia's Creative Nation policy, although the actual phrase "creative economy" was not used in the documents. Created in 1994 by the Labor government under Prime Minister Paul Keating, the policy explicitly announced, "This cultural policy is also an economic policy. Culture creates wealth."[65] Although the Labor government emphasized the importance of Australian culture and identity, and it also genuinely welcomed input from all directions, the economism that underpinned its cultural policy suggested that it was the economic potential of culture rather than its inherent worth that the government valued.[66] With a similar mentality, the British Labour Party's election campaign in 1997 focused on the term "creative industries."[67] Since this spectacularly successful campaign, the government of the United Kingdom has become one of the most active pursuers of the creative economy and in 2006 launched an initiative to develop a national Creative Economy Programme, drawn up by a team of experts tasked with exploring new ways to promote the U.K.'s creative industries.[68] But the status of this program remains unclear under the new coalition of the Conservative Party and the Liberal Democrats which came to power in 2010.

Concepts related to the creative economy are particularly attractive to smaller nations and regions. In those areas lacking global industrial or financial investments, the creative economy promises profits from tourism and smaller-scale cultural activities; for example, Maine and Vermont have been quick to make the creative economy the key economic engine in the New England region of the United States.[69] The creative economy is also extremely alluring to global financial cities such as Singapore and Hong Kong,[70] whose prime global positions are increasingly vulnerable to intense regional competition; thus their governments strongly push for the development of industrial bases to stabilize their future economies (see chapter 5).

Within such a system of expansion and proliferation, the real challenge for critics is to disclose the political dimensions of this creative economy, hidden by the façade of style and fashion. We need to rearticulate the forces making up this creative economy, both as a regime manipulated by those in power and as a site that productively shapes material and epistemological conditions of life and thought. Naomi Klein points out that corporate sponsorship has colonized all parts of our lives, from large religious gatherings to small community events, including even private weddings.[71] What we gain is not only financial sponsorship and material supply, but also the image and the new ideas provided. There is no longer an "outside" to the capitalist way of living if the dynamic process of creating is also commodified. The academic dilemma we face lies here as well. A simple dialectic of domination and opposition, of inside and outside, is no longer sufficient to politicize late capitalism, which has conditioned our entire lives.[72] Many contemporary critical scholars see their political task in the privileging of differences as respect and tolerance, aiming to promote plurality and condemn inequality. However, too much emphasis on the fluidity of the system renders critical studies impotent, and the consumer society operates precisely on the mechanism of differences. I believe the most important political task of this book is to locate and examine antagonistic structures pertaining to creativity in such a field of multiplicity and to explore how such antagonisms are functions and excesses of the overarching system. While some sets of antagonism may have been reconciled by complex logics of hegemony, I believe there are always others retained or newly constructed. I am interested precisely in the dynamics between structures that are resolved and those that are not.

The main theoretical concern of this book is the dynamics between two antagonistic structures that imbricate each other. The more fundamental and defining pair of contesting logics conditioning the creative economy are economic logic and cultural logic, and they correspond, in my study, to the instrumentalizing tendency of the creative economy (creativity as object) and the uninhibited nature of creativity (creativity as subject), respectively. Although the economic and the cultural are competing logics, what really characterizes the creative economy is not the opposition between them, but their increasing exchanges. This set of contradictory principles, in other words, is increasingly reconciled, and their mutual conditioning has become a primary force that fuels the new creative economy.

Previously, very few economists would dare to approach questions about the economic value of a creative work, as their professional training taught them to refrain from scientifically analyzing anything that is not objective, whereas the field of culture is largely composed of subjective value judgments.[73] But the recent discursive development surrounding creativity attests precisely to the strong urge on the part of economists to find ways to "rationalize" culture.[74] What we are seeing is not a simple economization of culture, but its extensive interpenetration. Depending on how they are used and conceived, money and creativity could be both the means and the ends to each other, in that both economy and culture can presumably benefit from that interpenetration. Our global economy is increasingly ordered by relations between consumers and products and services, and a key momentum of the creative economy is the constant proliferation of such relations in company image, branding, exploitation of trends, and niche markets.[75] A new managerialist discourse has also arisen in the international business community that increasingly co-opts a cultural discourse of flexibility, human relationships, and knowledge.[76]

Inherent in this mutual conditioning between the economic and the cultural is, however, a more acute yet less imperative set of oppositions characterizing the creative economy, which is the IPR regime and its offenses. In the past decade we have observed a tremendous expansion of the IPR regime. The creative economy cannot operate without IPR control—just imagine a world where everything may be copied freely. More accurately, IPR controls the copying of creativity instead of creativity itself, although the two are intimately connected. It is true that all the IPR components—copyrights, patents, trademarks, trade secrets, and others—work within their confines and devise their own areas of exceptions to avoid monopolization. However, the recent development of the IPR regime sees increasing mutual invasions among these individual rights, so that, for example, the protection of ideas, originally disallowed by copyrights, finds shelter in patents, and the development of trademarks and trade secrets helps IPR owners to obtain permanent ownership by evading the public domain established by copyrights and patents. The creative economy is characterized by the way each of the individual rights fill the loopholes inherent in the others.

If the principal set of antagonisms in the creative economy, that is, the economic and instrumental in opposition to the cultural and proliferating, is increasingly reconciled and made mutually generative, the irreconcilable oppositional relationship between IPR and its offenses—which I believe stems from the first pair of relationships—is worthy of our attention. The creative economy seems to have incorporated the logic of the cultural, but the desperate criminalization of IPR offenses would tell us the limits of this incorporation, and it also shows the residues of creativity that cannot, after all, be incorporated into the creative economy. The opposition between IPR and piracy is the most prominent set of antagonisms in the creative economy, and it crystallizes the failure of late capitalism's desire for pluralization. The opposition between IPR and piracy provides us with a window through which the seemingly reconciled antagonism between the economic and the cultural can be viewed.

In their classic formulation of "radical democracy," Laclau and Mouffe theorize how multiple political subjectivities can be unified for political action. They argue that antagonism and differences are oppositional logics in conceptualizing society, in the sense that the logic of antagonism assumes that human relations can be shaped according to an objective and intelligible pattern, whereas our empirical experiences of society, particularly those that have arisen from postmodern conditions, correspond more closely to the logic of differences in terms of the plural coexistence of agents and subjectivities.[77] In reality, antagonism, as a set of unified oppositional structures, is empirically impossible within a society characterized by the proliferation of differences. But it is still our responsibility to identify antagonism in our capitalist society, seeing antagonism not as society's governing structure, but as its failure: antagonism witnesses the failure of capitalism that feeds on differences. Social antagonism should not be understood as a positive and corrective force located outside the social, but the structural failure of that social. As such, it is important to hold on to antagonism because, simply speaking, it is where political intervention is still possible.

The key challenge, or impossible mission, of post-Marxist critics is to continue to provide anticapitalist critiques in this late capitalist society, which has grown to be so flexible and unstructured that it can subsume or make irrelevant all criticisms. Fredric Jameson believes that this is also the burden of Theodor Adorno, who, like Laclau and Mouffe, is committed to thinking of the social as the totality that can only be slit open internally. Adorno is highly critical of "identity," or "concept," which subsumes a great variety of different, really existing objects and ideas into a falsified coherent structure, through which the subject is made to believe that the outside world is submissive to one's own knowledge and control. In order to provide room to imagine beyond "concept," Adorno surprisingly advocates a commitment to the thinking of totality, or system, not in the sense of understanding, and therefore controlling, a totality as a universal subsuming all particulars, but as a solution to the closure of identity. Jameson writes, "System is very precisely that outer face of the concept, that outside forever inaccessible to us, evoked above." Knowing that the system is beyond our reach, we cannot let it go at that, but continue to talk about it, think about it, and "de-conceal" it, which governs our reason and abstract thought. Consider capitalism as that totality which increasingly encircles us and defines all our activities: the more we find we cannot escape from this system, the more we need to explain it, to wrestle with it. But the access to the totality remains in the particulars, and we need to keep "interpreting" the historical particulars in order to reach and modify the totality. The particular is not interpreted in light of the universal, "but rather in the light of the very contradiction between universal and particular in the first place."[78] Although Jameson does not use the concept of antagonism here as Laclau and Mouffe do, they all try to struggle with the totalizing system, injecting it with room for politics.

I find these post-Marxist attempts relevant to our understanding of the IPR antagonism. How can we offer any effective criticism of the creative economy as a totalizing system? We can consider IPR offenses as those particulars that can bring us to the contradictions or failures of the creative economy, or late capitalism, as the universal. We cannot characterize IPR offenses as being germane to revolution, but they are parasitic to the existing capitalist structure. They are not the opposite of late capitalism, but they are the result of the pluralizing tendency of late capitalism, in that piracy and counterfeiting are simply other forms of consumption. Our creative economy supports the pluralist model of consumer society, whose multiple identifications make any unified politics impossible. Arising from late capitalism, IPR offenses, however, are also the indocile residues of the same structure. They have become the most prominent enemy of the creative economy because their proliferation will directly erode this economic order. As Jameson writes, "The attention systematically directed to the particular, to the text or phenomenon to be interpreted . . . finds that what has been said, unexpectedly, addresses that totality itself and modifies it."[79] Therefore IPR offenses can be seen as witnesses to the fantasized unity of late capitalism, and they are also excesses of the logic of culture that must be repressed. Not only are they structural to the creative economy, but the creative economy also needs to construct and aggrandize this "enemy" to legitimize its own rhetoric and control. The ability of the late capitalist economy to draw all creative activity and knowledge production into its service cannot but be a myth, and IPR offenses are the fetishistic embodiment of its fundamental blockage. The criminalization of piracy and the counterfeit, therefore, has helped conjure up the need to pursue IPR by all means.[80] In this book I choose to focus on and identify with IPR offenses because they represent the excesses attributed by the creative economy to the logic of mimesis and the logic of culture that the creative economy exploits in the first place. The proliferation of IPR offenses demonstrates culture's resistance to being completely incorporated into the realm of economics, and of creativity's resistance to being incorporated into the creative economy. At a time when we can foresee no more breaks, when creativity cannot bring us any shocks of the new,[81] I hope that we can gain a different understanding of the relationship between the established and the new by reverting to the logic of copying.

Laclau and Mouffe believe that through the establishment of equivalences, we are able to connect the logic of equivalence and the logic of differences, allowing diverse subject positions and particular events to be connected in imaginary antagonistic unity to achieve universal claims or even emancipations.[82] It is not my intention to romanticize China's IPR offenses, and I do not believe that these acts can unify discrete political struggles. More specifically, most IPR offenses are not political in nature, and there are no conscious political views behind them that can be united with other struggles. However, we might continue to investigate and emphasize the connections of these seemingly discrete acts, giving us an alternative perspective from which to understand the operation of macrosocial discourses. For Laclau, the more productive politics against the current global oppressions must be those constantly sliding between the particular and the universal:

> The more particularized a demand, the easier it is to satisfy it and integrate in into the system; while if the demand is equivalent to a variety of other demands, no partial victory will be considered as anything other than an episode in a protracted war of position. . . .
>
> The central point is that for a certain demand, subject position, identity, and so on, to become political means that it is something other than itself, living its own particularity as a moment or link in a chain of equivalences that transcends and, in this way, universalizes it.[83]

In order to politicize Chinese experiences in the new creative economy, these experiences are studied not only for their own sake, but, as Laclau claims, they will turn into moments and links in a chain of equivalences, which in turn will inform our politics against larger global structures and dominations. To be more precise, I hope the following chapters can show us that we can hold on to these criminalized yet pervasive activities to, first, gain access to the structural failures of late capitalism, and second, find room for transformation and emancipation based on the logic of mimesis that is an essential part of the humanities. As a particular case caught in such universal polemics, China is both unique and not unique, and Chinese experiences offer us insights into the global operations of the creative economy. As suggested earlier, China's own sociopolitical development is constantly affected by global and regional conditions. Actual events in China, a postsocialist country fast-forwarding into late capitalism, reveal how powerful global forces are shaping national development, yet an enormous amount of local friction is also produced to delay or actualize these global forces.

At a time when the world has recognized and approved, willingly or unwillingly, the dominant position of China in the global future, it is even more urgent for those of us studying China to look into this myth. It is clear that contemporary China has attracted much scholarly attention recently, but we must resist staying on the descriptive level. My task is as much epistemological as political, and it applies not only to my study of the creative economy but also to my study of China. There are, unfortunately, still scholarly prejudices against the study of non-Western cultures as "cases," whereas things happening in the West can be taken for granted as "universal." Non-Western scholars might participate in academic theoretical discussions only by providing cultural examples to support or refute established theories, whereas the actual theorization is generated primarily from Western examples. If my focus on China is seen as a particular case study, the numerous and transient (anti)creative acts taking place in China and their products are particulars of a particular, whose theoretical values, so to speak, are ostensibly even lower. However, these small acts and objects attract my attention not just because they manifest the failure of the dominant ideological structure, but because they also embody the most radical structure of opposition. It is my ambition to retrace the links between seemingly meaningless piracy acts or counterfeit objects and the dominant socioeconomic structure of late capitalism, and I hope that my dual emphases on dominant ideologies and the microreading of small objects and activities will allow me to achieve this difficult task.

Structure of the Book

This book is separated into two parts: the three chapters in part I combine to provide an interdisciplinary theoretical background on the sociophilosophical conditions and problems of the creative economy. There are two main purposes of this part. First, in light of the indefinable nature of creativity, I believe the current manifestation of creativity can be understood as a series of related dialectics. Second, I want to show that the creative economy is a continuation and an intensification of Western modernity and capitalism. Part II is divided into two sections, which examine the actual renditions of creative industries and IPR offenses in China. I explore how the state and various sectors foster creative industries and promote IPR consciousness, with offenses and contradictions abounding. Chapters 4 to 6 discuss Lijiang's cultural tourism, Hong Kong's film industry, and Beijing's fine arts scene, exploring the wide range of China's creative industries in both its regional diversity and its industrial diversity. Chapters 7 to 9 analyze the many events and meanings pertaining to IPR offenses, from which I want to reestablish the intimate connections between culture and copying. The two sections, focusing primarily on the theoretical and the empirical, are closely related and are meant to provide a schema that connects and complicates the universal and the particular.

More specifically, in chapter 1 I demonstrate how the dominant manifestation of Western modernity shows a strong desire to tame human creativity instead of encouraging us to explore our relations with others through creative acts. This tendency is made possible by mythologizing creativity as uncontrollable and contingent, which stems from the secularization of divine creation in the West and characterizes the modernity project. In order to resist the modernity project's fetishization of creativity, we should understand creativity as also practice and text, which is the task of the next two chapters.

In chapter 2, I shift my critical focus from modernity to capitalism and provide a Marxist analysis of the creative agency conceptualized by the new creative economy. Analyzing the differences and continuities between the creative economy and the traditional industrial economy, I explore how creative labor is selectively invested with the logics of both artistic production and industrial production, so that the creative economy might operate and proliferate amid tensions between scarcity and abundance.

Chapter 3 continues, this time from an IPR perspective, to explore creativity's dual dimensions, in that it is generated by an author but it also eludes the author's control. Therein I examine how problematic it is to understand creative works according to the logic of property. The domination of the discourse of rights in the current form of IPR fails to recognize how creativity proliferates. These three chapters can be seen as my general effort to reexamine the notion of authorship or, more accurately, the relationship between the human subject and creativity.

Commencing part II, chapter 4 is devoted to the overall development of cultural policy and the IPR legal structure in China. I want to show how China's policies and its legal environment increasingly adapt to global conditions. Focusing on cultural tourism in the World Heritage city of Lijiang, I demonstrate how China's creative economy escapes Aihwa Ong's theorization of "exception" as related global and state interests converge not at geographic locations of exception but at the heart of numerous local economies, allowing the creative economy to penetrate and prevail.

In chapter 5 I shift my attention from cultural tourism to cinema. I explore the kinds of cultural and social infrastructural changes that pertain to the transformation of Hong Kong cinema from a traditional cultural industry to a new member of the creative industries, and how creative industries can organize a city's cultural activities to promote a brand identity. Through the reconceptualization of the films, the filmmakers, and the viewers, Hong Kong cinema no longer produces place-based texts but engages in transnational cinema, which tends to dematerialize the films.

In chapter 6 I continue to develop the concept of city branding, but I travel from Hong Kong to Beijing, and from mass media to high art. I focus on the development of two art spaces, Factory 798 and Songzhuang, to demonstrate how the city craves abstract branding, yet the realization of such images also demands the violent transformation of the city. Caught between abstract branding effects and concrete spatial politics, art easily loses its ability to come to terms with its place.

The next three chapters pay close attention to pirated objects, congealing the intimate connection between creativity and copying. Chapter 7 focuses on a Chinese magazine dedicated to the Japanese anime master Miyazaki Hayao. All materials in the magazine are copied or modified from other sources. Through a close reading of this pirated object, I argue that cartoon culture serves as a unique example to demonstrate the relationship between copying and sharing, which are both feared and criminalized by the creative economy. But cartoon culture also gives us another perspective on copyright, since a lack of copyright protection in Japanese anime culture has actually promoted the culture's dynamism, and it also demonstrates a model of transcultural communications not subject to IPR rule.

Chapter 8 is a theorization of the counterfeit product. Through a close engagement with Benjamin's idea of mechanical reproduction and the actual Chinese counterfeiting situation, I analyze how we can read such a seemingly meaningless object as a convergence and a dodging of social and cultural discourses in order to highlight a textuality that is resistant to control. I believe a commitment to reading is also a political commitment, which demythologizes the ways piracy, and China, are condemned.

I conclude in chapter 9 by focusing on the slippery relationship between knockoffs and appropriation art, and I hark back to chapter 6 for a critical rereading of the flourishing art scene in China. I compare two pieces of contemporary artwork—both touch upon the issue of piracy—in order to demonstrate the relationship between creativity and technology, also offering another perspective to understand the Heideggerian notion of *techne*. The comparison of the two works provides an alternative perspective from which to examine how creativity is run, and how creativity runs on its own. My analysis of the artworks also recaps the overall thesis of the book, reconnecting creativity and humanity by revealing the continual relationship between creating and copying, between individuals and community.

PART I

Understanding Creativity

Creativity as a Problem of Modernity

I devote chapters 1–3 to the theoretical explication of the meanings of creativity before analyzing the actual renditions and discontents of the creative economy in China. Our various understandings of creativity are characterized by the tensions and dynamics between freedom and control, art and design, textuality and industrialism. I believe the entangled relationships of these contradictions are rooted in the modernity project, adopted and reinforced by the creative economy as its latest manifestation.[1] These three chapters provide an elaborate discussion of the ramifications of these dialectics in the operation of this creative economy, an economy as abstract as it is concrete. In chapters 2 and 3 I illustrate how creativity—largely through economic and legal mechanisms—is both mystified and made into a concrete property for today's global capitalism. In this chapter I go back to history a little bit to begin my analysis of creativity, along with a genealogical study of the concept in the context of Western modernity. Readers might find this chapter too distant from today's events in the world and in China, but I think it is important to lay a philosophical groundwork to understand the relationship between divine creativity and secular creativity in the West, which directly conditions how creativity is conceptualized and utilized globally today.

As it is widely studied, the modernity project is characterized by a particular Western epistemology, which, on the one hand, is driven by human desire for control over others and the world and, on the other hand, represents humanity's own insecurity about this sovereign position. There is a clear tendency among human beings in recent history to order and subdue the world through industrialization, colonialism, and capitalism, and this incessant desire also demonstrates the enormous amount of anxiety involved. The drastic leap we see in this current phase of global capitalism is not a departure from this modernity project, but is its extreme manifestation, to the point where creativity, which has been most resistant to instrumentalization, is made into a tool for its own alienation. Critics tend to describe the age of creative economy and the space of flows created by late capitalist societal networks as postmodern.[2] I would argue instead that this economy is not a breakaway from modernity, but its most saturated manifestation, which therefore also contains the seeds of destruction.[3]

To understand the relationship between creativity and modernity, we might need to go back to history. In the development of modern Western culture, the divine creative power has been secularized into two human capacities: artistic creativity and epistemological knowledge. But the two are not simply dichotomized: the latter has manifested into a strong tendency to control the former, whereas artistic creativity retains some of the mythic components of divine creation. The tensions and dynamics involved characterize, at least partly, the formation of modernity. I believe an investigation of the genealogy and various conceptualizations of creativity in Western modernity could bring to light the repressed links between creativity as a trans-sociohistorical force of creation and creativity as an individual author's production of artistic works, which the creative economy utilizes selectively in part or in pairs. Establishing such links can help us to deconstruct the current modernity hegemony and to rediscover the indocile element of culture that is both germane and resistant to the logic of the creative economy.

In this chapter I analyze an array of understandings of creativity by prominent Western philosophers and thinkers. My purpose is neither to assert the supremacy of Western origin nor to conjure up a sense of continuous canonical thinking, but we must recognize that our global modernity is characterized by the hegemony of a particular Western thinking. With the global triumph of Western modernity, what grounds the development of China's and other developing countries' current socioeconomic development is not the culture's own philosophical history but that of the West. One way to tackle that dominion is to confront the core of Western tradition and its repressions. Therein we shall find complex dialectics of suppression and complicity, as well as possibilities of alternative thinking.

Modernity and the Creative Economy

In the West creativity was not understood as a form of personal aptitude until the advent of modernity. We can trace this development back to the Enlightenment, from which point creativity has been secularized with an eye to privileging anthropocentric epistemology over humans' ontological existence. In *Keywords* Raymond Williams defines the original meanings of creativity: "The word ["create"] was mainly used in the precise context of the original divine creation of the world: creation itself, and creature, have the same root stem. Moreover, with that system of belief, as Augustine insisted, 'creatura non potest creare' — the 'creature' — who has been created — cannot himself create."[4] Williams then summarizes the secularizing process of creativity in the West, passing from the hands of God to man. The decisive development took place in the nineteenth century: in the beginning of the century the creative act was understood as conscious and powerful; by midcentury it had become conventional. Creativity, a general name for that faculty, followed in the twentieth century. Williams's brief account points out the close connection between modernity and the democratizing process of creativity: creativity had been owned solely by God; with the advent of modernity the power to create was first given to the artist through his or her spiritual communion with Nature, and by the twentieth century anyone could be creative.[5] The development of capitalism supported by the Protestant ethic also plays a key role in fusing creativity and progress. As Max Weber showed us, in the West the productivity of work in the capitalist sense was infused with the Protestant ethic of striving for the kingdom of God.[6] Creation is transformed into productivity, which gradually becomes an end itself, to be supported by all kinds of innovative measures. With the moderns' increasing desire for control and wealth, divine creativity materialized into an epistemological and economic endeavor through the forces of secularization and capitalism. The spiritual dimension of human creativity is therefore maintained in a contrived way: divine creativity must be secularized as human aptitude, but the secularized form becomes a manifestation of God's grace. The philosophical tensions and structural leaps involved in this secularization process are intense, which I believe also inherently manifests a modernity problem.

Let us examine this history with some details, however scanty. In the Judeo-Christian tradition, creativity originally belonged to God. A simple dichotomy, as Williams points out, is thus established between God as the creator and humanity as the created. Given the direct equation of God with creation, humanity can create when empowered as God's vehicle. In the Greek tradition, however, the notion of self-creation does not exist. The Platonic order is a manifestation of preexisting rules of Being, and Plato's great architect, Timaeus, is a mere executor; he does not possess the creative power of the Creator God in the biblical tradition.[7] In other words, there are two main models of creativity that inform Western modernity: Plato's understanding of creativity as rational reproduction of the intelligible and logical Being, and the willful Creator God of the Hebraic tradition.[8]

Simply stated, a major task and motivation of the Enlightenment was to come to terms with these two traditions and, not surprisingly, to subject the divine creative power of the Judeo-Christian tradition to Greek philosophy. It is mainly Platonic epistemology that has driven the ongoing development of Western modernity.[9] The modern subject—specifically, that theorized by Descartes—does not aspire to be God, and he knows very well his limitations, in that he cannot grasp the infinite. But it is precisely this knowledge of both his finitude and the existence of the infinite that characterizes modern subjectivity. The unity of the modern subject is established less by his ability to create than by his ability to control a unified discursive field, or point of view, of the created world.[10] The most important secularization project of Western modernity turned out to be not creating but understanding, since with knowledge humans can control what has already been created.

But the secularization of creativity continues its course, and is manifested in several different ways. The Judeo-Christian sense of divine creativity is passed down largely to become acts of art, and God's moral dimension is maintained in the realm of law and ethics. But generally speaking, when capitalism pairs up with the Protestant ethic to turn creativity into productivity, it is the domain of knowledge that is assigned the key role in advancing modernity. We thus have a split between aesthetics and knowledge—artists create, scientists discover—but artistic creation is not put on a par with scientific discovery, and the latter remains the normative drive of modernity. Scientific discoveries are placed in a protected realm, ideally to be free from economic and moral considerations. It is true that the notion of the creative genius applies not only to the master artist; the most celebrated scientists are also hailed as geniuses who rebel against the status quo and are able to see things we ordinary people cannot. But only a small number of very original scientists receive the renown of the artist or the poet (thus possessing the mysterious divine link); in general, the creativity manifested within the realm of epistemology is understood as innovation, as opposed to artistic creativity that cannot be understood and calculated rationally. The mythic power of creativity is largely contained and curbed within the realm of art in order to prevent its corruption of the order of rationality. After Kant we see the rise of positivism, according to which truth and value are understood as discoverable, and philosophers were interested in the process and method of uncovering them. On the other hand, from the romantic to the modernist movements, artists

were increasingly encouraged to plunge deep into interiors; interiority is conceptualized as the effect of a complex relationship between psychological and
formal aesthetic values. Such entanglement is probably most clearly observed
in nineteenth-century music.

This marginalization of art and the complete separation of the discursive
realms (epistemological, moral, and aesthetic) are central modernity issues
examined by Jürgen Habermas.[11] Weber believes that knowledge, justice, and
taste, which can all be seen as aspects of the divine, were originally unified as
a coherent worldview in premodern society, but they are increasingly differentiated in modern society into autonomous fields of reasoning, to the extent that they become mutually incompatible, excluding moral and aesthetic
ideals from modern social and political life. Habermas follows up on and
criticizes this triangular structure of modern reasoning. He promotes intercommunication among the realms, which he believes would bring about a
"better" form of modern rationality that could prevent the irreparable split-
ting of society into competitive value spheres as posited by Weber. Habermas
believes that modernity promises, instead of precludes, intercommunication
among the three fields, so that the arts can speak to the social once again. The
three spheres should be made relevant to each other, so that art can fulfill
modernity's promise of critical self-reflexivity.[12]

Although Habermas criticizes the increasing marginalization of Western
arts, in reality artistic creativity has always attracted philosophers' epistemological and moral investigation. Beginning with Kant's *Critique of Judgment*,
Western aesthetic theory has been preoccupied with the pursuit and analysis
of the meaning of art: to engage in its definitions; to explore the experience
of reception in categories like pleasure, pain, or the sublime; or to examine
art's sociopolitical functions. Although aesthetic judgments are probably the
most radical kind of reflective judgments among those theorized by Kant, and
are also the most difficult to understand, Kant's strong desire to understand
artistic creativity clearly demonstrates an epistemological tendency in this
aesthetics. Acknowledging the impossibility of circumventing the full meaning of art by some kind of empirical or transcendental framework, Kant still
struggles to find ways to understand art in the form of knowledge, resulting
in the extremely dense circular rhetorical movements in his third critique.[13]
A long and elaborate tradition of aesthetic philosophy follows. Even Alain
Badiou, who is highly critical of the Western philosophical tradition of aesthetics and calls his theory of art "inaesthetics," finds "truths" in art.[14] He
condemns the avant-garde's false fusion of art and politics, as he believes
that the truth claims of politics and the truth claims of art are entirely differ-

ent. But through the mechanism of negation Badiou still wants to articulate how art and politics can be connected, particularly in critiquing late capitalism. Many critics with Marxist or feminist backgrounds are more willing to argue and establish the strong relationship between art and society.[15] Such eminent social critics as Theodor Adorno and Georg Lukács regard authentic works of art and literature as being able to express conflicts within the larger sociohistorical process from which they arise and to which they belong, although Adorno emphasizes the autonomy of arts much more so than Lukács does.[16] There is a long and prominent tradition of scholarship in the West that provides links among art, knowledge, and ethics. Whether these efforts are manifestations of Habermas's Enlightenment ideals I do not know, but it is important to emphasize that they are not in fact simply marginal to but are prominent in Western philosophical traditions. Although there is a long tradition of Western artists painstakingly constructing fields of autonomy from other realms of control in the name of aesthetic independence, the domain of art is never completely independent, but is alive with epistemological desire stemming from the domain of knowledge and ethical desire from the domain of justice.

This surely is too simple a recounting of Western aesthetics, and it is not aimed at reducing a complex philosophical tradition into a simple narrative, but I want to point out the entangled relationship among knowledge, politics, and art, and that art is both autonomous and not. Art, as the progeny of divine creativity, is assigned a separate realm of subjectivity irrelevant to social praxis, but the Western modernity project is also characterized by an epistemological drive to unearth, and therefore control, the "truth" of art. There is such a strong desire to tame artistic creativity precisely because of its preservation of the mythical components of divine creativity, which are very powerful and alluring.

In fact Habermas's advocacy of interrealm communication could also be understood accordingly, that the real danger is not the autonomy of artistic creativity, but the "wrong" usage of art. There have been strong criticisms of aestheticism, which, as Walter Benjamin demonstrates, could become a political tool for fascist purposes.[17] Or, as Fredric Jameson proclaims, aesthetics is manipulated by the consumer culture to blind people and prevent their engagement with the social.[18] While Benjamin and Jameson are vigilant against any domination of aesthetic identification that might dilute people's autonomous rational thinking, Habermas promotes the intercommunication between the cultural and other realms to also prevent cultural modernity from servicing conservative traditions. Accordingly Habermas is not a critic of Western modernity, but his thinking is located at the very heart of it. Art, whose roots can be traced back to the Judeo-Christian conception of divine creativity, is nonrational and potentially dangerous; in order to make it socially productive, aesthetics must be contained within proper epistemology and morality.

Resistant to Meanings

As demonstrated, central to the modernity project is a desire to use and control creativity rationally, and creativity is so alluring yet threatening precisely because it retains part of the mythic power of divine creation. Its unpredictability and indocility make artistic creativity both resistant and germane to the modernity project. Not surprisingly, while there is a strong tradition in Western philosophy devoted to the understanding and therefore control of creativity, there is a dialectical side of the same tradition exploring the relationship between creativity and freedom, which we find in the writings of F. W. J. Schelling, Gilles Deleuze, and other philosophers as well as in more recent studies of modernist arts and culture by prominent critics such as Jameson and Mary Ann Doane. Their work and passion show that the desire to maintain the autonomy of arts from any epistemological control is more than latent in the Western tradition, and some thinkers' will to be in command of creativity cannot be understood apart from others' yielding to its liberating potential.

Let us start with Schelling, whose ideas of divine destruction laid the groundwork for many later thinkers in understanding the relationship between creativity and freedom. In a way, Schelling's philosophy belongs squarely within the German idealism tradition, which privileges the controlling ability of human agency, corresponding to the tendency described in the previous section. As Schelling writes, his view "removes the inconsistent notion of the contingency of individual acts." He believes that "true freedom is in accord with a holy necessity, of a sort which we feel in essential knowledge when heart and spirit, bound only by their own law, freely affirm that what is necessary."[19] However, dialectic to such German idealist convictions, Schelling's philosophy is also characterized by a strong urge for freedom, which attracts and is carefully studied by later critics, such as Heidegger, Habermas, and Žižek.[20]

Many critics are interested in Schelling because to Schelling, evil is not foreign to God, but God arises out of a struggle between two primordial antagonistic forces, one constructive and one destructive. According to Schelling, the true Beginning is not God Himself, but the passage from the "closed" rotary motion of the struggle between the two antagonistic forces to the "open" progress, in which the notion of God arises. The actual God belongs to the realm of "existence," which is "grounded" by a blind force of striving from the prior rotary forces. To Schelling, pure freedom is conceivable only within this primordial rotary motion of the mutual conditioning of the two antagonistic forces. If God arises out of this rotary motion, then pure freedom is prior to God, and it must be understood as a negative and contractive force, which is a Will that actively, effectively wants "nothing." In other words, this primordial Freedom is a will that annihilates all positive, determinate content in order to retain that nothingness. Žižek, for example, finds Schelling so attractive largely because Schelling allows divine creation to go beyond the enlightenment framework, escaping the confine of rationality and morality. To Žižek, the primordial form of creation that Schelling describes is pure contraction, which constantly slides into the vortex of divine madness. Therefore Schelling's God has its roots in madness. If we understand God as the perfect masculine subject, He is grounded in some kind of female madness providing the potentiality for God to actualize. Žižek is most interested in this "dark" side of Schelling's God. Situated in both the domains of "closed" rotary motion and "open" progress, this God is in fact a "psychotic" God, and "this all-destructive divine vortex remains even today the innermost base of all reality."[21]

The contemporary philosopher who is most indebted to this understanding of creativity might be Deleuze, who is devoted to the demonstration of the dialectic construction and destruction of time and space. Schelling's idea of divine madness finds a distant reverberation in Deleuzean theorization of capitalism. To Deleuze and Guattari, capitalism, among other creative forces, most vividly embodies the dialectics of construction and destruction, and they believe that capitalism and its challenges are both built on the constant rupture of established categories. In *Anti-Oedipus* they argue that capitalist production arrests the schizophrenic process and fashions its own chaos and death, but it also binds the schizophrenic charges and energies within interior limits, so the capitalist axiomatic is both destructive and constructive.[22] In *A Thousand Plateaus* they describe that core to capitalism is a logic of the assemblage, which, as a general model of life formation, is composed of two mutually conditioning forces: territorialization and deterritorialization.[23] Territorialization refers to the process that increases the internal homogeneity or the degree of sharpness of the boundaries of an assemblage, while deterritorialization refers to the opposite process. Capitalism is only one of the many historical forces that interest Deleuze and Guattari, and it is a general process of becoming that really characterizes their work. As Jacques Rancière argues, core to the Deleuzean thought is a particular aesthetic thinking, which is in a constant process of dissensus, resisting both the artist's intention and its material form.[24] Peter Hallward also argues that Deleuze's entire philosophy might be summarized as a philosophy of creation—one which is, however, constantly drifting toward disembodiment and dematerialization. Hallward summarizes Deleuze's thinking thus: "Creation itself generates internal obstacles to its own continuation. Virtual creatings are obstructed by the actual creatures they produce, [therefore we need] to develop the means, from within our actual or creatural constraints, of overcoming these same constraints."[25]

Whereas Hallward finds Deleuze's ideas too devastating, Žižek finds Schelling's theory of creativity to be not destructive enough. To Žižek, Schelling ultimately fails to come to terms with the enormous potential of the new thinking he opens up, and ends up retreating into the safe waters of the Aristotelian ontological frame because "he is unready to accept the fact that God's freedom is also the freedom of a forced choice, the gesture of freely assuming an imposed necessity."[26] In contrast, Hallward believes that Deleuze's "subtractive" philosophy points all human activities, through creativity, toward disintegration, and that Deleuze fails to provide us with a constructive view of social life. With their different concerns, both Žižek and Hallward locate the destructive potentiality of creativity in their studies of key philosophers, and they both gesture to a way to turn such negative power into something more productive. In general, the destructive dimension of creativity, although marginal to Western modernity, has been very attractive to thinkers, in the sense that the strong desire in Western modernity to control creativity stems precisely from the danger of creativity.

Schelling's theorization of God echoes Deleuze's analysis of capitalism, as they both concern creation (of things and of capital), and they both demonstrate how creativity must be simultaneously understood as destruction. In addition to its destructive components, creativity is uncontrollable also because it is contingent, and we might say that some early modernist art is most devoted to the exploration of the relationship between creativity and contingency. As mentioned earlier, art becomes the embodiment of divine creativity in modern times, and modernist art incarnates most vividly the desire for freedom and the resistance to meanings that are fundamental to the enlightenment. In his recent book Jameson applauds the contingent dimension of early modernist art, but he finds most of the later established modernists' celebration of creative force a pretense and a failure, precisely because these artists do not recognize art's contingent aspects as their predecessors unconsciously did.[27] Contingency is another concept that resists instrumentalization.

Jameson uses the notion of contingency to distinguish between the two kinds of modernist art: classical modernism, whose practice was untheorized and nameless at the time of its various creations, is preoccupied with chance and accident, but late modernism tames creativity by focusing on the formal and representational problems of contingency. In his words, "Contingency is thus the word for a failure of the idea, the name for what is radically unintelligible, and it belongs to the conceptual field of ontology, rather than that of various epistemologies that succeed and displace an ontological philosophy in the 'modern' period (or since Descartes)." The component of contingency actually made creativity more powerful and alluring, because contingency is not governed by knowledge and order, and it also shows the destabilizing dimension of creativity. Jameson demonstrates that although modernist art claims to celebrate the liberating force of creativity that breaks down modernity's boundaries, most of it actually freezes time by internalizing the past models it disavows. By not confronting true alterity, later modernist artists take refuge in form, which closes down all political possibilities: "Modernism is seen as originating in an ever-keener distance for what is conventional and outmoded, rather than an exploratory appetite for the unexplored and undiscovered."[28] In the name of celebrating creativity, modernist art strives to overcome, but at the same time also preserve, older content and technique.

In fact contingency has always been a problem for modernity. To incorporate culture under its order, the modernity project must monitor and control contingency. In her recent studies of early cinema developed between the end of the nineteenth century and the early twentieth century, Doane argues that modernity is characterized by two dialectical desires: the desire for contingency and the desire for structure. The first decade of cinema development demonstrates the gradual surrendering of the former to the latter.[29] As many film historians have pointed out, the earliest occasional films (those which record the unstructured form of reality, like Lumière's *Exiting the Factory*) were devoted to the documentation of everyday life, displaying the camera's potential for recording. The images recorded are not necessarily "meaningful," but they re-present how we experience our lives. The earliest extant occasional films therefore expose an early affinity between modernity and contingency and demonstrate that this affinity is advanced by the new technology of cinema, which opens up people's sensory aptitude.[30] They are called "occasional" films because they demonstrate a fascination with contingency. But very soon early filmmakers began to ask how they could present contingency in interesting ways, to conceive film not as photographic recording but a series of images with "syntax." Complex editing techniques were developed in order to cut away boring "nonevents," leading to the development of classical cinema, which condenses space and time. As Doane argues, the structuralist desire of modernity can be seen as a battle against contingency.[31] The classical Hollywood cinema model, for example, can be understood as anticontingency par excellence.

Both Jameson and Doane, through their different studies of modernist art and early cinema, conclude that modernity bears the potential to open up contingency and multiplicity, although this dimension is also largely repressed by modernity; modernity bears a dialectic tendency of promoting order and disorder. To Jameson, the works of earlier modernists, whose freedom is utterly blind and groping,[32] are much more fascinating than the works of late modernists, and the latter anticipate their "creativity" in advance through the recognition and disavowal of earlier modernist masters and of the name "modernism" they carry. To Doane, occasional films, being the dominant form of filmmaking in its formative years, were doomed to be suppressed once filmmakers developed a more sophisticated control over the technology and the form. Once the category of "modern" was actualized into specific narratives and forms, the "modern," as Jameson and Doane suggest, lost its sensibility to the power of contingency, and therefore the power of creativity. But at the same time the unrepresentable vision of the ceaseless flow of the absolutely new produced sheer terror; as Jameson stresses, no one can survive under the flux of perpetual change, and we all need a persistent identity over time to gauge our being.[33] So the new is both desired and feared, not only by modernity, but by humanity in general.

Creativity as Social Practice

As demonstrated, modernity shows strong anxiety about and an equally strong fascination with artistic creativity, due precisely to its own components of unpredictability and contingency, which, as Schelling argued, might be directly passed down from divine creativity. This dialectic makes art both powerful and powerless, and it also indirectly explains the creative economy's desire to tame and exploit artistic potentials. In general, I believe that the current creative economy is characterized by certain kinds of modernity logic, albeit intensified. Gianni Vattimo has written that "modernity is defined as the era of overcoming and of the new which rapidly grows old and is immediately replaced by something still newer, in an unstoppable movement that discourages all creativity even as it demands creativity and defines the latter as the sole possible form of life."[34] The contradiction he points out is an important one: although modernity is fueled by creativity, it also makes creativity impossible. In the framework of modernity, Vattimo cautions, although newness is celebrated, it cannot be radical, but must fit into a teleology of progression, so that creativity, already conditioned by the logic of innovation, is always already epistemological. The same mechanism is currently running the creative economy. In the double logic of autonomy and functionalism, artistic creativity becomes powerful and usable, and the two oppositional forces of suppression and fetishism are fed into the same system, making creativity useful for capitalist development.

Not only does the creative economy reconcile and incorporate the oppositional understanding of creativity inherent in Western modernity, but it also, coming back to Habermas, overcomes the modernity segmentation among the aesthetic (fashion, novelty, and flexibility), the epistemological (knowledge and information), and the moral legal (largely in the form of neoliberalism and IPR). As such, creativity has become not simply something to be controlled and manipulated; what we have seen in the past two decades are complex mechanisms and legal conditions allowing ever more intense mutual conditioning between creativity, knowledge, and laws. George Yúdice terms this phenomenon "culture-as-resource," which he argues is the lynchpin of a new epistemic framework in which culture becomes a site to be invested in by all kinds of interests.[35] While this concept has received plenty of academic attention in its usefulness for describing current events, certain critics, such as Peter Osborne, are very critical of it. Osborne argues that the concept of culture-as-resource negates the autonomy of culture from politics, therefore negating also the critical function of metacultural discourse in deploying "culture" against "politics."[36] If culture becomes just a pool of resources for everybody to use, then cultural studies, whose criticality is made possible by the logic of culture, becomes inconceivable.

I agree with Osborne that we cultural critics should hold on to the critical potentiality of culture instead of surrendering it too easily to the epistemic desire of various forces exploiting culture as their own resource. We are seeing many scientific ways of rationalizing and utilizing the creativity potential of culture, not only to maximize profit but also as knowledge to be applied to other realms, so that culture has become a means of "humanizing" both capitalist productivity and political control—often called "cultural turns" in other fields. The workforce is managed in increasingly flexible ways, wherein concepts of leisure, culture, and interactive human relations are introduced, resulting in at-home workers, domestic-style offices, and flexible work schedules and patterns.[37] Political realms have also been transformed. As I mentioned in the introduction, in Australia and the U.K. reformers in the 1990s defined their new politics in cultural terms, emphasizing consumer interests, cultural opportunities, and community life. Accompanying this "aestheticization of politics" is the rise of a new cultural policy discourse underpinned by a strong IPR rhetoric, so that culture can become an economic tool. Generally speaking, knowledge is packaged with creativity for easier consumption, whereas the presentation of culture is heavily engineered by practical knowledge for marketing and functionalist purposes. A legal regime also arises not only to provide order but also to reinforce a new IPR morality. At the same time, production and consumption mutually invade each other, so that we need a feeling of play at work (the need to "humanize" our working environment) and a feeling of work at play (the need to spend our leisure time productively). Such very personal experiences are made to circulate around the world, and the pursuit of individual pleasure fits well within the general neoliberal milieu. When culture becomes resource, culture also loses all its critical potentiality.

We might ask whether alternatives to such omnipotent structures are possible. Clearly one way of thinking is to follow the modernist movement, which stresses the autonomous space occupied by the field of the aesthetic expressive, in the name of art for art's sake, to prevent the encroachment of instrumental reasoning into the field of art. However, Habermas has already rightly pointed out the resultant impotence of art in engaging with the social and the political. Another way of thinking is precisely the Habermasian assertion of the integration of the three realms, but such integration runs the risk of turning culture into resource, which supports today's creative economy. What Habermas ignores in his wish to complete the project of modernity is the tremendous power of the capitalist economy, which is now able to bridge the various realms for the sake of turning a profit.

Here I would like to present a third way of understanding creativity, also within Western philosophy, which casts a new light on the dialectics between control and freedom. In her reading of Giambattista Vico's classic *The New Science*, Sandra Luft does not treat creativity as unpredictable, but as basic to human nature.[38] Luft argues that models of divine creativity in the Hebraic and Greek traditions were appropriated by different Enlightenment thinkers to form drastically different ways of understanding creativity. Great classical thinkers such as Galileo, Descartes, and Leibniz followed Plato's conception of mimesis, but Vico provides a model of the human world that secularizes the Hebraic notion of divine creation to shape people's worldviews. In Vico's model there are three distinct conceptions of creativity, which correspond to three generations of being. First, there is the age of the gods, who create. Second, there are the first peoples, the heroes, who respond to the gods' creation by uttering their first words, with a "corporeal imagination," an originary language inseparable from deeds and things, out of ignorance and fear. Third, we, the people of "the third age," have made ourselves subjective beings.[39]

Luft's interpretation of this model is characterized by her two main arguments. First, the Hebraic tradition, as documented by Vico, provides a different way to understand the original creative power; Vico's god is more a creator than a knower. Second, we should not understand Vico's historical schema as a developmental one, and we must avoid considering the "instrumental" third people to be more advanced than the "poetic" second people. Instead they are connected genetically, so that the people of the third age are also equipped with the poetic ability of the first and second ages: "For Vico the poetic event originates a patterned and recurrent process unfolding genetically through three ages." Being direct descendants of the first peoples, people of the third age are also creators, and their creativity is never other than that of being in the world. In contrast, the metaphysical tradition that Western modernity inherited from Plato emphasizes humans' epistemic ability. If Descartes describes the modern subject as the knower, Vico describes him or her as the creator: people can create without knowing. Vico's tale is a powerful one, breaking the Platonic dichotomy between making as fictive and knowing as real, and it reminds us, according to Luft, that "humans are never other than creators, their reality never other than artifactual and finite, their 'truths' never other than fictive."[40] By demonstrating how we came from the first Gentiles, who were poets precisely because they were not knowers, Vico locates the originality of humanity in which we are always ontological beings who creatively respond to what arises in our social historical world.

While in the metaphysical story creativity is subdued in the course of secularization, Vico provides an alternative vision, helping us see a concrete creativity rendered as people's poetic and vulnerable responses to the world, like the utterance *pa* to express one's fear of thunder. This utterance is a recognition of the original poverty of the human condition, and, according to Luft, such "primitive" creativity continues to be embodied in the social practices of modern people. Vico's model, in which knowledge and subjectivity cannot be separated, also helps us interrogate modernity's segregation of creativity into instrumental reasoning and aesthetic sentiments. There is nothing mystical about creativity, and it does not belong only to a select few. Because we are always already creative, and through creativity we express ourselves and connect to other people, there are no grounds for fetishizing creativity.

Vico's understanding of the intimate relationship between divine creation and human praxis finds an interesting echo in a branch of theological thinking. It is true that the mainstream understanding of creation within Christian studies is of a dichotomy between chaos and order, in which the Christian God creates by providing order. Many of the current mainstream theological studies therefore tread the similar epistemological path of Western modernity. However, even in contemporary theological studies there is a model of divine creation, known as the "serendipity of history," which complements Vico's ideas in an odd way. Instead of explaining how human creativities are responses to and results of divine creation, the theologian Gordon D. Kaufman argues just the opposite. He asserts that the common conception of the Christian God is actually drawn from the way people understand human activities. It is mostly our everyday experience of being humans as individual agents in modern Westernized society that shapes the conception of God as Creator: "This conception of God is clearly constructed on the model of the human purposive agent, capable of self-conscious creative work." Kaufman finds this model a limiting one, polarizing the creator and the created in the mechanism of control and also reinforcing the conception of the self (on the part of the creator) as freestanding and metaphysically self-sufficient. Thus Kaufman demonstrates an alternative model of divine creativity, one which is based not on the notion of sufficient and controlling human agency, but on the complex development patterns of culture, language, and society: "This capacity or feature of history, to produce vastly more than we human inventors and creators and purposes expected or intended is what I call the 'serendipity of history.'"[41] Based on the ways human civilization has unfolded, divine creativity can therefore be seen as an enormous and nonlinear expansion of effects that are not determined by any original intention, although humans fully participate in it. Just as history unfolds in surprising ways, divine creativity also goes in all kinds of directions.

Although Kaufman is concerned not with modernity as such but with the understanding of the Christian God, the predicament he is trying to resolve is relevant to Vico's project, as he also finds problematic the connection between creativity and the control of human agency. While Vico posits a different understanding of divine creativity in order to provide an alternative conceptualization of our human world, Kaufman suggests that the complex ways the human world has evolved shed light on our comprehension of divine creativity. Therefore Kaufman's idea can be understood alongside Vico's non-epistemological poetic creation. Creativity is not controlled and ordered by some willful agency, but interacts with the subject (divine or human) to mutually define each other.

Most important, Kaufman's analysis posits that man's desire to understand God can also be a creative act: either we apply our own instrumentalist desire to God, or we associate God with the serendipity of historical unfolding. In this sense, we can relate creativity not only to production but also to understanding. Introducing the notion of understanding in my framework of "creativity as social practice" is important, because a community cannot be formed without a continuous and complex relation between production and reception, encoding and decoding. The ways creativity functions in culture comprise both that involve making and understanding.

"Creative understanding" is a notion Mikhail Bakhtin has used to refer to the dialogic encounter of people with different cultural backgrounds. In order to understand, a person should be located outside the object of one's creative understanding, not pretending that one has either incorporated the other or forgotten oneself, both ways demonstrate the epistemological desire characterizing western modernity. "Creative understanding does not renounce itself, its own place and time, its own culture; it forgets nothing."[42] This idea of creative understanding is intimately related to his more famous concept of "dialogism," referring to the many languages at work in a community, making both understanding and diversity possible.[43] The two notions link meaning productions and meaning receptions, through which Bakhtin emphasizes the plural expressions produced in a community that do not hinder but in fact contribute to the formation of a community. Bakhtin's use of the term "creative" is particularly illuminating, and can be related to Kaufman's model of divine creation. Creation is an act involving not only action but also reaction, and the object of creation will be transformed and re-created by those who receive them creatively. This chain-like model emphasizes the irreducible existence of both oneself and the other: to be creative is to remember that we are not isolated controlling intellects but social beings constantly caught in the intercourse between ourselves and others. Kaufman's and Bakhtin's models of creative understanding endorse social intercourse, mutual respect, and the existence of other possibilities, connecting creativity with social praxis.[44] This understanding of creative acts is different from the way we have understood Western artistic genius, and the idea that creativity is a matter of social practice can be seen as an effective challenge to both the modernity project and the creative economy. Both the modernity project and the creative economy celebrate creativity as the making of "new" ideas and products, but only to the extent that creative energy will not exceed the control of human beings. The sense of uncertainty inherent in the new is therefore tamed, and the rich potentiality of creativity is also radically depleted.

In order to critically challenge the instrumental manipulation of creativity, what we need is neither a Habermasian call to render art relevant to society, nor a simple claim of creativity as uncontrollable. Instead we need a more profound understanding of creativity—one that both builds and destroys, one that connects individuals and also points toward one's own alterity, and one that belongs not only to a few gifted individuals but to all of us. It is our willingness to grant, or simply acknowledge, the full potentiality of creativity that might help us to counter the late capitalist desire for total control. Therefore it is not my aim in this book to dichotomize creative industries and intellectual property rights offenses, whose opposition is largely a discursive construction of the creative economy, but to explain their continuity in relation to creativity's multifaceted manifestations.

Creativity as a Product of Labor

In the preceding chapter I located the ideological roots of the creative economy in Western modernity. To understand the complex lacework of the ways creativity is used economically, in this chapter I would like to shift my focus from modernity to capitalism, from creativity as freedom to creativity as a product of human labor. The critical stance I took against the instrumentalization of creativity in chapter 1 does not imply an uncritical celebration of transcendentalism or naturalism. While Vico's *pa* might reflect human beings' spontaneously creative and fearful responses to the wonders of nature, the creativity celebrated in the creative economy does not just happen; it involves elaborate industrial manipulation. The creative economy relies on, but also readily dismisses, the materiality of creative labor. My objective in this chapter is to uncover the labor factor that makes up this creative economy, although there is also a danger in privileging the industrial aspect of creativity, which will be treated in greater detail in chapter 3. First I will deal with the notion of creative labor.

One of the most important theoretical works on the concept is Maurizio Lazzarato's "Immaterial Labor," in which he argues that the old dichotomy between manual or material and mental or immaterial labor has failed to grasp the new nature of production activities. According to Lazzarato, the late 1970s witnessed a new phase of capitalist production that emphasizes the value of communication, which in turn acts as the interface negotiating the relationship between production and consumption. It is also in this new kind of commodity and commodification that the dichotomy between material and immaterial labor falls apart. At the end of the essay, Lazzarato demonstrates two models of immaterial labor: Simmel accepts the division of labor founded on the opposition between manual and intellectual labor, whereas Bakhtin defines immaterial labor as the diffusion of the two.[1] Lazza-

rato argues that Simmel runs the risk of legitimizing the regulation and mystification of the social process of creation and innovation, because in Simmel's
model members of the upper middle classes create fashion, and the lower
classes attempt to imitate them. Lazzarato finds Bakhtin's call to supersede
the division between material labor and intellectual labor more productive,
in that it offers a view to understanding how creativity is a social process.

Of greatest significance in Lazzarato's essay is his advancement of a new
theory of social production that diffuses the boundaries between manual and
intellectual labor, which, he believes, would also provide room to demythologize the division of the two classes to which the two kinds of labor supposedly
belong. However, I believe the increasing overlap of the two kinds of labor
which Lazzarato identifies is not maintained by mutual diffusion: the two
logics exist simultaneously in new global conditions, and their coexistence
does not cancel either out, but intensifies both. Unlike Lazzarato, I would
argue that creative labor does not embody the disappearance of boundaries
between manual and intellectual labor, but it is a unique function that demonstrates the intensification of the contradictions between the two logics.

In fact the current creative economy is saturated with an abhorrence or
ignorance of traditional manual labor.[2] People in the West lament the moving of factories to developing countries, but the fact is that fewer and fewer
educated people are attracted to routinized production work. The migration
of monotonous assembly line work is in part willed by the citizens of wealthy
nations, so that they, and particularly members of the younger generation,
can partake in more "innovative" and "rewarding" careers. Alvin Toffler's
claim—that traditional labor has become less important in the new information society, and the new hero is the innovator, who combines imaginative
knowledge with action—is clearly naïve.[3] Traditional labor is not less important; it is just less visible. Sweatshops are exported to faraway lands, rendering
them invisible to most of the developed world, which retains only the most
"desirable" sorts of work.

Toffler also describes the disappearance of labor exploitation in the new
economy: industrial workers were exploited because they owned the few tools
of production, but today the most powerful wealth-amplifying tools reside in
workers' heads, making the workers irreplaceable and therefore unexploit-
able.[4] But we know that exploitation of the creative class continues to inten-
sify in the developed world. In the new economy, labor is seemingly bifurcated: regressive, exploitable manual labor is considered obsolete and should
be replaced and displaced by creative works and knowledge production. In
the affluent parts of the world, the new economy dematerializes not only com-

modities but also labor, in the sense that work is packaged as leisure, and hardship and boredom are effaced by the promises of creativity and satisfaction. This eradication of traditional labor and the romanticization of creative labor in the West are made possible by the exploitation of Third World labor (or Third World populations in the First World). Labor exploitation has become impossible to discuss among the new creative workers, as exploitation is thought to have vanished.

The problematic dichotomization between the First and Third Worlds leads to, or is partly justified by, the false dichotomization of the two types of labor; intellectual and manual labor are concentrated in completely different geographical locations and political economies to allow the opposite logics to operate alongside each other.[5] The developed world therefore is empowered by the works of "symbolic analysis," to borrow Robert B. Reich's term; scientists, researchers, and designers in the West busily sell their ideas and discoveries and plan globally.[6] Abstracted and isolated either as figures of jobs lost in the developed world or as human exploitation in the developing world—both of which could be used to justify claims of globalization—actual labor vanishes, or is distorted, in the formulation of the creative economy.

While Lazzarato and his *futur antérieur* fellows are right to point out the false dichotomization between the two types of labor, focusing on the immaterial labor in the contemporary West they tend to privilege the vanguardism of the "intellectual proletariat" without examining more closely its ideological formation.[7] Herein I wish to reconnect the relationship between creativity and labor. It is important to bring labor back to the investigation of the creative economy in order to demonstrate that creativity is not just an aesthetic concept but also a social praxis and to examine how the new creative economy continues to harbor exploitation while investing in fantasized notions of creativity. The notion of the creative economy should not mislead us into believing that creativity has replaced capital as an end unto itself. As long as this economy remains firmly grounded in capitalism, the ultimate object remains capital, and labor is an essential form of input.

The Artist versus the Creative Worker

As I discussed in the previous chapter, the modernity project celebrates the individualistic controlling subject, which in the domain of art and culture is the artist genius. The artist's expressions are believed to be the result of his or her unique talents, expressions whose creativity cannot be replicated. This notion of the artist can be seen as the ideological antithesis of, on the one hand, alienated industrial workers who lack opportunities to engage in their work creatively, and, on the other hand, the masses who revere, or are ignorant of, artwork. However, the actual economic conditions governing the creative worker currently are vastly different from any idealized world of art: creative commodities are produced for the consumption of the masses. Whereas the notion of the artist suggests autonomy and freedom, creative labor operates under the division of labor, so that no individual can claim complete ownership of a product. The two logics are not dichotomized in the new economy, but logics of aesthetic production and industrial production simultaneously structure creative labor, whose products can be considered both artistic and accessible to the masses. A careful investigation of the tensions and negotiations of the two strains of logic should give us a unique angle from which to understand how the current creative economy incorporates creativity as a new condition of late capitalist production.

I believe that any criticism of the creative economy must start with a careful analysis of the author function.[8] As Martha Woodmansee argues, the artist or author as creative genius did not fully emerge before the eighteenth century,[9] but then became dominant in Western society. The concept of moral rights is steeped in this Romanticist understanding of the artist, with a strong possessive connotation based on the premise that the author owns the work. We should guard against the exploitation that results from distributor-based copyright discourse,[10] but a nostalgic return to the notion of the autonomous artist does little to help us analyze the creative economy, which is only a continuous development of author-based modernity.

The creative economy continues to rely on the Romantic notion of the genius artist to reify creativity, while at the same time overcoming the "inefficiency" associated with the artist discourse. The creative worker might still be characterized by his or her personal artistic sensibilities, but he or she also rationally weighs both creativity and business considerations to produce salable products. The main activities in the late capitalist economy are centered on consumer desire for identification and self-expression, and this economy advances subjective and unpredictable evaluations of taste, making styles and trends extremely volatile—but profitable. The creative worker is mythologized as the source of these transient but priceless ideas, and the consumer buys freedom and self-realization from the producer in the form of the commodity. The discourse of talent built around creative labor has afforded the worker entry into a privileged class, perpetuating the illusion that it is the creative class, instead of the capitalists, that leads the way in the current economy. However, while the discourse of the genius persists, the concept of artistic creation is also the most estranged by the commodification of creativity. Marx suggests that the more the logic of exchange values dominates the production process, the more laborers will be alienated.[11] This condition of industrial labor now applies to creative labor: artists, who supposedly produce for the sake of their own self-expression, are estranged by their own products, which are subject to capitalist logic; these works are no longer ends in themselves, but are meaningful only in their exchange values.

The simultaneous existence and mutual reinforcement of the logics of art and commerce are not new and have been structured over the course of the development of modern art in the West, in which the art market developed in tandem with the discourse of the genius artist.[12] Since the seventeenth century the commodification of art and the discourse of the master artist have mutually penetrated. What distinguishes the uniqueness of our current creative age is not only the mutual support of the two domains of art and commerce, but also how the new category of the creative worker simultaneously embodies two seemingly oppositional logics. The master artist, although embedded in the art market, remains at a distance from commercial activities pertaining to his or her work due to the supposed separation of artistic production and reception. But the creative worker does not have this privilege; his or her labor is situated squarely in a dense economic reality. A recent Hollywood film offers us a glimpse of the complex intertwining — and mutual rejection — of the artist discourse and management logic simultaneously embodied in the same creative worker. I choose to discuss a Hollywood film as an illustrative example here, instead of a real social case, because there have been many empirical studies already conducted (see the introduction) and also because of the unique ideological value Hollywood cinema maintains and which is constitutive of the creative economy. This film has the quality of both aggrandizing the phantasmagoria of creative labor and subtly revealing the repressed exploitation.

The Devil Wears Prada (directed by David Frankel, 2006) evokes the glamour as well as the gloom of the working environment of the creative economy. Miranda Priestly, chief editor of the prestigious fashion magazine *Runway*, embodies the most powerful type of creative labor, because it is her aesthetic taste that determines which designers get media exposure and she dictates global fashion trends. She is not an actual designer, but the arbiter of "taste." She is both manager and artist, and she uses her talent and power to control global fashion. The film revolves around the trust that develops between Miranda and her new assistant, Andrea, who initially disdains the pretentiousness and the lack of social importance of the fashion business. In spite of Miranda's ruthlessness and the submission and transformation of Andrea, the film is a clear endorsement of the power and glamour of fashion, indirectly reinforcing Hollywood's role in constructing fashion.

But both the aura of art and the brutality of commerce loom large in the characterization of Miranda. Miranda's career is inherently linked to a diversified range of labor, from designers to factory laborers, and her power is based on the hierarchy among these different forms of labor. In one of their early confrontations, Miranda lectures Andrea on the sacredness of her work, stating that any single decision she makes will determine the livelihoods of thousands of people working at the various levels of the fashion industry. In the hierarchy of the new global division of labor, Miranda epitomizes the pinnacle of work (or nonwork), which controls and coordinates the actual production taking place in, say, Third World factories. But the film is not just a glorification of this position, and it can also be seen as an effort to strip Miranda of her aura by exposing fierce competition behind the scenes. She not only possesses the aura of the artist, but also embodies the treacherous entrepreneur. She is set against Nigel, the magazine's creative director, who has helped Miranda to make creative decisions in the past. But when Nigel thinks that he can finally leave Miranda and embark on a creative life of his own, Miranda makes a scapegoat of him in order to preserve her own job; Nigel's new job is then given to Miranda's rival.

Not only Miranda, but also the film itself, vacillates between the glorification and the condemnation of fashion. The morality of the film seemingly can be summarized in Miranda's accusation of Andrea: "You sold your soul the first time you put on that pair of Jimmy Choos." At the end of the film Andrea decides to abandon fashion and embark on a journey of self-realization. But the thrust of the film is clearly Andrea's coming of age through her life in the fashion industry, and the film's narrative structure and visual pleasure are clearly organized around the display of fashion. We could therefore read two different sets of ideological values in this film: fashion as capitalist vanity ultimately to be discarded, and fashion as creativity, freedom, and self-realization, which characterize the essence of creative labor. This dual set of values assigned to fashion makes up Miranda's subjectivity. The struggles between Miranda and Nigel, or those between Miranda and Andrea, can be seen as externalizing Miranda's own internal tensions: she is torn between the logic of art and the logic of commerce she simultaneously embodies. In spite of, or perhaps due to, her arrogance and selfishness, Miranda absorbs the complete attention and devotion of the people around her. But the artistic aura she embodies is also demythologized by her own submission to power. Like all creative workers, she possesses a split personality because she must both self-actualize and fulfill competitive market demands at the same time. The film resolves these tensions by separating Miranda and Andrea. However, in reality the actual operation of creative labor cannot be differentiated between "good" artistic qualities and "bad" market calculations—and this, I think, is a unique feature of creative labor that merits further exploration.

Creative Labor: Input and Processing

Marxist discussion of raw materials is valuable to our understanding of creative labor, because the new economy is characterized by the feeding of creativity—as one more type of raw material—into the chain of production. In classical Marxism, there are three elements necessary for capitalist production: raw material, labor power, and machinery; these are the material embodiments of the "self-expansion" of capital. Simply speaking, the value of an exchangeable good is determined by the labor and the machinery required to transform raw materials into commodities. In other words, labor and machines are treated largely as tools employed to transform raw materials into commodities.

$$\text{Raw Materials} \xrightarrow{\text{Industrial Labor + Technology}} \text{Tangible Commodity}$$

In the production of intellectual property, the input is not tangible raw material but intangible knowledge, ideas, or expressions, which are provided by the creative worker and transformed by technological mediation into commodities, whether something as "simple" as writing down musical notation or as complex as putting together a Hollywood movie. In the creative economy the factory is replaced by a computer, so that industrial labor disappears into the creative worker working comfortably on his own.

$$\underset{\text{(Creative Labor)}}{\text{Ideas}} \xrightarrow{\text{Technology}} \text{Intellectual Property}$$

The two formulae differ most clearly in the form of input: tangible raw materials in traditional industrial production are replaced by abstract ideas and knowledge conceived and organized by a creative agent to produce intellectual property. Theoretically, a creative idea is not depleted after exploitation, and a single idea can be applied to an infinite number of products. The ever renewing trend of "glam" in the fashion industry, for example, derives partly from 1970s glam rock, whose visual dimensions were highly influenced by pop art of the 1960s. David Bowie himself can be seen as a specter perennially haunting the fashion business in different forms. Glam, in an abstract way, can be seen as a raw material to be applied in different creative processes for different creative products. We could describe this characteristic as "nonrival," as an idea that can be shared infinitely. The economics of intellectual property, therefore, might be described not in terms of scarcity, but of abundance. Many argue that this inexhaustible dimension of intellectual production is the key feature of the creative economy, in contrast to industrial capitalism's basis in competition for limited resources.

However, a simple differentiation between scarcity and abundance does not truly describe the differences between the creative economy and the traditional industrial economy. First, we must note that in Marxism, traditional raw materials also have an inexhaustible dimension. According to Marx, "The object of labour counts as raw material only when it has already undergone some alteration by means of labour." To Marx, raw materials differ from natural resources: natural resources are those means of production supplied by nature without human assistance—such as land, wind, and water—and create use-value without contributing to the formation of exchange value. In all other operations of capitalism that create exchange values, raw materials themselves must be understood as products of labor, meaning that they are already processed. Raw materials, in other words, are both products of labor and means of production. Cotton, for example, is both a product of industrial extraction and a piece of raw material for further industrial manipulation. "Hence we see that whether a use-value is to be regarded as raw material, as instrument of labour or as product is determined entirely by its specific function in the labour process, by the position it occupies there." His interest lying not in the primitive process of animalistic survival but in the ways an advanced economy functions, Marx emphasizes that raw materials are not collected to be consumed, but are embedded in the chain of production. They must be constantly used and reappropriated, because it is through the incessant process of production and consumption that surplus values are created.[13] Therefore, in the chain of production, raw materials do not stay unchanged, but are constantly transformed, consumed, and reappropriated to facilitate the production of capital.

I want to emphasize that Marx does not understand raw materials in terms of abundance or scarcity, as they are not inert and waiting to be exhausted, but are always worked over by labor. Raw material in itself does not interest him; it is the applied labor that is vital to our understanding of capitalist production. It is in the processing of raw materials by labor that capitalism generates and recoups its energy. Marx describes the capitalist mechanism of raw material production:

> On the one hand, the immediate effect of machinery is to increase the supply of raw material: thus, for example, the invention of the cotton gin increased the production of cotton. On the other hand, the cheapness of the articles produced by machinery and the revolution in the means of transport and communication provide the weapons for the conquest of foreign markets. By ruining handicraft production of finished articles in other countries, machinery forcibly converts them into fields for the production of its raw material. Thus India was compelled to produce cotton, wool, hemp, jute and indigo for Great Britain.[14]

While labor of the developing world continues to be exploited, production efficiency is greatly improved by industrial machinery. They both help reduce prices, and therefore expand markets. This process of constant harvesting of raw materials then drives colonialism and imperialism, which further expands the production of raw materials, and therefore capital.

This Marxist understanding of raw material as continuous, inexhaustible, and constantly transforming applies also to intellectual property, and our understanding of creative labor would be productively enriched by taking into account the continuous nature of raw materials. To return to our second formula, the labor factor is effaced in the production of creative commodity because ideas are thought to be produced effortlessly. But on a closer look, labor is required both in the production of ideas—in the various forms of training and experimentation, as well as group discussions and collaboration—and, like all other modern forms of commodities, in the transformation of ideas, as raw material, into commodities.

Therefore the labor factor in the production of intellectual property is manifested into at least two connected forms: labor that initiates ideas (CL^1) and labor that transforms creative input (CL^2):

$$\text{Ideas} \xrightarrow[\text{(Creative labor / } CL^1)]{\text{Technology + Creative Labor / } CL^2} \text{Intellectual Property}$$

Marx argues that raw material is not the origin of production but is embedded in the incessant chain of production; as such, labor is also embedded in the raw material. The production of intellectual property follows a similar logic, in that there is also no absolute origin of the creative idea as implied in the traditional artist genius discourse, and therefore the two types of creative labor (CL^1 and CL^2) cannot be separated. The new ideas one is able to come up with are necessarily versions of the products of previous cultural productions, and both CL^1 and CL^2 involve selection, processing, and recycling of "old" ideas into "new" ones. Be it tangible commodity or intangible intellectual property, the production input must be an output of a previous production process, but at the same time the material is consumed and transformed in order to produce surplus value. Therefore, as is the case in the capitalist mode of production, creativity, like traditional raw materials, cannot be simply understood as either scarce or abundant, but needs labor input to introduce it to the capitalist system.

I am not arguing that the logic of creative labor is identical to that of traditional labor, but we know that the labor involved in the production of intellectual property is much more complex than that of traditional property, as the identity of a creative worker not only resides in his or her output, but he or she is also consumer and tastemaker. In his discussion of the creative class, Richard Florida not only describes its work, but he also elaborately documents its lifestyle. The creative class is admired not only for its labor but also for its consumption, as well as the intricate overlap between work and leisure manifested among this group of people.[15] Members of this creative class consume their own products, and they themselves define what style is. Due to the quasi-artist status given to creative laborers, not only are they passive consumers, but they are also their own critics, and they shape and endorse trends. In the case of advertising, a profession which heavily manipulates the notion of creativity, the success of agencies and individuals is directly linked to awards received; the power to dictate and shape creativity is governed by the profession itself.[16] This phenomenon is described as "peer regard." Andy C. Pratt argues that "peer regard works most effectively in fuzzy, fast-moving environments that are about 'quality' not 'quantity': industries driven by fashion and consumption changes are a good case."[17] I agree with Pratt that in the new creative industries it is the common task of peers to shape what style is and what creativity is, but I believe that not only quality but also quantity must be highlighted in the creative economy, in the sense that abstract creativity and rational calculation constantly negotiate with and complement each other.

Contemporary creative workers also exhibit strong entrepreneurial ability. Creative workers tend to be freelancers, or have a job that is short term and insecure. In general, they are responsible for their own careers, so they need to take risks, develop their own networks, and readily adapt to changing markets. In order to maintain their own competitiveness, they need to be innovative, flexible, and sometimes aggressive in order to gain access to the latest knowledge and opportunities provided by the market. At the same time, they need to maintain good interpersonal skills, build trust networks, and offer and receive peer support.[18] As a result, many creative workers lead lives very similar to those of entrepreneurs, and they manage their career more as entrepreneurs than as artists, constantly coping with risks while remaining open to new career breaks. Dialectically they manage their careers as much as they are managed. As Stefano Harney argues, the creative industries are primarily a manifestation of the logic of management, organizing labor in such a way that it is not art being commodified, but the creative industries commodifying those who produce art.[19] Between the dynamics of management and the dynamics of self-management, the creative worker is both empowered and disempowered.

Despite, and because of, the trend toward flexibility, spaces for independent work are actually shrinking. It is clear that the components of creative freedom and individualism inherent in the traditional artist discourse are not compatible with the components of peer evaluation and collective contribution in the discourse of creative labor. The notion of freedom continues to be circulated, but it does not really describe the mode of production of the creative worker so much as it legitimizes job insecurity.[20] In fact creativity poses hidden threats to our creative economy, and discipline must be enforced to keep creativity contained. To be commodified for mass consumption, the components of freedom associated with creativity must be restrained.[21] Marissa Ann Mayer, vice president of search product and user experience at Google, justifies the company's exploitation of its creative labor by arguing that creativity triumphs over and benefits from "rules." By delimiting how many designers work on each new product and for how long, management limits the company's investment. Mayer argues that this limitation is in fact good for creativity, as their designers come up with better ideas and throw away bad ones faster: "Constraints shape and focus problems and provide clear challenges to overcome. Creativity thrives best when constrained."[22] While this creative economy craves creativity, it also recognizes strong incentives to tame creativity. Creativity can be a most time- and capital-consuming activity. If we indulge in it, it can eat up the entire support of the economy. In other words, although this late capitalist economy relies heavily on creativity, creativity—as an unraveling of potentialities and unfamiliarity—is also a natural enemy of capitalism, whose principles are efficiency, productivity, and management. I believe the theory that "creativity loves constraints" is not only Google's justification for exploiting its creative workers, but a dialectical demonstration of the threat of unrestrained creativity.

The simultaneous dichotomization and intensification of intellectual and manual labor is manifested within not only identical creative agents like Miranda in *The Devil Wears Prada* but also the creative class. We know that the creative class is composed of a hierarchy of workers ranked largely by their level of creative input: there are glamorous designers who make key decisions, and there are also strata of less creative workers suffering from low job security and high career risk. Research suggests that in the rapid expansion of the service sector in the past two decades inequality grew within the sector, not simply between sectors.[23] As critics explain, "'Hot' industries and 'cool' jobs not only normalize, they glamorize risk, and the entrepreneurial investment required of individuals seeking these jobs leads to a structural disincentive to exit during difficult economic times. The image of glamorized risk provides support for continued attacks on unionized work and for ever more market-driven, portfolio-based evaluations of workers' value."[24] Such an illusion is clearly a result of the aura accorded the creative dimension of the creative class. In spite of the actual complex manifestation of creative labor, the glamour of creativity continues to prevent us from seeing the intimate relationship between industrial labor and creative labor, allowing the creative economy to privilege spontaneous creativity as being naturally more valuable than the labor required to change raw creativity into commodity, although it is labor that really makes up the creative economy.

A radical subjectivism is still retained in the creative economy, in the sense that creative energies supposedly emerge from a creator's self-exploration, and the creator's expressive power derives from imaginative depth. At the same time, creativity can now be planned, exercised, and executed by careful formulation and coordination, and it has become a collective product. The creative agent, then, is no longer an autonomous individual artist who exercises creativity for her own sake; nor does she follow rigid rules to perform her duties. But this agent combines both logics, maneuvering a diversified mode of thinking and training in order to produce both creatively and industrially. Endowed with both the elite status of the artist and the consumption pattern of the leisure class, the popular imagination of the creative worker effectively conceals her actual labor circumstances.

The Democratization of Creativity

In the logic of the creative economy, there is a dialectic relationship between creativity scarcity and creativity democracy. In order to justify their property status, contrary to the other commonsense understanding that intellectual property is "nonrival," intangible materials like ideas and creativity are understood to be exhaustible, so that activities related to sharing and copying can be delegitimized. Owners do not want to share their creative ideas with others because, they claim, ideas can be exhausted through sharing and copying. It is believed that the value of a creative idea decreases with each successive iteration.[25] In order to apply the notion of exhaustion to creative ideas, these ideas must be understood in temporal terms: fashions come and go; creativity becomes a sparkle doomed to fade away. Increasingly medical discourse is also built upon concepts of competition; constantly mutating diseases and viruses continually make drugs obsolete. In addition to fetishizing newness, IPR owners also artificially create scarcity. In her analysis of film collecting in the VHS and DVD era, Barbara Klinger demonstrates that digitally reproduced films can never become rare. But in order to raise the desire for ownership among videotape or disc buyers, the language of scarcity (e.g., limited editions or rare items) permeates the discourse of video releases.[26] In order to conjure up the brand aura in spite of infinite production capacities, many companies, from Louis Vuitton to Nike, persistently introduce new "limited edition" products to the market to keep the retail price high and the queuing line long. The myth of exhaustion is most trickily revealed in the case of publicity right, which is based on the assumption that celebrity can become exhausted, so that the one who owns the public image can claim property rights to the image. As Landes and Posner assert, "The trademark and right-of-publicity cases . . . recognize that intellectual property can be diminished by consumption."[27] As I have mentioned earlier, while the image of David Bowie is constantly alluded to in the fashion industry to give value to new products, publicity right also assumes that Bowie's value will decline with constant use. Obviously both sides have their own audience.

The scarcity discourse of creativity is intimately related to the fetishization of creative labor. To return to the formulae analyzed earlier, the creative worker seems to be situated at the origin of the production process, which places him or her in a more privileged position than the industrial laborer, who is only a tool. The scarcity myth of creativity can be maintained in this age of creative economy only by the exalted position of the creative agency. In examining the digitization of film culture, Michele Pierson asks to what extent special effects are still special, if computer-generated imaging (CGI) effects are taken for granted in current Hollywood productions, and whether these so-called special effects only serve to meet the demand for photo-realism.[28] Pierson argues that a discourse of scarcity is still maintained, but in the sense that only a certain group of people (i.e., Hollywood) can produce such images. The aesthetics of scarcity continues to dominate Hollywood's fetishization of CGI, which produces the effect of impressing upon viewers that special effects are still special, and they are owned exclusively by Hollywood. While creative workers employed by Hollywood studios or related corporations are subject to the constraints of marketing strategies, company profiles, deadlines, and teamwork, the decoy of the Hollywood brand unifies them as the abstract author of commercial films, thus reifying the values of this creative class.[29] The gay population is now sought after by the notoriously conservative Singapore government on the assumption that gayness equals creative talent, and many formerly prosperous and up-and-coming American cities are also investing in cultural infrastructure to attract creative workers and (re)vitalize urban areas.[30] In general, the creative economy justifies the scarcity of creativity by conjuring up the scarcity of creative agents in order to legitimize the discourse of creativity ownership.

However, the myth of the scarcity of creative workers is both contradicted and supported by the opposite discourse of creativity democratization. Responding to the rise of the creative economy, Florida articulates a new framework of the "creative class," which is unified by the values of individuality and meritocracy, as well as the recognition of diversity and openness.[31] The elitism embedded in the discourse of the genius is discarded, which limits the availability of the creative source. In this sense, Florida's work contains a hidden tension in his formulation of the creative class, as he argues that creativity is both intrinsic to all, a biologically and intellectually innate characteristic in all human beings, and realized only selectively. He is most disturbed by the fact that only one-third of the workforce is employed in the creative sector, in which employees are often treated much better than those in the manufacturing sectors. So he advocates expansion of the creative class. I infer that Florida believes in the mutual reinforcement of the growth of creativity and the growth of economics, both of which have no limits. In other words, he uses a capitalist mind-set of development to understand creativity. He argues that "the role of culture is much more expansive, that human beings have limitless potential, and that the key to economic growth is to enable and unleash that potential."[32] Although creativity is innate to all, within the capitalist framework the competitive dimension of the creative economy must be retained and further emphasized, thus Florida's self-contradictory discourse of fetishizing something that's supposed to be universal. Now competition rests not in the discovery of individual geniuses, but in the democratization and intensification of creativity, so governments need to promote the teaching of "creativity," and there should also be a more extensive merit system to reward the creative ones.

Since the rise of the creative economy, creativity can no longer belong only to a talented few, but must be democratized to expand the creative labor force. John Seabrook observes that as the mainstream becomes ever more homogeneous, the fringes have also become ever richer in cultural offerings, with an enormous increase in niche markets as well as "artists": "Virtually everyone under twenty-five I met at MTV was an artist of one kind or another."[33] This phenomenon is reinforced by the IPR legal regime, which has also loosened the qualifications of authorship. Jane Gaines observes:

> All works of authorship are original. Why? Because they originate with authors. . . . Every work is an original work, regardless of whether it is aesthetically unoriginal, banal, or in some cases, imitative. Every individual person is also a potential "author" whose "writings" will be as "original" as those of a renowned or acclaimed literary figure. . . . Copyright's minimal point of origin requirement, which considers light fixtures and belt buckles as "works of authorship," performs a critique of traditional theory's notion of authorial originality. Copyright law is a great cultural leveler.[34]

As Gaines suggests, copyright's loose demands on the qualification of authorship help democratize authorship, so that everybody can now be a writer or an artist in the legal sense. With various new production (cheap cameras and easy editing programs) and distribution (YouTube and other online sites) technologies available, everyone can make and exhibit moving images, dramatically increasing the number of legitimate video artists worldwide. While Gaines is right to point out the impact of this cultural democracy on the traditional understanding of the artist, we cannot assume this "cultural leveler" will lead to a more egalitarian society. This democratization of creativity also supports current economic conditions, so that the proliferation of creativity, with the help of the legal protection of IPR, continues to fetishize the capitalist value of creativity, and the competition toward creativity only intensifies, as implied in Florida's arguments.

The idea that everybody produces is not new to us, as the Birmingham school of cultural studies has demonstrated that consumption can be active and political; this is most easily observed in the ways that fans not only exchange and accumulate ideas, but they also poach and create values.[35] But the drastic democratization of art production training and art-performing experience is an altogether completely different phenomenon, as creativity is not only democratized but also fetishized by our education system and popular culture, to the extent that each of us is fed the illusion that "I" am uniquely talented. Seemingly contradictory ideas of creativity—elitist and democratic—can also be found in today's popular culture, in which fans think of celebrities as gods. The structure of fan culture remains largely hierarchical: the audience reveres the artist. But the coexistence of different conceptions of creativity is more intertwined: although an artist may be so unique as to be worthy of mass worship, the worshippers themselves may one day become idols in their own right, as demonstrated by the global popularity of reality TV programs such as *American Idol*. In other words, the creative economy's celebration of the democratization of creativity is manifested in the individual fan's fantasy of being an idol. Such creative democracy does not demythologize notions of talent or deconstruct the associated hierarchy, as the Birmingham school strives to do. It only reinforces competition and naturalizes the social ladder based on the myth that everyone is equal. Going back to my discussion in the previous chapter, creativity should not be revered only as a production drive; we also need to acknowledge the creative dimension in reception in order to recognize creativity as a process of social intercourse.

The reification of creativity as a form of personal aptitude permeates not only discussions of creative labor but other, even oppositional discourses. Eva Hemmungs Wirtén rightly observes that a major problem of recent critical discourses against IPR expansion is the resurrection and reinvention of the author under names such as "hacker."[36] The hacker becomes just another romanticized form of artist, whose hacking exercises are considered his or her own personal productions and expressions of creativity and freedom. As a result, we continue to mythologize creativity, ignoring the actual labor involved. Although Florida introduces the concept of class to address the collectivity of creative labor, which seemingly takes away the individualist dimension associated with the artist, he essentializes the supremacy of creative labor over other forms of labor. Class is a highly constructed concept; it is not simply a structural category based on the nature of property ownership, but is always politically and ideologically constructed. The notion of class therefore requires a constant reflection on power. But today's discourse on the creative class is grounded on the assumption that creativity is the natural property or immanent capability of a selected group, or "aristocracy." If we are to hold on to the collective notion of class to understand the new creative labor, we must also be alert to various contrived ideological matters related to identification and representation, which Florida simply casts aside.

When we incorporate culture into economy, economy must take human dimensions into account, and there are inevitable tensions between the two logics that might result in a plethora of consequences. It is true that creative labor might introduce noncapitalist economic notions of collaborative networks and creative ecologies. As some scholars argue, the community of the creative workers might generate a collective resource which exists independently of capital, "providing a mezzo-level structural defence for autonomous artistic labour, and a politics of autonomy within and beyond the commodified cultural sector."[37] Other scholars have also emphasized that the intimate entanglements between creativity and economy in current society actually offer opportunities to develop working communities in which economic activities are subordinated under wider social and cultural imperatives, so that the economy can no longer afford to be blind to human affect and social relationships.[38]

However, there is also a danger of romanticizing the exercise of creativity as liberation, which runs the risks of idealizing the working environment and ideological limitations associated with this form of labor. The exaltation of "taste" and "beauty," for example, can be extremely intellectually constraining, and such sensational appeals also make the works readily available to be appropriated by different political interests. In discussing the role of a photographer in the age of commodification, Walter Benjamin argues that the photographer easily becomes "illiterate," unable to read his own pictures because his production of the "beautiful" prevents him from seeing the political content captured in his own pictures. Being lured into the production of the beautiful and capitulation to the fashionable, the photographer can never discover the full meaning of his own work. In a period characterized by aestheticization, Benjamin believes, people are too paralyzed by the "beautiful" to use critical thinking to discern social ramifications. He praises photographers of an earlier generation, such as Atget, who was able to turn his photographed space into a crime scene: "Isn't it the task of the photographer—descendant of the augurs and haruspices—to reveal guilt and to point out the guilty in his pictures?" However, the photographer, who was able to reveal to us the optical unconscious in the nineteenth century, increasingly serves the status quo by producing "the beautiful world." The "creative" therefore covers up political maneuvering. Benjamin claims, "The more far-reaching the crisis of the present social order, and the more rigidly its individual components are locked together in their death struggle, the more the creative—in its deepest essence a variant (contradiction its father, imitation its mother)—becomes a fetish, whose lineaments live only in the fitful illumination of changing fashion." The crisis Benjamin refers to here is certainly fascism, but I think his insights can also help us understand our present situation. He uses the term "creative" pejoratively in the quote above, as he equates the creative to the production of the beautiful, and therefore to insensitivity to any other forms of knowledge. He argues that because current photographers no longer manifest the physiognomic, political, and scientific interests shown among earlier generations of photographers, the photographs produced become "creative."[39] In general, Benjamin believes that photographers must be driven by the desire for engagement with the world, instead of indulging in "creative" activities to legitimize their indifference. As the earliest generation of photographers shows, social engagement and craving for knowledge can be manifested in many different forms—only through the submission of one's creative efforts to other social pursuits can the photograph be enlightened and captivating.

I will continue to explore Benjamin's understanding of creativity in chapters 8 and 9. Here let us be careful to avoid equating the creative with aesthetics, which might uncritically endorse the transcendental discourse of the artist. It might essentialize one's ownership of one's work and dissociate the work from its social embedding. The creative economy employs the creative in exactly the way Benjamin criticizes it. In order to carry on Benjamin's critique, our task is not to brush aside the materiality of creative productions altogether and to consider them ideologically regressive, but to take creative labor more seriously and understand it as a site of contestation. Creative labor is informed by both the logic of modernist art and the logic of capitalism, and this new form of labor is equipped with a wide array of aptitudes and values. At the same time, it is also under a broader spectrum of pressure and exploitation.

A problem of Benjamin's argument is the way he takes production for granted and associates labor as political. But the property logic, which is predicated on the relationship between labor and product, works precisely to depoliticize labor. I will follow up on this in the next chapter; but for now, it suffices to consider the almost religious devotion to labor in traditional Marxist thought. While property rights in capitalism are legitimized by the Lockean thesis of the unalienating relationship between a person and his labor, Marx conceptualizes labor (not labor power) along similar lines, in the sense that labor is a basic condition of human existence and mediates the relation between man and nature, and therefore human life itself.[40] Marx believes that human relations are largely defined by people's labor and the sociopolitical structures that instigate it.

Hannah Arendt launches a full-fledged criticism on this Marxist understanding of labor in *The Human Condition*: "In all stages of his work [Marx] defines man as an *animal laborans* and then leads him into a society in which this greatest and most human power is no longer necessary. We are left with the rather distressing alternative between productive slavery and unproductive freedom." Arendt is most critical of the private dimension of the common understanding of labor: "Of all human activities, only labor, and neither action nor work, is unending, progressing automatically in accordance with life itself and outside the range of willful decisions or humanly meaningful purposes." Therefore, instead of labor, Arendt emphasizes public actions, which distinguish humans from animals, from which politics arise. She points out that Locke develops his property rights theory by using the notion of labor.[41] Locke claimed that by adding our labor to a certain piece of the common life, we appropriate that piece into our private possession, and it is the private nature of labor that legitimizes property rights. Arendt is disappointed that Marx did not interrogate this logic but continued to privilege this private site as the base of his political theories.

Following Arendt's criticism, I must emphasize that labor should not be privileged for the sake of its private relationship with the laborer, because it runs the risk of preempting the social and the political (thus my criticism of the discourse of rights, to be elaborated in the next chapter). But I think Arendt also misses the point that instead of emphasizing the personal nature of labor as Locke does, Marx stresses the social relations labor elicits. Through labor people enter into definite social relations with each other, whether positively as members of the same community, or negatively, propelled by capitalism, as slave or master, lord or serf, or capitalist or wage earner.[42] But the creative economy works precisely to render creative labor radically private and therefore apolitical. An urgent task for critics of the creative economy is to explore the collective nature of creative acts, therefore the indissoluble relationship between CL^1 and CL^2, in terms not only of industrial collaboration but also of meaning production. Creative labor cannot be substantiated as one's isolated toil, but is always embedded within the chains of industrial production and meaning production, processes which are much more complicated than the current concept of the author or artist can grasp.

In his studies of the intercourse between students and factory workers in nineteenth-century France, Jacques Rancière demonstrates the mutual desire of the two groups for the liberating possibilities inherent in the other's material labor situations.[43] The confrontation between two different kinds of workers and different modes of production could point out the deficiencies and repressions in the different sets of social and subjective conditions, providing both of these groups with a new perspective from which to understand desperation, social unrest, and revolution. Within a Marxist framework, Rancière seeks to reconceptualize the actual political meanings of industrial laborers, who were considered the only people who could lead society to revolution; it was not the nature of their labor or material hardship, but their predetermined quality of life that was the real source of agitation. By the same token, Rancière also "rescues" the notion of intellectual production from the damnation of orthodox Marxists as nothing but "false ideology." Most important, he demonstrates that the confrontation between different forms of labor is politically productive, as such confrontations often help to denaturalize the working environment one is too mired in to see beyond.

As such, the simultaneous embodiment of artistic and industrial logics in creative labor is potentially revolutionary, as we can see the value of creative labor in its ability to bring to crisis the inherent limitations of both logics. Instead of following Florida's uncritical celebration of creative labor, we might choose to complicate the constituents of creative labor and see such complexity as politically confounding, because it constantly incorporates and interjects different kinds of labor and different ways of thinking, although it also means that workers are exposed to exploitation on different fronts. The creative economy seems to have provided the infrastructure to realize the democracy of creativity, which allegedly addresses the innate creative ability of all people and promises to provide enough incentives and training to allow all individuals to turn their innate creative ability into not only means of self-realization but also forms of cultural capital. But the myth that everybody can be creative uncritically endorses the superiority of creative labor over other forms of labor, fulfilling the human-centered modernity project in a different way. Instead, if we can discern the complex social embedding of creative labor, we will not fetishize creative labor as a "higher" form of labor, but understand that it actually embodies the site where contradictions of late capitalism operate. Labor does not evaporate in the creative economy, but it is only more intricately shaped to accommodate and justify a condensed and twisted economic logic.

Creativity as a Construct of Rights

In recent discussions of IPR, particular rights—around issues such as territories, ownership, and negotiations among different rights holders—are often the key site of contestation. But most fundamental to such discussions are the author's rights. Distributor's rights are safeguarded under contractual transfer of author's rights, so that the distributor should be seen as a function of the author,[1] and user's rights are often formulated under the promises of further creativity and innovation. The protection of author's rights has become a common moral principle for IPR critics of all positions, but the concept also raises the question of creativity ownership. Highlighting the author's rights might reestablish the connection between creativity and labor, but it also reduces creative acts to products negotiable among discrete individuals, running the risk of turning all aspects of humanity into property. The author's autonomy seems to be protected: because the products of one's labor supposedly belong to the laborer alone, one can sell it to others at one's discretion. However, such autonomy is most fragile within a hegemonic structure, and these individual exchange activities are easily manipulated by the dominant class. We need a much more complex understanding of the author in order to arrive at a proper understanding of the production of creativity that can resist commodification.

In the previous chapter I argued that we must consider the author as (constructed as) both an artist and a laborer. Here I demonstrate that author's rights should also be put under critical scrutiny—it should not be understood as natural and inalienable, but must be negotiated along two lines of logic: the public nature of any rights and the spontaneous and diffusive tendency of the signification of signs, that is, textuality. Both logics emphasize connectedness through differences in terms of people and in terms of signs, and their juxtaposition reminds us of the mutual conditioning between people and their ideas. Only by rescuing the uniqueness of human creativity can we resist viewing creative products as controllable social products, and therefore relocate the liberating dimensions of art and culture. Chapters 1, 2, and 3 demonstrate the intricate relationship between the two logics of art and labor in the forging of the creative economy and the subversive meanings of creativity to this overarching system. While the creative economy dialectically manipulates the tensions between artistic production and industrial production to turn creativity into a new condition of production, creativity is liberating because of the mutual conditioning and rejection between textuality and industrialism.

Between Economy and Ideology

As individual modern legal concepts, trademarks, patents, and copyrights all have long and separate histories in the West, let us first revisit briefly how IPR developed in order to distinguish earlier forms of IPR from current forms in their different economy-ideology relationships. According to Christopher May and Susan K. Sell, trademark protection was the first form of intellectual property in Europe that resembled current patterns of law, when guilds developed methods of differentiating guild-sanctioned goods from others and of enforcing their chartered monopolies in the Middle Ages. In the twelfth and thirteenth centuries early forms of patent evolved when sovereigns began to reward those who introduced new knowledge or industrial practices into their territory, particularly in the form of technology transfer that reduced imports and expanded exports.[2] Most copyright scholars date the emergence of modern copyright to 1557, when the members of the English book trade received a royal charter and became the Stationers of London, although it is also certain that some form of copyright had been developed earlier.[3] Unlike trademark and patent, which refer to commercial and industrial practices and knowledge in a general sense, copyright is related to the invention of a specific technology: the moveable type printing first used by Gutenberg in 1451 in Europe. A. J. K. Robinson demonstrates that exclusive rights to print certain books were granted by the Senate of Venice to individuals as early as 1469, eighteen years after mass printing was invented.[4]

As industrialization and commercialization continued to develop rapidly, these primitive IPR concepts were constituted in national laws and enjoyed stronger protection. The first patent law dates to 1474, when Venice enacted its first patent statute decree, requiring the inventors or manufacturers to register their new and inventive devices in order to obtain the right to prevent others from using them. Print capitalism began to drive the socioeconomic development of Europe in the sixteenth and seventeenth centuries,[5] and the first copyright law, the Statute of Anne, was passed in the U.K. in 1709, which soon led other European countries to pass their own versions of copyright laws. In 1787 the U.S. Constitution enacted its Patent and Copyright Clause (Article I, section 8, clause 8), which grants Congress the power to promote the sciences and arts by ensuring the rights of authors and inventors. Trademark is treated separately in the U.S. Constitution, as part of the commerce law, while European countries enacted individual trademark laws, such as the Trade Mark Registration Act in 1875 in the U.K. and Legislation Relating to Commercial Marks and Product Marks in 1857 in France. Each of these legal concepts was a necessary byproduct of the new industrial and market conditions, and they individually and collectively witnessed the expansion of capitalism.

In spite of the increasing attention given to intellectual property legislation among Western countries, in the nineteenth century there was not a clear set of international standards all countries needed to follow. The diversity of intellectual property policies among countries was in part a function of their different stages of development.[6] Individual IPR-related laws were developed to introduce foreign technologies or artistic works to a country and to provide incentives for domestic innovation and creativity. In other words, these national laws were international in scope but driven by national interests. As capitalism continued to develop, patents and copyrights were increasingly conceptualized as trade issues that involved grave international commercial and political interests, and a dense network of bilateral treaties began to emerge in the nineteenth century. Out of the complexity and confusion arose a quest for broader multilateral agreements. At the same time, individual inventors like Thomas Edison and Werner von Siemens and their corporations, as well as established authors like Victor Hugo and Mark Twain and their publishers, pressed for higher standards of international patent and copyright protection.[7] With the active involvement of these interested parties, particularly the lobbying efforts of large predatory corporations, multilateral patent and copyright treaties were developed; the most important ones were the Paris Convention for the Protection of Industrial Property of 1883 and the Berne Convention for the Protection of Literary and Artistic Works of 1886.[8] In the early twentieth century, with extensive national and international IPR laws in place, lawsuits abounded, along with growing international competition.[9] Although these treaties might be seen as evidence that some forms of globalization existed before the 1970s, the scope and power of these treaties by no means matched those of the Agreement on Trade-Related Aspects of Intellectual Property Rights, to be discussed later.

Underlying this legal history, which was heavily manipulated by commercial and political interests, was a parallel history of philosophical discussions among thinkers and critics concerning the meanings and values of IPR. Adam Smith contended in 1762 that "the property one has in a book he has written or a machine he has invented, which continues by patent in this country for fourteen years, is actually a real right."[10] But the combination of the individual concepts of patent, copyright, trademark, and the like into a coherent concept of "intellectual property" occurred only in the nineteenth century. Borrowing John Locke's ideas of property rights to articulate the ownership of abstract ideas, prominent nineteenth-century moral and political philosophers such as Herbert Spencer, Lysander Spooner, and Thomas Jefferson wrote of IPR as an abstract philosophical concept;[11] thus the concept of IPR must be traced back to Locke. According to Locke, people have a natural right to the things they have removed from nature by their own labor, and people should be protected by the state from any—including the state's—infringement on their property: "The labour of his body, and the work of his hands, we may say, are properly his. Whatsoever then he removes out of the state that nature hath provided, and left it in, he hath mixed his labour with, and joined to it something that is his own, thereby makes it his property." Given the logic of the inalienable relationship between a person and his labor, property rights are intrinsic to human beings and should be applied universally. To Locke, the role of the state is to enforce, instead of legitimize or negotiate, this universal right. Property was not created by government, but it was the source of government. As a result, "government has no other end but the preservation of property."[12]

Two centuries later, Spooner, who is considered the first person to use the term "intellectual property" in print, argued that concepts of property rights apply to intellectual property as well: "When a man digs into the earth, and finds, and takes possession of, a diamond, he thereby acquires a supreme right of property in it, against all the world. . . . By the same rule, when the scientist, in his laboratory, discovers that, in nature, there exists a substance, or a law, that was before unknown, but that may be useful to mankind, he therefore acquires a supreme right of property in that knowledge, against all the world."[13]

In Locke's moral philosophy man evolves by conquering nature;[14] the nineteenth-century notion of IPR is also individualist in nature. Celebrating man's material and intellectual reign over nature, both property rights

and intellectual property rights promote competition to drive social development. This is particularly evident in nineteenth-century IPR moral philosophy, which celebrates social progress and individualism by arguing that intellectual property—primarily human ideas—epitomizes social development
through diversity and selection. In general, we can say that the seventeenth-
century discourse of property rights and the nineteenth-century discourse of
IPR are both rooted in a certain "possessive individualism," which is driven
by the concerns of human freedom and market relations. As C. B. MacPherson explains, in possessive individualism one is human only insofar as one is
free, and free only insofar as one is a proprietor of oneself; therefore society
can only be a series of relationships between sole proprietors, i.e., a series of
market relations.[15] As a result, market logics are legitimized by the ideology
of individualism.

Echoing MacPherson's logic, Nicos Poulantzas argues that modern property rights law is manifested, not directly as an instrument of the dominant
class, but indirectly through dominant values such as liberty and equality.
Accordingly legal norms can be granted a wider validity, effectively subordi-
nating everybody to the interests of the dominant class.[16] MacPherson and
Poulantzas are correct in identifying liberty and equality as the key ideological
components of the property rights concept, but in the era of global capitalism,
economic forces have now gained a much more powerful role. Economics directly interfere with the operation of IPR, without resorting to its legitimization by existing modernity concepts such as freedom and justice. Instead of
promoting new ideas, the current IPR legal system has a tendency to protect
monopolies, secretly allowing market competition to wither. Herbert Spencer
celebrates the concept of intellectual property as a manifestation of free competition that leads to evolutionary progress, but today's IPR legal regime often
deters competition and favors monopolies.

I am not arguing that the notion of possessive individual rights no longer
applies to the current regime; in fact the ideology is only reinforced by transforming and aggrandizing individual interests into corporate interests. This
new global order is epitomized by the latest monopolization of IPR by the
Agreement on Trade-Related Aspects of Intellectual Property Rights (TRIPs),
which incorporates the standards of protection embodied in earlier multilateral IPR treaties like Berne and Paris and adds the new considerations of
global markets and new technologies.[17] The most significant contribution of
TRIPs is in the realm of enforcement, because it is administered by the powerful World Trade Organization (WTO), which directly links IPR to the chains
of trade.[18] The Agreement entitles a member country whose nationals are in-

jured by another member country's failure to comply with TRIPS standards to file a complaint with a WTO panel; if the panel finds noncompliance, the victim country can employ otherwise proscribed trade sanctions against the offending country.[19] Enforced by the WTO, IPR, and others such as the General Agreement on Trade in Services (GATS),[20] has become the most important global regime to regulate the transfer and commodification of intangible materials. While IPR history can be seen as progressing from the national to the global, it is also characterized by the move from competition to monopoly, contradictory to our commonsense understanding of globalization as market-driven. The nineteenth-century concepts are based on individual freedom, but the new IPR regime is driven by corporate interests, and it is meant to maintain the present global order instead of promoting change. In the words of Samir Amin, "The WTO's plan for world economic government is an ultra-reactionary project in the full sense of the word: it means returning to earlier forms of the international division of labor."[21] It is largely through the keen pursuit of a number of private enterprises that TRIPS and the resultant IPR regime can organize these once rather discrete treaties and concepts into a new global regime; TRIPS may be seen as a stunning triumph of the private sector in shaping global IPR rules and in enlisting states and international organizations to enforce them.[22] Many of the WTO's treaties can be understood along the logic of dispossession, as strategies of current neoliberal capitalism to usurp everything, tangible and intangible, from the public to the private.[23]

The economic determinism of classical Marxism, by which some Marxists boil everything down to simple results of economic logics, has been widely criticized. But the new phase of global capitalism might prove once again the validity of this strand of thought. Logics of global capitalism have now infiltrated all parts of our lives, and the wide spectrum of the social and the cultural is indeed increasingly and directly conditioned by economics. The enormous legal power inherent in IPR also clearly supports the new global capitalism. We need to be reminded that late capitalism "is a system which is no longer governed by any transcendent Law; on the contrary, it dismantles all such codes, only to re-install them on an *ad hoc* basis."[24] The IPR regime is such a system: it is so powerful, but it is also full of contradictions and room for negotiations, so that stakeholders can advance their benefits. In contrast to the nineteenth century's IPR philosophy of individualism and competition, the underlying agenda of the WTO is to further strengthen the comparative advantages transnational capital already receives. But this does not mean that the current IPR regime is devoid of all normative values. The difference between nineteenth-century philosophical discourse about IPR and today's

WTO regime resides in the different relationships between the legal and the moral: the previous IPR discourse legitimized itself by resorting to already accepted normative values of modernity, whereas the contemporary IPR discourse needs to enforce a new set of moral norms in order to validate this global legal regime.

It has been widely assumed that ideologies are first articulated in existing customary rules and moral standards, which are then incorporated into law. Once a formal legal rule has been announced, it often subsumes existing customs, and members of the society look henceforth to the legal rule rather than to customary practices for guidance. Legal regulation, according to Hugh Collins, is a more precise and advanced articulation of the requirements of the dominant ideology, instead of embodying anything new.[25] The recent advent of the IPR legal regime might demonstrate an opposite movement: IPR laws are designed not to supersede but to condition new customary practices demanded by a new economic structure. The creative economy cannot operate without people's voluntary respect for IPR, but this new norm is extremely difficult to establish, in part because the copying and the sharing of intellectual property have been made much easier by newly available technologies. The IPR morality might deter certain law-abiding global citizens, but IPR offenses are still part of the everyday for many people. Piracy and counterfeiting cannot be eradicated, in spite of fervent attempts to do so.[26] Contrary to Collins's argument, the IPR legal regime is not designed to take over existing practices, but to enforce a new but "unnatural" global ideological structure. It is therefore both ideological and legal: its aim is to perpetuate respect for intellectual property ownership, but its legal dimension demonstrates how difficult this ideological task is, in that it has to resort to the threat of punishment to stop people from copying. If the concept of property rights needs such ideas as individualism or progress to legitimize its advocacy of ownership, the new IPR regime resorts to the already normalized property rights logic to infiltrate a new moral system.

There is a clear artificiality about this IPR regime, and some Marxist scholars describe IPR as another form of reification.[27] In order to protect the wide range of intangible materials appertaining to the current phase of capitalism, IPR deals with extremely diversified matters embedded in very different social, cultural, and political contexts, while at the same time coordinating capital and knowledge flows within and between the developed and the developing world to maintain global order. Tarleton Gillespie describes the new copyright system as a "regime of alignment": the alignment of distribution systems through material and legal constraints, the alignment of allied institutions through technologically enforced licenses and ideological linkages, and the alignment of access, use, and consumption through a network of restrictions and facilitations.[28] This logic can be expanded to explain the current manifestation and power of IPR in general, which further aligns the different rights components of patents, trademarks, copyrights, and so on. The seemingly unrelated issues IPR has to deal with include online media piracy, developing countries' access to medicine, and the effects of transnational brand names on global consumers, to name a few. Although IPR does not work to conflate and reduce all these relatively autonomous social and cultural fields into simple structures, it effectively organizes these disparate matters by promising and endorsing the unified moral discourse of respect for ownership, "Thou shalt not steal."[29] At stake is the conflation of old property rights morality and new IPR discourse. The strong component of rights in recent IPR discussions allows moral topics to evade actual economic logics to form a new global common sense. The notion of rights, I believe, is both the ultimate goal and the magical element holding the artificial IPR system together, which also indirectly holds together the creative economy.

Authors' Rights and Creative Commons

There are two prevalent approaches to dealing with IPR. First, there is the positivist approach, with which legal experts and lawmakers try to perfect the legal system. Such discussions involve a careful balance of interests and various contexts of events, and as such make the discussions highly technical. Copyright, for example, might be among the most incomprehensible and self-contradictory modern laws, because it is full of exceptions and room for argument.[30] The IPR legal regime in general is a quintessential example of a modern technocratic device because of its extreme technicality.

Recently IPR discussions have proliferated in public space, particularly on the Internet. Based on the amount of critical public commentary IPR has received, some argue that no area of the law has been under more fire. However, these discussions are confined among a relatively small group of interested and informed individuals, and their pervasive discussions have not yet led to general public comprehension of the real implications of IPR on global politics.[31] Most depressing, these discussions have had minimal effects on actual legislations. While the Sonny Bono Copyright Term Extension Act of 1998, which provides twenty more years of monopoly to copyright owners, has attracted much criticism in the past ten years, the U.S. Supreme Court is still unmoved by a recent constitutional challenge to the law led by a team of esteemed international economists and law experts.[32] As a cultural studies scholar, I am wary of taking the positivist approach to critically deal with IPR, in spite of my appreciation of the tremendous efforts esteemed scholars and activists have devoted to educating the public about the social meanings of IPR. As Herbert Marcuse pointed out as early as the 1940s, in our modern society, which honors technological process as a new rationality and a new standard of individuality, the free economic subject is "rationalized" into the system.[33] It might be futile to interrogate the IPR regime through its technicality because that would only lead to the perfection of the system, instead of nurturing a critical position from which to reflect on the taken-for-granted notions of property and of rights. One IPR expert admits that the more she is drawn into the study of intellectual property, the more she speaks the language of the law and develops her critique based upon the law, and therefore the more she becomes "co-opted" by the law.[34]

The second dominant approach in current IPR studies focuses on the discussion of rights, or more precisely, the balance of interests among stakeholders. These critics can be categorized into two opposing camps. Those advocating strong IPR protection claim that the protection of the rights holders and the fostering of creativity is basically the same thing: by protecting existing work from infringement, creators' financial rewards are maximized, thus encouraging further creative acts. Collective well-being and social advancement will ultimately be achieved through the protection of individual rights holders. Those promoting a weak IPR regime argue that the more easily ideas and expressions can be accessed and circulated, the more creative products will result. They criticize tight IPR controls for being hegemonic and for fortifying the uneven global distribution of wealth both on the individual and international levels.[35] They believe that the purpose of intellectual creation is to serve all humankind, which is better fulfilled by allowing the fruits of knowledge and creativity to remain public.[36] While the advocates for strong IPR tend to identify with the rights holders and those supporting weak IPR with users, what is taken for granted in both camps is the endorsement of the "author": among IPR advocates the author is understood strictly as the idea originator, while those promoting weak IPR see users as potential authors who should be allowed to adopt existing ideas to create new ones. This is clearly evident in the logic of Creative Commons.

Creative Commons, which emphasizes sharing rather than owning, is one of the most influential alternative copyright programs. The project aims to develop alternative approaches within the legal framework of the current copyright system to handle copyright licensing that encourages contributions to the public domain.[37] Johanna Gibson is right to point out that Creative Commons challenges the dominant model of creativity, which promotes adherence to the original form and the mythology of the creator. Creative Commons demonstrates that creativity and knowledge can be transferred and developed in processes of viral form.[38] It confronts the ways creativity has been industrialized, and the license also dilutes the economic drives of creative acts that underpin the current IPR regime.

However, Creative Commons is ultimately also a project for the author and supports IPR's underlying property rights and possessive individualism rhetoric. In Creative Commons, the author is considered both the copyright holder and the user: the author retains the rights to her works and also accesses others' works to produce additional works. Within specified limits, people may use the works licensed under Creative Commons without paying royalties, but all current Creative Commons licenses require that users and copiers supply attribution in the manner specified by the original author or licensor, and they also state that the author's moral rights cannot be affected by the license. Authors who choose to license their work with Creative Commons and similar alternative programs do not forfeit their names, but the licenses allow their names to travel more freely, and the authors can see their work distributed on the Internet and other media more effectively. Presenting one's work under a Creative Commons license or other alternative licensing option does not mean giving up authorship rights—quite the contrary. These licenses can be seen as reinforcing the author's control by allowing her to tailor her own copyrights, as Creative Commons licensors can stipulate how their works may be used and quoted.

In a way, this understanding of the author as both the rights holder and the user protects both the stakeholders and the public domain. But the two are tied together in the sense that the public must first of all endorse the concept of the individual author. An author's moral rights are held supreme in Creative Commons, and I believe that it is precisely this thinking that needs to be reexamined. Hannah Arendt believes that rights are not something inborn, but that they are always negotiated within a political community and given to individuals by that community, and she warns us that the notion of the private should not be taken for granted but be the dialectic other to be disparaged or negotiated by all meaningful political discourses.[39] By emphasizing the moral rights of individual authors, Creative Commons tends to decontextualize their works from the common social conditions in which the authors are caught, in spite of its opposite claim. What I find problematic about the project is that despite its publicized aim of promoting sharing, the authors remain isolated individuals.

The persistent themes of Adorno's criticism of popular culture—the standardization of commodities, consumers' submissiveness to authority, and the manipulation of mass consciousness through entertainments—have been deemed obsolete in the late capitalist economy, because people are no longer considered separated into the two discrete categories of producers and receivers, but all are producers and receivers in some sense. Everybody participates in the affective economy, so that power is dispersed and simple control is impossible. The rhetoric of Creative Commons, in which everybody is free and equal, seems to fit this new scenario much more aptly than Adorno's oppositional model can. But when everybody is considered a private subject equal to everybody else, it is impossible to conceptualize politics. Arendt states that because humans are not born equal, we need to come together and do our best to build a fair community out of the inequalities provided. Politics therefore should be about publicizing and socializing private conflicts, broadening the scope of matters concerning individuals to allow collective bargaining.[40] Creative Commons tends to facilitate the reverse: sharing is possible only after the recognition of the author's private and privileged position, which can be occupied by each of us. This gives us the dangerously false impression that both authority and coercion have disappeared.

Equality is not given but must be painstakingly negotiated and constructed among inequalities. Creative Commons does not play the public role of revealing and negotiating the interests of different groups; it is conceptualized simply as an inert platform facilitating an author's organization of his or her own rights. The celebration of individuality is in accord with our capitalist society's emphasis and manipulation of differences and liberty to promote the unrestricted exercise of individual goals, which not only breed apolitical relationships and perpetuate social hierarchy, but also hinder the conceptualization of alternative politics. I support the way Creative Commons helps authors find alternative copyright options, but we should not expect it to challenge the underlying logic of IPR; quite the contrary, Creative Commons is only one of IPR's effects, giving us yet another copyright option in the age of flexible accumulation. The acts of negotiation that Arendt treasures are simply not structured in Creative Commons, which therefore excludes politics.

A structural limitation of Creative Commons resulting from its nonconfrontational politics is its noncommercial nature: it is stipulated that the licensed work cannot be used for commercial purposes. This rule is not forced upon Creative Commons by the commercial world, but it is an internal recognition that the license can only function this way. Consider that once a Creative Commons work becomes profitable, those authors who locate their earlier contributions to the work could ask for a share, and goodwill would collapse. By imposing a noncommercial environment, Creative Commons will remain marginal and nonoppositional to the mainstream copyright cultures.

One alternative to the Creative Commons project is hacking. However, as I pointed out in the previous chapter, the dominant imagination of the pirate, the quintessential figure of antilegality, is extremely individualistic, and its romantic image is built around the discourse of agency.[41] The contemporary reverberation of the romantic pirate figure is most obviously detected in the hacker discourse, in which figures such as Linus Torvalds, the Finnish university student who developed Linux, are celebrated as heroes.[42] In fact the hacker discourse is largely a representational product, fictively in popular films and literature, or socially in hacker publications. In Hollywood representations, for example, while hackers might be positioned as dangerous and sometimes naïve, the characterization of the hacker as hero is also extremely common. The release in 1983 of the hacker thriller movie *WarGames* (directed by John Badham), which features a teenage computer genius who accidentally hacks into the Pentagon's defense system and initiates a countdown to the Third World War, both produced and reflected the formation of a new hacking culture emerging at that time. Many young males were attracted to the smart and good-natured protagonist and started to model themselves after him. One first-generation hacker recounted, "I'll admit it, my interest in hacking was largely influenced by [*WarGames*]."[43] Hollywood's subsequent enthusiastic adoption of the hacker narrative is the best demonstration of the heroic dimension of the common hacker discourse, attesting to Wirtén's criticism of the resurrection of the author in anti-IPR discourses.[44]

The reality is that hacker culture is highly collective in nature, which has not been properly documented in mainstream representations. Hackers form communities through different public fora, from print pamphlets and electronic bulletin boards in the era before the Internet, to various online means such as email lists and blogs. They also announce new hacking methods and document their hacking experiences in these public arenas. Their fame is constructed from "forbidden knowledge," in the contradictory sense that it is both private (an illegal and solitary experience) and public (knowledge made known to others).[45] What is privileged in mainstream representations is not communal activities but the visibility of the hacker hero.

In fact these hacker and open source software communities are much more destructive to the current IPR system than programs like Creative Commons. I find Christopher Kelty's remark enlightening, that free software should be rethought as a collective, technical experiment rather than as an expression of any ideology or culture.[46] Although Kelty is also interested in Creative Commons because of its practical approach to solving real problems instead of engaging in ideological entanglement, I believe it is open source software like Linux that is more germane as a real alternative to the dominant IPR logic because of its technological and negotiation dimensions. First, at stake in open source software is the technology that strives to advance potentials, not the will of individual agents to realize control over the technology. Second, the participants constantly interact and negotiate during the process, and they give and take in ways that form a community. Although in this software the human dimension is clearly essential, the participants are mostly nameless volunteers, and they find a sense of satisfaction in contributing their creativity to the project, often without any financial reward or fame.

Besides operating systems such as Linux and Android, the vigorous subtitling activities taking place online demonstrate another open source development. Many illegal sharing activities found in the Chinese cyberworld concern the uploading and downloading of contemporary foreign television programs, particularly those from Japan and the United States. The uploading can be extremely systematic and efficient, almost simultaneous with the program's first broadcast in the original countries. While these activities demand uploading efforts by residents in foreign countries, core to these activities is subtitling, as most Chinese people do not understand the original dialogues. As such, a number of subtitling groups have arisen in Chinese-speaking communities, such as subpig, TVBT, FRM, and YTET, and they are extremely efficient and mutually competitive in subtitling the programs. Kelly Hu provides an intimate study of the operations of these groups; she finds that almost all participants are voluntary, and they remain mostly anonymous. There are core members in each of these groups who constantly recruit and train volunteers, and the volunteers in turn work cooperatively and responsibly without any real financial reward. Such fan labor is driven by a number of factors, including passion for the programs, the sense of belonging to the group, and the sense of satisfaction driven partly by the competition among the subtitling groups.[47] These subtitling activities, as I have said, can also be understood as part of the open source movement, as the addition of subtitles modifies the content and helps distribute it to a wider audience. Not only can such non-profit sharing intervene and disturb the commodity society, but the participants also develop bonds by sharing their creative labor, therefore reconnecting the content recipients' individuated experiences conditioned by the modern mass media environment. However, these activities are not radically severed from mainstream society. Hu, interestingly, describes the work ethic of such labor as neoliberal, as they are affective, flexible, and mediating. But Hu does not explain how the absence of personal financial gain can be factored into this neoliberal work ethic. Or is this form of labor a critique of neoliberalism? Also the reputation earned in such activities is very different from that of the traditional author, which ascribes the cultural products to personal ownership. It is the new communal connections brought about by these activities which most interest me.

Reexamining the logic and assumptions of the author's rights is a fundamental challenge to the current IPR hegemony, and also encourages examination of the piracy and counterfeit cultures. Anthropologists have incessantly reminded us that the notions of "authenticity" and "rights" in the IPR discourse are not universal, and that different people understand counterfeiting and piracy in a wide range of ways. Research shows that Vietnamese consumers of counterfeits care less about brand or product authenticity than quality or affordability, while Indonesian indie fashion designers engage in bricolage to respond to and become part of a new transnational youth culture.[48] East Indians understand "real" and "fake" in immigration terms: buying American brands, although in the form of counterfeit products, helps them to access the foreign and a better place.[49] Instead of holding on to author's rights as inviolable, we need to explore how appropriations and circulations can be understood and practiced differently so that we can expand the repertoire of politics against the hegemony of "originality" and beyond the IPR confine. These activities are vivid examples showing us the limitation of using the economic rationale in understanding culture, and they also demonstrate that we do not need to take the author's moral rights for granted.

Beyond Rights: Connections of Humans and Signs

The IPR regime focuses so narrowly on the author because it is the author who produces signs and expressions. A more pertinent question to ask is whether signs or text can be owned. In connection with the practices of community and technology just discussed, the notion of textuality also directly challenges any blind endorsement of the author's rights. According to Saussurean linguistics, no text is created or owned by one author, but all significations are related synchronically and diachronically; thus the notion of textuality. Roland Barthes, arguing the death of the author, asserts, "A text is not a line of words releasing a 'theological' meaning (the 'message' of the Author-God) but a multi-dimensional space in which a variety of writings, none of them original, blend and clash."[50] All texts are necessarily incomplete, and meanings necessarily proliferate, which is particularly evident on the World Wide Web, which more ostensibly demonstrates how meanings are produced and related to others in complex, multilayered ways. Textuality therefore provides a model for us to understand meaning production completely different from the dominant IPR discourse. We do not need to mythologize text as a living organism that grows on its own, but human participation and communications are always an essential part of the textualization process, echoing the serendipity discussed in chapter 1.

While the basic unit of a text is the sign, individual signs also have textuality, preventing their meanings from being contained. Trademark laws are designed to legalize and protect ownership of trademark as sign, and it is widely argued that the culture of signs has increasingly fashioned our present-day "disorganized" capitalism, in which people are actively shaping and being shaped by the expressive component of commodities.[51] Through the commodification of signs, everyday life is aestheticized. Cultural relationships can now be produced and manipulated by the culture industry, which constructs and circulates signs and affects. At the same time, this global order must be maintained by shifting structures of cultural differences to legitimize the inequality essential to globalization.[52] We might say that globalization is characterized by the mutual conditioning of the production of "culture" and the production of "cultural differences"; such mechanisms make signs the fundamental components of today's global order. However, the strong ideological desire to control signs is always resisted by the sign's own textuality—the tendency of proliferation and reordering, and signs signify by engaging in the metonymic transfer and exchange of meanings. If we could displace the ownership discourse into a textuality discourse, the subversion of IPR could be realized without identifying any subverting subject position, allowing us to resist taking the simple discourse of rights for granted.

Branding is a major manifestation of the ways sign is used and exploited by multinational corporations, but, as Naomi Klein demonstrates, global branding also helps unite diversified "antiglobalization" coalitions and agendas. Due to the sheer scope of impact and the global ambitions of multinational corporations, their fame and success also facilitate the "creative" coalitions of activists: "So you can build a single campaign or coalition around a single brand like General Electric. Thanks to Monsanto, farmers in India are working with environmentalists and consumers around the world to develop direct-action strategies that cut off genetically modified foods in the fields and in the supermarkets. Thanks to Shell Oil and Chevron, human rights activists in Nigeria, democrats in Europe, environmentalists in North America have united in a fight against the unsustainability of the oil industry."[53] Unlike appropriation artists such as Hans Haacke and Dorean M. Koenig, who appropriate famous brand names to protest against copyright hegemony and the corporate control of culture,[54] these programs call attention to the brand itself rather than the artist function. In such movements, the driving force does not come from a hacker or a pirate; it is the brand itself that activates the energy. These activist activities indirectly witness the fantastic and all-encompassing nature of brands and trademarks, which unite diversified and always changing products under a single image. And with their metonymic effects brands also negatively help bring together originally quite disjointed political projects.

Globalization relies on representations for the circulation of meanings and power, yet these border-crossing globalized trademarks are transgressive in nature and can be usurped by other players in ways subversive or not. While oppositional programs can be organized around a brand name, appropriations of famous trademarks can take place in different contexts. In a recent article Paul B. Bick and Sorina Chiper call our attention to the swoosh sign and the name "Nike" carved into a gravestone in Haiti, where the visual sign, more than the name of the dead, designates the deceased. While the swoosh's multiple and idiosyncratic recontextualization does not suppress its source meaning, in the sense that its intended suggestions of freedom, speed, and grace continue to signify here in the tomb, the trademark has also become a convenience object, a collective symbol that anyone can feast on, whose meanings both multiply and impoverish.[55] Signs transgress because they build new connections and open new horizons, waiting to be understood and rewritten.

Not just signs, but even information tends to proliferate in the creative economy, which is characterized by the urge to aestheticize information and knowledge into a stylistically, or even emotionally, pleasing experience. Therefore dry knowledge and information must be turned into enjoyable consumption—whether as experience, feelings, or emotions—so that information is given a humanistic veneer. But softening its edges also incurs the production of residues that are of no use. Alan Liu describes a "politics of cool" that is recently evidenced in design and popular culture. "Cool" refers to stylization, but this politics of stylization is also a politics of inefficiency and ineffectiveness; residues are cool. "Cool is information designed to resist information — not so much noise in the information theory sense as information fed back into its own signal to create a standing interference pattern, a paradox pattern."[56] Precisely due to "creative" components, although late capitalism promotes the circulation and production of knowledge and information, its efficacy is defined not by its "useful" but by its "pleasurable" consumption, so that the continual circulation of knowledge and information is conditioned oftentimes by the ineffectiveness of its consumption. This is attested to in many current advertising campaigns; between presenting information and presenting style, there lies a constant tension over how each would bring the other into crisis. Liu's model demonstrates the "failure" of the creative economy to come to terms with creativity, and it also avoids the subjectivist dimension of the author function, privileging neither the control nor the agency of the people. This politics of cool, in which the creative economy is invaded by creativity itself, is structural. The underlying force of creativity is as destructive as it is constructive. As a style instead of an art, cool is purely formal and residual, and it therefore evades the traditional aesthetic baggage of finding truth.

Tarleton Gillespie criticizes modern people's blind faith in technology to fix social problems.[57] I also trust technology, but my faith lies in the exact opposite of its utilitarian functions: technology also has its textuality, which can corrupt the modern concepts of control and efficiency. I think technology as text also has its own "creative" dimension. As Friedrich Kittler illustrates, in order to match our everyday language, computer codes have a tendency to infinitely expand, and so redundancy will increase: codes will grow wild, no matter how economical or orthogonal their first design may have been.[58] The perfection of technology therefore can lead to excess and become subversive of technological control itself. Most counterfeiting and piracy activities are not willed by politically conscious agents, but are in part products of our technological world. Piracy and counterfeiting are particularly prominent in developing countries, as globalization encourages the equalization of cultural tastes but promotes unequal distribution of wealth, while the availability of cheap technologies helps bridge this gap. More often than not, piracy is not the act of a lone hero but a function deeply embedded within the new economy made possible by technological development.[59]

This logic of textuality can indeed be understood as the logic of the network. Our creative economy is densely located in our network society, and this network society might facilitate the pluralization tendency of textuality, which the IPR regime works to tame. Today's network society might give rise to the managerial and negotiation frameworks of global trade and finance coordinated by multilateral trade organizations, new political and military alignments among different nation-states, a hierarchy of geographies based on labor migration, and knowledge networks set up among major universities and research centers.[60] However, we do not want to equate networks with capitalism, as networks both precede and are the result of the phenomena attributed to late capitalism. As Scott Lash argues, "Information and communication are neither instrumentalities nor finalities: information and communication build networks, and they make connections. Information and communication are now—in what is no longer an industrial society, but now primarily a media society—prior to both instrumentality and finality."[61] Our network society encircles us with privatized human expressions, confers economic rights to copyright owners, and develops a new economy around the circulation of copyrighted materials. However, it also makes room for many other forms of circulation and signification beyond the control of the dominant power, such as the rampant media piracy seen on the Internet. As the major result and site of power of the current network society, the WTO, the global platform and organization that facilitates most global economic negotiations and policing, is in constant crisis.[62] The many multilateral treaties that the WTO negotiated are both powerful and vulnerable. If network society is the ground from which global capitalism sprouts, the former also always puts forth seeds that subvert the capitalist order. The WTO crisis is a natural result of its own ambitious project, and the difficulties of locating common interests among countries will always be roadblocks for the WTO. It is in this overall cultural economic framework that the IPR regime functions and wields power, and it is also in this framework that the IPR regime might witness its own implosion.

The notion of networks brings us back to Arendt, whose influential theory of human rights endorses not the individual human as such but the human community. As Étienne Balibar succinctly explains, "[Arendt's] idea is that, apart from the institution of the community (not in the sense of 'organic' community, another form of naturalistic myth, but in the sense of reciprocity of actions), there simply are no humans."[63] Politics is so important to Arendt's philosophy precisely because each one of us is connected to and made meaningful by someone else; likewise the interconnectedness of signs and meanings is important. The notion of IPR is so problematic because creativity and knowledge, whose production and reception are caught up in chain relationships, are isolated into discrete objects for private ownership. We must reexamine how "correlation" can be reconceptualized, in terms of both humans and signs; thus my discussions in this section.

It is impossible to return to a precapitalist folk culture in which the relationship between cultural productions and their producers was supposedly not alienated by consumer culture. But the social embeddedness of cultural productions should not be articulated in market terms only, and there are still acts of copying and sharing in today's culture that evade private property logics. To bring my discussions in the previous chapters together, in order to contest the overblown discourse on authors and property, what we need is not only a politics of labor, but also a politics of text, or a politics of network. Whereas the politics of labor diffuses the artist function, the politics of text resists any attempt to set up the subject position of the owner. We must resist any simple discourse of control in understanding human expression if we still want to give humanity room in this all-encompassing late capitalist society. I believe that a respect for textuality, which sounds obsolete since the fall of deconstruction, is one way to counter the IPR privatization tendency; it is also an ethical position we must hold on to in order to assert the meanings of the humanities in the age of late capitalism.

PART II

China's Creative Industries
and IPR Offenses

Cultural Policy,
Intellectual Property Rights,
and Cultural Tourism

Throughout the history of capitalism, legal and policy supports have been essential for the expansion of new economic logics.[1] This is particularly the case for the ascendancy of global capitalism, which is not just composed of activities in the economic realm, but is pushed by international regimes and national governments working closely together despite the intricate negotiations and tensions involved. For global influences to perpetuate, the active pursuit and adaptation by the state and the local are essential. The recent pursuit of the creative economy in many parts of the world demands and triggers the transformation of local policy and legal and bureaucratic infrastructure, constructing a complex interactive network for global regimes, state governments, and local governments to communicate. Commencing my investigation of China's creative industries and IPR offenses, this chapter concerns the collaboration and mutual conditioning between China's national cultural policy and its IPR environment within such a context. The viewpoint adopted in this chapter is both macroscopic and microscopic: trying to produce an overall picture of China's position in the new global creative economy, I do not examine in detail the actual piracy activities or creative workers' conditions until later chapters, but I do zoom in on a creative industry of a local place, Lijiang, and its cultural tourism to examine the local manifestations in both national and global terms.

Cultural policy and IPR appear to fall into separate domains. In the Western model of separation of powers, policy is formulated by the state, while lawmaking is a matter for legislative councils and congresses, and the two areas are free from each other's influence. Even in China, policy and law are under separate domains, the Chinese Communist Party and the National

People's Congress, respectively. However, the actual mutual conditioning between policy and law, particularly in China, is pervasive. As Mary Gallagher argues, the CCP's turn to the rule of law is at its foundation not an ideological choice but pragmatic. Legal reform helps the state's integration into the world economy, and it also helps the government to control and manage domestic social change.[2] The CCP needs to resort to the rule of law to legitimize its post-socialist rule, so the adoption and understanding of law are intimately related to the government's policy.

The separation of cultural policy from IPR is also distinguished, seemingly, by their areas of concern. Cultural policy attends only to cultural matters, whereas IPR laws include those related not only to culture (copyright), but also to commerce (trademarks, trade secrets, and geographic identification) and science and innovation (patents). This assumption is also problematic, as a most important IPR development of recent years is the increasing convergence of these different rights, alongside cultural policy's alignment with the rhetoric of economics, so that the concerns of the two discourses gradually overlap. The mutual interference between cultural policy and IPR demonstrates precisely how culture and economics, politics and law, increasingly condition each other, and how the realms of national sovereignty and global control intersect. By focusing on these intersections, I hope to demonstrate how global and state interests converge at the level of the local economy, in this case Lijiang, which allows the creative economy to penetrate and prevail.

Chinese State Policy on Culture

Cultural policy has a long tradition in the West. Toby Miller and George Yúdice trace the roots of cultural policy in Europe back to the fifteenth century, when English displaced Latin and French as the national language of England.[3] Tony Bennett locates the origin of Western cultural policy in the birth of the museum, which provides appropriate tutelage in national identity.[4] Since the modern state emerged in the West, cultural policy has been understood as an essential instrument for state governance, which depends upon a national culture for the legitimization of its national sovereignty. Until recently cultural policy has been mainly a state enterprise, and many governments have special councils or agents to address the formulation and implementation of cultural policy. However, the political instrumentalist approach has never gained a completely dominant position in Western countries because it is also believed that in modern societies, culture and the arts should be autonomous from political and economic controls. State concerns are always affected by public opinion, and cultural policy in the West also stresses the value of multi-culturalism and the recognition of differences.[5] Meandering between governmental and civil approaches, cultural policy in many Western countries has mostly taken the form of protectionist intervention through funding, preservation, and education to cultivate cultural identity and cultural diversity.

China, however, has never taken a civil approach to cultural policy, even in name; its cultural policy conflates the people and the nation, and it is an instrument of political propaganda and a means of political control. When the Chinese Communist Party was established in the 1920s, cultural propaganda was a major component of its political rhetoric, particularly during the Anti-Japanese War period, when political solidarity was absolutely demanded.[6] After the Liberation, Mao Zedong's famous talks on art and literature in 1942 became official state ideology,[7] and his wartime rhetoric and strong position on the politicization of arts defined Communist China's cultural policy. Between 1949 and 1955 the state's priority was to secure a new socialist order, and the regulation of culture was an important element of this pursuit.[8] On the one hand, the state advocated respect for culture to ensure cultural workers' identification with the new regime;[9] on the other hand, the cultural scene was kept homogeneous to prevent negative views from arising.

The Hundred Flowers Campaign of 1956 was originally a political maneuver intended to reverse constraining tendencies and to promote the diversification of national culture, but it quickly turned into the ruthless Anti-Rightist Movement. On the eve of the Cultural Revolution, cultural policy became radically political. The Cultural Revolution might be seen as Mao's, or Jiang Qing's, aggressive program of cultural policy, intended to develop a culture divergent from that of capitalist modernity, one that could transcend bourgeois democracy and Western liberalism to realize a truly Communist future for the ancient country. The Cultural Revolution was also the result of a long series of fierce internal power struggles within the CCP. As Paul Clarke demonstrates, during the Cultural Revolution, culture was the point of convergence of ideological and political fanaticism, although culture also found its own way to flourish in the aesthetic perfectionism of the model plays.[10] If we understand culture in its broadest sense as people's values and ways of communication, cultural policy became the entirety, or the essence, of the governance of the time, which equated the cultural with the political. The scope and the impact of cultural policy (if we can call it that) during this period could not have been more overwhelming.

The Chinese art scene has been given a completely different set of conditions of late. Richard Curt Kraus writes that these new developments can be partly explained by the changes in leadership: Deng Xiaoping, Jiang Zemin, and Hu Jintao have shown no special interest in the arts, in sharp contrast to key figures in Mao's generation, who had strong aesthetic ambitions.[11] Joel Andreas points out that engineers are ruling the country now, as the majority of the members of the Standing Committee of the Party's Political Bureau were trained as engineers.[12] While the new leaders may no longer support the intimate relations between culture and politics, the more fundamental social conditions underlying these changes are defined by the rise of the market economy, which no longer allows the kind of governmental financial support and ideological dictation of cultural production seen in the previous era.

Beginning in the 1980s, the state gradually realized that a new mentality of cultural governance was needed, as the people began to conceptualize culture in terms of leisure and culture became connected to entertainment and consumption more than to politics. However, in the wake of the Cultural Revolution, the PRC government continued to be highly sensitive to the political malleability of culture, and thus did not welcome its complete marketization. As such, instead of using culture to support official ideology, the government's new role was to regulate and depoliticize culture, so that culture could be saved from the forces of commodification and politicization. After decades of heavy political agitation and protection, art was more or less left alone in the 1980s, although artists were still largely shielded from fierce market competition, at which point all kinds of new explorations and experimentations began to spring up.

But this does not mean that the government's control of culture has decreased; it was in fact reinforced by the Tiananmen event in 1989. Compared to the 1960s and 1970s, when censorship was ubiquitous and taken for granted, the PRC in the 1990s worked to institutionalize and systematize different kinds of censorship so that they were not exceptional to law but subjected to it. The New China News Agency (Xinhua she 新華社) continues to occupy the top of the information hierarchy and coordinates the national distribution of news. The two major censoring authorities are the State Press and Publication Administration (Xinwen chuban zongchu 新聞出版總處) for printed matter and the State Administration of Radio, Film, and Television (Guojia guangbo dianying dianshi zongju 國家廣播電影電視總局) for broadcasting and cinema. The CCP's Central Propaganda Department (Zhongyang xuanchuan bu 中央宣傳部) controls media reportage and discussion of "delicate" political issues that might affect state security, such as Taiwan, Tibet, and even the Sichuan earthquake in 2008. Other censorship units include the Ministry of Information Industry (Xinxi chanye bu 信息產業部), which oversees web content; the Ministry of Public Security (Gong'an bu 公安部), which, among other assignments, filters and monitors the Internet; the Ministry of State Security (Guojia anquan bu 國家安全部), which has the authority to arrest or detain people who disseminate news and opinions that threaten state security; and the General Administration of Customs (Haiguan zongchu 海關總處), which can confiscate any publication that is deemed dangerous to the government. In spite of depoliticization efforts, contemporary cultural policy remains overtly political regarding certain sensitive areas, such as separatism. But this censorship apparatus should not encourage us to see the PRC state as exceptionally authoritarian, as similar situations can be found in many other countries, including the United States—particularly after its declaration of war on terrorism—which supposedly considers freedom of speech its central value.

Parallel to the new censorship system gradually taking shape, a new discourse of "cultural management" also appeared in the 1980s. The Ministry of Culture's College for Cultural Cadres established its Teaching and Research Section on Cultural Management in 1983, and in 1985 the college launched the first related academic journal in China, *Cultural Management* (Wenhua guanli 文化管理). A series of research activities were organized to investigate related issues, but most of these activities continue to be heavily ideological, emphasizing the importance of political leadership and social stability.[13] A key turning point took place in 2000 and 2001, when the promotion of cultural industries became a major state policy. In October 2000 the term "cultural enterprises" (wenhua chanye 文化產業) appeared in the document "Suggestions for China's Tenth Five-Year Plan" in the fifth plenary section of the fifteenth Chinese Communist Party meeting. The document clearly announces the state's stakes in "improving cultural enterprise policy, strengthening the development and management of cultural markets, and promoting the development of related cultural enterprises." The document also indicates the government's responsibility in promoting mutual support between information industries and cultural industries. In March 2001 the document was accepted by the fourth meeting of the Ninth National People's Congress and officially entered China's Tenth Five-Year Plan.[14] The PRC's commitment to cultural diversity became an official state policy in Jiang Zemin's "Three Represents" theory, which was embraced by the country in the PRC Constitution of 2004, and it reiterated the short-lived but recurrent Maoist doctrine of "letting a hundred flowers blossom and a hundred schools of thought contend" as once again the principle of state cultural policy.[15] But the underlying assumption differs greatly: in the late 1950s Mao showed a strong belief in the political potential of culture, but in postsocialist China, culture is engineered for economic gain and depoliticization.

However, I do not want to exaggerate the rupture between now and then. Unlike many Western countries whose cultural policies have to concur with the dominating ideology of liberal democracy, the Chinese government, even now, never emphasizes the value of autonomy in the realm of culture. Quite the contrary: unity, harmony, and national development are stressed, only with a different social context. The PRC's current cultural policymakers are trying to strike a balance between economic development and social stability. Jing Wang demonstrates that while the WTO requires the PRC to liberalize its retail and distribution sectors, the content industry has not been liberalized by the state, and this situation encourages new kinds of joint ventures and the search for loopholes.[16] Michael Keane also criticizes the PRC's reluctance to forgo tight media censorship, which allegedly jeopardizes the exercise of creativity and therefore the well-being of related industries.[17] However, censorship can also be seen as a protectionist policy, drastically reducing the number of foreign products from entering the country and protecting certain law-abiding local creative industries from international competition, allowing them to develop rapidly.[18] A simple discourse of cultural freedom tends to dichotomize the state and the private sector, and it ignores the state's active participation in the forging, as well as the control, of the domestic creative industries. Creative industries are increasingly highlighted in the development discourse not only in terms of their contributions to the GDP, but also in terms of their overall functions of originating, selecting, and retaining new ideas, which ultimately facilitate the flow of information and ideas and promote the development of open systems of coordination.[19] We can understand why the PRC has shown keen interest in cultivating and controlling selected national creative industries, which could contribute profoundly to the nation's economic development and political stability.

The elaborate government apparatus maintained by the CCP is aimed at supervising culture by creating self-censorship and double or triple censorship (censorship of the same materials by more than one agency). But an elaborate bureaucracy has also evolved, and new cultural content is particularly prone to bureaucratic intrusion. The game industry, for example, is simultaneously supervised by the Ministry of Information Industry, the Ministry of Culture (Wenhua bu 文化部), the State Press and Publication Administration, and the General Administration of National Sport (Guojia tiyu zongju 國家體育總局); these departments all claim censorship and management rights in the production of new digital games. But the balance of power is harder to maintain than claimed; for instance, the online game *World of Warcraft* (魔獸世界) was recently banned by the State Press and Publication Administration for its negative influence on youth, causing a sudden plunge in the stock price of its distributor, NetEase, on the Nasdaq.[20] The Ministry of Culture very quickly responded to the incident by reasserting the approval it had already issued and accused the State Press and Publication Administration for its lack of authority in superseding the ministry's decision. Although this elaborate censorship system has the advantage of creating seamless control to weed out undesirable elements, we can understand why the central government is willing to streamline the system in response to cultural industries' frustrations. In 2004 the state selected nine cities to house local General Offices of Culture, Broadcasting, Press and Publication (Wenhua guangdian xinwen chubanju 文化廣電新聞出版局), which were set up to manage the cultural industries of these regions so that they can bypass the elaborate national system.[21] Additional cities and regions have followed suit, although cases like *World of Warcraft* continue to happen.

To facilitate the development of cultural industries, efforts are devoted not only to the conditional loosening of state control, but also to the implementation of a new economic logic and vocabulary. In 2003 the National Bureau of Statistics established a high-profile Working Group in Topics Related to Cultural Industries Statistics and Research (Wenhua chanye tongji yanjiu keti gongzuo zu 文化產業統計研究課題工作組), responsible for steering the development of the nation's cultural industries.[22] In January 2006 China's State Council released an important policy document, "Guanyu shenhua wenhua tizhi gaige de ruogan yijian" 關於深化文化體制改革的若干意見 (Several opinions on the deepening of the reform of cultural industries), which stresses the economic and social values of culture in national policy, elevating culture to perhaps its highest official status since the Cultural Revolution.[23] The government document suggests promoting cultural industries as a prominent national asset, in particular fostering, through privatization and conglomeration, a number of flagship cross-media corporations that are competitive not only nationally but also globally. It also recommends a thorough revision and reform of national cultural policy and law, so that the government can effectively manage and direct development and private companies can grow under the protection of a healthy policy and legal infrastructure.[24] In general, what we have witnessed in the past two decades is a gradual shift in state interests toward a cultural policy which downplays political control to emphasize culture's economic value, and which embraces the global discourse of creative industries.[25] Or, as Keane argues, state policy has evolved from an "engineering" culture to one embracing culture as industry.[26] But in such a rapidly transforming discursive environment, in spite of clear efforts to de-politicize art, state involvement in culture persists. As such, we need to be aware that the PRC's current reforms are not any less political than those of the previous socialist regime, but are characterized by a more contrived conspiracy between the political and the economic. It is in the dynamics between cultural control and market liberalization that we gain a unique perspective to understand the operation of late capitalism in this postsocialist country.

The Global IPR Regime

China's cultural policy has always reflected state interests, but the IPR situation seems to have exceeded national confines. The two seem to follow their own independent trajectories. Some scholars argue that the earliest copyright concepts were formed in ancient China; in the Spring and Autumn Periods (approximately 750–450 B.C.) authors started signing their writings; during the Song Dynasty (A.D. 960–1279) actual copyright statements and descriptions of copyright disputes appeared in official documents.[27] Others argue that Chinese notions of patent can be traced back two thousand years, when emperors granted individual merchants the right to smelt iron, distill salt, and mint coins.[28] But there are also scholars who are skeptical about the Chinese roots of copyright and patent concepts and who argue that so-called copyright disputes in the Song Dynasty pertained to censorship instead of attempts at author protection, and that premodern China did not have a cultural environment comparable to seventeenth- and eighteenth-century England, the birthplace of modern copyright.[29]

In light of the strong historical evidence, it is undeniable that written materials reproduced without the consent of the authors were rampant in the Song Dynasty, a time when mass printing began in China.[30] It is clearly documented that these authors were angry about this practice, and they brought cases to court to protect their names.[31] Piracy always accompanies new publication and distribution technologies, and it should be no surprise that print piracy first appeared in Europe in the sixteenth century, about six hundred years later than in China, coinciding with the availability of large-scale mass printing technology in the two civilizations. However, piracy does not necessarily lead to copyright, which is a legal concept shaped by Western moral political discourse to make sense, dialectically, of the piracy activities already in existence. The modern European concept of copyright and IPR did not exist in China, not because there was no piracy there, but because modern copyright's underlying motivations—commercialism and private property—were not emphasized as much in premodern China.

As I have discussed in chapter 3, the present IPR global regime is a legal and ideological product specific to Western history and deeply entrenched in the development of modernity and capitalism. Although a few angry writers during the Song Dynasty may have protested piracy's detrimental impact on their names and incomes, modern copyright did not take root in China until the country was forced to open its doors to Western imperialists and Western legal morality. It is true that seeds of capitalism can be found not only in Protestantism but also in Confucianism. Peter Berger has argued that although in imperial China Confucian education did not encourage attitudes and habits conducive to modern economic activity, the potential of the tradition for capitalism was dramatically triggered by specific historical events, such as emigration to Southeast Asia and recent PRC economic reforms.[32] But these recent events cannot be dissociated from the capitalist conditions already developed and embedded, and we should not confuse potential from actual flowerings. China's IPR development cannot be traced back to the invention of mass printing in Song, but to the nineteenth century, when capitalism in the West was a social structure already expansively developed and was crawling all over the world to violently search for potentiality.

Components of IPR were exported to China in the late 1880s as part of both imperialist and nationalist agendas. Scholars demonstrate that the first modern patent concept was advocated by a Taiping Rebellion leader, Hong Rengan, who in 1859 introduced concepts of Western modernity and capitalism to the short-lived Taiping regime.[33] The first Chinese patent rules, "Zhenxing gongyi jijiang zhangcheng" 振興工藝給獎章程 (Regulations on rewards for the promotion of technology), were established in 1898 as part of Emperor Guangxu's Hundred Days' Reform. China's first copyright law, "Da Qing zhuzuoquan lü" 大清著作權律 (Copyright act of the Great Qing Dynasty), was enacted in 1910.[34] The first modern copyright event in China involved Yan Fu's translation of Adam Smith's *Wealth of Nations* in 1899; $2,000 plus 20 percent of the profits were paid to the copyright holder.[35] Under pressure from Western countries, the Qing government also enacted the "Shangbiao zhuce shiban zhangcheng" 商標註冊試辦章程 (Provisional regulations of trademark registration) in 1904; it did not become law until 1923.[36] Intellectual property rights, as Peter Feng explains, "came with such inventions and novel ideas as the gunboat, opium, 'most favored nation' trading status and extraterritoriality."[37]

In the early twentieth century, the ruling Nationalist Party (Guomindang) did make plenty of efforts to merge the country into the international IPR environment.[38] In 1928 and 1930 the Guomindang implemented copyright and trademark laws, both of which conformed to the general international standards. However, all laws enacted by the Guomindang were abrogated upon the founding of the People's Republic of China in 1949. Among the greatest legislative transformations in the new nation were land reform and the overall abolition of private property. Although lingering concepts of patent and copyright still existed to encourage invention and creative effort,[39] identifying these efforts as private property is fundamentally incongruent to socialist ideology. Patent, due to its direct relationship to technological advancement, might have been the IPR component most tolerated by the communist regime, but by 1963 the property components of patent were also officially abolished; only the system of remuneration for inventors remained.[40] In the mid-1950s a series of regulations forbade Chinese publishers to pay royalties to or seek permission from copyright holders when translating, using, or appropriating foreign works, although financial arrangements could be made with authors in "brother" socialist countries, progressive organizations, or authors in capitalist or colonial places.[41] According to socialist principles, individual innovation and creation in the arts and sciences do not belong to the creator; they are the fruit of collective endeavor and should be shared by all. This notion was fiercely upheld during the Cultural Revolution.

Two major historical moments signal the complete revision of the CCP's collectivization efforts: Deng Xiaoping's reform in 1978 and China's accession to the WTO in 2002; they also mark the trajectory of Chinese IPR reform. The earliest IPR restoration activities of the late 1970s were motivated by specific national needs and aimed at cultivating a more congenial environment for innovation and creation. But very soon efforts shifted toward the pursuit of international recognition, as they had in the Nationalist era. Between 1980 and 1994 China signed nearly every major international IPR-related contract and joined the important international organizations in order to become a member of the international IPR community (including the World Intellectual Property Organization, the Berne Convention, the Paris Convention, and the Patent Cooperation Treaty).[42] By 1994 IPR reform in China was basically complete, and the Chinese IPR system generally follows Continental European practices. Since then the country has been a strong protector of IPR, and it is compatible with the rest of the "civilized" world.

In spite of global demand that China enact more stringent IPR legal controls upon its accession to the WTO, there was not much China could do in the late 1990s, at least in terms of legislation; changes introduced then were generally remedial in nature and aimed to comply with updated specificities of TRIPs or to streamline existing registration processes to avoid lengthy and unpredictable decision making. For example, China's first patent law was enacted in 1984 and was amended in 2000—with some minor modifications in between—to expand the scope of protection to include chemical and pharmaceutical products, as well as food, beverages, and flavorings, and to extend the term of patent protection to twenty years after the filing date, following TRIPs requirements. China's first trademark law was adopted in 1982 and was also revised in 2001 to meet TRIPs requirements; the new trademark law extends registration to collective marks, certification marks, and three-dimensional symbols. Chinese copyright law, first established in 1990, was also amended in 2001, when China acceded to the WTO. In spite of its symbolic significance, the country's WTO accession did not bring drastic transformations to existing IPR legislation in China, because much had already been done in the previous two decades in light of the PRC's drive to join the global IPR community.

As shown in China's Internet Copyright Regulations, which are modeled after the Digital Millennium Copyright Act but enforce even more stringent control in anticircumvention (see chapter 5 for more about DMCA), China's current IPR laws often simply copy those in the developed countries, and they fail to take into account the specific circumstances and disadvantages of China as a developing country.[43] The PRC is ready to submit to global scrutiny in order to gain a legitimate IPR status; however, no one can deny that rampant IPR offenses take place throughout China every day. As government-supported research shows, 46 percent of interviewees admitted that they have knowingly purchased pirated publications,[44] and doubtless the actual figure is much higher. Censured worldwide as an intellectual property thief and often forced to make commercial concessions to mitigate such complaints, the Chinese state finds the enforcement of IPR so difficult a task that they can only helplessly tolerate international manipulation. The country seems to remain relatively unharmed by the regional financial crisis of 1997 or even the global crisis of 2008; its poverty rate decreased from 53 percent in 1981 to 8 percent in 2001,[45] and it hosted arguably the most spectacular Olympic Games in history. But it cannot eradicate piracy and counterfeiting, as demanded by the international community. The rampant piracy in China does show that the Chinese state is not the powerful regime it is feared and imagined to be, and it also demonstrates that piracy cannot be completely controlled by the global IPR regime.

The enormous number of IPR offenses taking place in China is not the result of its weak legislation. Many, both scholars and the U.S. government, blame the PRC's weak enforcement, as the PRC relies on administrative instead of criminal measures to combat IPR infringement.[46] Many Westerners also lack confidence in the ability of the Chinese courts to arbitrate legal disputes.[47] Other factors contributing to China's piracy problems include corruption and local protectionism at the provincial level, limited resources and training available to enforcement officials, and the lack of public education regarding the economic and social impacts of counterfeiting and piracy.

These observations might be valid, but they ignore the most fundamental factor behind the country's pirated production and consumption, which is the public. Piracy and counterfeiting have helped to enrich people's cultural and social lives at low cost and allow people to stay current with the latest popular culture and fashion around the world; piracy activities have also provided employment for a large number of Chinese people. Many of those involved in piracy production and retail are forced retirees from national enterprises or migrant workers, and they are among the most disenfranchised by the country's capitalist conversion. In order to gain sympathy from law enforcement, some women who hawk pirated movies on the street actually bring their babies to work.[48] In China and many other developing countries, piracy has become a substantial part of people's material lives.[49] Based on his fieldwork in various Chinese cities, Jack Qiu observes that the buying and selling of pirated DVDs have already become an essential part of the local economy and entered the people's networked connectivity; vendors selling pirated DVDs are situated next to cybercafés, mobile operator shops, long-distance phone bars, and digital camera and computer rental shops.[50] If copyright did not take hold in the Song Dynasty due to a lack of capitalist interests, we might expect current IPR logic to also fail to come to terms with China's actual situation, with its capitalist conditions that are a far cry from those in the developed West. After all, as the world's factory, China is still an IPR-poor country, and IPR morality is too far removed from people's everyday lives.

Between the National and the Global: Lijiang's Cultural Tourism

State interests dominate the formulation of China's cultural policy, from the extreme political radicalism of the Cultural Revolution to the current celebration of creative industries. In contrast, IPR legislation is made to comply with global demands, and national interests are neither highlighted nor justified other than as reflections of the general desire of the state and the people to join the global economy and the international community. There is little international media or political commentary on China's new cultural policy; instead the focus is—sometimes too heavily—on IPR violations. It is generally assumed that IPR legislation is meant to safeguard international interests, whereas cultural policy protects national culture only. However, the development of creative industries demands an infrastructure composed of both appropriate cultural policy and IPR legal morality, and late capitalism cannot operate without the support of both national governments and global regimes. I believe the two domains of cultural policy and IPR, as well as the interests of state and global regimes, interact and diffuse most broadly on local levels.

Let us examine the recent development of Lijiang, which, like many places emphasizing cultural tourism, has found its local economy heavily intertwined with cultural policy and IPR. Lijiang Prefecture is a Minority Autonomous District located in Yunnan Province. In 2002 the total population of the prefecture was about 351,000; 58.6 percent were Naxi, 24.43 percent were other minorities, and 16.97 percent were Han.[51] The Naxi nation has been credited for the ancient Dongba (東巴) culture, which is distinctly different from Han's. The Naxi people are also considered a model minority because of their historically easy relationship with the Han people and the PRC government.[52] They have been the subject of heavy anthropological investigation by Chinese and Western scholars alike, due to their rich, advanced cultural background (embodied in the Dongba hieroglyphic script) and alternative gender structure (the Mosuo matriarchal structure).[53] The Lijiang area is also known for its beautiful scenery as well as its people's passionate personalities. Romantic images of Lijiang are presented in both Chinese and foreign cultural productions, such as James Hilton's novel *Lost Horizon* (1933), which depicts an English consul finding romance and peace in a remote Chinese land called Shangri-La, presumably modeled after Lijiang,[54] and Bai Hua's novel *Yuanfang you ge nüerguo* 遠方有個女兒國 (The remote country of women, 1988), a romantic tragedy that unfolds within Mosuo's matriarchal structure.

After a major earthquake in 1992 destroyed much of Lijiang's splendor, the PRC invested heavily to rebuild the place into a tourist spot, for both economic and political reasons. Accompanying the state's efforts was UNESCO's decision to register the ancient city of Lijiang as a World Heritage Site in 1997. The recent development of Lijiang is an exemplary instance of close collaboration between the PRC and UNESCO. Tourism and cultural conservation go hand in hand, and state and local governments' collaboration with UNESCO is responsible for the place's recent economic boom; in 1995 the prefecture's income from tourism was an estimated 160 million RMB, and in 2002 the figure jumped to 2.5 billion RMB. The prefecture's GDP per capita also increased from 510 RMB in the late 1980s to 4,867 RMB in 2002.[55]

Cultural preservation and global trade seem to be contesting regimes. On the one hand, UNESCO promotes cultural diversity by working proactively with national governments to design and implement related cultural policies; on the other hand, the WTO is vigorously reshaping cultural understanding according to the logic of international trade. Recent developments in global culture have given rise to a tug-of-war between the economically competitive WTO model and the responsive UNESCO protectionist model. Conflicts between the two mind-sets are most clearly seen in the WTO's General Agreement on Trade in Services, which states that all forms of artistic expression are services to be governed by GATS, and as such, WTO members are to refrain from subsidizing the arts in any form.[56] The GATS has therefore stripped national governments of the ability to protect their national markets from being totally monopolized by a narrow variety of mainstream cultural productions. The implication is that the countries subscribing to the WTO mandate will have to oppose those policies to protect their national cultures, which UNESCO strives to cultivate.

The WTO and UNESCO operate under different, and sometimes opposing, ideologies.[57] Both are global in organization and interests (notwithstanding the manipulation of the WTO by certain dominating national powers), but the relationships between UNESCO and individual national governments are often more complex. World Heritage Site nominations are initiated by individual countries, and once a place is granted World Heritage Site status, the country must preserve the site according to standards set by UNESCO, which provides technical assistance and professional training to aid its maintenance. Most of the time UNESCO skillfully collaborates with individual national governments instead of ruthlessly meddling; state interests are generally highly regarded in UNESCO policies, and many scholars and critics are attracted to UNESCO's views as alternatives to the WTO's mandates.[58] As James Louis Hevia shows in his study of Chengde, another World Heritage Site in China, the PRC has a strong political interest in making Chengde symbolic of the unified, multicultural China. Hevia states that "however uncomfortable UNESCO may have felt with this seeming politicization of its notion of heritage, the organization was willing to accept the PRC definition of the site."[59]

While the relationship between UNESCO and national cultural policies around the world has always been intimate, economic interests and cultural interests conflate. This is particularly obvious in the case of cultural tourism, where there are economic benefits in the formulation of cultural policy. Recently the PRC has officially recognized cultural tourism as a part of its creative industries, and it is investing more than 100 billion RMB to develop cultural tourism.[60] UNESCO also plays a pivotal role in this "modernization" process; it has begun its first East Asia World Heritage Guide training program in Yunnan, granting certifications to tour guides who successfully undergo the program, which imparts not only specific skills but also the mentality of long-term sustainability and partnerships with private, cultural, and national networks.[61] In light of this, UNESCO might embody global interests (in the plural) in the most sophisticated and diffusive manner, and policy might also have stronger impacts on society than law does. While global legal regimes, such as the WTO, are considered ruthless and anxiety-provoking, because the laws seem to embody a top-down approach that is enforced by means of threats and punishment, UNESCO's cultural policy might be seen as congenial to and protective of local development, in that it provides flexibility in terms of actual social and cultural conditions. However, such cultural policy is also often formulated to shape local cultures according to global conditions, and it can exert pervasive influence on actual social institutions and everyday life.

It is often in cultural tourism that we see the most intimate collaboration between IPR and cultural policies, as indigenous cultural products often function as export or tourist commodities, and rituals are modernized to become tourist entertainment. In many cases IPR and cultural policy fulfill each other's promises, in spite of their different interests and ideologies. The World Heritage Committee's rationale, for example, can be considered the exact opposite of IPR logic; the former emphasizes the sharing of culture, that we have responsibility to protect our valuable heritage and share it with everyone, geographically and historically. The UNESCO World Heritage Centre website states explicitly, "What makes the concept of World Heritage exceptional is its universal application. World Heritage sites belong to all the peoples of the world, irrespective of the territory on which they are located."[62] However, when it comes to actual operations, almost all World Heritage Sites are supported by and designed for tourism. This emphasis on tourism and commodification can be problematic for cultural conservation, as export-oriented economic growth strategies only accentuate the dominant development discourse that is destroying so many cultures in the first place.[63] Furthermore tourism easily shifts the responsibility to protect the endangered communal or national cultures from governments to the marketplace, which is extremely effective in wiping out the "noncompetitive" cultures.

Recent developments in Lijiang demonstrate precisely such a rationale.

In 2005 the Standing Committee of the Ninth People's Congress of Yunnan Province adopted "Regulations on the Protection of Dongba Culture in Lijiang Naxi Autonomous Prefecture of Yunnan Province." The focus of the regulations is on cultural protection; the government is not listed as the sole agent of conservation, but a major government task is to encourage the development of Lijiang's cultural industries and the marketing of cultural commodities.[64] The regulations also highlight the need to crack down on the proliferation of counterfeit cultural products in the market, as well as advocate for film and television adaptations of Dongba stories. All these demand a sound IPR infrastructure, which, not surprisingly, has developed quickly in the past few years; Lijiang has its own IPR office to coordinate local regulations and registrations and to serve as the legal enforcer of IPR.[65] Lijiang Prefecture was also one of eight places first selected by the PRC, as mentioned earlier, to set up a local General Office of Culture, Broadcasting, Press, and Publication to support the development of local cultural industries.

In addition to promoting patent and copyright registrations of all sorts, local officials also encourage the promotion of Naxi traditional music, which has gained international attention in recent years. However, this has prompted other regional music in China to be labeled Naxi music, thus infringing on the "geographical identification" of the "authentic" music. There are many attempts to protect the local music from IPR infringement through legal actions.[66] Most recently, a Naxi musician, Dapo Abo (達坡阿玻), with his company, Naxi Music, filed a copyright infringement suit against one of the largest Chinese film companies, Huayi Brothers, accusing one of its films, *Limi de caixiang* 李米的猜想 (The equation of love and death), of using three pieces of traditional Naxi music without his consent as the copyright holder.[67] I am not arguing that UNESCO's efforts in protecting Lijiang damaged the position of its traditional music; quite the contrary, I believe that the so-called Naxi music in its present commodified and IPR-protected form is an invention of Lijiang's newly conferred World Heritage Site status. Musicologists have identified multiple sources of Naxi music, which is not pure in any culturalist sense. As Helen Rees argues, there is a "double anomaly" in Naxi music: it has contradictory ethnic affiliations, and it has been adapted from its original religious purpose to become secular entertainment for the booming Lijiang tourist industry.[68] This double anomaly mocks any IPR legislation of this music. Also, if World Heritage Sites belong to all people, how can we justify claims of ownership of Naxi music through IPR concepts? In spite of the obvious logical contradictions, the two sets of logic need each other, however problematically, to fulfill their own missions.

Many have called for IPR protection to prevent the disappearance of traditional Dongba cultural products. One successful example involves the famous Dongba paper. Because of its specific local ingredients, the paper lasts much longer than other types of paper, and thus has preserved a large number of ancient Naxi manuscripts.[69] However, by the 1970s, the costly, labor-intensive, and relatively low-quality handmade paper traded in non-Han areas was completely displaced by industrially produced paper.[70] Dongba handmade paper has made a comeback in recent years, thanks almost completely to tourism, because it is sold as souvenirs. Dongba zhifang 東巴紙坊 (Dongba Paper Workshop) now has eleven chain stores in the old town of Lijiang. These stores sell Dongba paper products such as bookmarks, notebooks, and stationery; tourists can also observe and participate in the making of "authentic" Dongba paper. Dongba paper itself and the Dongba script imprinted thereon have been revered by archaeologists and anthropologists because of the advanced culture they embody. Today this paper-making industry, embodying everything from direct commodity consumption to experiential tourism, exemplifies contemporary tourism.

The IPR protection of the paper is obviously closely related to tourist activities, which obscure the problematic underlying logic. Traditional Dongba paper is made from the bark of a particular species of tree that is on the verge of extinction, and traditional ways of making Dongba paper vary regionally.[71] Protection of this paper may be driven by the desire to guarantee the paper's cultural authenticity, but both traditional practices and present-day environmental damage make any claims of authenticity impossible. Ironically the impossibility of making the actual traditional product does not deter but actually promotes IPR activities. Recent years have seen a number of patent registrations related to the making of Dongba paper, and they all claim "new" methods of making this "old" paper.[72] Cultural tourism discourse, which fetishizes ancient culture, is ironically realized in patenting, which celebrates new ideas and development. Once patented, traditional knowledge and skills (plus whatever "new" components justify the patents) are no longer confined to the community, and traditional craftsmen might be threatened by legal risks. Logical conundrums such as these are not specific to Dongba paper, but this case reveals the ideological conflicts inherent in the seemingly happy marriage between IPR and cultural conservation. IPR is actually a discourse of development, promoting and rewarding innovations—and therefore opposing inertia. This rationale fundamentally contradicts the logic of cultural conservation.

At stake when patenting indigenous knowledge is not only the conflicts between old and new, but also those between public and private. Indigenous knowledge is both public and private, yet it is neither one exclusively. Indigenous culture is shared within a specific community or tribe, but the customary authority also controls its use by those outside the community.[73] So the community's boundary is prominent. But patenting radically redraws the line: knowledge is privatized to make ownership possible, while it is also publicized to become global knowledge for a global public. The private and public boundaries are both pushed to the extreme, evaporating the original confines and disinheriting indigenous people of their cultural resources. Juggling the public and the private, IPR protection allows commodification, so that the unique and original product can be mass-reproduced to generate profits. John L. Comaroff and Jean Comaroff explain that the ethnocommodity "has a 'strange' capacity to conjure an open-ended dialectic in which ethnic subjects and cultural objects, genetic endowment and elective practice, constantly configure each other; to render those cultural products and practices in 'naturally' copyrighted intellectual property, owned by dint of indigenous knowledge or innovative elaboration; and to retain its auratic value even under conditions of mass-mediated replication."[74] The patented Dongba paper is situated at this perplexing crossroads between private and public, between new and old, between singular and plural. The magic and the problems of IPR are precisely its drive to merge the contradictory logics together, isolating cultural products from their changing historical and cultural continuum to make commodification possible.

The identity of the Dongba paper is defined not only economically, but also politically. In the name of collectivizing traditional family-run businesses, the early PRC government reactivated the Dongba papermaking industry, which was sidelined as a private family business during the Nationalist era. However, because of its premodern, preindustrial form, Dongba papermaking came to a complete halt during the Cultural Revolution. A major contribution of PRC's third-generation leaders of the 1990s was their emphasis on economic motivations—in addition to political coercion—to promote effective ethnic integration.[75] Dongba paper came back as a tourist item in precisely such a political milieu. Dongba papermaking went through both a demise and a resurrection in the name of economic development, from Fordist mass production to post-Fordist niche consumption. However, this economic logic also clandestinely supports state politics in different periods, allowing economics and politics to legitimize and infiltrate each other.

Underlying the conspiracy between local economic development and ethnic policy is the depletion of local culture's richness, and the entire Dongba culture is now tokenized in the form of a few commodifiable items. Heritage tourism involves bridging the past and the present; otherwise, historical arti- facts remain unconnected to most contemporary visitors. Aside from visitors' emotional identification with the constructed meanings of historical artifacts through their cultural embedding,[76] the temporal connection is also made possible by commodification: the historical Dongba paper is valuable now because it can be bought. Local scholars call our attention to the fact that, in spite of the thriving tourist economy, the overall Dongba culture is on the verge of extinction. Mainland scholars demonstrate that Dongba culture is facing a critical moment of crisis: although there are many organizations de- voted to the conservation of that culture, many of them focus on teaching selected dance styles and ignore the more arduous studies of classics and reli- gious rituals. It is lamentable that most of the cultural conservation activities around Dongba culture are instrumental in nature, valuing only those com- mercial activities that are part of tourism.[77] Although there has been much serious scholarship devoted to the study of Dongba culture in recent years, and tourist activities have led to the establishment of museums and the pro- tection of artifacts, the tourism industry lures many outsiders to migrate to the Lijiang area, and urbanization is bringing irreversible change to the re- gion.[78] Han imagination dominates the transformation of Lijiang, and the Han people participate actively in the actual cultural commercialization. Field studies show that approximately two-thirds of goods sold at Lijiang's souvenir shops lack local characteristics. The majority of shop operators are temporary residents, who run more than 80 percent of the stores selling spe- cialties from elsewhere.[79] In workshops managed by immigrant Han people, prices are at lower levels, and overall sales figures are higher.[80] The local Naxi people and their traditional culture cannot be described as displaying suffi- cient independent initiative in the creation of new industry, and it is the im- migrant Han people who commercialize contemporary Dongba crafts as a trade. Not only are IPR and creative industries unable to deal with these more fundamental cultural crises, but they often achieve the opposite effect, as they protect only selected commodifiable products and knowledge, directly con- tributing to the truncation of the culture.

Not all items that cannot be sold disappear in the commodity society; selected rituals and everyday life practices are fetishized or spectacularized by creative industries into performances or cultural productions to be consumed by tourists or audiences abroad. Here the problematic entanglement between creative industries and cultural tourism is most directly revealed. As demon- strated in the "Regulations on the Protection of Dongba Culture," the Yunnan government is actively promoting cultural productions featuring local stories and scenery. We have seen the popular TV drama series *Yimi yang-guang* 一米陽光 (One meter of sunlight), Zhang Yimou's transnational film *Riding Alone for Thousands of Miles*, the ten-part film project "Chinese New Cinema: The Yunnan project,"[81] as well as theatrical productions like *Yinxiang Lijiang* 印象麗江 (Impressions of Lijiang), also by Zhang—all of which feature the actual scenery of Lijiang and enjoy the active support of the local government. As described in the media, "The Zhang Yimou brand with the Lijiang Snow Mountain brand bring about the new *Yixiang Lijiang* brand."[82] Creative industries and their logic participate in every aspect of Lijiang's cultural tourism, which entails not only visits by tourists, but also the commodification of Lijiang as an object of entertainment.

Cultural critics have argued for closer collaboration between cultural policy and IPR in the protection of traditional culture.[83] But the limitations of IPR regimes in protecting traditional knowledge are also widely recognized. Some critics have advanced new forms of legal protection to safeguard both biodiversity and indigenous peoples' political autonomy and cultural identity in the face of modernity.[84] I applaud these efforts, but it is clear that most of the time we are seeing contestation instead of collaboration between the two goals. Although the overall standard of living in Dongba has improved and its people are respected for their autonomous cultural identity, traditional Dongba culture is rapidly deteriorating. I am not privileging or essentializing premodern cultures over modern ones, but I believe that if we want to employ IPR as a tool of cultural preservation, it is important to realize the unavoidable gap between IPR's economic fetishization of novelty and cultural conservation's ultimate goals.

Depoliticization and Neoliberalism

Cultural conservation, which is often related to ethnic minority policy, is a particularly troublesome area in China. Although multiculturalism has occupied a prominent position in national cultural policy since 1949, ethnic policy is highly political, and harmony among different ethnic groups in China is always understood in terms of political stability rather than cultural rights.[85] An important theoretical basis of current state policy is the idea of pluralistic unity promoted by the anthropology professor Fei Xiaotong; he argues that the unity of China as a nation-state is not only complementary to but also fundamental to China's multiethnic composition.[86] China's multiculturalism and state unity mutually define each other, so its multicultural policy is necessarily political. A recent document released by the Ministry of Culture on the protection of ethnic cultures states explicitly that one of the main objectives of China's multicultural policy is to fight against "certain Western enemies who try to use culture to infuse our ethnic regions with the aim of 'Westerniz-ing' our ethnic groups and promoting 'separatism' in our country."[87] The gov-ernment's political control of the ethnic groups against "Western interests" relies specifically on depoliticizing the people and their culture.

Cultural tourism and creative industries are warmly embraced by the gov-ernment, not only because of their economic promises, but also because of their instrumental function in depoliticization. The political strategies of mi-nority governance and general attempts to depoliticize culture find the per-fect vanishing point in the promotion of global tourism and cultural conser-vation. What these strategies show is not a simple postmodern assimilation of differences into fragments and chaos, but the conflation and reinforcement of discrete ideologies through their confrontations.

China's depoliticization is manifested most intricately in the economiza-tion of local ethnic culture, whose enormous political potential is depleted by the overall neoliberal drive. Both IPR and cultural policy regimes play a role here. IPR legislation and enforcement are not necessarily top-down—that is, forced upon local areas by the WTO—but IPR infrastructure is actively pursued by local economies. As seen in China, the intersections between the global and the national are often most vibrantly and contradictorily located on the local level, in which we see the direct confrontation between rampant IPR offenses among the people and the fervent pursuit of the transient cate-gories of creativity and spectacularity in the local economy. In terms of IPR, the government and other interested parties want to possess, while the people want to consume, so that the widespread piracy activities currently taking place in China are accompanied by an equally epidemic desire to mimic the IPR form on the state level. Neither one directly complies with the wishes of IPR-rich countries, but they are manifestations of the same creative economy.

In the past few years we have seen an explosion of IPR offices all over China, ranging from those instigated by the state and provinces to those established on the city and even prefectural levels. There are currently fifty-eight regional intellectual property offices directly under the State Intellectual Property Office, but city and prefectural governments also establish their own IPR offices. Each of these IPR offices might differ vastly in structure, consti-tution, and function. Some offices report directly to the State Office; some share offices and cooperate more closely with the Ministry of Culture. Pre-cisely because of hasty local implementation of IPR, there is also significant regional discrepancy, resulting, ironically, in ineffective communication and enforcement.

In the area of cultural policy, neoliberal depoliticization might be seen as a parallel structure of (failed) control and mimicry. At least on the surface, China's cultural policymakers try to downplay ideology to highlight culture's economic value, so that the earlier emphasis on close textual analysis (particularly in terms of censorship) is no longer pronounced. Instead we are seeing an emphasis on the quantification of culture, that culture is composed not of ideologically laden text, but of politically neutral data. In 2004 and 2005 the Working Group in Topics Related to Cultural Industries Statistics and Research published two documents, "Wenhua ji xiangguan chanye fenlei" 文化及相關產業分類 (Classification of culture and related industries) and "Wenhua ji xiangguan chanye zhibiao tixi kuangjia" 文化及相關產業指標體系框架 (Framework of the indexical structure of cultural and related industries).[88] Combined, these constitute the first systematic categorization and statistical model for China's cultural industries. This has triggered a wave of action among city governments trying to map the cultural industries of their own regions, with the aim of implementing new policies to nurture these industries.[89] These two documents play a pivotal role in encouraging local adoption of the creative economy, and they provide a system of classification that can serve a number of important functions. They offer a general definition of cultural industries and encourage local government offices to develop related promotional policies, and they also illustrate collection methods and the kinds of statistical data that can help the central government get a complete picture of its national creative economy. Most important, such data collection has fueled competition among cities and regions whose achievements can now be quantified and compared. Instead of directly controlling local government activities, the central government only defines a statistical and comparative framework that allows researchers and local governments to embark on creative economy discourse. This strong comparative tendency is not unique to China, but it is intrinsic to the global creative industries discourse, which is defined not only according to its contribution to a country's economic activities (GDP), but also for the establishment of an international standard that facilitates global comparisons.[90]

I believe the rapid implementation of the creative economy in China through a dual mechanism of top-down mandates and bottom-up mimicry could aid our understanding of China's seemingly contradictory coexistence of neoliberalism, which emphasizes deregulation, and nationalism, and which is an ideology of unification. Aihwa Ong explains the situation in terms of the "exception." She argues that neoliberalism, external to its socialist state ideology, functions in the operation of China's Special Economic Zones. The concept of the exception could help scholars explain the coexistence of abundant contradictions in sovereign powers. But using this concept to understand the PRC's relationship with the world might run the risk of dichotomizing the forces of globalization and the integrity of the state. Ong argues, "In Asian milieus, the option of exception has allowed states to carve up their own territory so they can better engage and compete in global markets."[91] But the rapid development of the creative economy in China does not entail any territorial slicing, and the new global logic no longer needs a Shenzhen or a Hong Kong to enter China. As shown in the rapid transformation of IPR and cultural policy infrastructures, the new economic discourse is actively pursued at the local level, meaning transformation is carried out from within.

Many scholars have pointed out that there are so many forms of neoliberalism being implemented around the world that it has become almost meaningless to pursue the meaning of neoliberalism.[92] But this proliferation of its different versions has also made neoliberalism a force of extreme success and its power enduring. As Lisa Rofel has argued more pointedly, neoliberalism is never a coherent structure but rather a form of desire among people in the developing world to fantasize their pursuits and participation in the global order.[93] As an anthropologist, Rofel situates the effects and affects of neoliberalism not in any social institutions but in individual subjectivities. What interests her about China's recent changes, therefore, is not a top-down institutional model of neoliberalism, but the ways subjects create their own subjectivities by desiring and consuming the new neoliberal era. If we see neoliberalism as a structure of desire, regulation and deregulation belong to two sides of the same coin, characterizing people's different tactics in pursuit of the global. Wang Hui explains that the rapid development of the neoliberal market economy in China does not entail the withdrawal of state involvement, as "the actualities of market economics and the process of globalization cannot be implemented other than by State intervention."[94] Given the importance of the state, what remains to be fully analyzed in Wang's studies is the actual operation of the local economy under state control. I believe it is the actual participation of local governments and people, which are never under the complete control of any sovereign force, which marks the real success of the new economy.

Depoliticization is a key condition of neoliberalism, whose enormous success thus far is largely due to its mobilization of people at all levels of society. Pierre Bourdieu describes neoliberalism as a Darwinian world: "It is the struggle of all against all at all levels of the hierarchy, which finds support through everyone clinging to their job and organisation under conditions of insecurity, suffering, and stress."[95] When people are most enthusiastically engaged in the neoliberal pursuit, they are also the most personally stressed (in terms of career insecurity) and politically docile (in terms of the reign of consumption). Ong's territorial model fails to grasp the political implications of the neoliberal economy, which depoliticizes not only certain parts of China, but the entire country—including the ethnic minorities, whose cultures have become ever more vulnerable to political and economic forces.

Cinema as a Creative Industry

In chapter 4 I examined the relationship between the two discourses of cultural policy and IPR and their intertwining conditions as manifested in local creative industries. In this chapter I focus on the effects of creative industries on traditional media and how IPR offenses arise accordingly. It is widely recognized that the promotion of creative industries is one of the key forces motivating the rapid development of both the copyright regime and the new phase of global cultural policy reform in the past few years, but how traditional cultural industries welcome and are challenged by the new creative industries has not yet been adequately studied. While in chapter 4 I took a broader perspective to study institutional and historical changes, in this chapter I provide a close analysis of the challenge of an established cultural industry, Hong Kong cinema, which struggles to adapt to the new creative industries environment. I then explore in general how the audience is conceptualized in the creative industries discourse.

From Lijiang, the ancient city deep in the country's western rural land, I come back to my home, the metropolis Hong Kong in the southern tip of China. It is important to demonstrate that not only developing areas, but this global financial center, one of the most advanced cities in the world, struggles to adopt IPR and foster creativity for its own economy. Despite the enormous differences between Lijiang and Hong Kong, the two cities share common desire for the creative economy, which demonstrates how alluring and ambiguous the concept is and how China is both one and many. Generally speaking, the discourse of creative industries is more systematically adopted in the Hong Kong Special Administration Region than in the PRC mainland, but Hong Kong cinema still manifests its uneasy transition to adapt to the post-Fordist creative economy environment. The wide spectrum of creative industries includes both cultural tourism, which is primarily made up of small enterprises and relatively independent workers, and the mass-media film industry.

Specifically, I investigate two main areas of changes effected by creative industries on cinema, the flexible-transnational and the digital, and cinema has to confront the loosening of its identity in two areas: its place and its media. I explore how the working conditions of filmmakers and the conceptualization of the audience are transformed accordingly. While governments develop transnational creative industries and adopt global IPR policy, the place-based specificity of films is being emptied out, and filmmakers also need to adapt to a much more competitive market and industrial environment. Also, creative industries advocate the merging of media, and the technologies associated with cinema have undergone substantial changes, specifically in the areas of distribution and reception. Commercial film companies have to resort to a variety of IPR-related legislation to resist the new freedom viewers have in this digital environment. "Destructive" technologies are demarcated from "productive" ones, so that creative industries can have tighter control over the use of their content. Combining the two parts, I demonstrate the differences between cultural industries and creative industries, in that the latter are much more diffuse, adaptable, and controlling than the former.

Creative Industries and Hong Kong Cinema

The adoption of the creative industries discourse by Hong Kong cinema has its own history, and the marriage between them is by no means a natural one. As I mentioned in the introduction, the notion of creative industries first appeared in Australian and U.K. policy circles in the 1990s, most prominently in the Labour Party's election campaign in 1997, which promised to renew Britain's cultural image through the development of the national creative industries. Using the British definition, the creative industries encompass (1) traditional cultural industries, such as cinema, music, publishing, television, and radio; (2) arts and crafts, such as the performing arts and souvenir and antiques markets; (3) new media, such as leisure software and games; and (4) other industries that require the input of creativity, such as advertising, design, and architecture. The discourse of creative industries emphasizes the convergence and collaboration among these originally autonomous industries and cultural forms and demonstrates how they combine to become an economic force powerful enough to drive regional and national economies. I call creative industries a discourse because its immediate popularity among governments attests to a strong discursive power, and various governments adopt and repackage it to cater to their own national situations and give the term specific national appeal.

Creative industries as a discourse is embraced not only by governments but also by many skeptical cultural critics for its celebration of individual creativity and the rare opportunities provided to articulate new forms of cultural politics and creative activities even within a capitalist framework.[1] However, in order to infuse these products with market value, the creativity in the creative industries must be governed by complex contractual relations over intellectual property.[2] Accordingly, individual creativity is conditioned by its potential for wealth, and the ultimate aim is to exploit creativity in the form of intellectual property. Creative industries would collapse without the required copyright and trademark support, so an essential part of the discourse is raising copyright awareness and condemning piracy.[3] Cultural organizations that rely less heavily on the protection of the IPR legal regime are those that cannot generate profits on their own. As they depend more on public subsidies or sponsorship to survive, they are usually considered closely related to but distinct from true creative industries. Museums, for example, add value to creative industries through indirect factors such as social coherence and city branding.[4]

Creative industries have become particularly valued in East Asia. Inspired by the successes in Britain, Canada, and Australia, many Asian countries have begun to investigate creative industries in recent years. Taiwan, for example, named 2003 the "Creative Industry Year," and in the same year the government also designated creative industries as the second most important target of investment in its ten-year plan.[5] Recognizing the cross-institutional nature of this "new" economic sector, many Asian governments have set up their own think tanks or agencies, modeled in large part on the U.K.'s Demos think tank, to investigate development strategies suitable for their own national situation. High-profile institutions such as Taiwan Thinktank Cultural Forum, the Korea Culture and Content Agency, and Singapore's Workgroup on Creative Industries aim to integrate culture, industry, and public policy to boost their national creative industries. The notion of "content industries" (similar to creative industries) is also slowly gaining currency in Japan, specifically through the current "Cool Japan" boom, which refers to the recent trend of young Japanese starting their own companies in various cultural industries. At least seven government committees and organizations were established in Japan between 2000 and 2005 to promote popular culture.[6] But there is basically an absence of national policy on creative industries in South Asian countries, in spite of their close relationship with the Commonwealth. The Indian government, for example, is still more interested in promoting its information industry than branding the country or exporting the sari as modern fashion.

Lily Kong and her colleagues have provided a useful comparison of creative economies around Asia.[7] They trace the uneven diffusion of this discourse among different countries, demonstrating how this "translation" occurs through the movements of "experts," the consumption of popular books by such authors as Florida and Landry, the dissemination of all kinds of online information, and the promotion of official multilateral policymaking forums like the WTO. Hong Kong's is one of the Asian governments most eager to investigate how to strengthen its economic infrastructure by emphasizing creative and entertainment products. Chief Executive Tung Chee-Hwa acknowledged the link between the arts and the economy as far back as 1998.[8] In his Policy Address in 2003, Tung advocated the creative industries as an important strategic area whose development is vital to the city's economic future, a point he repeated in his following Policy Addresses.[9] Responding to the recent global financial crisis, the current chief executive, Donald Tsang, identifies six priority industries, and among them are cultural and creative industries as the key targets of government support to broaden the city's economic base and to add new impetus for sustainable growth.[10] Commissioned by the Hong Kong government's Central Policy Unit, the Centre for Cultural Policy Research at the University of Hong Kong completed the *Baseline Study on Hong Kong's Creative Industries* in 2003 and the *Study on the Relationship between Hong Kong's Cultural and Creative Industries and the Pearl River Delta* in 2006. The *Baseline Study* clearly states that in order to develop Hong Kong's creative industries, the people must learn to transform creativity into tradable deliverables and services, and the linchpin in this transformation is the deployment of intellectual property.[11] This is an almost word-for-word reiteration of the U.K. model, once again demonstrating the mimetic nature of the entire global creative industries phenomenon.

The creative industries portfolio of individual countries and cities does not always include cinema; that depends largely on the well-being of the existing filmmaking industry. In Hong Kong cinema is a major stakeholder in the cultural sphere, and it has enjoyed much attention in the aforementioned reports as well as in general discussions of creative industries in the city. But generally speaking, cinema, straddling between culture and commerce, is situated easily yet also uneasily within the creative industries discourse.[12] Internationally there is a prominent critical trend disfavoring government meddling in cinema. Negative measures such as censorship are always criticized. State

control in Third World cinema is particularly condemned for its totalitar-
ian intentions and results, which often become causes for national cinemas'
waning artistic and commercial vigor.[13] But even protectionist policies such
as subsidies are seen as preventing films from being responsive to the market.
Some scholars also believe that direct government support for the film industry can protect an economic sector from its own internal weakness.[14] For example, the Australian government provides significant government funding
to its film industry through tax concessions and direct subsidies from institutions such as the Film Finance Corporation. But scholars observe that once
these publicly funded producers become aesthetically dominant within the
industry, they prevent the vision of independent artists from emerging.[15] It is
argued that the Taiwan film industry, which has also been largely supported
by the government in the past two decades, suffers from a lack of market sensibility because the government tends to nurture award-winning auteur filmmakers who take the name of Taiwan to international film festivals. Other
critics contend that the recent success of Korean cinema is due not to government funding but to private investment.[16]

But the fact is that direct government investment in the commercial film
industry was rare. In certain Western countries, such as France and Canada,
cinema is an item in the state's cultural policy, but the support of domestic
films is usually rationalized as cultural protection against Hollywood instead
of as a means for profit-making. To legitimize government support cinema
is often seen as a national art instead of a commercial activity. The creative
industries discourse has altered this scenario. The U.K. Film Council was created in 2000, not in the name of protecting British film as art but to "help
make the U.K. a global centre for film in the digital age." Managing a large
annual budget of around £17 million lottery sales, the U.K. Film Council has
backed more than nine hundred films, shorts and features, since its creation.[17]
The New Zealand Film Commission set up a new fund in the same year with
the clear mission of investing in larger-budget New Zealand films. The German government set up its German Film Promotion Fund in 2007 with the
explicit goal of promoting the German film industry. In 2007 and 2008 the
Fund sponsored 198 productions with some €118.5 million.[18] The South African government is also starting to recognize both the growth and the employment potential inherent in its film industry and has set up a variety of finances
and incentives to support film-related activities.[19]

Direct government support has also been observed in Hong Kong cinema,
which until recently was left entirely on its own by a government that practiced laissez-faire. A major reason for this policy shift is the recent demise of

commercial Hong Kong cinema and the drastic and continuous drop in the number of productions (see table 1).

It is generally believed that the heyday of Hong Kong cinema has passed and that it might head toward the perpetual slump in which Taiwanese cinema is now caught. However, the city is still producing a steady stream of commercial films, although in much smaller numbers than it did in its prime. While annual film production peaked in the early 1990s, with 242 films in 1993, its rapid decline has not yet substantially weakened Hong Kong's role as a regional film center. In 2000 Hong Kong's film industry, with an annual output of 150 films, still ranked third in Asia, after India and Japan.[20] While the decline in the past decade is huge, a few commercial hits, like *Infernal Affairs* (directed by Andrew Lau and Mak Siu-fai, 2002), *Kung Fu Hustle* (directed by Stephen Chow, 2004), *Initial D* (directed by Andrew Lau and Mak Siu-fai, 2005), and *Ip Man* (directed by Wilson Yip, 2008), swept local or regional box offices, and the rapidly expanding mainland market continually brings investment into the city's film industry. Many of these blockbusters are now transborder productions incorporating mainland funding, talent, and markets, but the Hong Kong components are also prominent enough for this local cinema to carry on its legacy.

The creative industries discourse has come to Hong Kong's film industry at an important moment. In spite of its previous success without any public support, Hong Kong's film industry is actively seeking government backing to come to terms with the new mainland market and related policies, and the creative industries discourse comes in handy for producers to legitimize such requests. In order to implement the overall creative industries policy, the government also actively seeks and positively responds to these demands. The Film Services Office was set up by the government in 1998 with an overall mission to create and maintain an environment conducive to the long-term and healthy development of the film industry.[21] In 1999 the Hong Kong government also assigned around HK$100 million to set up the Film Development Fund to support local productions, but the utilization of the fund has been extremely low, allegedly due to its heavy restrictions. The industry also complains that the fund cannot be used directly on production, but only serves as a guarantee fund to assist local film production companies to obtain loans. In response to the industry's strong lobbying, Chief Executive Tsang promised to step up government support for the film industry,[22] and the Hong Kong Film Development Council was set up in 2007 for this purpose. The government's HK$300 million Film Fund invests directly in small and midsize film productions. Another major apparatus is the successful Hong Kong–Asia Film

Table 1. Chinese-Language Films Screened in Hong Kong
and Their Box Office Revenues, 2001–2007

Year	Number of Chinese Films Screened in Hong Kong	Box Office Revenues of Chinese Films (in million HK$)
2001	151	383
2002	133	476
2003	92	350
2004	77	366
2005	63	383
2006	52	284
2007	50	229

Source: Hong Kong, Kowloon and New Territories Motion Picture
Industry Association (MPIA)

Financing Forum (HAF), which strives to match global investors with Asian
filmmakers, without a specific emphasis on local production.[23]

While the government was busily debating and learning how to assist its
commercial filmmaking industry, a headline-grabbing news item seized the
city. On 12 January 2005 a jobless thirty-eight-year-old man, Chan Nai-ming,
was arrested at his home by Hong Kong customs officers. He was accused of
uploading the BitTorrent (BT) "seeds"—data that can be used by others to
download a media product—to the Hollywood movies *Daredevil, Red Planet*,
and *Miss Congeniality* onto the bt.newsgroup.com.hk forum just two days
before his arrest.[24] Online the copyright infringer called himself Guhuo tian-
wang 古惑天王 (King of the Tricksters),[25] a reference to the movie series *Young
and Dangerous* (*Guhuo zai* 古惑仔), which glorifies a triad of young street
gangsters as heroes. The news made local headlines as the first ever BT piracy
arrest in the city. Three months later the case attracted even wider media attention because the Hong Kong government and the Hong Kong film industry worked together to bring a criminal lawsuit against the King for copyright
violation of the three Hollywood movies. Unsurprisingly, he was found guilty
and sentenced to three months in jail.[26] The case is the very first criminal con-
viction for international online film piracy, and has been followed by similar
legal and moral disputes worldwide.[27] Hong Kong filed the world's first criminal charges against BT movie piracy to attest to its status as a global film center
and a leading IPR supporter.

The arrest took place in January 2005 and the criminal charges were announced at a press conference on 27 April, attended by famous directors and

movie stars and organized by an ad hoc committee composed of filmmakers and the Film Industry Response Group (Dianying gongye yingbian xiaozu 電影工業應變小組). The arrest of the King was an interesting climax to a series of international events, Entertainment Expo, which was jointly organized by the film industry and the government to position Hong Kong as a regional center of Asia's creative industries. The Expo included the twenty-ninth Hong Kong International Film Festival, the twenty-fourth Hong Kong Film Awards presentation, the second Hong Kong International Film and TV Market (FILM-ART) festival,[28] and the third HAF. These key events are all related to cinema (music, television, and game industries were gradually added to the Expo in subsequent years). The Expo has two major purposes: to attract international media attention to Hong Kong cinema and to develop Hong Kong as a media finance center. The two missions are related, in that the first furthers the second. Given that the glamorous nature of cinema naturally attracts media attention, it is reasonable to speculate that the BT criminal charges, which were announced immediately after the Expo, were timed to support the Expo. The symbolic meaning of the arrest for the position of Hong Kong as an IPR center is confirmed in Magistrate Colin Mackintosh's problematic statement that began his six pages of judgment against the King: "Hong Kong carefully guards intellectual property rights. These rights are not illusory. . . . They are valuable and they amount to genuine property."[29]

In spite of their close collaboration, while creative industries protect local industries, IPR is supposedly region-blind and tends to privilege the market dominator against its struggling or emerging competitors. The case of the King seems to indicate that Hong Kong cinema and Hollywood both occupy the front line against piracy. However, because of its larger market share, Hollywood is mostly the beneficiary. Historically Hong Kong films were more popular than American products in the local market, but recently the domestic film industry has started to lose ground to Hollywood films.[30] Similarly most of the BT files available on Hong Kong's BT forums and newsgroups are Hollywood films, along with games, television programs, animation, and computer software from other countries; only a few are local productions.[31] Hong Kong residents, both the online community and ordinary theatergoers and disc buyers, are less and less attracted to Hong Kong films. Ironically the major rival of Hong Kong filmmakers will continue to be Hollywood, but the local film industry only helps its American rivals—and themselves to a much lesser extent—by eradicating copyright violation.

When discussing Hollywood's increasing diversification and transnationalization, Paul McDonald and Janet Wasko argue that there is still a very definite foundation to the Hollywood film business: "Films may enter the market in many forms, but at its core Hollywood remains a business which is not really based on the production of things so much as the control of the rights to use those things."[32] More accurately, it is no longer films but IPR which has become the fundamental commodity produced by Hollywood. This is not true in Hong Kong cinema yet, but obviously the allure is strong. This battle against BT piracy, which protects the global IPR infrastructure instead of local film industries, is considered strategic to the survival of Hong Kong cinema even as the logic of why IPR is essential to the film industry remains entirely fuzzy. The result is that while copyright-poor nations are encouraged to heavily police local piracy, the immediate rewards are reaped by copyright-rich nations (particularly the U.S.). These anxious copyright-poor countries are rewarded with the hope that if only a stringent IPR framework were imposed, they could attract trusts and future creative industries investment, and then the creative industries will finally make these handicapped countries copyright-rich. But the fallacy of this reckoning is the connection between future creative industries investment and current IPR legislation and enforcement, which is established by nothing but a leap of faith.[33]

Cinema and Place

Many local viewers have strongly supported Hong Kong cinema because of its intimate reflection of the city's collective ethos, and many international critics celebrate its place-based productions as opposed to Hollywood's America-centric transnational hegemony.[34] Historically the films made in Hong Kong were largely conditioned by actual events in the city and by the people's collective emotions, which naturally provide topics, incentives, and a keen sense of style to Hong Kong filmmaking. In spite of its quasi-independent status, Hong Kong cinema's "national" identity can never be taken for granted due to the city's specific colonial and postcolonial status. Hong Kong cinema in the 1980s and 1990s was particularly blessed by the handover in 1997, which enforced the assumed dichotomy between the PRC's nationalist incorporation and Hong Kong's cosmopolitan and postcolonial subjectivity. Critics suggest that the fear surrounding the handover defined and enlivened the wonders of Hong Kong cinema of the 1980s and 1990s—forcing filmmakers to reflect on the city's fragile identity and resulting in a unique and vigorous self-reflexive cinema.[35] A favorite topic of recent Hong Kong cinema scholarship is the relationship between the city and its cinema and how the films directly or indirectly bear the collective identity of the people.[36]

However, Hong Kong cinema as a place-based cultural industry whose products are designed for a specific domestic and diasporic audience is at odds with the transnational creative industries discourse. Instead of emphasizing the cultural affinity between the producer and the receiver, the creative industries discourse reconceptualizes the relationship between cinema and place in two other ways: as creative sectors and city branding. Largely inspired by recent studies of the creative city and creative clusters,[37] many film and geography researchers have found that film production is part of a network, and different sectors of the industry work together in a contractual, flexible manner.[38] Scholars also demonstrate that successful film industries display evidence of clustering, both in terms of local agglomeration and transnational connections.[39] Different filmmaking subsectors collaborate, and creative ideas are generated in innovative ways. The study of creative clusters as such might be difficult to apply to Hong Kong cinema, because the city itself is extremely complex and the institutional collaborations are hard to chart geographically. But increasing attention has been paid to Hong Kong's coproduction culture with the mainland, and scholars are interested in the flexible nature of related transborder flows of capital, ideas, and personnel. Many "Hong Kong" films are no longer made in the city, but local companies have to work closely with people and companies in different parts of China, so the coproduction culture could be seen as another version of the creative cluster trend. I will discuss transborder coproduction in the next section.

The discourses of creative industries also link filmmaking with city branding. In the case of Hong Kong cinema, the values of its films are calculated not only according to the actual profits generated but also according to the degree that films build an image of Hong Kong as a media hub or a global city, as shown in the works of the Film Services Office. Under the continual development of global capitalism, cities are not only strategic sites for the production, circulation, and consumption of commodities, but they are themselves intensively commodified, insofar as their constitutive sociospatial forms are sculpted and continually reorganized in order to enhance the profit-making capacities of capital.[40] Accordingly the Hong Kong film industry produces not only films as commodities, but also the image of the commodified Hong Kong. The connection between movies and city image is particularly obvious in Hong Kong cinema, as most people around the world know Hong Kong through its films. Hong Kong cinema has been given the burden of saving itself and the city by attracting both tourists and investment to the city.[41]

Strangely, with the advent of the creative industries model, Hong Kong cinema is now conceptualized without the city's viewers, and sometimes without the films themselves. As seen in the efforts around the Entertainment Expo, while the branding of Hong Kong cinema is highlighted, Hong Kong cinema is tokenized and dematerialized, but only as a means to attract media attention and investment. As the city is repositioned as a finance center rather than a production center, Hong Kong's interest in the arrest of the King of the Tricksters is manifested on the abstract plane of "advertising effects." The global branding of Hong Kong cinema needs the lure of award-winning directors and stars, like Wong Kar-wai and Tony Leung Chiu-wai, as well as an IPR-loyal image. The rise of creative industries is one result of the fall of cinema as a traditional cultural industry.

As a result, Hong Kong cinema has radically new meanings in the creative industries' discursive context, in that it becomes an empty brand name designed to attract capital, whether in the form of direct investment in local or regional productions, or whether to turn Hong Kong into a finance or distribution center where the headquarters of transnational media corporations are located. Hong Kong needs to continue to produce award-winning films that can claim some space on the pages of the New York Times, and the seductive stills of Zhang Ziyi in 2046 and other films must continue to circulate globally to attest to Hong Kong's "film power."[42] As a brand name, Hong Kong cinema can organize and participate in many transnational productions aimed at global markets. It has been transnational for decades, but only recently do we see it turning into an abstract brand name instead of the producer of concrete place-based productions.[43]

This displacement of Hong Kong cinema directly impacts the production scene. The rapid development and modernization of the local industry can be traced back to the early 1960s, when the Shaw Brothers constructed Movie Town, with twelve sound stages and sixteen outdoor sets. The studio adopted vertical integration in the manner of Hollywood majors, employing fifteen hundred contract workers and producing an average of forty films per year in the mid-1960s.[44] Golden Harvest replaced Shaw Brothers to become the dominant force in Chinese commercial cinema by the late 1970s. Although the younger studio began to outsource its production and to finance independent filmmaking, it operated an intact production line and trained and provided secure employment to a staple of filmmaking professionals. By the late 1990s the older studio system dominated by the Shaws and Golden Harvest was rapidly replaced by the rise of smaller independent production houses.[45] Unlike their predecessors, these smaller studios usually operate with small budgets and therefore tend to have very short life spans in the recession period. Most of the workers in the industry are forced to turn freelance.

Although the transborder Hong Kong–China coproductions continue to lure investors and major creative figures, the once prosperous film industry is under the threat of extinction because most of the actual production now takes place in mainland China, where filmmaking is cheaper and closer to the target audiences. Currently there are only two or three projects in Hong Kong on any given day, far from enough to provide jobs to the many professional film workers this industry has attracted and cultivated.[46] While Hong Kong's film industry continues to operate, unemployment and underemployment are now the norm.

There are local reasons for this situation, but the conditions are not unique to Hong Kong. In the name of generating innovative ideas and encouraging new methods, the creative industries discourse privileges flexible accumulation and competition, and smaller independent filmmaking has become a prominent development in the new transnational film scene. However, while the transnational flows of culture have become more complex, inconsistent, and unpredictable, they also generate new kinds of power, which are even more difficult to pin down and engage with. With the proactive participation of governments and film festivals, many transnational funding platforms are now available, and filmmakers are given more chances to match their projects with diversified public and private investments. But many of these investors, unlike the major commercial studios in the old days, are not willing to shoulder the entire budget, and current film projects are often financed by multiple sources. Under such conditions, filmmakers have to become entrepreneurs and cater to changing market conditions. At a time when Hong Kong cinema is so rapidly approaching an unknown destiny, fostering new creative talent is among its most urgent tasks, but filmmakers are also under increasing pressure to survive on their own.

The working conditions of new directors are emblematic of the overall creative industries environment. The creative industries discourse favors small enterprises for their flexible structure and innovative ideas, and the new global cinema also tends to privilege small studios and new directors. Many national and regional film funding agencies, like the German Film Promotion Fund, the U.K. Film Council, Taiwan's Government Information Office, the New South Wales Film and Television Office, and the New Mexico Film Office, administer specific grants to new filmmakers. In Hong Kong, although its Film Development Council does not show clear preference for young filmmakers, the industry continues to provide opportunities for new directors. Major commercial film companies, such as Mei Ah, EDKO, Sundream, and Filmko, continue to invest in films directed by newcomers. A few smaller companies, like Focus and Irresistible Films, are openly committed to discovering and providing opportunities to new directors. The robust mainland economy has also bred many new capitalists who have developed an interest in filmmaking, for legitimate or illegitimate reasons; as long as they have the connections, both established and new directors are tapped for spontaneous projects of this sort. But this seemingly prosperous reality for new filmmakers is challenged by an insecure freelance job environment.[47] Under the new creative industries discourse, they are the first generation of Hong Kong directors—at least in terms of commercial cinema—who have to sail through the post-Fordist environment, where job security is extinct. The fetishization of newness, a prominent feature of the late capitalist economy, also characterizes this new cinema, making newcomers quickly unattractive, because they will no longer be new after making one or two films.

These new directors are considered precious new blood desperately needed by the failing Hong Kong industry, and they are still sporadically trusted with projects by investors in spite of the extremely high risks involved. However, with legendarily low wages and insecure job conditions, many of these new directors also have to work as freelancers for various media in order to earn a living, while spending most of their time and energies working for future projects which never seem to be realized. One young director who has already directed two feature-length commercial films admits that his average monthly salary is about HK$8,000 (about U.S.$1,000), lower than a full-time production assistant. This salary barely pays the rent. To look for projects some have to move constantly between Hong Kong and China, and they have to deal with all kinds of investors and producers who do not always honor their contracts. Many of them have directed one or two films only, but they have chosen filmmaking as their sole career, and they struggle to hold on to it as much as they can. Under the aegis of a flexible mode of operation, these new directors are usually not attached to any studio, so they have to secure simultaneously their income and career prospects, which do not tend to overlap. Directing music videos, advertisements, corporate videos, educational television, and other media projects, they also need to liaise with investors and other filmmakers, constantly writing up new projects and participating in discussions, although most of the time these projects never come to fruition. The new market conditions and risks in the transnational coproduction scene, including volatile censorship in China, multiple financial sources, constantly changing film policies, and incomprehensible film festival politics, are all matters new directors have to deal with which were not relevant to the older generation. Caught in an industry which is at the edge of disappearance, almost all commercial filmmakers are struggling with conditions as complex as the meaning of their professional identity and as simple as making ends meet.

As it is well known, a special feature of the current digital age is the widespread image-making activity among global youths, who can now easily produce (with a simple DV camera and editing software) and distribute (through online sites like YouTube) their work. But for those working in the industry, they have made a decision to turn their hobby into a career. A thirty-year-old director who has made a few independent videos and a commercial feature film explained that young video makers tend to face the same dilemma upon hitting the age of thirty: either to opt out or to try to move up to the commercial film world. After directing a film or two, they are already in their mid- to late thirties, finding it extremely difficult to start another career. New filmmakers in Hong Kong are caught in its unique local and global sociopolitical circumstances, in which filmmaking is both easier and more difficult. Their career is existentially intertwined with the industry, as critics and audiences burden these new directors with the future of Hong Kong cinema, while the filmmakers themselves only hope for the industry's continued prosperity.

Given a volatile global film culture with no job security, a career in filmmaking is increasingly competitive. In spite of the glamour associated with the filmmaking business, young directors are exemplary creative laborers, who are exposed to an increasingly volatile environment with no career safety net. The creative industries' emphasis on agglomeration and flexibility actually deprives workers of a stable creative environment in which to engage with filmmaking more meaningfully. Among the young directors I talked to, almost all were nostalgic for the old studio era, when directors only needed to direct.

Bad Technologies and Indocile Consumers

The creative industries discourse not only diffuses the concept of place and deprives filmmakers of a stable working environment, but it also conflates the medium: digitization levels all cultural forms. In this section we will further explore elements of place in the film industry by focusing on the audience, particularly the impact of digital technologies on cinema globally. As a major purpose of this book is to investigate the intricate relationships between creative industries and IPR offenses, here I would also like to emphasize how the two are connected digitally.

Almost all creative industries rely on digital technology in production, although some less heavily than others. The rise of creative industries is clearly intertwined with the rise of digital technology in areas of product design. However, digital technology is not as enthusiastically embraced in the realm of product distribution, particularly for traditional cultural industries. Almost all traditional cultural industries (film, music, and television) distribute their products in digital form; this causes a lot of anxiety to copyright holders because of easy duplication. Today digitization of media products means the radical dematerialization of reproduction costs—but high production costs, including astronomical advertising fees, keep the retail prices of the goods high. Almost by nature some people, attracted to certain products, will resort to less expensive—and increasingly easy—piracy to copy these products for their own use. Digitization and piracy almost go hand in hand, because retail prices are markedly higher than the real reproduction costs. An interesting development in commercial filmmaking in recent years is 3-D production, whose 3-D effects cannot yet be replicated outside the theatre, although the rapidly developing home theatre technology will ultimately also benefit the pirates.

In fact the high-profile arrests of online copyright infringers such as the King of the Tricksters point out the great anxiety over the audience that is inherent in the creative industries discourse. Online distribution is most feared, and concerned industries, particularly cinema, have shown great reluctance in embracing this part of digitization. Like the passionate subtitling labor found in the Chinese cyberculture, the web is characterized by fervent downloadings and uploadings, filling the Internet with useful data and knowledge as well as censored materials diligently made available by netizens on websites and networks. The impulse of sharing is characteristically prominent on the net, and there are a few reasons contributing to this tendency. First, digital content is not based on rivalry, in the sense that more than one individual can consume the same goods without diminishing its value. Digital sharing therefore is not conducted in the form of giving, as the uploader continues to possess the entirety of the uploaded materials. Second, with the current technology and popular online groups available, digital distribution is extremely easy and effective. The anonymous nature of the web also means that uploaders and downloaders can often avoid ethical responsibility and criminal consequences. Most important, sharing forms bonds. Many of the cybercommunities, illicit or not, are formed by the activities of file, data, and information sharing, providing members with a sense of connection not easily found in society.

Currently a major battle in copyright discourse is taking place in the digital realm, where distribution makes control over the mobility of cultural goods most difficult. IPR measures, particularly antipiracy measures, are highly inefficient in such areas, because piracy is almost an inevitable result of the current technological environment. The IPR regime becomes a necessary but largely strained legal structure to counter the new digital environment's natural predisposition to share and pirate. Ironically this inefficiency also makes IPR one of the most urgent and appealing issues on the creative industries' agenda. In order for creative industries to garner maximum profits, their products must be protected from illegal reproduction and distribution, which is made extremely easy by new technology. This explains the embarrassment surrounding the high-profile arrest of the King of the Tricksters in Hong Kong. In order to make the legal threat clearly felt, right after the arrest the film industry and the government cooperated to expand the scope of investigation and harassment to criminalize not only uploaders but also downloaders. Close collaborations among various government departments, the film industry, and Internet service providers resulted in intensified surveillance on online file-sharing activities. The Customs and Excise Department also launched the scheme entitled "Youth League for Monitoring Internet Piracy" to enlist the help of some 200,000 members of 11 local youth uniform organizations to reduce the flow of BT seeds on the Internet.[48] However, there was only a 20 percent drop in online file-sharing activities in Hong Kong immediately following the widely discussed arrest, meaning that this case had only a minor deterrent effect on online piracy.[49] There are no current data available, but obviously BT movie piracy is still taking place in Hong Kong, particularly on mainland Chinese sites.[50] In fact many Hong Kong and mainland netizens are watching entire television programs and feature films directly online through sites like Tudou.com without having to download them, although Tudou has been diligently deleting copyright-problematic files and buying rights from film companies for their featured programs since 2010. Debates about IPR, the guardian of the new economy, have become so intense partly because IPR is meant to fight against a propensity of this very economy: expediting and reducing the cost of information circulation, which makes piracy easier than ever before.

For cinema to embrace the new creative industries environment, digitization seems to be inevitable. However, the more film industries delve into digitization, the less they can escape from its tendency to diffuse their institutional control. It is true that digital effects rendered as visual or audio enhancements are considered a productive tool to boost a film's commercial value. Film industries around the world have found themselves painstakingly chasing after Hollywood's digital effects, with the vain hope that their films will equally impress and enthrall global viewers. However, online digitization is treated much more carefully, as it is not only a liberation from celluloid, but it is also a liberation from the medium. It could drastically change the present mode of spectatorship, discursive formation, profit source, and the industrial control of commercial cinema, thereby diffusing the specificity of the medium that film practitioners and scholars of the past century tried very hard to fortify.

A common ideological predisposition among film scholars and fans is their acclaim of the public nature of cinema as a shared experience of a large number of audiences conditioned by the singularity of a film text, which has been celebrated as generative of productive social and political forces.[51] Unsurprisingly, many still consider TV or direct-to-video releases second-rate or marginal compared to commercial or art films screened in theaters.[52] The prejudices against online distribution entail realistic financial consequences. In fact, in spite of the availability of technology, the film industry still is largely reluctant to distribute films online.[53] Those few companies interested in exploring online distribution often create a division devoted solely to the new process.[54] In 2000 George Lucas claimed that film images would be beamed via satellite into theaters across the country in a matter of a few years, but in 2005 he was still bemoaning the slow growth of digital cinema.[55] In spite of the initial digital exhibitions of *Star Wars: Episode III: Revenge of the Sith* (2005), his promise of dematerializing celluloid remains largely unfulfilled, and satellite and online distribution of first-run mainstream commercial films is still a prophecy.

Cinema has always shown great resistance to nontheatrical releases, from television in the 1960s, to VCR and VHS in the 1970s and disc and online distributions in the 1990s. Cinema has tried very hard to safeguard its own institutional control from the encroachment of other media and distribution means. One film distributor's strategy to delay online distribution is to mimic cyber interactivity on the disc format, which, given the global adoption of the technology, is now the major vehicle for home movie viewing. Much of the initial experimentation of interactive cinema is now available on DVD, and Laura Mulvey states that interactive features such as commentaries and interviews on DVDs have already allowed for a very different mode of spectatorship.[56] However, this is a diluted form of interactive spectatorship, because all is contained on a disc, and the disc remains a single commodity format. Although the disc form requires the film text to be turned into digital code, many strategies have been created to prevent these already digitized contents from being copied and distributed online. Copyright owners use Content Scrambling

System (css), an access control system that encrypts the content stored on DVDs to prevent illicit copying. In response, pirates have created a proliferation of DECSS, or circumvention, programs, which are designed to crack such codes.[57]

The use of DECSS technology is banned by most governments.[58] But there was no legal apparatus to criminalize digital technology until the World Intellectual Property Organization of the UN passed the influential WIPO Copyright Treaty in 1996.[59] The treaty requires signatory countries to take steps to improve the legal protection of copyrighted materials in digital form. The treaty legalizes copyright owners' protective technology and protects these technologies from other circumventing technologies.[60] The WIPO Copyright Treaty was followed by the Digital Millennium Copyright Act (DMCA), passed in the United States in 1998, and the European Union Copyright Directive in 2004.[61] The technical applications and commercial implications supported by the WIPO Copyright Treaty and all related global legislation are generally known as Digital Rights Management (DRM), which has been so controversial largely because of the fear that it jeopardizes "fair use" as a key principle of international copyright laws since the Berne Convention of 1886.[62] By differentiating good technology from bad, DRM could evade fair use by privatizing technology, therefore privatizing all "uses" of copyrighted materials.

In fact we can think of DRM as a legal system that indirectly encourages hacking, because the fair user who wants to reproduce a work that is encrypted can rely on no legal tools. All those who access encrypted technology automatically become hackers; or, to put it another way, only hackers can prevail. As a result, these laws indirectly help not only to romanticize hackers—because their actions are illegal—but also to legitimize them, because only they can break down the system and realize fair use. If fair use is the legal space in which the rights of the user and the rights of the owner meet and negotiate, recent digital copyright laws simply efface fair use and render a simple dichotomy between legal use and illegal hacking, realizing the ultimate nightmare of many copyright scholars.

But the impact of DRM on movie viewers is felt unevenly around the world. The disc market in many parts of the developing world is dominated by VCDs, which cannot be encrypted; in fact some DVDs sold in these regions are also without encryption to keep the sales price low. For example, all legal Hollywood DVDs sold in Hong Kong are encrypted, while many local films are not. The three Hollywood films the King uploaded on the web were VCDs, not DVDs. With the availability of "inferior" technology, it is much easier to upload these Hollywood films in the developing world than in the developed world, although the two worlds are connected in cyberspace. The difference is also felt in the sphere of downloading. Many who purchase BitTorrent media content legally through official sites such as BitTorrent Video Store complain about DRM-related problems, as the DRM protections are so specifically defined that very little deviation is allowed.[63] But those who download BitTorrent files illegally on the web do not face the same problems precisely because DRM is absent. The logic is weird: those who can afford a higher price are actually supervised more closely, and the price they pay includes a set of restraints conceived by the owners, while those who cannot afford the high price are set free.

Instead of punishing crimes that have already occurred, DRM works to impose technological barriers for the purpose of preventing crimes. But Tarleton Gillespie explains that whereas copyright law leaves the discretion to act in the hands of the users, allowing them to determine whether to risk activity that might result in legal penalties, DRM forecloses such discretion, allowing only those actions deemed appropriate in advance by the information producer.[64] Not only is fair use made impossible, but a basic principle of the rule of law—the possibility of defiance—is also evaded. But in many developing countries, where many cannot afford the pricy products with DRM, the fair use is maintained, honoring a basic principle of copyright. This comparison demonstrates clearly the technological base of the creative economy: it is characterized by a sophisticated and utilitarian use of technology, which controls not only creative products but also technology itself.

DRM's erosion of the fair use doctrine in copyright also illuminates the conversion of traditional cultural industries to creative industries. Our creative economy, supported by the IPR regime, is developing a schizophrenic attitude toward the customer: although the customer is the ultimate object of desire, she is also a potential pirate. Such fear of the customer in the new creative economy is observed in the "first sale" doctrine of the copyright regime. Under this doctrine, the buyer can sell or transfer the "ownership" of the copy she owns, but she is not allowed to copy the work, which would infringe upon the rights of the true copyright holder.[65] "Ownership of a copy" and "ownership of the copyright" are clearly demarcated, resulting in the awkward situation in which we can resell a DVD we buy, but we cannot copy it or show it publicly without the consent of the copyright holder. The "first sale" doctrine functions less to protect than to confine the rights of the customer. We should not be surprised to discover that the major part of the copyright legal regime is designed to police the customer instead of the pirate. As Gillespie laments, with the many new technological innovations concerning copyright protection, film and music distributors are going far beyond what the software in- dustry had once imagined, to govern not only whether we copy their work, but also how we buy, share, experience, and interact with it.[66]

Cultural commodity is not destroyed in the act of consumption, but dur- ing consumption the commodity enlarges, transforms, and creates the ideo- logical and cultural environment of the consumer.[67] The creative industries discourse promotes continual innovation in the forms and conditions of communication, so it should also produce and materialize the consumer in terms of needs, images, and tastes.[68] Theoretically the consumer should be empowered by creative industries, which allows one to interfere with the pro- duction process in a more direct way. However, focusing on economic issues like finance, markets, public support, and employment, the creative indus- tries discourse chooses to ignore or even repress these cultural relationships.

There is a clear decline in cinema attendance among Hong Kong people. Hong Kong's average annual cinema admissions per person dropped from 12.7 in 1981, at one point one of the highest in the world, to 3.1 in 2006, a drop much sharper than most other countries experienced during the same period.[69] But the various creative industries' reports fail to mention this ten- dency and provide no solutions, and the author-based IPR ignores consumers. Johanna Gibson argues that in the dominant copyright discourse, the agency of the reader or viewer is dismissed as mere "projection" and denied any sub- jectivity in the construction of meaning.[70] But at the same time, the consumer is feared by the producer, who panics about the new kinds of technology con- sumers are equipped with to consume and invest in the cultural commodity, to the extent that the control of the producer could easily be usurped.

In this context, the transition of cinema from a traditional cultural indus- try to a part of the creative industries is not an easy one. It has to loosen up the cultural identity of place-based productions in order to address trans- national markets and finance. It has to deprive its committed workers a rea- sonable working environment to cultivate projects. It also has to succumb to and come to terms with the pluralization tendency of the digital culture. The flexible nature of the creative economy necessarily challenges the institutional autonomy of cinema, and the changes involved could be extremely disruptive.

Branding the Creative City with Fine Arts

We are seeing branding in everything around us, from universities and armies to water and soil.[1] The fervent demand to create a positive and aesthetically pleasing image for almost any institution or entity demonstrates the extreme competition in the new economy, not only between rival members of the same sector, such as Coke and Pepsi, but also, more diffusely, among unrelated institutions and ideologies, like the military's fight for youths' admiration in this pluralistic and "effeminate" contemporary culture. From Lijiang and Hong Kong, I now come to Beijing to explore the many relationships between city branding and the creative industries in the complex situation of China, not only in terms of geographical divergences, but also in terms of the wide range of cultural forms and logics involved. In this chapter I explore how the fine arts is incorporated into city branding.

City and national branding is one of the most sophisticated forms of contemporary branding, as the branding of a place must incorporate an extremely diverse set of conditions—historical, cultural, economic, political, and geographic—into a unified image that can be easily communicated. While national branding tends to be most reductive in manipulating global abstraction, the local environment, and stereotypical cultural and traditional images,[2] city branding involves more careful macro top-down engineering that has increasingly become the duty of city government. If it is simply impossible to shape a nation, many city governments are working hard to remodel their cities to attract global interest. A unified image, not only as myth but rendered by actual urban design, is exalted to subdue or control, although never easily, the unruly chaos of an urban space and culture that resulted from historical contingencies and the overlapping of multiple life patterns.

Gerard Wigmans's overview of the urban policy in Rotterdam in the past three decades might help us understand the general rhetoric of city branding. He begins his essay this way:

> A new approach to city planning in the inner city of Rotterdam was introduced in 1974. This strategy was based on a coalition between organizations of local residents and local authorities, known as "building for the neighborhood." . . . In this participation model there was a strong commitment between the citizens of the city and the urban policy based on social democracy. Solidarity and equality of opportunities were expressed in the statement of "the city as a collective arrangement for living" which had to be equally accessible for every citizen. However, in doing so, economic activities were driven out of the districts.[3]

The last sentence specifies the key problem Wigmans deals with in his study, and the beautiful egalitarian picture he draws in this paragraph is precisely the source of the problem. Wigmans shows that "fortunately" a corrective policy change was resurrected in the late 1980s, which was able to promote an economic and cultural revitalization in Rotterdam. According to Wigmans, the previous policy, based on social democracy, only engendered a parochialism which was wisely corrected by the city's new cosmopolitan and globally minded economy. Wigmans tries to demonstrate a direct relationship between economy and culture: only a certain culture leads to a flourishing economy, and this global metropolitan culture can be compartmentalized and summarized as "the availability of an attractive housing environment and cultural climate, a complete and varied package of facilities, adequate services, and good accessibility."[4] Culture is understood in two ways as related to capital: a culture which can attract preferred immigrants, visitors, and consumers, that is, a comfortable lifestyle; and a culture which can attract investment and produce profits, that is, the development of creative and other industries. The two logics combine to form today's creative cities.

As a result, a city's culture is no longer a natural manifestation of the collective taste and values of a given people, but tourism in a broad sense. While financial control is a global city's key aptitude, these powerful cities also tend to be cultural hubs, hosting the fine arts and popular culture alike. The global city can be seen as operating under a specific tourism strategy: tourism promotes a mishmash of culture and economy, of sight and power, and city branding works by exactly the same logic. Simply speaking, culture cannot exist on its own as ordinary reflection of the ways people organically live, but must be engineered and monitored, with specific purposes in promoting economic opportunities of the city in general.

From "Glasgow: Scotland with Style" to "Toronto Unlimited," and from "Hong Kong: Asia's World City" to "Pattaya: The Extreme City," the discourse of city branding has gained wide global currency. But the marketing and promotions involved can be radically diverse. While "Asia's World City" is abstract and vague enough to describe Hong Kong as a late capitalist city,[5] the many walks of life, human feelings, and spatial practices of Pattaya are summarized in terms of extremity. Obviously the two cities project two different sets of desires: Hong Kong invites transnational capital, while Pattaya seduces global tourists seeking exotic but highly regulated excitement. We are seeing the radical abstraction of myriad urban experiences to simplified statements and images for various marketing purposes. The city's culture, in turn, is inevitably altered, to various degrees, to correspond to such images.

The Global City and Decentralization

The global city concept is definitely new to the ancient city of Beijing. An industrialized Beijing gradually emerged out of its imperial relics and traditional clan-based housing in the 1960s, but this Maoist Beijing was not a glistening metropolis presenting spectacular images; it lacked urban landmarks other than the traditional architecture that had managed to stay intact. A new set of urban policies developed in the beginning of the 1980s, but their primary aim was to eliminate the city's industrial components and turn it into a modern national capital. Not until the 1990s did Beijing start to be obsessed with its global image, which supposedly attests to the rising Chinese power.[6] Skyscrapers sprout as if they are dropped from the sky, burying all traditional housing, no matter how old. Ever renewed modern visual elements manifest profusely as fashions, commodities, advertising materials, and cool designs in general. Along with the Olympic vogue is a clear branding force looming large around the presentation of Beijing to the world, as Yomi Braester thoroughly demonstrates in his recent book.[7]

The Beijing government has taken an active role in promoting the cultural scene in recent years.[8] Since 1996 Beijing's city government has been in competition with other cities for the title of China's cultural industry center, and there has been a clear policy shift toward developing the "tertiary sector" in place of heavy industry; the city has also made vigorous efforts to capitalize on historical and cultural tourism.[9] At the end of 2005, at the eleventh general meeting of the Ninth Party Committee in Beijing, the cultural industries were officially declared the pillar of Beijing's ongoing development, and the first Beijing Cultural Industries Expo was held in November 2006. Beijing also announced ten designated cultural creative clusters at the end of 2006, showing, as Michael Keane describes it, the city's commitment to the creative zeitgeist.[10]

Beijing's city branding is conducive to the new global order, in which global networks of capital and commodity flows are organized around global cities.[11] While the measure of economic achievement increasingly shifts from national to city-based indicators, cities vie with each other to register in the highly hierarchical global network. As our global economy becomes increasingly an economy of affect and persuasion, and economic strength is based more on facilitation than production, the discourse of the global city is inevitably linked to its own branding. Creativity becomes an impulse belonging to a particular type of global city,[12] of which Beijing strives to be a legitimate member.

However, the ascendancy of city or region branding in China is not entirely a global event, but should also be understood as part of the PRC's own political trajectory of administrative decentralization. Following the Soviet model, socialist China before 1978 was ruled by a centralized government, yet such centralized power could no longer be legitimized by the political economic disasters it brought about by the mid-1970s, and a series of policies were formulated and implemented to decentralize administrative power to different levels of regional governments. The current global market economy further fuels the decentralization demands in the name of flexibility and localization. In fact the PRC's political history since 1978 can be characterized by the tensions between central control and decentralization. While decentralization is the trend, the PRC government is also very anxious about the power increasingly channeled toward local governments. Fierce intranational competition is taking place among cities and districts, indirectly promoting the economic hierarchy among regions.[13] It has also been argued that decentralization has led to corruption, as the central government has lost its ability to detect the bad behavior of local officials and capitals are now controlled by relatively autonomous local officials and specialized bankers.[14]

Politically, decentralization might also provoke regional autonomy, feared particularly by the nondemocratic one-party CCP governance. The central–provincial relationship, similar to the state–people relationship, is formulated almost entirely on direct power transfer and struggles, as political power is not conceptualized as rights but as ownership of the central government to be selectively distributed to the regions and the people only as a gift. City branding, which flags cultural differences more than political autonomy, seems to bypass some of these anxieties, and it is considered far safer for a local region to promote its cultural instead of its political or economic identity. The depoliticized creative economy becomes a safe haven for decentralization to continue its course in China. But at the same time, the new global economy privileging cities more than nations also fuels China's decentralization, encouraging regional governments to engineer their own development against the state's central planning.

Shanghai's creative industries discourse was initiated first by the private sector and was soon overtaken by the city government, which now coordinates all related activities under the aegis of its Creative Industries Centre.[15] Hangzhou focuses primarily on its cartoon industry, while Yunnan advertises itself as an overall cultural province. The Yuexiu regional government of the city of Guangzhou launched a Creative Economy Forum in January 2007— the first of its kind in the region—in hopes of transforming the Yuexiu region into a "national creativity center."[16] By 2006 Beijing, Nanjing, Shenzhen, Guangzhou, Qingdao, Hangzhou, Xi'an, and Chengdu had all been involved in setting up their own creative industry zones. In Beijing, in addition to the Beijing Creative Center in Dongcheng District, construction of five new such districts is under way. In Shandong Province, Creation 100, the province's first creative industrial zone, is now under construction in Qingdao; it will feature advertising, design, film, and television businesses. Nanjing is putting up its first creative industry zone, called Window of the World, and the municipal government plans to set up ten more such areas over the next three to five years.[17]

Less prominently, elite tastes are also increasingly incorporated into modern spectacle to become valuable elements in city branding. This is reflected, for example, in various Chinese cities' recent enthusiasm for hosting major international events, and these events in turn become both justifications and deadlines for completion of the city's own urban and cultural development. Thirty-two major new museums were planned in Beijing alone in the lead-up to the Olympic Games in 2008;[18] many of them were actually constructed, and there are now 108 museums operating in Beijing. Shanghai aimed to open 150 new museums in time for the World Expo in 2010.[19] They are not quite there yet, but there were more than 80 museums operating in Shanghai in 2011. Another example of the branding effects of art is seen in Shanghai's new Zhangjiang High-Tech Park, which in late 2006 hosted the art event "City Present Tense: Live in Zhangjiang" (城市進行式: 現場張江). With a total investment of more than ten million RMB, the Park invited some of the most prestigious contemporary Chinese artists to construct public art at the site for permanent

display. These works will supposedly add value to the Park's future development, in terms of both real estate and the ability to attract creative talent.

We have also seen the development of art spaces, such as Shanghai's M50
(莫干山路 50 號), Guangzhou's Red Brick Factory (紅磚廠), and Kunming's
Chuangkuyuan (創庫原), which are composed of studios and galleries, nicely
packaged as bohemian and touristy. The artist village is by no means unique
to contemporary China, as artists need spaces for production and exhibitions,
and there is a general tendency of studios and galleries to seek each other
out for opportunities, mutual support, and public attention. City branding
carves out such art spaces, as they often give a city an aura of culture and creativity. They also correspond to the economic concept of clustering, which
refers to the geographic concentrations of interconnected firms and institutions to promote both cooperation and competition; in the name of collective efficiency, clusters can support the economic viability of a region.[20] Let us
focus on two major art spaces in Beijing—Factory 798 and Songzhuang—to
see how they negotiate between contemporary art and the discourse of city
branding, and explore how business concepts are applied to the fine arts.

Factory 798 and Songzhuang: The Production of Creativity

Shanghai was once the country's cultural hub in the Republican period, but
the city quickly lost its glamour after Liberation in 1949, as the CCP government immediately seized on the arts as political and pedagogical tools, and
Beijing quickly positioned itself as the national cultural center, a hegemony
that is still felt today.

With the exception of a few expatriates, such as Cai Guo-qiang, the country's hottest Chinese artists currently live in Beijing. As shown in table 2,
record sale prices for artworks were reached in the past few years; the rapid
upward trend is phenomenal, particularly considering that all these artists
are still actively producing. Beijing is developing a vigorous contemporary
art scene, adding to the city's overall branding value. But art is also caught in
myriad social discourses and cultural significations in ways probably more
entrenching than in the authoritarian eras.

Factory 798 (originally called United Factory 718), which is now also known
as the Dashanzi Art District, is an enormous industrial site on the northeast-
ern edge of Beijing, occupying 640,000 square meters. The CCP government
envisioned it as a model industrial project showcasing the new socialist era,
and in the early 1950s the CCP invited the best engineers from the German
Democratic Republic to design and build a state-of-the-art industrial com-

Table 2. Chinese Contemporary Works of Arts: Top Prices (as of November 2009)

Auction Date	Artist	Artwork	Auction Price (million US$)	Auction House
24 May 2008	Zeng Fanzhi 曾梵志	*Mask Series 1996, No. 6* (1996)	9.7	Christie's HK
25 Nov. 2007	Cai Guo-qiang 蔡國強	Set of fourteen drawings for APEC (2002)	9.4	Christie's HK
9 April 2008	Liu Xiaodong 劉小東	*Battlefield Realism: The 18 Arhats* (2004)	7.9	Sotheby's HK
24 May 2008	Yue Minjun 岳敏君	*Gweong-Gweong* (1993)	7	Christie's HK
9 April 2008	Zhang Xiaogang 張曉剛	*Bloodline: Big Family No. 3* (1995)	6	Sotheby's HK
12 Oct. 2007	Yue Minjun	*Execution* (1995)	6	Sotheby's London
13 Oct. 2007	Zeng Fanzhi	*Xiehe Hospital Series* triptych (1992)	5.5	Phillips de Pury, London
7 Oct. 2007	Yue Minjun	*The Massacre at Chios* (1994)	4	Sotheby's HK
20 Sept. 2007	Zhang Xiaogang	*Chapter of a New Century— Birth of the People's Republic of China* (1992)	3.2	Sotheby's New York
25 Nov. 2007	Zhang Xiaogang	*Portrait in Yellow* (1993)	2.9	Christie's HK
21 Nov. 2006	Liu Xiaodong	*Three Gorges: Newly Displaced Population* (2004)	2.9	Poly International
27 May 2007	Yue Minjun	*Portrait of the Artist and His Friends* (1991)	2.8	Christie's HK
25 Nov. 2007	Yue Minjun	*Life* (1999)	2.7	Christie's HK
2 Dec. 2007	Wang Huaiqing 王懷慶	*Gold Stone* (1998)	2.7	Ravenel

Sources: Sotheby's; Christie's; Phillips de Pury; Ravenel; Poly International; and others.

plex for the new China. At its peak there were twenty thousand workers employed by the factory,[21] and many of them lived there along with their family members. Some urban studies scholars characterize the dominant urban planning model in China between 1949 and 1978 as that of the "Maoist city," in which "cities were to become production centres and a new stress was placed on rapid industrial development. . . . Places of employment (*danwei*, or work units) were encouraged to become self-sufficient communities within the city, providing not only work and housing, but also health care, food distribution, and other basic social services."[22] Factory 798 was a direct product of the organic and self-sufficient urban planning that stressed the mutual support of and proximity between working and living. Materials produced by the factory complex were extremely diversified, ranging from spacecraft to street lights, and from weapons to everyday utensils. Scientists and engineers claim that Factory 798 contributed significantly to China's industrial growth and prosperity.[23]

But the socialist mode of production according to which Factory 798 operated failed quickly in the 1980s. Much of the factory space was soon deserted, and the enormous space and its low rent soon attracted poor artists and intellectuals. As evidenced elsewhere around the world, the development of art space could also be good for the real estate business, allowing used land to be recycled. Run-down inner-city neighborhoods often are attractive to artists, who move in because of low rents and an abstract sense of authenticity. The increasingly bohemian character of the area gradually attracts more affluent young urbanites, who eventually edge out the earlier arrivals.[24] The development of 798 followed a similar path,[25] but a more significant stage in its development was the arrival of foreign artists and investors in the late 1990s, when there were more Westerners than locals stationed at 798. Some of these residents, such as the American Robert Bernell, who founded the Timezone 8 Bookstore and the website Chinese-art.com, were active in bringing international attention to 798.[26] Currently 798 is mainly a space for Chinese artists, although it is still permeated by a strong Western aura.

Today 798 is a key cultural establishment in the city. There are still factories operating in the area, but the central part of 798 is almost completely occupied by activities directly or indirectly related to the art business, housing more than forty studios and forty galleries, as well as a number of bars, restaurants, printing houses, bookstores, and many retail shops (figure 1). It has become a sensation in Beijing, attracting thousands of domestic and international tourists every day. While the factory complex houses some of the most famous and important art studios and projects in China, such as the

1. Beijing 798 Art Zone. Photo by Wu Zhi.

ambitious Long March Space, it is also a highly commercial place, which has hosted numerous shows sponsored by companies such as Sony and Omega.

The history of the spatial development of 798 is complex. Originally a top-down design facilitating the socialist mode of production, 798 was gradually transformed into something completely foreign to the original design. But this transformation should not be romanticized as subversive, as there is still a certain ideological link between the two phases of its spatial use. The highly organized spatial design of the original factory complex allowed 798 to be easily turned into a consumer area, and one would find strikingly similar experiences between walking around 798 and around many megamalls, except that 798 is even bigger. Shops and restaurants are located next to fancy galleries, and there are clear signs and directions for various locations (figure 2). Few cars are permitted to enter 798. Strollers are at ease walking down the spacious roads lined with pleasant trees (figure 3), and they can also turn into small alleys which lead to more galleries and shops (figure 4). The indoor space is blessed with the factories' huge windows and high ceilings, which provide plenty of natural light and headroom to enliven the space (figure 5). Most important, the overall area of 798 is vast; bounded by walls and trees, it

2. Signs and directions in 798. Photo by Wu Zhi.

3. The main road in 798. Photo by Wu Zhi.

4. A corner of 798. Photo by Wu Zhi.

5. A gallery in 798. Photo by Wu Zhi.

is a little village of its own and gives those inside a feeling of protection against outside forces, which explains why so many Beijingers still do not know of this place. The original space of socialist production finds itself at ease with the current space of late capitalist consumption, in the sense that they were both structurally designed to facilitate functional space use, easy spatial conversion, and, most important, self-sufficiency.

New industrial sites developed in eastern and central Europe after the Second World War were often seen as iconic sites of socialism, venerated and admired in official propaganda as much as the workers themselves. To epitomize their material as well as ideological functions, most factories were constructed around a single workplace set at the end of a long impressive avenue behind a monumental entrance.[27] The 798 Art Zone, however, was not designed in that fashion; it resembles the architectural style and rhetoric of the Bauhaus, focusing on actual function and rationality. Reportedly, 798's German architects did suggest a Soviet style of architectural grandeur, which was rejected by the Chinese planners, who were concerned that the new China was not sure what its national style should be.[28] As a result, we can still experience a sense of unadorned formalism and humanism in the current 798, which was not only a collection of factories but, to many, a home. Clearly the original designers gave a homey, leisurely aura to the industrial site, which naturally appeals to contemporary shoppers and tourists. These factors all reinforce the traditional modernist idea of art as liberating, autonomous, and egalitarian.

The Beijing city government is very interested in the promotion of art and culture, and it has commissioned large-scale research with the aim of fostering a fine cultural environment for economic growth.[29] Behind the burgeoning development of 798 is also the active participation of the city government, which has prevented the landowner, Seven Stars Group, from reclaiming the space for development. It was widely reported in 2003 and 2004 that the Seven Stars Group was interested in redeveloping the factory complex.[30] But since the high-profile endorsement of 798 by the city government at its meeting in 2006, everyone believes that 798 will remain an art community. It is reported that this is a result of the direct involvement of the top city government officials, including the mayor himself.[31] The government's strong interest in 798 is clearly related to city branding. It has been widely touted in Chinese media that the American magazine *Newsweek* included Beijing among the top twelve world cities in 2003, and in the report 798 was hailed as a key cultural establishment that demonstrated the city's value.[32]

In 2004 the American architect Bernard Tschumi and his company proposed a theoretical project: a huge megastructural lattice that would be built over the factory complex. The idea was to maintain the neighborhood while allowing new real estate development in the area.[33] We can also safely deduce that this project was conceived in accordance with the government's interests, as Tschumi's company has undertaken several major architectural projects for the Beijing government. The city government also commissioned two reports by Congressman Chen Dongsheng (陳東升) and the art historian Li Xiang-qun (李象群), which substantiated various cultural and economic reasons for keeping 798.[34] Although it is claimed that relative to other major Chinese cities, Beijing is the most committed to a careful urban renewal program sensitive to preservation,[35] with the fervent developmentalism dominating China and the Olympic frenzy, the entire city has been plunged into a festive mode of reconstruction. Clearly, without strong backing from the city government, 798 might easily have been demolished and rebuilt.

The 798 Art Zone is mainly a gallery space; the largest residential art community in China is currently Songzhuang (宋莊), located in Tongzhou (通州), an hour's drive east of Beijing. More than one thousand artists live and work in the area, which is a combination of four main villages and a few smaller ones. Upon first visiting Songzhuang, one would find it far less tourist-friendly than 798, and there are many fewer fancy galleries and restaurants. Songzhuang is largely a provincial village, and artist residents are still a minority. Geographically Songzhuang is only a satellite city, and it is much less accessible to visitors, whereas 798 is situated in a core development area of Beijing.

Songzhuang is largely a successor of the Yuanmingyuan (圓明園) artist village, considered to be the first of its kind in China since the Open Door Policy, a ground zero for China's contemporary art scene from 1984 to 1995. Witnessing the birth and the dramatic development in the 1980s of the highly energetic Chinese arts, Yuanmingyuan was considered the mecca of not only contemporary Chinese artists but also of the new avant-garde dissidents. Yuanmingyuan was as chaotic as it was revolutionary and attracted much negative attention from the government. As the story goes, in May 1995 a painter urinated on the dining table at a dinner party, outraging guests who were there to pay homage to the painter. He was twice detained by the police for this behavior, and the art community was also closed down by the police in the name of stopping crime.[36]

A number of the original Yuanmingyuan residents, including the now internationally sought-after Fang Lijun (方力鈞) and the critic and curator tycoon Li Xianting (栗憲庭), moved out of the central Beijing area and took up residence in Songzhuang because of its cheap rent and distance from the city center. The art community of Songzhuang has expanded in the past few years, largely due to the considerable international fame of some of its residents, such as Yue Minjun and Zhang Xiaogang; their works have earned top sales prices, and the prices of works by other famous residents, like Liu Ye (劉野) and Wang Guangyi (王廣藝), follow suit. It was estimated that in 2008 the number of artists residing in Songzhuang exceeded two thousand. Allegedly, Songzhuang has exceeded other art villages in the world in size and significance, including Barbizon in France and the East Village in the U.S.[37] If Factory 798 is largely an exhibition site, Songzhuang is China's biggest art studio, where important and emerging artists supposedly lead solitary but communal lives devoted to making art. While those artists whose works actually make it into galleries and auction rooms are extremely small in number, most others attracted by these successes who have moved to the village still lead meager lives.[38]

As Songzhuang was largely an extension of the legendary Yuanmingyuan art communities, the new art village community continues to assume certain liberal and nonconformist attitudes. In contrast, 798 has no obvious links to Yuanmingyuan, and it is also largely devoid of any dissident aura and remains upbeat and trendy. But it would be a gross mistake to romanticize Songzhuang as an anticommercial space. Currently China shows great promise in the world's art market as a source of both contemporary works and potential buyers. Songzhuang, which represents China's contemporary art, has become a brand in itself. Every day art brokers and agents, sometimes with potential buyers in tow, travel to the village, and through them the artists are directly connected to the world's art market. The Songzhuang government has been particularly committed to promoting its art-related businesses. The provincial government has sponsored six annual Songzhuang culture and art festivals intended to be media events. The second of these officially opened with a live concert by Cui Jian, the father of Chinese rock 'n' roll, in October 2006, and it juxtaposed various fine arts exhibitions and the Sixth Generation films with many other commercial activities. The third event was a collaboration with the Second China (Beijing) International Cultural and Creative Industry Expo; the most recent one, held in September 2010, was given an excessively commercial theme Crossover (figure 6). In its official press release it is clearly stated that the festival of 2010 is a response to the government's call for building and exporting the country's soft power, and Songzhuang claims to be China's youngest and most passionate representative of its soft power.[39]

6. Poster of the Sixth Songzhuang Culture and Art Festival.

Songzhuang has also hired a Taiwan licensing agency, Artkey, to help artists distribute their works and secure proper copyright protections.[40] However, Artkey has not made much progress, largely because of the many local and international art brokers already active in the place.

The magical success of Songzhuang is not just an accident; the realization of this art village was made possible largely by the country's overall support of cultural industries, as well as the foresight and efforts of local officials. Cui Dabo (崔大柏), the Xiaobaocun (小堡村) Municipality's chief Party secretary, has trusted artists and curators to design Songzhuang and facilitated related policy support accordingly. He discloses his vision in an interview: "To me, Xiaobaocun (of Songzhuang) is developing a new model, trying to make profits from the end of the art production chain. We run galleries, arrange auctions, and we are agents to the artists. We also establish hotels and promote tourism. As long as there are artists, and we provide the related service industry, Xiaobaocun has a lot of opportunities, and all the residents will obtain long-term benefits from the cultural industry."[41]

As demonstrated by the rapid development of 798 and Songzhuang, Beijing has successfully incorporated the fine arts into its city branding. Art and culture are seen largely as cultural capital which the city markets to residents, tourists, and investors. Art space has a special affiliation with such development because it combines both exquisite taste and consumption, providing a sense of culture congenial to late capitalist aesthetics. It is true that the two art spaces developed with separate historical trajectories, so that 798 became more touristic and bourgeois, while Songzhuang has a stronger local and bohemian aura. However, the two spaces are connected with each other in the common government supports they have garnered, and both are the result of the advent of the creative industries and both involve land policies. Despite their own independent development they have become related to each other under the banner of Beijing's city branding, so that not only is art produced, displayed, and sold in Beijing, but art is also abstractly carved into the image of the city to become its cultural capital. In terms of the cultural capital gained through the fine art scene, Beijing outranks its major regional rivals, Shanghai, Hong Kong, and Singapore.

City Imagination and Real Estate

The late capitalist economy heavily relies on abstract images and immaterial entities to further propel production and consumption that already saturate the market; city branding is a key manifestation of this. However, while the economy of late capitalism continues to be immaterial, a parallel, equally spectacular trend of growth resides on the land, the archetype of traditional property. In the logic of the creative economy, concrete land must be turned into abstract image, but abstract images must also be embodied in concrete materials. A new city image can be realized only by altering the real landscape, which can no longer be simply conceptualized as a place where people live together. Under the logic of branding, civic space, as Sue Curry Jensen explains, becomes calculative space, space that is constituted by marketing data and decision making rather than conceived in terms of social relations or governance.[42] One of the most important factors in city branding, in spite of its emphasis on immateriality, is precisely the land, witnessed in the intimate relationship between art and real estate in the development of art spaces like 798 and Songzhuang.

Let us start with the changing imaginations of the city, from the nineteenth-century modern metropolis to the twenty-first-century global city. The former is an imagination, an attitude, and a psychological effect, while the latter is a product and a site of economy. As James Donald illustrates, the rise of the modern city required people of the nineteenth century to completely reimagine space, which became too vast and sprawling to be captured in a panoramic view; replacing it were montages of random figures and events. The contemporaneity, the nowness of a city suggests a style of living in the present, and this style entails a specific psychological response. According to Donald, this experience of immediacy and fragmentation necessarily turned the city into an abstraction, and the city became an imagined environment, reflected in various literary and art works of the time.[43] This model of the modern metropolis still informs certain images of today's Beijing. As shown in some contemporary film and literary works, artists are the romanticized citizens of Beijing, and their floating lives demonstrate some essential characteristics of the city.[44] In these cultural imaginations, Chinese artists, like their European counterparts in the nineteenth century, are often poor, but they are highly intelligent and observant, so they are equipped with the ability to read the city from the perspectives of both the oppressed and the elite. They are not tied down by fixed work schedules, and their works give us glimpses of fragmented city life. They are portrayed as free spirits, whose flânerie and pertinent insights offer us disjointed views of the city.

However, the global city is conceptualized very differently: while the chaos and the shocks of the modern metropolis can never be fully comprehended, the global city must be organized and managed to become a strategic site on the global map. If the former modernist imagination informs certain cultural productions, the later global city model dominates the actual functioning of urban development and management, in which Beijing is a product that can be produced and managed rather than a vast area of urban space where people dwell. In the words of Saskia Sassen, "Global cities are strategic sites for the management of the global economy and the production of the most advanced services and financial operations that have become key inputs for that work of managing global economic operations."[45] The city becomes a site again, but this site is a strategic and therefore fictive one. In other words, the city's materiality is not redeemed in the new global city discourse, but the city is seen as a player—or more abstractly, a potentiality—that can be placed and manipulated within a larger economic plan. In this sense, the global city is imagined completely differently from the modern metropolis theorized by Walter Benjamin or Georg Simmel.[46] The key components are no longer psychological responses to disjointed space and experiences, but the instrumentalization of spatial practices as a form of cultural capital.

While a modern metropolis cannot be branded, a global city can. While the spectacle the nineteenth-century flâneur beheld was fragmented and shocking, the urban planning and mega-events organized in global cities are exercised by more powerful and coherent forces, so that the spectacles are continual and correlated. Arjun Appadurai has studied carefully the transformation of Bombay to Mumbai in the 1990s, which is an excellent example of such transition from the modern metropolis to the global city. Appadurai characterizes Bombay as a chaotic city where people have to struggle every day to lead their lives. Like many other megacities in the world, people have to travel long hours from home to work. There is a large number of homeless people due to the unreasonable rise in rental prices, and people from the countryside continue to flood the city, whose "colonization" disrupts middle class lives. All such chaos results from modernization, yet it also reflects a certain cosmopolitan reality where different ethnic and religious groups live together in a relatively peaceful manner. However, such grassroot cosmopolitanism is increasingly considered intolerable to the new global city of Mumbai. Real estate comes to clean up the unpleasant sites, and ethnic and religious minorities must be swept away, homogenized and organized into Hindu public space. Hindu Puritanism embraces the discourse of global city dearly, as both formulate a hatred of otherness.[47]

Bombay still exists under Mumbai, but the former is repressed as the uncivilized other, constantly purged and punished by the latter. The recent urban development of Beijing might not be easily comparable to Mumbai, which is culturally and religiously more diverse, but the Chinese city also suffers from its own global city dream with its own cultural specificities. In order to take the express train of the Olympics to depart from a second-class capital and arrive at a global city, Beijing must supplement, or replace, its national culture with global connections and order, and its space must be disciplined into something that can be managed and connected to the new late capitalist economy. The 798 Art Zone and Songzhuang are both such renditions: buried beneath the order and appeal is an older, unattractive Beijing, and permeating the global city dream is also real estate opportunism.

Real estate, which deals with actual pieces of land, plays an enormous part in such global conversions, reflecting how the true magic and devastation introduced by globalization are manifested in local sites. The virtuality of the global network is supported by the drastic alternation of everyday spatial practices, so that locality can be disciplined and made relevant to globality, both in terms of capital production and social facilitation. Therefore, dialectical to the formation of the global city network is the heavy investment in actual pieces of land, and real estate becomes the most powerful agent and economic force of spatial production in late capitalist society.

The research of Joe Studwell shows that a large amount of overseas Chinese investment arrived in China right after Deng Xiaoping's historical Southern Tour in 1992, and much of it went directly into real estate.[48] Local capitals followed suit, and domestic millionaires were bred by the real estate boom in the country. Richard Walker and Daniel Buck also demonstrate that city governments have played an important role in China in the commodification of land in the past two decades. The amendment to the land management law in 1998 stipulates that all leasing of state lands to commercial development has to pass through the hands of the municipalities. The city governments are also motivated by rents and revenues from land taxes to speed up urban redevelopment and suburban expansion.[49] Currently 47 percent of Beijing's GDP comes from real estate–related activities. The danger of this is obvious to everyone.[50] Both the national and the city governments have, half-heartedly, tried to intervene in the unhealthy development of the real estate market, which only continues to expand. Luxury apartments and condominiums dominate this market, many of which are bought to be sold, and the haunting emptiness of many new apartment buildings is a common sight. Those traveling two or three hours every day from home to work are greeted with the sight of these beautiful buildings with empty rooms right in the heart of the city.

Capital is also flowing from real estate to other sectors. Critics argued earlier that investment in industrial commodities would be directed to real estate only in times of recession, and industrial capitalism still dominates our new economy.[51] But in contemporary China, whose economy is surging every day, real estate speculation has become the principal source for the formation of capital. Currently in China there are two main ways for real estate money to reach the art scene: through investment in private collections and investment in related enterprises. Many Chinese entrepreneurs have begun to include the fine arts as a part of their overall investment plan: they buy and sell artworks, primarily paintings, just as they buy land and sell houses.[52] It is reported that many of these buyers are new investors; not wishing to see prices plummet, they are eager to manipulate the market, resulting in a huge bubble in the art market that some critics simply call "madness."[53] It is also reported that a massive amount of private capital from Wenzhou (溫州), the famous entrepreneurial city, has reached Beijing, primarily targeted at national enterprises, particularly traditional cultural industries.[54] In fact the Beijing government actively seeks such investments; whereas an alleged 30 percent of London's GDP comes from the creative sector, creative industries contribute only 6 percent of Beijing's current GDP, and Beijing's government finds strong reasons and ample opportunities to channel some of the real estate money into the cultural sector.[55]

In order to brand a global city, local space must be usurped. Real estate speculation is particularly devastating in contemporary China, as all land and enterprises were once the property of the socialist government, which, having entered the capitalist phase, is quick to collaborate with real estate partners in the name of urban redevelopment.[56] Older spaces must be relocated, factories and ghettoes must be demolished, and industries and poor people must move to outlying areas. Given the enormous financial benefits at stake, developers and local governments have been known to resort to violence and fraud to ensure effective and often unfair land deals, and land disputes have been one of the key sources of China's social instability.[57] For example, Formula One racing was introduced in Shanghai in 2004; two years later the central government arrested its chief manager and promoter, Yu Zhifei, for bribing officials in order to arrogate peasants' land and benefiting from rising property prices in the surrounding areas.[58] Such land usurpation is a prime example of Harvey's demonstration of "accumulation by dispossession." Harvey argues that the current New Imperialism is driven largely by the overaccumulation of capital. Investors are now desperate to find opportunities for profitable investing, which are often "manufactured" by the reversion of common property to the private domain.[59] China's current land reform provides a most suitable enclave for these looting practices.

The New Phase of Land Reform

The current urban development of Beijing is related to a traditional hierarchy of power distribution: the farther an area is from the city center, where the political power is located, the less developed it is. In contrast to certain suburbanization tendencies seen in other large Chinese cities such as Shanghai and Guangzhou, Beijing's outskirts are still significantly poorer than the central municipal area.[60] This traditional spatial politics still in place does not accord well with the overall late capitalist competitive mentality. Although each of these districts has been given its own distinct economic and cultural role (a legacy of economic planning), internal competition among them, reflecting the overall intercity competition, is fueled by the overall developmentalist milieu, and each has its own urban plan aimed at surpassing the other areas.[61] The central Beijing area is composed of four main districts, and outside there are four inner suburbs (798 was founded in one of them, Chaoyang) and ten outer suburbs (Songzhuang is situated in one of these, Tongzhou). The inner suburbs are now already more or less part of the city, while the outer suburbs remain largely provincial. These outlying towns and villages struggle to urbanize themselves, and one of the most common and direct strategies adopted by their provincial governments is to convert farmland for other uses, such as factories and service industries.[62]

The Songzhuang municipality has been one of the more aggressive governments in the larger Beijing area, but unlike other towns trying to urbanize through traditional or service industries, it is particularly keen on developing a land-use policy congenial to the growth of the arts. It has devised a land-ownership program for artists, allowing them to rent a hectare of land for fifty years for 10,000 RMB to build their own studios (figure 7). A new privately funded museum was also established in Songzhuang (figure 8); the land was supplied by the local government free of charge, and the local government also promised to invest in the corresponding infrastructure.[63] Fueled by both capitalist competition and China's own property rights reform, land has become the largest asset of regional governments. Collectively owned farmlands or factories, which were violently usurped by the Communist government in the 1950s from their original landowners, are now vacant again, sometimes through even more violent means, for remarketization. Most regional governments have little vision in such land development, although some regions have become production centers, and a few use their land to produce late capitalist assets like knowledge and creativity.

We might contrast the fate of Songzhuang to that of Xiaoguwei Village (小谷圍村) in another major Chinese city, Guangzhou. Xiaoguwei became an art community around 1994, when some teachers from the Guangzhou Fine Arts Institute began to establish studios there, and since then it has acquired the name Xiaoguwei Art Village. In 2004 residents were expelled from the area to allow for the development of a university city. Water and electricity were cut, and residents were threatened and bullied.[64] As official documents attest, the residents' land claims were completely legitimate, and the community could have been preserved with only minor alterations in the overall University City design.[65] However, in contrast to the local government's active support of Songzhuang, Xiaoguwei Artist Village disappeared forever from China's contemporary art scene. It seemed the Beijing and Songzhuang governments are much more willing to protect and cultivate art, and therefore

7. Land in Songzhuang waiting to be rented to artists. Photo by Wu Zhi.

8. Songzhuang Museum. Photo by Cui Yanli.

are more accepting of culture and community building. But on closer examination, the governments in Beijing and Guangzhou both demonstrate similar
late capitalist insights. While 798 and Songzhuang help brand Beijing as a city
of art, Guangzhou's University City now houses ten colleges of different sizes
and types, helping brand Guangzhou as a city of higher education. Instead of
turning the art villages into real estate projects for quick disposal and income,
not only the Beijing but also the Guangzhou government developed the land
for noncommercial use; art spaces and universities are not considered capitalist endeavors in the traditional sense, but are now prime components of the
new creative and knowledge economy. The development of 798, Songzhuang,
and Guangzhou's University City represents China's entrance into a new late
capitalist awareness.[66]

Ironically the surging real estate development of Songzhuang came back to
haunt its art establishment, which created the town's image in the first place.
As land prices climbed rapidly, those villagers who sold or rented their land
to artists years ago at relatively low prices now want their land back.[67] This
has happened to the painter Li Yulan (李玉蘭) and at least twelve other artists,
who purchased home studios in Songzhuang and have been taken to court by
the villagers from whom they purchased the properties originally.[68] Li Yulan
bought a small house for 45,000 RMB from a Songzhuang villager, Ma Hai-
tao (馬海濤) in 2002. Four years later Ma took Li to court and claimed that
the deal was illegal. Ironically it is the lingering socialist land policy that has
become the legal tool for those original landowners. Since the 1990s, leases
of thirty years have been granted on many agricultural lands, but farmers
are still unable to use the land as collateral for loans or to sell it, because in
theory these lands are still state property. The earlier Songzhuang contracts,
which were signed along with these leases, are illegal in spite of the official
endorsement by local governments and village chiefs at the time. Claiming
the earlier contracts were illegal, villagers now hope that the new property
rights law, which was passed in March 2007, will allow them to sell their land,
this time legally, for higher prices, although the current version of the law
only allows city urbanities, not rural residents, to buy and sell property with
leases of between fifty and seventy years.[69] As expected, Li lost the case to
Ma in December 2007, but the court demanded that Ma pay Li a compensation of 93,808 RMB, stating furthermore that Li has the right to seek further damages through civil actions. Li did, and sued Ma for compensation of
480,000 RMB.[70]

While land disputes continue, some of the most prominent Songzhuang
residents, like the painters Yue Minjun and Fang Lijun, have already threat-

ened to move out if they find the environment not right for their creations.[71] Structured by sheer financial interests, real estate contributes to cultural development only under the condition of financial return, however indirectly, and many of the so-called win-win collaborations between culture and capital are not based on mutual respect; more often it is the money side which dominates decision making. We have seen too many cases of regentrification in which artists are ultimately expelled from their original dwellings, although in this case the situation is complicated by the bargaining chip of the already financially powerful artist elite. I do not intend to take the side of either the villagers or the artists to become entangled in their different sets of personal interests. What strikes me is the difficult positioning of contemporary Chinese arts, which have become so deeply entrenched in the privatization desires for both traditional property and abstract images.

Art and Place

In order for art to uphold its autonomy while continuing to engage with the dense texture of the social, the artist must maintain an acute awareness of her "place." China's demographic policy is characterized by its *hukou* 戶口 (registered permanent residence) system, which, generally speaking, segregates the vast population into urban and rural types in order to stop people from the provincial areas from moving to the cities.[72] Although they are generally deprived of access to channels to transfer their residency, artists continue to be highly mobile in China. The early Communist government made sure that young artists trained in major art schools went to other parts of the country, under the premise that culture belongs to the people, not only to urbanites. Therefore, from the 1950s on, artists were some of the most mobile citizens in a demographically rigid country.

However, the earlier centrifugal force has been replaced by an opposite set of movements since the 1980s, and artists from every part of the country now flood a few metropolitan areas, particularly Beijing. The Yuanmingyuan community, composed of artists from all parts of the country, was the first of its kind in China since 1949; this centripetal force also drastically renewed China's contemporary art scene. In today's Songzhuang, for example, many of the artists are not native Beijing residents; they came from different parts of the country to seek opportunity.[73] However, it is notoriously difficult to apply for a *hukou* in Beijing.[74] So there is still a great sense of mobility and rootlessness among poor artists in Beijing. They are attracted to places with low rent and increased opportunities, and now that rents in 798 and Songzhuang have become too high, many of them are trying their luck in cheaper, adjacent areas, forming smaller artist villages in Suojiacun (索家村) and Caochangdi (草場地).[75] From Yuanmingyuan to Songzhuang to other outlying areas of Beijing, there is a clear nomadic history among this generation of young Chinese artists, who constantly search for a space of their own.[76]

In response to the rapid urbanization and the destruction of existing communities, in the 1990s artists like Zhang Dali (張大力), Zhu Fadong (朱發東), Rong Rong (榮蓉), and Zhang Wang (張望) demonstrated in their works a critical sensibility toward the deterioration of urban space.[77] However, in the recent works produced in Songzhuang and 798, I find little trace of such place sensitivity. With some exceptions, many emerging artists continue to follow established genres, particularly Pop Art, which were made internationally famous by artists in the 1990s. The two most commonly seen images are the dislocated human face and the human body. While Fang Lijun's and Yue Mingjun's empty and hysterical faces, symbolizing the contemporary Chinese psyche, continue to be bestsellers in the international art market, many controversial experimental artists have been obsessed with the torture of human bodies.[78] We have seen too many bodies submerged in a sea of commodities and emotional void, and there are too few subjects in intimate contact with or with critical reflections on their own place.

The recent vibrant development of art spaces in China might prevent artists from embodying the space organically and affectively. I have spoken to a few Chinese artists who are currently conceptualizing or are involved in the development of art spaces in conjunction with various local governments. For example, Li Xianting, China's most respected art critic and curator, says that running Songzhuang is his most important duty, and he believes that Songzhuang is the true realization of the Yuanmingyuan community's dream of artistic freedom. However, he also admits that Songzhuang is run in accordance with the new creative industries model the Chinese government supports. The construction application of the Songzhuang Museum was twice rejected until the new policy of creative industries was in place, and Li also admitted that Songzhuang's rents have risen tremendously in the past few years as a result of the rise in the profile of the artist village.[79] Although Li and other artists in other art spaces deny that these are real estate enterprises, almost all of these projects are infused with strong economic rhetoric and consequences. To my surprise, many Chinese artists remain devoted to the ideology of city branding and creative economy as a way to convince others and themselves of their relevance to contemporary Chinese society, which necessarily tames any antagonism invested in the arts. The most oppositional place in

Songzhuang is allegedly the independent film establishment, including a film archive, a film studio, and the acclaimed Xianxiang website, put together by Li Xianting and Zhu Rikun. But the vibrant hub was closed down by the government in March 2011 in fear of the ripple effects of the Jasmine Movement, meaning that the government is still in full control of Songzhuang. If artists occupy the position of the urbanist, who plans and designs spaces from a managerial level, they are running the risk of ignoring the subject matter and the materiality of place in their own works.

We should not essentialize the spatial identity of an art space, as art coordinates and facilitates flows of ideas instead of serving as a simple tool of social reflection. But this does not mean an artwork should be aloof to the materiality of its place, particularly in the age of the creative economy, which has a tendency to melt all concreteness. A socially engaging piece of artwork should be equipped with the forces to constantly question and break away from its surrounding environment, while being continually nurtured by the same environment in which it is deeply involved. Peter Osborne insightfully articulates the tensions between art and space:

> Contemporary art produces (or fails to produce) the non-place of art-space as the condition of its autonomy and hence its functioning as "art." That is, autonomy is not an external condition of art, but must be produced anew, on the basis of its external conditions, in each instance, by each work, by its immanent negation of place. Art cannot live, qua art, within the everyday as the everyday. Rather, qua art, it necessarily interrupts the everyday, from within, on the basis of the fact that it is always both autonomous and "social fact." It is the continued search for a productive form of this duality that has driven art beyond the literal physical space of museum and gallery into other social spaces.[80]

Osborne says that a piece of artwork should be acutely conscious of its positioning, constantly struggling between the embodiment of and the contestation against its own place. This is a particularly urgent question for this generation of Chinese artists, who are witnessing spatial transformations on a daily basis. Modernization and globalization prompt major land reform, witnessed not only in the escalation of real estate development but also in the advent of migrant workers, who leave their rural hometowns to become temporary workers in urban areas. We are seeing the largest population movement, or floating lives, in China's history. Globalization, through the reordering of spatial functioning and massive social uprooting, has dramatically changed the notion of place in many Chinese people's psyche. Should art be content to follow, and therefore endorse, the underlying global forces, or should it respond to and reflect on such transformations?

Lefebvre uses the spider and its web to show that one does not occupy a transcendental position to design and create one's living space, but, like the spider, produces and occupies the space of one's web, of one's stratagems, of one's needs. He also explains that a seashell is beautiful not because of the work of a divine designer or spirit, but as a result of the seashell producing its own body and space according to its actual needs and way of life. According to Lefebvre, Surrealist art is of special value in the understanding of space, because the leading Surrealists "sought to decode inner subjective space and illuminate the nature of the transition from this subjective space to the material realm of the body and the outside world, and thence to social life."[81] To Lefebvre, the beauty of Surrealist art lies not in the artists' rational reflections of the outside world, but in their embodied experiences of their everyday reality. The illuminating and antagonistic value of art cannot be separated from the artist's subject position intimately within the questioned social reality. However, in the age of the creative economy, when creativity is, however indirectly, absorbed into the capitalist machine, we can no longer easily substantiate this embodied position of the artist (or the spider) which produces through his or her own space.

Animation and Transcultural Signification

As I have demonstrated, the creative industries discourse is highly contagious, particularly in East Asia, where related rhetoric and strategies are quickly absorbed and integrated into the national economy. However, Japan, with some of the most prominent cultural industries in the world, has been relatively slow to engage in such discourse. The global success of the Japanese cartoon industry, one of the most influential cultural industries in the world, was achieved largely uninformed by and aloof from the creative economy, and it also breeds a viewership different from that conditioned by the logic of creativity commodification. Furthering my deliberation of the creative industries discourse, starting in this chapter I examine pirated objects more closely, as well as the dynamics between creativity and copying. Ironically cartoons as a representation form and Japanese manga and anime as a culture can be connected to piracy in subtle ways.

In the functioning of the creative economy, copying is cast as the opposite of creativity. In its many forms of piracy, plagiarism, and forgery, copying does not produce any new ideas, and it is demonized as unimaginative, lazy theft, so that the consumption of such products is also classified as bad taste. However, as we all know, industrialized creativity is actually a function of copying, and the commodity is never truly unique. Copying is now even more convenient and effective due to the availability of different digital and cyber technologies, and new commodities often result from the reappropriation and conflation of existing ideas and designs. On the opposite end, different kinds of IPR offenses are elaborately labeled and classified in order to facilitate legal condemnation. A site that attracts intensive discursive interests, the pirated product, no matter what it is, also is semiotically rich.

In fact IPR does not curtail sharing and copying, but stipulates legal access, in terms of both encoding and decoding, by first privatizing them. As acts to establish human relationships, encoding and decoding are now governed as profit-making activities. However, a more primitive, noncommercial nature of sharing and copying is still observable in today's Japanese cartoon culture, and in this chapter I argue that there are connections between its pirated receptions in China, the nature of cartooning, and related fan activities around the world. By exploring the patterns of sharing and copying as revealed in the Chinese piracy of Japanese cartoon products, I show that there are different ways to articulate transcultural connections and creativity beyond the current creative economy rationale. Henry Jenkins points out that there is always a creative and subversive side to fan culture, because fans often poach (interpret, recycle, and appropriate) original sources in imaginative and socially embedded ways;[1] the pirate culture and the fan culture I address herein are even more indeterminate because the texts themselves are highly amorphous, realized through piracy and fans' appropriation. Analyzing the sharing and copying activities related to the Japanese cartoon culture in China and in Japan, we might be able to understand the specificity of both piracy and cartooning, and more broadly the antagonistic relationship between the creative economy and societal bonding.

Sharing: The Piracy Culture of Anime in China

One of the major incidents marking China's Open-Door Policy was the signing of the Treaty of Peace and Friendship between Japan and the People's Republic of China (中日和平友好條約) in 1978, and one result was the selective introduction of Japanese television programs to China. Among the first imported programs broadcast by China's Central Television were Tezuka Osamu's *Astro Boy* (1963) and *Kimba the White Lion* (1965–66), and Japanese anime became the first batch of popular culture reaching the Chinese masses.[2] As happened in many other East Asian countries, Japanese anime soon became vastly popular in China but they are no longer widely shown on Chinese television because of the protective measures recently implemented by the state to encourage the broadcasting of local children productions. Recent research shows that more than 80 percent of Chinese youths prefer Japanese anime to any other cartoon form.[3] However, no feature-length Japanese anime films have been shown on official Chinese screens.[4] In China the import of foreign cinematic content has been much more strictly limited than television content, and the quota of imported revenue-sharing films has been almost entirely filled by Hollywood and Hong Kong blockbusters.[5] Most important, Japanese studios have not shown much interest in the Chinese market; its domestic market, and to a lesser degree the markets in the West, are of primary concern—a point I will revisit later. A few anime films have been shown in festivals; e.g., Oshii Mamoru's *Innocence* and Shinkai Makoto's *The Place Promised in Our Early Days* were shown at the Shanghai International Arts Festival in 2005.[6]

There are a small number of legally distributed Japanese manga in the Chinese markets, but it is still primarily piracy that makes Japanese cartoon culture available in China. It is argued that piracy outperforms legal distribution of manga because pirates usually have access to better local distribution networks and work much faster and therefore are better able to keep up with trends.[7] For example, the manga of Tezuka Osamu was legally distributed in China for the first time in 2007, by which time these works were already considered classic. Japanese anime is not represented by official distributors (except television) in China. If anime available online or on disc has Chinese subtitles, it is almost certainly a bootleg copy. According to some Japanese sources, about 2.1 trillion yen worth of pirated anime are sold in China each year.[8] Although television continues to show anime in China, many more viewers watch Japanese anime on the Internet or on pirated discs. Manga, on the other hand, has always been pirated. According to some blogs, Japanese manga was first made available in China in the early 1980s in the pirated copies printed by Hainan Press of Photography and Arts (海南攝影美術出版社), which was ordered to close down in 1998. As shown in these blog discussions, the name of this press remains part of the collective memory of Chinese who are now in their twenties or early thirties.[9] Other publishing companies specializing in pirating manga include Huaqiao Press (華僑出版社) and Yuanfang Press (遠方出版社). It is, however, generally understood that the Chinese government was aware of and even approved these pirated publications, evidenced in the presses' self-censorship, deleting some of the most blatant erotic scenes in *Ryo Saeba* 寒羽良 and *Saotome Ranma* 亂馬. Currently most pirated anime and manga are available for sale on the Internet, and the diversity of materials accessible to the Chinese population has grown exponentially.[10] As a form of pirated material, knockoff manga has provided not only entertainment but also information about sex to youths in a puritan society. Without piracy and online sharing, the two major means by which Chinese youths reach the outside world today, Japanese popular culture might have a very different face in China.

Many of these copyright-infringing activities have commercial interests at stake. Today traditional disc and print piracy continues to prosper, and new digital-printing technologies have enabled more efficient and higher-quality mass reprinting of manga. But online sharing, which is mainly a social and leisure activity with no financial reward, cannot be viewed directly from an economic perspective. An incredible amount of material is distributed online free of charge, ranging from anime and manga to all kinds of peripheral information about Japanese cartoons, made accessible through specific peer-to-peer applications or large servers.[11] This is not unique to Japanese cartoons; we are witnessing the rise of a new culture online, in which netizens diligently upload, download, and classify various materials.

The distinction between online and offline is increasingly problematic, particularly in Japanese cartoon culture. In general, disc and print piracy and online sharing have a great deal of overlap. Although abundant materials can be freely obtained online, pirates sometimes repackage them as new commodities for profit. Activities range from reselling online materials in print or disc form, to creating popular magazines and periodicals that collect material online without citing proper references. While online materials can be sold offline for a profit, pirated materials can also be distributed free of charge through the Internet. Many current Japanese television programs are available online immediately after their broadcast in Japan—usually with Chinese subtitles already added, thanks to the generous efforts of the bilingual and technologically informed members of the subtitling groups I have mentioned in chapter 3. Some online materials are remakes of existing anime or manga adapted by their appropriators. With the aid of new technologies such as digitization and online circulation, piracy has become a much more adaptable and widespread activity in many people's lives.

What does this pirated popular culture look like? I recently purchased a pirated volume published in mainland China in a bookstore in Hong Kong: *The World of Miyazaki Hayao*, by Fei Yuxiao (figure 9).[12] The book came with eight bookmarks and a pirated soundtrack of *Howl's Moving Castle*, and its retail price was 35 RMB (517 JPY, US$4.30). The price is low by Japanese or Western standards, but it is on the expensive side for the general Chinese consumer, and no doubt targets young, upper-middle-class urbanites. Obviously this is a counterfeit product, and it comprises many levels of piracy. The CD was copied directly from a legally produced disc, and the many images collected in the book were captured from different sources. The author compiled the text by consulting different online and print materials without citing his or her sources. As mentioned earlier, none of Miyazaki's films has ever been screened officially in theaters in mainland China. However, according to research involving 3,355 mainland Chinese youths, Miyazaki is their favorite cartoon author, and the popularity of Japanese comic materials significantly

9. Cover of *The World of Miyazaki Hayao.*

exceeds that of American content in China (among the ten most favorite items, only one comes from the U.S., while the other nine are all Japanese).[13] Obviously Miyazaki's works have become popular in China largely through pirated discs. We can safely deduce that customers are attracted to this book because they have watched pirated Miyazaki movies. Ironically the copyright page ascribes copyright to Fei Yuxiao and indicates that no one may copy or appropriate materials from the book without the author's consent (figure 10).

Many of the images collected in this book are captured from different sources: some directly from online pages, some from Japanese anime magazines, some (more crudely) from discs or television, and some from Chinese sources which themselves are compiled from pirated materials.[14] The pictures are not only a collage of attractive images, but they are also carefully selected, illustrated, and juxtaposed, and obviously much editorial effort was involved.

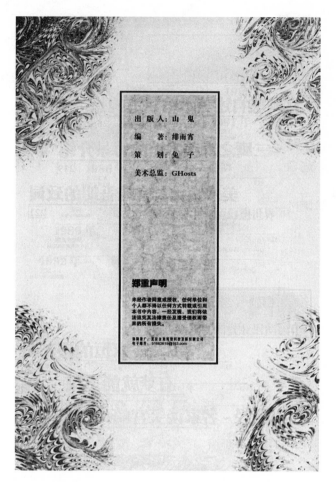

出 版 人:山 鬼

编   著:绯雨宵

策   划:兔 子

美术总监: GHosts

郑重声明

未经作者同意或授权，任何单位和
个人都不得以任何方式转载或引用
本书中内容，一经发现，我们将依
法追究其法律责任及漫受侵权而带
来的所有损失。

10. Copyright
page of *The World
of Miyazaki Hayao*.

The information provided is rich and diverse, including standard promotional materials such as film descriptions, film analysis, interviews, and behind-the-scenes reports. It also provides detailed biographies of those involved with the films, including not only important associates of Miyazaki such as the film producer Suzuki Toshio (p. 197), the composer Joe Hisaishi (p. 199), and the publisher Tokuma Yasuyashi (pp. 202–3), but also the likes of Jonathan Swift, the eighteenth-century British author whose work inspired *Castle in the Sky* (p. 53), and Miyazaki's protégé, the late Kondō Yoshifumi (pp. 189–91). There is also an elaborate description of the famous Ghibli Museum, Mitaka, which features Miyazaki's works and which has become a minor tourist attraction in Japan.

Of course the text cites no original sources for such rich information, and it is not my intention here to figure out where the materials came from. But I can say that many of these materials came directly from Japanese sources, both online and in print, although the author has also freely made alterations and added information for Chinese readers. For example, in the section introducing Miyazaki's environmentalist thinking, the author discusses the theories of the Japanese botanist Nakao Sasuke, who allegedly heavily influenced Miyazaki (pp. 131–33). The section is clearly copied from a Japanese article available online, "*Nausicaa of the Valley of Wind* to *Princess Mononoke*: The Thirteen-Year Collaboration of Miyazaki Hayao and Studio Ghibli" by Kanō Seiji.[15] But the Chinese translation is not completely loyal to the original. Perhaps due to the absence of copyright concerns, the author seems to feel free to add his or her ideas anywhere and in any way he or she likes. For example, in a passage describing foods the ancient Japanese loved, the Chinese author adds that Japanese eating practice is very similar to that in the Yunnan area, a comparison not mentioned in the original article. This connection echoes the always existing Japanese–Chinese cultural connection that this book would like to stress, a transcultural tendency that supposedly also grounds Miyazaki's own works. This book was published at a point when the Sino-Japanese relationship was at its worst since the Second World War; anti-Japanese demonstrations were seen everywhere in major Chinese cities. Thanks to these diverse cultural networks, cultural connections between the two countries can no longer be singlehandedly manipulated by political discourse.

This Miyazaki collection involves the actual selection and manipulation of materials produced by the official Miyazaki industry, but they are also heavily rearranged and reassembled. Although delicate editorial work is evident in the pirated volume, the production editor is also erroneous at times. Mistakes and confusions abound, making reading difficult. There is, for example, an unexpected combination of typesetting styles. In general, Japanese typesetting follows the traditional Chinese way of arranging words in vertical lines from right to left. But contemporary typesetting in mainland China follows Western practice: horizontal lines from left to right. This pirated book oddly combines both practices. The overall typesetting design is a modern Chinese one, but there are a few pages deliberately modeled after the original Japanese. Since the front and back covers were similar, I was confused as to where to begin reading the first time I flipped through the pages: Do I read the book as I would a standard mainland Chinese book or a (pirated) Japanese book? After some effort deciding where the beginning was, I found the reading experience similarly bizarre. After finishing the section on Joe Hisaishi in modern Chinese typesetting (pp. 198–201) (figure 11), I was thrown completely

11. *The World of Miyazaki Hayao*, pp. 200–201.
Typesetting is horizontal left to right.

off by the section on Tokuma Yasuyashi that followed, because it was set in Japanese style (pp. 202–3) (figure 12), and the first line of this layout begins not at either end but right in the middle (the page moves forward from left to right, while the lines run from right to left). Ironically Tokuma is a publishing tycoon, distributing not only Miyazaki's works but works from a large part of the country's print and cartoon industries. This typesetting mistake makes Tokuma, among all the figures introduced in this book, the most "incomprehensible" person of all.

The reason for the use of Japanese typesetting might be mimicry, in an effort to evoke the experience of reading authentic Japanese magazines. Unless this is a design specifically intended to confuse readers (which I doubt, because the design of the volume is much akin to ordinary popular magazines), this typesetting is a result of carelessness, and the typesetter is probably too keen on producing Japanese effects to have committed such a serious editorial mistake as the juxtaposition of different typesetting styles. This kind of editorial mistake can probably be seen only in hastily published pirated materials, and it most unexpectedly destabilizes the information that this book tries to offer. Information is no longer transparent or pleasurable to take

12. *The World of Miyazaki Hayao*, pp. 202–3. Typesetting is vertical right to left.

in. I appreciate the author's efforts in collecting, editing, and even fabricating materials from divergent sources, but I am most amused by the careless mistakes that resulted from the typesetter's hurried appropriation of these different materials.

Today knowledge is intimately associated with consumerism: the more consumers are educated about specific products, the more fervent is their desire to consume them. The Miyazaki collection shows that entertainment is no longer easily distinguishable from information, and the popularity of Japanese anime in China is accompanied by a large amount of fan knowledge available online and offline, so that fans are able to obtain a wide range of information about the texts and their producers. The side products included in this collection—soundtracks and stationery—might be as important as the films in forging cultural bonds and fandom. Tie-ins, as this collection demonstrates, are given much weight in the creative industries because they form myriad networks in which the commodity can signify and circulate, and they tremendously enrich the cultural value of the commodity through association with other objects, subjects, and affects.

Although the Japanese cartoon industry, as far as I know, has never been truly concerned with the Chinese market, its products are tremendously popular and widely pirated in the country. Beijing's Shijingshan (石景山) theme park was recently accused of copyright infringement, as it displays cartoon figures very similar to Disney's and Sanrio's.[16] It is probably the only theme park in the world where one can see a parade including both Mickey Mouse and Hello Kitty. However, the Beijing park asserts that the accused Mickey Mouse is actually one of the four big-ear kittens selected from a national competition, and all the cartoon figures featured in the park were trademarked. Such a counterfeiting and piracy culture is a challenge to the creative economy partly because it redistributes and re-presents copyrighted and brand-name materials as well as their related knowledge and information in ways that the IPR owners have no way to control or even anticipate. The Miyazaki book is a collection of pirated materials from different sources, while the rundown Shijingshan theme park manipulates the highly popular Japanese and American cartoon figures in order to claim them as its own. Such a creative combination of materials is considered an enemy to true, that is, profitable, creativity.

The overwhelming popularity of Japanese anime in China forces the government to curtail the fervor by implanting a protectionist quota system: regulations now stipulate that no more than 40 percent of the animation broadcast in China can be foreign productions.[17] In order to fill the remaining 60 percent of airtime, local industries are trying very hard to satisfy a television audience that craves Disney cartoons and Japanese anime. The Chinese government also recognizes the importance of the development of a national entertainment industry to reduce the economy's heavy dependence on manufacturing.[18] The city of Hangzhou, home to sixty cartoon and animation enterprises employing ten thousand people, calls itself the capital of Chinese animation,[19] but there are many other cities and regions also trying to claim this title.

Complicating the nationalist project is the offshore phenomenon. Animation is an extremely labor-intensive industry,[20] and Chinese craftsmen are in fact responsible for the actual production of many Japanese animations. More than 80 percent of the production of Japanese anime is outsourced offshore,[21] and we might say the entire Japanese anime industry relies on the labor of adjacent countries—mostly South Korea, the Philippines, and China. If creative industries are often associated with nationalist pride, offshore creative labor is not. But such subsidiary craft labor can allegedly help cultivate true creativity. South Korea has developed a national animation industry as a result of the offshore labor training it has received from Japan,[22] and China is close on its heels. As if to supplement offshore labor training, Chinese academics are also sent directly to Japan to study cartooning so that they can teach Chinese students and establish a cartoon industry based on the highly successful Japanese model.[23] Major national universities such as Beijing Film Academy, Communication University of China, and Renmin University of China have recently established their own animation departments to train animators at the university level, following the government's agenda to develop China's animation industry.

The first Sino-Japanese coproduced anime film, *Silver-Hair Agito*, was announced in China in 2005 as the first step in the development of the Chinese animation industry, but according to the film's credits, the Chinese contribution was largely labor-intensive work. One year later the first Chinese 3-D feature animation film, *Thru the Moebius Strip* (*Mobishi huan* 魔比斯環), was released in Chinese movie theaters, although it was greeted with little enthusiasm. *Thru the Moebius Strip* was solely produced by the Chinese studio Universal Digital (Huanqiu shuma 環球數碼), but the key production members were all foreigners. (It was directed by Glenn Chaika, who made *The Adventures of Tom Thumb and Thumbelina*, and produced by Steven D. Katz, an American filmmaker and author of two bestselling books on the subject of directing.) The nationalist protectionist agenda continues to fetishize foreign creative ideas and exploit domestic Chinese labor. But very soon the first truly successful home-grown animation series appeared on the market: *Pleasant Sheep and Big Big Wolf* (Xiyangyang yu Huitailang 喜羊羊與灰太狼). The television series first appeared in August 2005, and in four years' time over seventy stations in China have broadcast more than six hundred episodes. Its first feature film was screened in 2009 during the Chinese New Year, reaping close to 100 million RMB at the national box office. Many Chinese people are hopeful that China's own comic industry will rapidly develop and protect their children from the corruptions of Japanese and American cartoons.

Copying: The Production of National Identities

It is true that the alternative practices and circulation networks formed by the piracy culture do not necessarily constitute antiglobalization or anticapitalism, as most of the time IPR infringement does not lead to those economic and cultural flows that frustrate the dominant networks. The piracy of Japanese cultural products, for example, does not necessarily challenge the products' Japanese identity. The Miyazaki collection continues to sustain the revered position of Japanese popular culture in the global circulation of commodities. Counterfeit products often solicit underdeveloped markets for their acquiescence to the commodity and the promotion of the brand name. While counterfeit tie-in products like this Miyazaki collection are clearly situated outside the IPR order, the pirated book does not necessarily signify alternative transnational reception networks. Instead Chinese readers learn about Japanese products through this sharing of information, so the cultural hierarchy of production and reception in which Japan is at the center is not challenged, but might be further promoted, by these illegal practices. The global creative economy is a battlefield for regions and nations to take charge of style and innovation. One duty of the creative industries is the production of cultural identities that contribute to city and national branding. The Miyazaki volume in fact demonstrates a reification of the author function conjured up by the creative industries—the author being both Miyazaki and Japan. The book continues to exploit the basic reception structure in which Chinese viewers consume and admire Miyazaki and Japanese culture.

However, such parasitical activities corrode the dominant power from within, and the most destructive actions are often antipolitical in nature; they are not consciously constructed as oppositional politics but as everyday embodied experiences that transcend and overwhelm the structures which engendered them. In the case of cartoon piracy, a more basic question I want to ask is whether cartoons can be pirated. I find the Miyazaki volume interesting not because it has upset the global distribution of commodities, but because it reminds me of the correspondence between China's piracy culture and the Japanese cartoon culture in their common affinity for mimesis. There seems to be a very strong cultural identity attached to Japanese animation. But this association between Japanese national identity and its cartoon industry is also shaky, due to the specificity of the form of the cartoon culture and Japanese industrial practices. While the Walt Disney Company very consciously carves its authorial mark into its products, the Japanese cartoon industry seems to show less interest in this regard, and instead continues to respect the logic of copying.

First of all, cartoons are a visual form closely associated with copying. In its original meanings, a cartoon is a drawing made on paper as a study for another drawing, so a cartoon is always itself a copy. It is therefore very difficult to differentiate between creative copying and plagiarism in cartoons. The notion of originality and identity in cartoons is not only weak but alienating. The form's strong affiliation with copying enormously complicates any national and cultural identity produced thereby, because there is no such thing as authenticity. This is particularly the case for the Japanese animation culture, as Anne Allison explains: "The entire world here is built from a bricolage of assorted and interchangeable (machine/organic/human) parts where familiar forms have been broken down and reassembled into new hybridities."[24] Identities are always fluid in the world of Japanese manga and anime, and the idea of originality is more often mocked than fortified. While the current American animation industry is driven by the pursuit of verisimilitude, Hayao Miyazaki proclaimed that computer-generated images could not exceed 10 percent of his total work, and he desires the "less real, less accurate, and less perfect" of these images.[25]

It is true that cartoon's pictorial form, which is particularly apt to exaggerate values and ideologies related to the human body that are generally difficult to realize in photographic form, facilitates an emphasis on collective identity. For example, it is easier to represent and legitimize exaggerated masculinity and heroism in animation than in any live-action fantasy because animation has the capacity to render figures indestructible.[26] The same logic can be applied also to cultural identity, as cartoonists can also easily give common bodily features to characters to emphasize their race or ethnicity. However, the Japanese cartoon industry does not seem particularly interested in demarcating cultural differences among characters; in fact the Japanese artist Takashi Murakami characterizes Japanese animation as "superflat."[27] A major difference between Japanese anime and Disney cartoons is the lack of "personality animation" that American animators value. In Disney's works, the appearance and voice of the characters, as well as their activities and even mannerisms, differentiate one character from another.[28] In contrast, Japanese cartoon characters look very similar to each other. While gender identity is reinforced in certain cases, Japanese anime is also famous for its transgender tendencies.[29] Ethnic and racial identities are also seldom clearly demarcated in Japanese animations, with exceptions such as the emphasis of characters of African descent in athletic stories related to American settings. In fact many Japanese animators, particularly Miyazaki, set their stories and design their characters based on foreign models, and it is difficult for viewers to differentiate Japanese from foreign characters.

While the ethnicity of individual characters is seldom emphasized pictorially, neither can we easily identify a collective "Japaneseness" in Japanese manga and anime as a whole. There are clearly Japanese values, Japanese tastes, and in some cases specific Japanese social concerns structured in the texts, and there are many Japanese factors in the stories and their ideologies, but they are not essential to the pictorial "form," and we cannot take a certain Japanese animation style for granted.[30] Although there seem to be common attributes—rich and dynamic drawing, doe-eyed characters with feminine features, and expressive and exaggerated color schemes—there are too many exceptions to claim a unified style. Since by nature animation is free from indexical burden, the cultural or national identity of Japanese animation can be both easily constructed and easily evaded.

Because animation is essentially a culture of copying, the relationship between representation and reality within this form is most dynamic: we enjoy animation precisely because it is not reality. Animation is structured by the dynamics between the aesthetics of imagination and the aesthetics of copying—between abstract and realist models.[31] If our modern visual culture is largely characterized by the desire for photographic realism and the creation of the illusion of dynamic reality, animation is a major exception that can afford to play with reality and highlight the complex similarity-qua-difference mechanism of mimesis.[32] Among other forms of representation, animation might be the one most resistant to claims of essentialist cultural roots, allowing Disney to appropriate and exploit folk culture and to situate its works within a forged timeless tradition. Animation in general has been shown to be a culture of appropriation.[33] This is also the case with Miyazaki, who quite freely appropriates stories and visual materials from different historical periods and cultures to situate his works in a supracultural plane that supposedly belongs to all children of all cultures.

I am not suggesting that the Japanese comic culture lacks its own historical tradition. Caricatures of people and animals were found in Japanese Buddhist temples built in the eighth century, and humorous pictures of animals engaging in everyday human activities, parodying the decadent lifestyle of the Japanese upper class, were popular in the eleventh and twelfth centuries.[34] The modern manga industry evolved rapidly after the Second World War, when the suffering people in this defeated country were quite uncertain about their future. Manga became both an escapist entertainment and a public venue for people to release their overall frustrations.

It is true that contemporary Japanese comic culture developed organically out of its own sociocultural history, but the people's fondness for the form does not necessarily give it a cultural identity. Also, commercial logics have entered the field. We know that culture must first be established within a specific community, and cultural expressions are encoded and decoded by members of that community. One must belong to that particular community to enjoy access to its shared networks of meanings and experiences. But with cultural industries this natural relationship between the culture and its people can no longer be taken for granted. As Jeremy Rifkin argues, due to the relentless and successful efforts of cultural industries to separate cultural expressions from their community origins for the market, access rights migrate from the social to the commercial realm: "Access will no longer be based on intrinsic criteria—traditions, rights of passage, family and kinship relations, ethnicity, religion, or gender—but rather on affordability in the commercial arena."[35] Although the Japanese cartoon industry primarily targets the domestic market, we cannot assume it to reflect a national culture organically, because the extremely complex marketing logic carves and re-carves up the national market into various niche sectors, which both segment Japanese readers and connect them to those outside the country.

While it is ultimately futile to try to detect national identity in pictorial forms, I also find it difficult to locate a Japanese national identity in anime that is politically enforced, as in the case of Hollywood, which is backed by the U.S. government.[36] Policy and legal interference, as I mentioned in chapter 4, characterize the development of creative industries, but the Japanese cartoon industry has not yet revealed this tendency. It is argued that there are two very different sectors of Japanese production industries: Japanese firms are highly competitive and globally oriented in the manufacturing industries, but there is also a strong isolationism in many other aspects of Japan's culture and its economy. Many rules are in place to restrict the import of foreign goods and investment, and many Japanese firms are preoccupied by their large domestic markets.[37] The cultural industries belong mostly to the second category. As some critics argue, the Japanese animation industry has not progressed very far from its roots as a cottage industry of sensitive artistes, and domestic competition is simply too strong to allow them to explore other markets, to say nothing of "nonexistent" markets like mainland China.[38] Hiroshi Aoyagi discovered in his recent research that many Japanese youths are not aware of the vast popularity of Japanese pop idols and trendy goods in other parts of Asia, and those who find out after visiting these Asian countries are not only astonished, but are also enlightened by the ways Japan is perceived outside its borders.[39]

While Japanese manga and anime are popular and widely pirated in Asia and around the world, unlike the American cartoon industry or the Japanese electronic industry, which carefully protect their copyrights and patents, the Japanese cartoon industry has not yet shown much interest in IPR, and we have seen an enormous amount of fan activity which could be considered IPR infringement. Scholars have identified at least two reasons for this. First, due to the relatively low damage incurred by what are mostly fans' activities, it is not economically rational to bring suit. Second, the Japanese comic industry has not developed an elaborate global distribution system.[40] As Koichi

Iwabuchi argues, "The most serious shortcoming of the Japanese animation industry, despite mature production capability and techniques, is its lack of international distribution channels. Western (American) global distribution power is thus indispensable to make Japanese animation a part of global popular culture."[41] As I have reiterated, global IPR consciousness is intimately related to the rise of the creative industries discourse, which has not yet become fierce in the Japanese animation industry. As there is ignorance of the wide global reception of their products, the national identity of Japanese cartoons does not need to be highlighted; anime and manga are always Japanese.

While the Japanese cartoon industry is aimed primarily at the national market, the popularity of Japanese cartoon culture is spreading among anime and manga fans all over the world, specifically with the help of the Internet. Unique to Japanese cartoons, there is heavy participation in creative fan fiction, *dōjinshi*, a fan's self-published works that mainly copy and transform already published materials. As the flourishing *dōjinshi* culture attests, Japanese manga is mainly a culture of copying and sharing; fans not only consume the materials passively but actively contribute to their production and expansion, generally without any direct financial interest at stake. A major centripetal force of *dōjinshi* culture is the fans' loyalty to the originals: their reproductions must closely follow the plots, characterizations, and sentiments of the originals. But *dōjinshi* fans also draw for the sake of drawing differences, characterizing the dynamic interactions between identity and difference inherent in the *dōjinshi* culture.[42] I believe this communal bonding developed through copying most uniquely distinguishes the cultural values of Japanese animation. But it does not mean that this unique identity is "Japanese." First, as mentioned earlier, cartooning itself is a form of copying and lacks an identity of its own; this dimension is suppressed by today's capitalist logics and CGI development, thus the Pixar stereoscopic 3-D aesthetics which is driven by the constant search for the perfect representation of reality. Second, the *dōjinshi* culture is practiced among fans all over the world, particularly on the Internet, and such networks are diversified and international. More important, its spirit is adaptation and transformation, which both fortify and resist identity construction: *dōjinshi* therefore both reveres and deconstructs Japanese culture.

This is most obviously seen in the new cosplay phenomenon, which is flourishing among cartoon fans not only in Japan but in other Asian communities. Cosplay fans dress up as their favorite cartoon characters and perform in public. The strong connotations of performance inherent in cosplay mock any naïve national identification associated with Japanese cartoon culture.

Stunning demonstrations of the local Chinese appropriation of the cosplay culture can be found in a series of photographic projects by Cao Fei, titled "Cosplayers," "Cos-cosplay," and "Un-Cosplayers," in which cosplay characters are posed against the backdrop of cityscape, domestic environment, and construction sites in China's coastal cities.[43] The rich performativity of cosplay is juxtaposed with the barrenness of the sites, and the characters' aloof confrontation of China's "social reality" through these extravagant Japanese cartoon costumes and postures suggests an uneasy coexistence of time and space. Such transnational coexistence both blurs and reinforces the distinct Chinese circumstances and Japanese identities, and the sharp juxtaposition again reminds us of how easy and yet difficult it is to associate the Japanese identity with Japanese cartoon products (figures 13 and 14).

Another byproduct of the *dōjinshi* culture is slash fiction, a genre of fan fiction that rewrites existing stories with homosexual twists. In her study of slash fiction, the legal scholar Sonia Katyal suggests adopting performativity theories to counter concepts of property, because slash fiction challenges the assumed dichotomy between originality and copying, subverting notions of authenticity and challenging mainstream gender ideologies: "Performance theory suggests a sort of rival relationship between the performer and the audience. The two are interdependent but are also deeply conflicted with the possibilities of internal rebellion."[44] I would like to add to Katyal's analysis that the tensions between the performer and the reader both reinforce and blur their distinctive identities, and the heavy components of performativity in slash fiction again remind us of how difficult it is to attach Japaneseness to Japanese cartoon productions. In fact the genre of slash has flourished in the cyberworld, where agency can be greatly fragmented. If the slash performativity can subvert the IPR regime, this subversion resides more in the individual author's refusal to allow his or her identity from solidifying, and therefore refusing the author's desire to own the text.

Iwabuchi points out the contradictory manifestations of the popularity of Japanese cultural commodities in Asia. On the one hand, in order to avoid the cultural discount effects, the Japanese cultural presence is deliberately de-emphasized in certain commodities, such as cultural technologies and animation; on the other hand, Japaneseness is much more visible in many other cultural products, like popular music and television programs. Iwabuchi thus claims that globalizing forces "make transnational cultural flow much more disjunctive, non-isomorphic, and complex than what the center-periphery paradigm allows us to understand."[45] The *dōjinshi* culture embodies both the two seemingly opposite manifestations that Iwabuchi points out—that Japa-

13. Cao Fei, *cosplayers*, 2004, photographic work. Courtesy Para/Site Art Space.

14. Cao Fei, *Cao Fei: cosplayers*, 2006, installation art, Para/Site Art Space, Hong Kong. Courtesy Para/Site Art Space.

neseness is both desired and rejected in transnational cultural consumption. In a way the presence and the absence of distinct cultural identity do not cancel out but support each other in the logic of global capitalism, because this economy is based on both mass and niche markets, both the rejection and the fetishization of newness. At the same time, uniqueness and sharing do not necessarily contradict each other, as is clearly shown in contemporary popular culture. There might be many reasons for the inertia of the Japanese cartoon industry toward such IPR-violating activities, but we do know that the *dōjinshi* culture and the cartoon industry are mutually beneficial to each other.[46] This is something the current IPR logic is not yet able to comprehend, as the American Creative Commons advocate Lawrence Lessig asserts that the tolerance and respect for copying demonstrated in the *dōjinshi* culture is beyond the imagination of American creative industries and the U.S. legal environment.[47]

This brings us back to the Chinese Miyazaki collection, which not only reflects the current bricolage of the Japanese anime culture in China, but it is also a re-creation of the Japanese fan culture outside IPR concepts. I would argue that it is the book's affiliation with the Japanese *dōjinshi* practices, instead of the actual information collected in it, which makes this Chinese publication so akin to the spirit of the Japanese cartoon culture. Although the Chinese Miyazaki book does not include new creations modeled after Miyazaki's works, the rearrangement and new interpretations of Miyazaki produce effects similar to those of *dōjinshi*, diffusing but also unifying the collective identity of Japanese anime. This collective imaging can be highly subversive to the pseudo-individualization of today's post-Fordist products conjured up by commodity culture and protected by IPR.

It is true that there is a strong cultural identity inherent in Japanese manga and anime, to the extent that there are people arguing that the popularity of Japanese cartoons in China is another form of cultural imperialism, and one could make a similar case for the Miyazaki collection and see it as another piece of evidence attesting to Japan's cultural invasion of China. However, although there might be many reasons and efforts solidifying the Japanese identity of Japanese animation, none of them, as I have shown, is definitive. In view of the pictorial form, the weak export impulse, and the wide regional and international consumption and reappropriation, the national identity produced by Japanese cartoons is marked neither in the texts, in policy, nor in the cartoons' reception. In other words, the strong cultural identity of Japanese anime is composed of weak resemblances and lax distinctiveness, demonstrating both the paradoxical nature of identity in general and the specific form of cartoon that always meanders between identity and differences.

When Beijing unveiled its 2008 Olympic mascots, five Fuwa, criticisms abounded.[48] Instead of being a design of pure imagination, the five Fuwa are clichéd archetypes, including real and mythic creatures, like the giant panda and Tibetan antelope, and natural forms, such as forest, fire, and earth, and even Japanese cartoons. One could also call Fuwa a form of unimaginative symbolism, as the five figures are made to represent at the same time thirty-

eight sports items, the five circles of the Olympic logo, the Chinese "five elements," as well as nature, animals, and so on and so forth. Fuwa, therefore,
can be seen as an "uncreative" caricature which copies from everywhere, and
such easy symbolization is not appreciated by many critics.[49]

In a *New York Times* essay on the anti-China actions of the NGO Dream
for Darfur, the reporter gauges readers' negative emotions against Beijing's
Olympics through the mascots. The essay opens thus:

> On a morning in mid-February [2008], the four staff members of Dream
> for Darfur sat in silence in what they call their war room, contemplating
> posters of Beibei the Fish and her four fellow Olympic mascots taped
> to the walls. In this cramped office in a shared space on the 16th floor
> of a downtown Manhattan Art Deco building, Beibei smiled welcom-
> ingly, as did Jingjing the giant panda, Huanhuan the red Olympic flame,
> Nini the green swallow and Yingying the horned orange Tibetan ante-
> lope: anime-style drawings that regardless of name appear strikingly
> the same, Medusa hair fused on teddy-bear faces with little-girl expres-
> sions. . . . "I don't know about the rest of you," said Jill Savitt, Dream
> for Darfur's executive director, as she scanned the posters, "but these
> cartoon creatures creep me out."[50]

The writer does not explain why the mascots are "creepy," but this dismis-
sive aura lingers and dominates the entire essay. Many of those familiar with
American and Japanese cartoons might have found these figures familiar but
also different; they seem creepy because of their mimetic nature: they re-
semble too many and too little, or, they are just not as cute as the "authentic"
American and Japanese products are. The design of Fuwa takes into account
the principle of cosmic connection and resemblance in traditional Chinese
culture, and the implication of premodern totems is strong. This *New York
Times* reporter not only demonstrates a racist perspective—taking an unfa-
miliar object as representation of a group of people's cultural or moral inferiority—but also reveals the domestication of the cartoon form in our contemporary culture. While the mascot is made to represent the Olympic spectacle,
and the mascot, tamed through commodification, can only be cute, we have
forgotten that the mimetic nature of cartoon caricature has the capacity not
only to carry prescribed meanings, but also to perpetuate and transform
them.

The Olympics is probably the most sought-after event for city branding,
and there were particularly vigorous discussions about the promotion of Beijing's creative industries through the event.[51] John Howkins recommended

this approach: "The [Olympic] organizers should bring together artists, singers, athletes and top physiologists to let them discuss the links between creative process and successful athletic performance."[52] The "uncreative" nature of the Chinese Fuwa might topple the natural relationship between the Olympics and creativity that Howkins suggests. The Beijing Olympics was specifically invested in the discourse of national pride. The nature of caricature in this mascot invited us to rethink the principles of innovation and identity held supreme by the current consumer culture and creative economy. As the mascot is widely used as a fictional spokesperson for consumer products, its cartoon nature might also remind us of the metonymical nature of commodity (to be elaborated in the next chapter), that no consumer product is really unique as such. Currently the celebration, or fetishization, of creativity traverses almost all levels of Chinese lives, from education to R&D, from packaging to everyday life. Maybe we can hear a feeble voice of opposition in these Fuwa figures.

Coming back to anime, with the fervent efforts of adjacent countries to copy the success of the Japanese cartoon industry, the Japanese government finally began to adopt, although slowly, the creative industry logics. Kukhee Choo argues that in official government views, popular cultural products were looked down upon as "vulgar and childish" in supposed opposition to the "refined and mature" products of high culture.[53] However, in the face of Japan's declining economic power, the government recently moved to brand Japan with popular culture. In the name of cracking down on piracy, beginning in 2004 the Organization for Promotion of Overseas Distribution of Content began affixing a "Made in Japan" trademark to Japanese animation and video game packaging.[54] Prime Minister Shinzo Abe, in his first policy speech to the Japanese Diet in 2006, called for a "Japanese cultural industry strategy" to promote everything from film to cuisine, and a massive global rebranding campaign to market the country as the epitome of "cool."[55] As Nissim Otmazgin demonstrates, in the past few years the media and official discourses in Japan have indulgently borrowed from soft power terminology, promoting the country's cultural exports and advocating support for investment in Japan's creative industries.[56] Anime is now considered the flagship content of "Cool Japan," and Ian Condry argues that this policy change encourages the discursive privileges of economic issues to exploit the unique practices of this culture.[57] Implementing new creative economy logics, whether the Japanese cartoon culture will become a full-fledged member of the creative economy remains to be seen.[58] Most important, if the creative economy gains a foothold in the Japanese cartoon industry, we should be particularly vigilant against its effects on the *dōjinshi* culture and its implications for the vibrant community formed by sharing and copying.

As Judith Butler claims, alterity is inherent in every identity.[59] Without romanticizing piracy as conscious revolutionary acts against capitalism, nor essentializing cartoons as necessarily antirealism, we can still develop a mode of critical thinking on cultural alterity using cases like the circulation of pirated Japanese anime in China. This is relevant to both our new global economy, in which all cultural differences are equalized and relativized by money, and the many international conflicts based on nationalism, as shown in the recent disputes between China and Japan. I believe that both piracy and the cartoon culture invite us to reactivate a vibrant dimension of copying and sharing that is increasingly repressed by our current creative industries, and it also reminds us that regionalization might be most effectively developed outside the IPR framework.

A Semiotics of the Counterfeit Product

Copying is generally considered as destructive to profitable creativity, but the actual relationship between copying and creativity is much more intimate. In this chapter I continue to explore this bipolar structure of the creative economy, but I expand my horizon from a particular representational form to consumer society in general, as I want to investigate how such sanctification of creativity and condemnation of copying are related to the logic of the commodity.

In advanced capitalist societies, where people's basic needs are largely satisfied, the value of a commodity is increasingly determined by the level of knowledge and creativity it manifests or that is invested in it, so that the appeal of new commodities is often conjured up by the continual supplies of knowledge and creativity. The value of a Ferrari, for example, might largely come from the technology invested in it, whereas the value of a Prada bag is related to its design. But knowledge and creativity cannot be easily separated: the presentation of knowledge (the style of the car) and the engineering of product design (the nanomaterial used to make the Prada bag) also make the car and the bag worth their prices. Or, to put it directly, knowledge, creativity, and information are all marketing items to be circulated, recycled, and reorganized in new forms. Because of the ever increasing demand for the input of knowledge and creativity, the world's advanced industrial economies move to specialization: major firms in advanced countries choose to stick to a much narrower range of products, but they also have access to a wide and similar range of production technologies.[1] Specialized skills, fine quality, and ever renewed products of the same type of commodities become essential to the success of brands.

Precisely due to the high R&D and marketing expenses invested in the production of commodities, furious accusations and attempts at repression are directed at the counterfeit. But the major question of this chapter is whether it is really that easy to read and understand such an object. A legal framework only helps us name the product, but it does not demonstrate what and how the product signifies. In other words, I want to ask if the pirated product has a unique semiotics. As Roland Barthes says, current consumer culture functions through its heavy manipulation of significations, which he calls "myths."[2] In order to demythologize, we have to unveil the discursive framework that naturalizes culture. By studying the semiotics of the pirated product and the piracy discourse related to China, I confront two myths: the Western notion of China as a pirate nation, and the Chinese notion that creativity is the key to modernization. The two myths are unified in today's global creative economy, which dialectically reifies creativity and condemns mimesis.

One way to tackle the dichotomy between creativity and copying is to investigate the interconnection between them, and in this chapter I show that the semiotics of the counterfeit product and brand commodity share common connections with mimesis. I hope to provide a semiological perspective from which to interrogate the creative economy and examine whether mimesis can point us beyond the mechanism of control that characterizes Western modernity. I also hope that this examination of mimesis demonstrates a new rendering of the methodology of semiotics. Thanks to Barthes's seminal work, we have learned the skills of visual semiotics in understanding advertisements. Here I would like to supplement his analyses with the dimension of mimesis. In his analysis Barthes focuses primarily on a diachronic relationship between the commodity and the reader to understand how the commodity is understood; I want to add the synchronic dimension of mimesis to explore the relationships among commodities themselves. Let us begin with myths.

China the Pirate, Chinese the Uncreative

At a press conference in 2003 in Beijing, U.S. Commerce Secretary Donald Evans held up a bootleg DVD of *Kill Bill* as evidence of China's flagrant disregard for IPR.[3] The European Union repeated the act three years later; the "sublime object" that time was even more spectacular than Tarantino's violent film. With photographic evidence in hand, Franco Frattini, European commissioner for justice and home affairs, solemnly announced that the Chinese have finally managed to produce a fake Ferrari model.[4] The sensational news immediately hit the world media. This press conference was held to announce an EU proposal to adopt criminal legislation to combat intellectual property offenses, and the photo and accusation were calculated to attract media attention to an otherwise dry policy announcement. However, the accusation was a poor imitation of its American predecessor, as it turned out to be false: the "Ferrari" was actually produced in Thailand, another country famous for counterfeiting.[5]

Of the many pirated products frequently associated with China, this car stands out because of its spectacularity. First, it dissociates the stereotypical association between counterfeit production and female consumption (unlike counterfeit handbags, Ferrari is masculine through and through); second, which is more to my interest here, it effectively condenses the stereotypes and the mythos surrounding both piracy and China. There are two myths associated with this incident: that China is the chief pirate nation, and that copying is culturally inferior. Barthes argues that the signifier (in this case the pirated Ferrari) is both the final term of the linguistic system and the first term of the mythical system; the meaning arising from the first system is distorted and appropriated into the second system. In this case, the first (linguistic) system tells us that it is a pirated car, and the second (mythical) system itself is manifested as two myths: that China is the chief threat to the knowledge economy, and that China is backward because it makes copies.

From the perspective of the West, the Ferrari incident reflects China's current international image and its ambiguous position in the global economy. China has been stigmatized as the bootlegging capital of the world, a stereotype that the international community, particularly the U.S., has effectively exploited. Coercing China to play by international rules—that is, Western interests—is a major goal of current international diplomacy.[6] The stereotype of China as a pirate, regardless of how (in)accurate it is, is complicated by two other economic factors: China is the biggest foreign market for many international companies and is capable of producing any kind of commodity. In other words, China is tied to today's global capitalism in every sense.

It is clear that all major automobile companies and even governments are watching the Chinese market closely. The Congressional Budget Office of the Congress of the United States commissioned an elaborate report in 2006 to investigate how China's growing demand for oil, partly a result of the continually expanding car market in China, would have a considerable impact on the U.S. and global oil market, and thus on world order.[7] In early 2006 Ferrari held a high-profile exhibition in Shanghai's Henglong Plaza, featuring its most popular models; the intention was clearly to reach out to potential Ferrari buyers among the Chinese nouveau riche (Ferrari sold one hundred of its sedans in China in 2005).[8] But, to the frustration of many, China is not just a huge market; it is also a major competitor that does not necessarily play by the rules. The illegal car parts produced in China include routine replacement items like oil, fuel, and air filters, brake pads, and sparkplugs, but factories have increasingly been found producing more technically complex parts in large numbers.[9] Almost any commodity can be knocked off and reproduced in this "world factory," which makes many "genuine" products as well.

As Kelly Hu demonstrates, as a most powerful original equipment manufacturer in the global production system, China gains knowledge and skills from high-tech clients, who, however, maintain their monopoly on the most advanced technological knowledge, compulsory patent enforcement, and distribution channels. In order to realize its own technological modernization, China produces a vibrant internal economy by utilizing low-cost technology.[10] This explanation applies also to the car scene. On the one hand, China continues to be the world factory of auto parts. Many of the parts of a Ferrari are made in China,[11] making a made-in-China counterfeit Ferrari highly plausible. But in reality, Ferrari still makes the most technological advanced parts in their local plants, so China does not possess the knowledge and skills to replicate a real Ferrari. Instead China's car manufacturers develop a robust internal market with lower-end products. In 2003 China was not only the third-largest consumer market but also the fourth-largest automobile producer globally, and most of the Chinese-made cars are for the domestic market.[12] China produced some 10.8 million cars in 2008, while American car makers were projected to sell well under 10 million cars in 2009.[13]

The presence of foreign players in China's car scene is extremely diverse, from the direct import of real Ferraris to parts imported and reassembled in China, and from transnational collaborations—cars made specifically for the local market (e.g., Beijing Jeep, Guangzhou Toyota, Shanghai GM, and Beijing Hyundai)—to the manufacturing of car parts in China mainly for export. But a major sector of China's automobile market remains local; there are numerous local companies of varying sizes and brands with varying market values. While Japanese automobile companies have earned a great deal of profit from the Chinese market through direct sales and different forms of collaboration, many of them—such as Toyota, Honda, and Nissan—have filed IPR lawsuits against Chinese auto companies, claiming they have pirated their models.[14] Recently the competition has become so intense that while overseas car manufacturers sternly oppose the aggressive Chinese car industry, which allegedly steals their ideas and even copies entire models, fierce internal competition has left not one Chinese car company profitable. It's a lose-lose situation, concluded a Beijing car dealer.[15]

The EU's accusation of Chinese counterfeiting highlights how this international image of the "Chinese pirate" is inextricable from the enormous industrial production power China allegedly possesses. The powerful and demonic status of China, from both political and economic perspectives, is manifested and unified in its image as a criminal pirate, and this discourse of robbery supports and is supported by the fervent desire and fear of transnational capital. As a country keen on becoming a major player in the new economy, China seems to have internalized this pirate image. In response to the Ferrari accusation, an angry commentator wrote in *China Daily*, "The developed world is already wary of China's meteoric rise. It accuses us of undervaluing our goods and dumping them into other countries' markets. It imposes unjustifiable fines on 'made-in-China' products. It wants to save its domestic markets, but wants us to open ours fully. We are charged with wreaking havoc on the environment. In fact, we are made the scapegoat for every possible wrong that could occur in this world."[16] After these strong, emotional, and complex allegations, the commentator's conclusion and advice to the Chinese people is very simple: "Help China by not making and buying fakes." The rhetoric is straightforward: while China's position in international politics is too complex for ordinary Chinese to interrogate, they can at least give the international community less ammunition; in the end, the Chinese people are guilty of faking and buying fakes. But so is Celine Dion, who was caught purchasing over fifty counterfeit products, including bogus Louis Vuitton goods, before her concert in Shanghai in April 2008.[17]

With the reification of knowledge and creativity, a major ethical battleground of the current IPR regime is the protection of the author, as I demonstrated in chapter 3. The legitimate commodity has an author (or a team of them, or a brand), while the pirated product does not. If China is seen as a world pirate, the country then lacks an author or subject position in the eyes of the international community proper. Parallel to the international anxiety over and fascination with the stereotype of China's mimetic power is the Chinese people's own anxiety about their culture and their future in relation to creativity: In order to resurrect a legitimate Chinese agency in the global economy, we must create instead of mimic.

Unfortunately there is a certain degree of accuracy to this rather racist claim printed in the *New York Times*: "Even the Chinese will tell you that they've been good at making the next new thing, and copying the next new thing, but not imagining the next new thing."[18] As demonstrated in chapter 4, we are seeing a certain creativity syndrome in China. The Chinese academic database China National Knowledge Infrastructure shows a rapid rise in the

Table 3. Academic Journal Articles Published in
Mainland China Containing the Word "Creativity"
in Their Title

Year	Number of titles with the word "creativity"	Total number of journal articles	Rate (1/10,000)
1994	105	855,995	1.2
2000	291	1,387,282	2.1
2004	672	1,811,996	3.7
2008	2627	3,446,678	7.6

Source: China National Knowledge Infrastructure Database,
1994–2008.

number of academic journal articles that contained the word "creativity" (創
意 chuangyi). At more than a sixfold increase in the span of fourteen years,
the data indirectly witness China's hunger for creativity (table 3).[19]

Here we observe two interrelated causes of anxiety: there is a general fear
in the West of China's enormous industrial production capacity, whereas the
Chinese worry that they can only reproduce, and therefore are forced in directions determined by others. In other words, the West fears China's copying power, while China is concerned that it can only copy. Copying is feared
because it is both powerful and powerless, depending on where one sits and
what is at stake. As I mentioned in earlier chapters, the celebration of creativity and the condemnation of copying are foreign to traditional Chinese
culture. In fact this is not only an issue in China; the meanings of copying
and appropriation have also changed drastically in modern Western history.
As Jean Baudrillard argues, the concept of forgery is basically a product of
modernity; it was around the nineteenth century that copying began to be
considered illegitimate and no longer art.[20] Respect for property also has a
history in the West. Sea piracy was central to the foundational spirit of Western modernity; not long ago Dutch and northern piracy was the origin of ad-
venturism and expansionism, and many pirate activities in the sixteenth and
seventeenth centuries were in fact supported by colonizers.[21] The vigorous developments in the first decades of the twentieth century that made Hollywood
the international film center were also clearly achieved by diligent piracy of all
sorts.[22]

Let us now move from myth to the counterfeit product itself.

The Magical Power of Mimesis

Japan's Kirin Brewery Company, which owns not only its namesake beer but an enormous number of agricultural and pharmaceutical patents, has claimed that "offending IPR is China's specialty."[23] Underlying this criminalization is anger, a sense of insecurity, or even jealousy. But there is also an indirect recognition of a sort of magical power, in the sense that China can conjure up anything found in our present capitalist market, and this fascination and fear are driven fundamentally by the challenge of this copying capability to our modern rational world. I call this power the mimetic power, in line with a major stream in postcolonial criticism which challenges the legitimacy of an original power. As Homi Bhabha describes it, colonial mimicry mocks the founding objects of the Western world; for example, early nineteenth-century Bengalis gladly received Bibles because their pages could be used as wrapping paper.[24] Thus I use mimesis not according to the Platonic-Aristotelian tradition of mimesis as representation, but in the anthropological sense of mimesis as mimicry, which is prelinguistic and therefore zoologically antecedent to the Platonic sense of mimesis.[25] Mimetic activities, then, are social practices and interpersonal relations rather than results of rational processes of human agency—the making of models based on observations of the world. Mimesis as mimicry, as Walter Benjamin and René Girard explain, allows people to connect to other people and also invites one to locate one's own alterity.[26] Precisely because of its prelinguistic nature, this kind of mimesis provides a model by which to understand human relations that are not confined to the modern Western experience.

To understand a material object through the concept of mimesis, we might start with Benjamin's seminal essay "The Work of Art in the Age of Mechanical Reproduction." The concept of mimesis is not mentioned therein, but its central concern is precisely the changes in the function and mechanism of mimesis in the modern world, which can be summarized thus: "Mechanical reproduction emancipates the work of art from its parasitical dependence on ritual."[27] Ritual is primarily mimetic, but it produces differences. The emancipation of the work of art is based upon a drastic technological change from ritual (the past) to mechanical reproduction (the modern). The premodern form of mimesis must attach to ritual, of which every performance is unique, while mechanical reproduction autonomizes and perfects the mimetic mechanism, which produces identical products.

Benjamin's position in relation to the modern and premodern forms of mimesis is slightly ambiguous; he interlinks instead of dichotomizes the two.

But his concluding predisposition is well known: it is the mechanically re-produced art, specifically cinema, that is capable of politicizing aesthetics and releasing the more culturally productive force of technology. This thesis of mechanically reproductive mimesis can be juxtaposed to the contemporary image of China as pirate: piracy has been so painstakingly criminalized in the new creative economy because of its enormous reproductive capacities. China's pirate image seems to distantly echo Benjamin's vision. Unlike its Fordist predecessor, the post-Fordist commodity is increasingly individualized because of the creativity and originality supposedly invested in it. Piracy duplicates and proliferates such forces, giving a new reading and new application of Benjamin's theorization of modern mechanical reproduction, as it reflects a (post)modern mode of technological reproduction that is beyond control. It does not even matter if this particular phony Ferrari is mass-produced; an army of them will come, as implied by Frattini's fearful accusation. In other words, the authentic commodity is endowed with a kind of aura, and the counterfeit product destroys this aura.

However, piracy is not just a politicized art; we would overlook much of piracy's power if we understood it only as simulacrum. Benjamin dichotomizes mimesis as modern (mechanical reproduction) and premodern (ritual), and piracy effectively demonstrates the problems of such dichotomization. While it is clear that the impacts of piracy's mimetic power are destructive to the order of the creative economy, the causes of this destruction are not ideological. There is a certain magical power associated with, for example, the Chinese ability to conjure up a Ferrari. The Italians are proud of the intelligence, handicraft, technology, and even taste that have been built into the brand after many years of research and refinement. How could China produce a fake with such ease and wizardry? Using Benjamin's vocabulary, if the Italian car builder is a surgeon who cautiously and scrupulously penetrates the car's body and builds it bit by bit, the Chinese pirate is a magician who maintains the natural distance between the car and himself. Does she perform the magic by simply laying hands on some unrefined metal, or by casting a spell? There is also a mythical aura about the fake Ferrari that cannot be contained within the normalized logic of present-day capitalism.

Accordingly, piracy can also be understood as a "premodern" form of mimesis, which is not just a specter of the past. Piracy is the negative definition not only of the current IPR legal regime but also of the social and cultural structure of capitalist modernity, so that inevitably piracy is associated with both modern crime and premodern irrationality. The developed world's fear of China's piracy capabilities is real. The frightening and fascinating dimension of the counterfeit Ferrari resides not only in the damage done to the real Ferrari, but also in the difficulty of attaching any fixed meaning or value to the fake car. Piracy is associated with contradictory meanings, in that it is both postmodern, as self-reproducible simulacrum, and premodern, as magic, so that the counterfeit product is infused with meanings that can subvert the rationality and the order of modern society which safely houses the genuine brand-name commodity.

However, what I really want to demonstrate is not their absolute differ-ences but the intricate connections between commodity and counterfeit; the two are different from yet similar to each other. It is true that there is not a fixed discursive framework to teach us how to relate to counterfeit prod-ucts, in contrast to the seemingly more stable price and knowledge network grounding commodity: some people consume counterfeit products simply because of their price and function, and many want to appear to possess a particular brand, but others like these products precisely because they are not "real." Because counterfeiting is criminalized by the dominant legal eco-nomic structure, there is no legal basis for legitimizing ownership and proper consumption of counterfeit products. But we should not assume that the counterfeit is the opposite of the commodity. Appadurai argues that the pro-duction and the consumption of commodities require very complex social forms and distributions of knowledge, and the various types of knowledge define the commodities' "life histories." While much technological, social, and aesthetic knowledge go into a commodity's production, knowledge is also required to consume it appropriately.[28] To Appadurai, a commodity has a social life because it constantly interacts with the world through the changing knowledge invested in and extracted from it. In other words, a commodity ac-quires its identity through a process that is constantly transforming. Similarly a counterfeit product also has its own social life, but the kinds of knowledge apposite to a counterfeit product seem to be less controllable and predictable. As the interviews Shujen Wang conducted with many Chinese pirated VCD consumers show, consumers purchasing these items have extremely diversi-fied interests and intentions, but they all also demonstrate a desire and a con-scious decision, very similar to the consumption of authentic goods, to make sense of the fast changing world around them.[29] The empirical data drawn by Jason Rutter and Jo Bryce also indicate that patterns of consumption of counterfeit and piracy products echo that of consumption of legal goods.[30] While there could be research showing the exact opposite tendency, these findings remind us that the genuine commodity and the counterfeit product might share many common traits.

The value of a genuine commodity is allegedly governed by production costs and market demand; this is also true of a counterfeit product, with the complication that a counterfeit's costs and markets are only partly conditioned by the genuine commodity. In terms of production costs, there are two very different systems governing the value of the counterfeit, one based entirely on the original product, and one based specifically on the production of the pirated product, which might be extremely slipshod. In terms of market demand, the counterfeit has its own market, yet it also exploits both the marketing and the residual market of the genuine brand. It becomes very difficult, therefore, to assign a price to the counterfeit Ferrari. Should it be cheaper or more expensive than a counterfeit BMW? Should it be priced according to its condition and quality (use value), or its brand image (exchange value), or its secondhand market value (surplus value)? It is also more difficult to be certain of the hierarchy of brand names in the world of counterfeiting. The consensus among Chinese pirates is that the Prada nylon bag is the most profitable pirated item because it is extremely easy to make and the materials are cheap.[31] The production value of Prada bags might be extremely high, but the reproduction costs of the pirated bags are very low, thus allowing the brand name to pervade the pirated goods market. The unsettling and powerful counterfeit product—the mimetic object—is enchanted partly because it cannot be abstracted into stable value.

Of course, the counterfeit Prada bag is so pervasive in the piracy market also because of the power of the brand. Chinese people's common vocabulary of international brand names has increased exponentially in the past decade. International brand-name products proliferate in department stores, which are located in major shopping malls and on main shopping boulevards. But their effects are more visual than tactile, as these brand-name products are far too expensive for the average Chinese person; this echoes Benjamin's description of the shopping culture in nineteenth-century Paris, which privileged seeing over touching.[32] The vast Chinese commodity markets are not yet monopolized by megabrands and transnational corporations, as are Western markets. For example, "the rapidly-growing MP3 players market in China is crowded with more than four hundred brands, mostly local ones with most of them capturing less than 1% of market share."[33]

But this does not mean that the Chinese government does not care about branding, which is in fact one of the top items on the national agenda. China is now the second largest economy in the world, but in terms of per capita income, the country occupies ninety-second place on the World Bank list.[34] Missing in the formula, many would claim, is the ability of Chinese firms to combine their cost advantage in production with higher value-added activities such as branding. According to the Development Research Center of the State Council PRC, the strongest components of China's economy are the country's labor force and production costs, and the weakest is its brandscape.[35] Some national brands are emerging, and a few such as Haier and Lenovo, have been major successes. Internationally the Haier Group is the world's fourth largest manufacturer of electrical home appliances, while Lenovo is the fourth largest company in the worldwide PC market. Tsingtao beer has decided to relaunch itself internationally outside the overseas Chinese community by targeting Western mainstream markets. China Mobile also makes it to the ninth of the most valuable global brands in 2011. Even traditional cultures engage in the same pursuit, as demonstrated in the recent case of Shaolin Temple's failure to apply for a Shaolin Medicine trademark for the food products it produces.[36] The development of Chinese brand names could be the driving force in the advancement of the country's industrial and economic portfolio, and it is also believed to be an effective way to elevate China's global image.[37]

The world of branding is highly hierarchal, with certain Western brands being the ultimate objects of desire and local brands trying in vain to catch up. Such fierce competition can be understood as competition of signification effectiveness, backed by marketing programs of different kinds. In a way, the brand offers an authorial signature, endowing the product with a kind of originality; thus that the brand functions as a metaphor, providing a semantic link from the commodity to a concept or a quality in a fixed and direct way. However, the actual ways the brand signifies are more ambiguous. Brand is a concept and an entity which fits very well with Raymond Williams's understanding of the unfixed and multiple forms of exchange that permeate people's "structures of feeling," which are not personal but social and collective.[38] As Celia Lury elaborates, brand is at heart performative, in the sense that it is the interface promoting, realizing, and also unifying the many different consumer expectations for the product(s).[39] The kind of creativity celebrated in recent capitalist society must not be understood as an end but as a means—not realized through a specific material product but manifested as a constant mutation that prevents the arrival at any final product.

The reification of brand, then, is not unrelated to mimesis. According to Lury, the creativity invested in branding does not rest in the product as new, but in the brand image as performative: "Brand innovation need not derive or emerge from innovation in the organization of the production process. Instead, it may be produced in the practices of simulation or behavior modeling—that is, through qualification trials in which products are experimentally tested in relation to the goal or aim of reaching a target market."[40] Because the ultimate signified—consumerist desire—is extremely volatile, the kinds of creativity invested in branding cannot be directed toward individual final products, which are destined to be displaced quickly. Each commodity is imbued with a built-in mechanism that leads the consumer to desire another commodity: I buy this camera in order to buy the next new model, although the succession of new cameras is unified by brand significations in terms of image, technology, or knowledge, "the whole point of modernity and capitalist competition being that technology and manufactured products are made obsolescent by progress' forward march."[41] The magic of mimesis ultimately also defines the magic of consumerism as performative, and it promises (but always fails) to reach the ultimate signified. If I may link the performativity of brand marketing to that of pirated objects, we might observe an odd connection between branding and piracy: the brand-name commodity and the counterfeit product each carries a metonymical movement that constantly displaces itself.

Postcolonial critics are interested in mimesis largely because of its transformative potential, which generates effects that are destructive to colonial hegemony.[42] However, we need to pay attention to the fact that the commodity also has this dimension of metonymical displacement, which must be stabilized by the brand: the brand "is."[43] Metonymy is a teleologically controlled trope, which, on the one hand, conjures otherwise unrelated terms and images into a signification process, and on the other hand, is governed by an invisible force that eludes figuration.[44] This linguistic concept can also be applied to commodity: metonymy allows us to label dynamic interactions between part (the commodity) and whole (brand), in the sense that it is the brand which provides a unity for the commodities constantly displacing each other in the market. It is this kind of teleologically controlled movement that makes the brand commodity attractive to consumers: it is always new but not radically so.

Precisely due to this powerful mimetic process, consumerism, as Michael Taussig states, has replaced colonialism to become the main hegemonic force of contemporary culture.[45] Mediated by commodities, the old colonial system has been converted into a new form of commodity imperialism. The mimetic faculty continues to be manipulated by dominating powers, yet because of the displacement of power from colonialism's privilege of an original source to consumerism's ubiquitous dissemination, it has also become more difficult for the manipulated to recognize and escape their manipulation. The active consumer is lured into the belief that he or she is the originator of taste, not ordered by some powerful party like the colonial master, and is unaware that this master position is only replaced by the brand.

In light of the dynamic metonymical movements governing branding, we might be able to come up with a new understanding of the makeup of IPR. As I demonstrated in chapter 3, copyrights, trademarks, patents, trade secrets, and other items making up IPR are rooted in different cultural and historical contexts and different international treaties, and the IPR regime is a recent WTO construct that artificially conflates all these rights. This sweeping generalization and categorization of disparate rights are painstakingly put in place to legitimize the IPR regime. In terms of the dynamics between transformation and stability, we could group patent and copyright together as constructs to promote profits generated from new works and inventions, whereas trademarks, trade secrets, and geographical indications protect and perpetuate existing monopolies. In the case of Nike, the singularity of the swoosh is protected by trademark laws to perpetuate its market domination, while the company constantly applies for new patents to substantiate the brand's pride in so-called state-of-the-art shoe technology. For example, Nike claims that there are nineteen separate patents protecting its SHOX system, yet what really matters is not these patents but the differentiation between Nike and Adidas.[46] Our new economy needs protection from both directions, in that the enormous amount of R&D investment in ever changing product lines is protected by patent and copyright, and trademark and trade secrets laws guarantee the continued domination of the established brand names. A wholehearted embrace and encouragement of creativity could be drastically detrimental to the status quo, and the existing hegemony needs proper protection from such destabilizing effects. It is therefore not enough to isolate any one of the constitutive rights as symptomatic of the entire functioning of the new economy, but it is through their interactions and negotiations within the new IPR confines that the contrived late capitalist logic is perpetuated.

Benjamin understands premodern mimesis mostly from the perspective of the performative act, emphasizing that each performance, and each attendance, is different from any other. "Aura" is a result of such productions of differences and authenticity.[47] He therefore discusses the power of ritual mainly according to its temporal dimension and the changes it makes possible. But in the discussion of commodity and counterfeit products, we can explore how a stable material object can be mimetic on its own. In fact Benjamin also briefly mentions the power of static objects, and he suggests that many statues of gods and madonnas are hidden from the general masses because of their specific ritualistic use.[48] According to Benjamin, the veiling and seclusion of the religious artifact reflect the dichotomy between cult values and exhibition values: the less often it is seen, the higher its cult value. Underlying this dichotomy is the assumption that each exhibition is powerful and unique, and the meanings of the artifact are made anew each time it is seen or is involved in the performance of rituals. In other words, although the artifact is fixed and inert, its significations change. While Benjamin's criticism mostly concerns the clergy's exclusive ownership of works of art, we might extend his observation to an understanding of how an object might be endowed with mimetic effects, particularly if they are religiously defined.

In Christian thought, the sign (as iconic) is considered religiously more truthful than the symbol (as idolatry), because the sign points beyond itself to reach the divine being, whereas the symbol retains power and might provoke, attract, or encourage idolatry.[49] In Christian aesthetics, art should never stop moving, because the iconic, which is also mimetic, moves toward the divine, whereas idolatry invites the gaze to cease looking beyond the symbol.[50] Time and change are important elements in Christian thinking: while the ultimate signified—God—stays transcendental and permanent, all arts dedicated to it are moving, transient, and unreliable. It is precisely this motion and instability that makes the artwork powerful.

This understanding of religious art is not unique to Christian thought; many other religious traditions have similar views of their ritualistic artifacts, which are religious precisely because they cannot figuratively portray their gods.[51] If the artifact is aware of its "representation" of a higher "unrepresentable" being, it cannot be confident in itself because of the distance between readings and meanings dramatized in religious art. If a human being (whether producer or viewer) is aware of his or her own impotence in reaching the divine through a particular work, the signified cannot be fixed within the work. However, this does not mean that the signified of the iconic art is free-floating or empty. As Paul de Man explains, religious art is often understood on the basis of structuralist symbolism, which assumes that all cultural expressions are manifestations of a set of ultimate symbols or archetypal stories.[52] The iconic movement of Christian art is clearly structured.

Accordingly, our understanding of brand-name commodities might benefit from studies of religious arts. It is true that capitalism is more a way of life than a belief system, so that commodities are not religious, and it does not point to an ultimate signified as Christian art does. However, capitalism provides a cult system with its own elaborate set of beliefs and values (e.g., market as god, commodity as fetish), which promote social solidarity and stability.[53] So brand-name commodities are like religious symbols in their reliance on a secure system in which god and brand name stabilize the object's metonymical movement. We can take the Mao badge,[54] or other similar "secular iconic" objects, as examples to demonstrate the difficulties of such balances. Collected today as both a personal protecting charm and an item for capital appreciation, the Mao badge is doubly fetishized because it is both sacred and commercialized, both magical and collectable. But due to the two signification systems functioning simultaneously, both Mao's divine figure and the Mao brand become less stable than most other religious artifacts and commodities. Market value and supernatural value define and delimit each other, so that the badge becomes not really magical, yet not completely disposable.[55] The significations of the Mao badge, being both a commodity and a religious sign, are very difficult to pin down. The mysterious identity of the counterfeit product is like the Mao badge, in the sense that in both cases the signification evades the capitalist system.

Kenneth S. Rogerson argues that the information age is characterized by the tension between two dynamics: "first, the tendency of information to be free flowing and not to lose its value as it moves, and second, the tendency to want to control that flow of information in order to profit from its value."[56] We might use the same model to understand the creativity invested in brand-name commodities, in that their significations, however fluid, must be controlled to secure and benefit the dominant discursive system. The brand is set up to relate each commodity to another in diachronic terms, such as generation, or synchronic terms, such as niche market. Like the religious transcendental, the brand name also links the diversified receptions and consumptions to generate the desire of coherent consumption, although its ultimate signified is impossible to define.

The Politics of Mimesis

So far I have demonstrated that both the commodity and the counterfeit are signified metonymically; while the commodity's movements are governed by the brand, the counterfeit is based both on the original brand name and something more irrational and arbitrary, which is outside of capitalist control. The key question remains whether such counterfeit residue can effectively subvert the ultimate signified, that is, the capitalist order. I am not optimistic, and I do not believe that we could hold on to the actual social functions and effects of piracy as a kind of responsible subversion. The current trend of hacking activism relies heavily on a politics of liberty, in that hacking realizes a form of freedom specific to the information age.[57] Popular writers like Matt Mason also describe the contemporary pirate as the "guardian of free speech who promotes efficiency, innovation, and creativity."[58] I agree that hacking and piracy could both unsettle the dominant systems, but we cannot use a leftist liberal perspective to understand piracy, because most piracy is, to different extents, driven by the desire for the commodity. In fact some corporations are highly conscious of the advertising effects of piracy, and designers like Stussy, Hilfiger, Polo, DKNY, and Nike have refused to crack down on the pirating of their logos on T-shirts and baseball hats in American inner cities because, according to Naomi Klein, the big brands know that the wide presence of their logo in the right, namely black, neighborhoods could create an enormous advertising effect globally.[59]

We should recognize the cultural productivity of some of these IPR offenses; an entire new generation of Chinese filmmakers has been taught the art of cinema through pirated movies, and new video works made up of copyrighted materials proliferate on the Internet.[60] However, the actual effects of many of these forgeries cannot be romanticized. One of the most heartbreaking examples took place in 2004, when knockoff baby formula caused the deaths of twelve infants and serious malnutrition in more than 220 others in China.[61] And in April and May 2006 bogus Armillarisin A injections produced by Qiqihar No. 2 Pharmaceutical Company caused the deaths of at least nine people and kidney failure in many others.[62] That Chinese company is by no means a pirate factory, but a renowned state-owned company with more than three hundred registered workers. It just happened that a corrupt merchandizing manager purchased an important component of the injection, propylene glycol, from a pirate.

In fact counterfeit drugs are found all over the world, and people in developing countries are particularly at risk.[63] Those in the developed world find these fatal incidents shocking mostly because they have taken commodities for granted. Would any parent doubt the nutritional value of a beautifully packaged baby formula sold in supermarkets? Would patients question the medication they receive in hospitals? Consumer society, however diversified it has become, needs coherency, just as iconic arts need god. While it may be arguable to call medicine a commodity, we must admit the important position of the drug and the health industries in the new economy. As IPR concerns are most contested in drug-related fields, the simple romanticism of piracy would also prove the most problematic there.

In China the drug industry spends the largest amount of money on advertising. In 2001 eight of the top ten most-advertised corporations were pharmaceutical companies. In 2009 medical and health-related companies continued to contribute 37 percent of the annual growth of newspaper advertisement.[64] In China health products most frequently carry brand names, and the aforementioned fatal piracy cases are detrimental to China's pharmaceutical industry. However, this subversion is provisional and weak because it only challenges China's, not the global, medical industry. Hong Kong's retail drugstores, for example, benefit from drug frauds in China; thousands of mainland tourists go to Hong Kong every day to buy medicine and baby food. Widespread piracy does not dismantle people's trust in brands; more affluent Chinese simply shift their consumption activities to other places, like Hong Kong, a more abstract brand name they now trust.[65] Parents might not have faith in any brand-name baby formula found in China, but they trust anything sold in Hong Kong. In this case, the capitalist system does not break down, but in some sense is reinforced. Such minor crises only reinforce people's longing for a better capitalist system.

A counterfeit product might disturb global capitalism because of its illegal position, which escapes and subverts any form of macro control. But a pirated product, although negating the brand-name commodity, is ultimately parasitical to the original commodity, so that the consumption of a counterfeit product also indirectly reinforces the value of the model. Counterfeiting is a function, however distorted, of the brand name, and the disruptions it causes are easily remedied by the commodity market itself; it is only China's fault for tolerating piracy, not the fault of "the market." Bhabha's celebration of the Bengali use of the Bible as wrapping paper might not apply to the actual use of counterfeit products, as the Christian god is probably not signified in the use of the individual pieces of paper, but many are attracted to counterfeit products precisely because of the exchange value of the original brand.

I now return to the theme of demythologization. In July 2006 three people, including one Coca-Cola employee, were charged with stealing the Coca-Cola Company's trade secrets and trying to sell them to PepsiCo Inc. The two companies are perennial enemies, but when Pepsi received a letter from someone offering to sell Coke's trade secrets, it went straight to its rival, which initiated an immediate FBI investigation.[66] I am not surprised by Pepsi's righteous response, as this notion of trade secrets really holds together the soft drink industry to which Pepsi, of course, belongs. However, I remain extremely doubtful about the secrets contained in those documents. Considering the extremely large number and variety of soft drinks in the market, how could this market be held together without some kind of mythical aura? In a memo concerning the case, Coca-Cola Chief Executive Officer Neville Isdell writes, "While this breach of trust is difficult for all of us to accept, it underscores the responsibility we each have to be vigilant in protecting our trade secrets. Information is the lifeblood of the company." To be more precise, it is the company's ability to uphold the myth of trade secrets that allows its pseudo-individual commodities to continue to flood the market. By resorting to trade secrets laws, these soft-drink companies prevent their consumers from reading the products, and therefore from understanding the market mechanisms.

As mentioned in the beginning of the chapter, I am interested in exploring the semiotics of the counterfeit product in order to understand the logic of the negative meanings associated with copying. As I have demonstrated, both the counterfeit and its model are governed first by the semiotics of mimesis, and second by the capitalist drive. The two are connected in the sense that the metonymical movements comprising the objects' semiotics need the grounding of an economic system. Or, to look at the situation from another perspective, it is this constantly displacing economic system that needs the myth of creativity to hold it together. Barthes demonstrates two ways to counter mythologization: through the poetic language that proliferates, and therefore transforms the sign back into meanings, and through labor, which does not mediate but links oneself to the object directly.[67] The latter is the language of revolution, which is equivalent to an act of penetrating the object and destroying it. This is an option unconsciously taken by many IPR critics, who choose to focus on political economy or legal polemics to understand piracy and counterfeiting, in which the actual objects, either the commodity or the counterfeit, are there to be deconstructed.

I choose the poetic approach advocated by Barthes, because I want to take the material object more seriously. Instead of destroying it in a single stroke, I choose to politicize by poeticizing the object, so that it—both the counterfeit product and the commodity—can be transformed from a sign back to a contested site embodying multiple sources of meaning. But I also try to avoid Barthes's visual bias, as he tends to see the commodity as just a sheer surface or veil, waiting to be peeled off in order to reach the hidden meanings.[68] As Baudrillard writes, the magic of today's consumption culture is the assimilation of commodity and sign into an object form, "on which use value, exchange value and sign value converge in a complex mode."[69] What we need, then, is a politics of mimetic reading that refuses to be shut down by such a system of mimetic control. I believe this reading is particularly warranted in China, where too many people see commodity as the object of desire, and capital the ultimate signified.

Currently the discourse of *dajia* 打假 (combating fakes) pervades Chinese media and government policy.[70] There is a proliferation of media pro-

grams and news coverage to educate the masses on how to avoid falling victim to fraud. Objects of condemnation range from unsafe food to dangerous
electronic apparatuses, and from academic plagiarism to reporters falsifying
news. A most ironic case is a news report that aired on the highly popular television program *Transparency* (透明度 *Toumingdu*) on Beijing Television's Life
Channel, which reported that some dumplings sold in Beijing are stuffed with
the same materials that are used to make carton boxes.[71] The news shocked
dumpling-loving Beijingers, but soon the complaint was found to have been
masterminded by the television station's own staff, who asked a food stall
to make dumplings out of the stuffing already prepared in order to fabri-
cate another piece of scandalous news. Jing Wang argues that one major difference between advertising in the West and in China is the importance of
safety to Chinese consumers: "It is 'safety' rather than 'desire' that speaks to
consumers across regions and social strata in China."[72] I certainly agree with
Wang's insight into the importance of product safety among the vast Chinese citizenry, but I insist on understanding the mechanism of "desire" with
wider resonances. The dumpling event demonstrates that safety, and therefore the identification of forgery, has itself become a form of desire, to the extent that forgery must be forged in order to satisfy a mass audience obsessed
with condemning their "phony" nation. The dumpling event is not just about
food safety; it also reveals the Chinese people's modernization urge, that they
desire to detect and identify with the backwardness of their country in order
to give them a sense of control, not unlike the blockbuster-bashing phenomenon I mentioned in the introduction.

Chasing a modernization dream, the Chinese people form their identification around the commodity and are therefore mercilessly exploited by
the capitalist market. As suggested earlier, China is positioned as a pirate by
the developed world because there is no other position in which the country
can be placed. If piracy is merely a fast track, all the evils associated with the
capitalist system are manifested much more hastily and dramatically through
piracy. Piracy itself definitely cannot be romanticized as a Maoist guerrilla
action, as piracy largely demonstrates the disorder resulting from China's
frantic adoption of capitalism.[73] In order to counter such dense mythological
systems, we need to commit to a mythological reading, reflecting carefully
on the ways contemporary China is entangled in capitalism. The fanatic capitalist society found in China and all over the world is constituted by objects
encoded with a complex and glistering system of signs, which attract our attention and lure us into perpetual consumption and perpetual indifference.
I find counterfeit products an interesting case for interrogation because they

are an extreme manifestation of commodity obsession, and a careful reading of the object form of the counterfeit necessarily sheds light on the sign system of the commodity itself. I believe that we need to regain our reading capacity to understand the current creative economy that actually robs us of our ability to read. Precisely because mimesis can be so easily tamed, we need to *hold* on to a politics of mimesis that prevents us from falling into the trap of abstraction.

Imitation or Appropriation Arts?

This chapter focuses on the notion of appropriation. I hope that these three chapters provide a kaleidoscopic view, though far from comprehensive, of a wide range of counterfeit activities happening in China, from pirated media products and magazines to counterfeit Ferrari and Prada bags, as well as the knockoff paintings to be discussed in this chapter. This final chapter also continues my previous discussions of the common metonymic signification and mimetic movement of the commodity and counterfeit object, which will lead us back to a discussion of authorship. Appropriation arts is a genre of the fine arts that most ostensibly demonstrates a production of sliding meaning, and the authorship articulated in this art form is less conducive to the discourse of ownership. As this book is primarily a critique of creativity being incorporated into the apparatus of late capitalism, I would like to conclude with a commitment to the logic of culture, which should be built on relations instead of possessions. For this I will continue to investigate the meaning of the author.

While different national laws might define copyright in slightly different ways, in general, for a work to secure copyright protection, it must be (1) an expression instead of simply an idea; (2) original and authored by an identifiable agency; and (3) fixed in a tangible medium by some form of technology. In a previous work I elaborated the problematics of the expression-idea dichotomy.[1] Here my primary task is to analyze the economic structure that dominates the rational basis of copyright, so I focus on the second and third criteria, which I believe reflect the complex relations between author and technology, also making it possible for intangible materials to become "property."

At stake in the commodification of intellectual property is a certain author–

technology relationship that leads to the reification of the author function. Primary ownership of an immaterial product must first be established before it can be transferred and circulated, without which the commodification of this immaterial product is impossible. This primary ownership, conditioned within the logic of Western modernity, is defined by its first creation: the author as the owner.[2] The author is differentiated from a traditional laborer in the immaterial products that he or she produces.[3] But in order to substantiate the logic of ownership, the intangible product must somehow be embodied in a quantifiable and circulatable form, and herein lies copyright's paradox: "tangible form" refers only to the final product, while the very expression of copyright protection is necessarily intangible.[4]

According to this rationale, to make the necessary connection between the intangible source and the tangible product there must be, first, an agency identified as the creator-owner (which fulfills the second criterion), and second, agency must be reproduced through some kind of technological mediation into a tangible product (the third criterion). The role of the author and the role of technology are responsible for two important stages of the production of copyrightable material. The author first formulates expressions, which are to be transformed by technology into circulatable form; for example, a painter uses a set of techniques to express himself or herself on the canvas. Although not explicitly stated in the copyright definition, essential to the commodification of culture are the ways authorship and technology correspond with each other, so that it is authorship—instead of technology—that is being reified, although both are indispensable to the copyright concept. Technology is a neutral tool employed by the author to embody his or her expressions in tangible form, so that it is the photographer, for example, who is in command of the camera instead of the other way around. In this chapter I pose an alternative model for understanding the relationship between the author and the mediating technology, exemplified by the politics and characters of appropriation arts. Actively conversing with and integrating other cultural works, appropriation arts often embody the intimate and nonhierarchical relationship between the artist and the utilized technology, which brings us to reexamine the current problematic understanding of authorship. Two recent pieces of Chinese appropriation art intriguingly manifest many thorny issues related to mimesis, pertaining not only to art making but also to the current system of global cultural production in general. The two pieces also inform our understanding of contemporary China largely because of their strong social embeddedness. Before I begin my explication of these two pieces, let me first explore the political dimension of appropriation arts.

Appropriation and Style

Appropriation art has been understood in many different ways and can be connected to a diverse range of aesthetic intentions, such as mockery, homage, or social criticism, as long as the work refers to or draws on existing works. I define appropriation art as a piece of work which is aware of mimesis as its major component and reveals a strong consciousness of its relation with the appropriated, so that the act and the scope of copying are foregrounded instead of taken for granted. Accordingly, appropriation art is a genre very aware of issues of power and privilege.[5] Such relational awareness also prevents the work from being self-enclosed, which I believe is this genre's most important feature.

The notion of appropriation is important to many contemporary critical theories, such as postcolonialism, due to its transgressive and negotiatory effects.[6] Appropriation art is also often understood in political terms; the form can break boundaries and help artists question things usually taken for granted by the establishment. For example, the Dadaists' found objects are important to modern arts because they help us rethink the entire construction of art and the museum in the Western tradition. What Sherrie Levine, Barbara Kruger, and many other appropriation artists have done in the past few decades demonstrates how such awareness allows contemporary appropriation art to stay self-reflexive in its exploration of the nature of art. At the same time, appropriation art is often employed to call into question the logic of copyright, as the art form embodies the endless chain of creativity that the copyright regime tries to limit.

However, appropriation is also prone to being commodified. It is widely recognized that during the past twenty or thirty years, collage and appropriation works have been further appropriated by popular culture and have now become mainstream. This is clearly seen in music: while new mixing technologies and possibilities are integral to the development of new analog and digital formats, they are also utilized in commercial music to commodify the mixing practices and selected musical repertoires.[7] Appropriation has also lost its edge in the fine arts. As the art critic John C. Welchman summarizes, "By the 1990s, singular, or programmatic appropriation, focusing on the relatively unassisted citation of an individual image or object, was largely a thing of the past, and the language of postmodern appropriation, complete with a core of critical assumptions, had passed into something like general currency."[8] Acknowledging this general tendency, Douglas Crimp is skeptical of any political effect that appropriation arts might claim: "Appropriation, pastiche, quotation—these methods extend to virtually every aspect of our culture, from the most cynically calculated products of the fashion and entertainment industries to the most committed critical activities of artists. . . . If all aspects of the culture use this new operation, then the operation itself cannot indicate a specific reflection upon the culture."[9] Crimp's assertion is valid, and he points out a major dilemma in the discourse of appropriation: originally a critical response to the dominant hegemony, appropriation has now become the status quo. So widely employed in the arts and other cultural domains, the mechanism of appropriation has lost all its original political power, and commodification is a key factor behind this.

More to my interests here is not popular culture's ability to appropriate alternative cultures, but the concept of the author. It is very difficult to argue whether rap music, for example, is appropriation art or a form of fashion, not only because the musical form has been commodified, but also because rap is essentially a collective culture which embraces an open community of authors, allowing followers to participate in the creation of songs to easily make rap into a trend. A trend is not authored by a single artist, so it is not copyrightable, as indicated in the second copyright criterion. This leads to the interesting remark made by the experimental musical group Negativland: "Observing this now generally culture-wide acceptance of collage's appropriation methodologies, one would think that sympathetic laws of allowance would also emerge to encourage the practice and assure that it is able to proceed legally. But that has not yet happened."[10] Why? Because authorship is still essential in the creative economy, and without the author function transaction becomes impossible. The contemporary creative economy tackles this copyright dilemma by resorting to other IPR means, specifically the trademark, so that it is the brand name that extracts objects from the chain of appropriation into a self-contained form to be owned by a specific entity. When appropriation is appropriated by commodification, the stabilization force of the brand must be in place, as discussed in the previous chapter. Today's fashion industry relies on trademark alone instead of copyright to protect its styles.[11] The contradictory capitalist impulses of deterritorialization and reterritorialization can be accommodated by different components of IPR: copyright privileges the unified author function, and trademark privileges the unified brand function, so that the ownership of industrial products lacking identifiable authors can be conjured up through registered brand names.

In other words, style or fashion becomes a commodity only after its inherent transformative tendency is consolidated by trademark, and commodity society mitigates the pluralizing effects of appropriation by resorting to the pseudo-unifying effect of the brand name. Understood in this way, there is an even more urgent demand for appropriation art to resist these unifying effects. There might be different ways to resist the enclosure of the ownership-driven author function; I suggest a reexamination of the relationship between the author and its copyright counterpart, the technology involved, because the two are mutually conditioning. Copyright requires technological intervention to fix the intangible material into a tangible form, but technology can also achieve the reverse, releasing textuality to its proliferation, thereby also liberating the author function.

Authorship and Technology

Let us take a look at two key mass reproduction technologies: printing and photography. Modern printing technology, which is the foundation of print capitalism, can be utilized to fix creativity, but it can also unleash creative energy. As mentioned in chapter 3, the rise of both copyright and piracy in early modern Europe was a response to the advent of mass printing. Although printing technologies turn intangible ideas into tangible materials for mass consumption, the same technologies also release the diffusing effects of textuality, so that people other than the author can easily appropriate these ideas. The rise of copyright is situated in this paradox: printing technology both realizes and diffuses the concept of authorship. The copyright system confers upon the author the right to own his or her work, but this right is based on the recognition that writing is always a systematic practice of transgression, challenging any unified notion of the author. Paradoxically, as Foucault points out, the transgressive effects of writing are publicly recognized only through the legal establishment of copyright.[12] When new printing technology gave rise to copyright, it also realized the transgressive force of textuality.

The other pertinent technology for the mass reproduction of representation is photography. As Bernard Edelman explains, photographic representation allows us to transgress the boundary between public and private, appropriating something originally public as one's own.[13] Although the objects photographed, such as a street or a seashore, might belong to the public sphere, one can hold copyright to photographs of these objects because they meet the copyright criteria: they are authored by the photographer, and they are rendered into tangible form as photographs. In photography the authorial labor and the technological intervention take place at the same time, with the click of the shutter. It is the authorial click that defines the intangible essence of the intellectual property, and it is the technological click that fixes it in its tangible form. However, in addition to fixing authorial creativity in a tangible form, photographic technology also diffuses the authorial function by democratizing creativity. The easy operation of the camera allows everyone to be a photographer (or lately, video artist), so that the fine line between professional and amateur can easily be crossed, and whether photography is art is a debate as old as the form itself.

As the development of appropriation art attests, there is often an interesting connection between appropriation and new technology: appropriation is most aesthetically and politically powerful when a new technology is utilized to create a new art form. For example, the concept of appropriation art is intertwined with the systematic use of photography in conceptual art.[14] The attempts of such pop artists as Andy Warhol and Roy Lichtenstein, who creatively utilized existing technologies like photography and silkscreen printing as reference to and commentary on lifestyles and consumerism in the 1960s, initiated the first wave of contemporary appropriation art. While it took time for photography to rise to the level of fine art, video art flourished when video technology was first widely used in the 1970s, and video art is often related to acts of appropriation, as shown in the video works of Nam June Paik.[15] Video art has been highly self-conscious of its appropriative power largely because of its awareness of itself as a technological form. Thus the video screen is almost always used as a frame of quotation, whose meanings within the piece are mostly defined through technological mediation. With the advent of digital technologies, which allow all forms of cultural representation, from still images to architecture and music, to be digitized, and therefore altered, "corrected," and recycled, appropriation artists are given new energy in terms of both theme and technique.[16] Based on the new appropriation capabilities provided by the digital cinema, Laura Mulvey advances a revision of her previous film theory, in which she argued that the cinematic avant-garde was informed by the binary thinking between the commercial or fictitious and the avant-garde or realist.[17] Mulvey now believes that digital technologies, as a new form of appropriation, allow new negotiations between commercial and alternative arts by manipulating found footage, thus helping us visualize the construction of time and history.[18] Digital art can be politically potent precisely because of its highly appropriative capability, which can recontextualize the meanings of mainstream images.

This very sketchy account of the recent history of appropriation art is not meant to essentialize the art form, but it echoes Walter Benjamin's assertion that "technical progress is for the author as producer the foundation of his political program." In "The Author as Producer," Benjamin does not use "technical progress" to refer specifically to the mechanical technologies he discusses in "The Work of Art in the Age of Mechanical Reproduction," but he understands technology more broadly. He advocates that writers and artists adopt new techniques and technologies that "fetter the production of intellectuals." He believes that by intervening in the process of literary and art production "technologically," the author avoids taking his privileged author role for granted, and an active self-reflection in the production process necessarily betrays his privileged "class of origin." It is in this sense of self-reflection that Benjamin argues an inherent link between an author's political commitment and the "quality" of his works.[19]

To Benjamin, politics does not corrupt art; on the contrary, the more the author is politically committed to proletarian class struggles, the higher the quality of his work. He believes literary and artistic productions could lose their political edge by yielding to the artist's comfortable status quo, and a commitment to technology could save the author from falling into the trap of fascism. This agitation of class struggle, which might seem irrelevant to present social conditions, in fact harks back to the copyright criteria that reify the author, and Benjamin's critical vigilance against the dominant social structure remains largely applicable today. Both the fascist regime and the current copyright regime demonstrate how easily the author function can succumb to commodification. As Benjamin suggests, developing a technical awareness can fetter the production of bourgeois intellectuals, so an alternative approach to copyright control could be established by formulating a different author–technology relationship. Keeping art open to the unfolding of technology, I believe, entails important implications for our resistance not only to the fascism of Benjamin's time but also to the creative economy of our time.

Venice's Rent Collection Courtyard and Made in Hong Kong

I will return to Benjamin's argument later. Here I would like to introduce two recent Chinese artworks to demonstrate how art, author, and technology intersect in appropriation arts. Both works reveal a web of social and cultural intertextuality, making them good examples to show how creativity can be connected to a liberating understanding of technology. They were chosen also because of their divergences from each other: both provoke copyright debates, yet they also show different approaches to conceiving of art ownership, and a comparison of the two demonstrates the intricate dynamics between the artist function and the technology of art.

15. Cai Guo-qiang, *Venice's Rent Collection Courtyard*. Installation view at the forty-eighth Venice Biennale, 1999. Photo by Elio Montanari. Courtesy of Cai Studio.

In the Venice Biennale of 1999, a contemporary Chinese art installation entitled *Venice's Rent Collection Courtyard* (*Weinisi shouzuyuan* 威尼斯收租院; figure 15), curated and authored by the veteran Chinese artist Cai Guo-qiang (蔡國強), was said to plagiarize a Chinese Socialist Realist work entitled *Rent Collection Courtyard* (*Shouzuyuan* 收租院, 1965), collectively authored by folk artists as well as teachers and students of the Sichuan Fine Arts Institute.[20] It was Cai's intention to appropriate the highly influential and ideological Chinese work of class struggle for the Biennale, but he was not particularly concerned about challenging copyright as such. Instead he wanted to pay tribute to and reflect on the original *Rent Collection Courtyard*, and so he also invited one of the sculptors of the original work—Long Xuli (龍緒理), who was a student at the Sichuan Fine Arts Institute at the time and one of the nineteen artists from the Institute involved in the original work—to install the art on site (figure 16). According to Cai, he himself was most interested in exploring the relationships between art and history and between propaganda and viewer engagement.[21] However, when *Venice's Rent Collection Courtyard* earned the coveted Leone d'Oro award, the director of the Sichuan Fine Arts Institute,

16. *Venice's Rent Collection Courtyard*, 108 life-sized sculptures created on site by Long Xuli and nine guest artisan sculptors. Installation view at the forty-eighth Venice Biennale, 1999. Photo by Elio Montanari. Courtesy of Cai Studio.

Luo Zhongli (羅中立), accused Cai of plagiarizing the original *Rent Collection Courtyard*, and reportedly Long Xuli was also angry at Cai's refusal to share his cash award with the craftsmen putting up the new sculptures in Venice.[22] Cai is accused of having failed to seek permission from the Institute and all those artists involved in the original work before engaging in the new work, and the Institute threatened to bring the case to court.[23]

The original *Rent Collection Courtyard* comprised 114 (later increased to 119) life-size figures, and the whole work spread across a ninety-six-meter-long space. There were six parts to the enormous installation: "Bringing the Rent," "Examining the Rent," "Measuring the Grain," "Reckoning the Accounts," "Forcing Payment," and "Revolt"; together the parts tell a sensational narrative of class exploitation and socialist revolt. The installation was allegedly based on historical facts and took as its subject the feudal landowner Liu Wencai (劉文采), who severely oppressed his tenants. In keeping with its role as propaganda art, nearly every figure was collectively made and modified in order to ensure that no individual authorial input was identifiable in any of them. *Rent Collection Courtyard* allegedly attracted half a million viewers when it was first exhibited in Beijing, and some of the figures traveled to Vietnam, Japan, Denmark, France, Albania, and other countries to represent China's glorious revolution. It was a most typical and successful example of Chinese socialist pedagogical art, which claims to have fused artistic values with political meanings.

This history of the work immediately invites questions of ownership. While the original *Rent Collection Courtyard* was designed to be socialist propaganda, and its content and form were heavily invested with the doctrine of collective ownership, the Sichuan Fine Arts Institute has always claimed it as its own, and the installation is still featured prominently on the Institute's website.[24] The Institute was also the primary force behind the accusation of plagiarism. Retracing copyright in Communist China is extremely problematic, as private ownership was theoretically impossible between the Liberation and 1990, when the PRC's first Copyright Law was codified. The fact that legal action was not pursued is probably due to this complication.

However, in the author-based modern Western art world, Cai Guo-qiang was awarded the Leone d'Oro and reaped personal benefits, so the Chinese accusation of plagiarism for personal gain has an audience. Intimately linked with this authorship question are problems of cultural appropriation. Chinese academic critics belittled the work by describing Cai as a "green card artist" or a "banana man"—yellow on the outside, white on the inside.[25] In fact a major goal of that particular Venice Biennale was to introduce contemporary Chinese art to the West. The expatriate identity of Cai and the Western identity of the Venice Biennale support accusations of cultural appropriation within an Orientalist discourse, which is problematic in many ways. A major problem in such a discourse is its emphasis on the integrity of cultural identity. In discourses of intellectual property rights and cultural rights, what matters is the infringement of a certain subject, whether the position is occupied by an actual rights holder or rendered into a collective culture. The general criticism the Sichuan Fine Arts Institute directed at *Venice's Rent Collection Courtyard* is based precisely on the two subjectivist discourses of cultural rights and intellectual property rights. A closer analysis of the author function brought about by the work will follow; now let us turn to another work of appropriation art which also highlights issues of collective authorship.

While Cai's work is still located squarely in the realm of the fine arts, Leung Mee Ping's appropriation of the commercial painting industry in Dafen Village is much more ambiguous in its self-positioning (figure 17). The deconstruction of Cai's author function is largely a result of the unexpected copyright lawsuit that followed, but in her installation and performance work Leung highlights the ambiguities of authorship, because its subject matter, Dafen Village, is itself famous for its copyright violations. The exhibition is as much a collection of paintings as a piece of performance art, authored as much by Leung as by the anonymous Dafen Village collective. If Cai's *Venice's Rent Collection Courtyard* is appropriation art, Leung's *Made in Hong Kong* is a work of appropriation art about art appropriation, as it displays a large number of paintings produced in Dafen, alongside a video showing Leung's own learning of the mass reproduction techniques in Dafen.[26]

There are many references to copying in *Made in Hong Kong*. First, the piece highlights an extremely successful creative industry and art village that recently developed in Dafen Village, whose expertise is precisely copying. The roots of Dafen can be traced to Hong Kong, where an industry of tourist paintings began in the 1970s; the industry was particularly blessed by the availability of a sizable number of mainland émigré artists who were drawn to trade paintings for a humble living. Trade painting in Hong Kong at that time was a kind of cottage industry, with a few studios each housing not more than twenty painters, and the finished paintings were quickly taken to the street for sale.[27] There was also some export, but most of the time paintings were ordered by individual tourists. As Hong Kong's economy surged in the late 1980s, the industry gradually died down, and a Hong Kong dealer, Huang Jiang (黄江), tried to continue the business in the late 1990s by settling in Shenzhen, a mainland city bordering Hong Kong. As Huang later

17. *Made in Hong Kong*, by Leung Mee Ping, installation art, Hexiangning Art Museum, Shenzhen, 2008. Photo by Joey Lam. Courtesy of Leung Mee Ping.

admitted, he was attracted to Dafen Village mainly due to its inaccessibility, since trainees could not easily run away.[28]

Originally an apprentice of Huang Jiang, Wu Ruiqiu (吴瑞球), along with a few other entrepreneurs in training, began to develop the cottage industry into an international trade. Wu's Shenzhen Jiyiyuan Painting and Frame Art Limited Company (深圳集藝源油畫框藝有限公司), allegedly the largest company in Dafen, makes over 20 million RMB annually; a single painting can be reproduced in 200,000 versions, all hand-painted by the Dafen painters, and sold all over the world.[29] These trade paintings include knockoffs of famous Western classics as well as generic paintings of the most pedestrian type, which can readily be found in hotel rooms and fast-food joints. A recent UNESCO study shows that, surprisingly, China has become the third biggest exporter of cultural goods, preceded only by the U.K. and the U.S., and a large share of China's cultural exports are visual arts.[30] Although the report does not specify what the Chinese exported cultural products are, we can safely infer that Dafen's productions contribute heavily to the overall data. The annual sales of Dafen Village reached 343 million RMB in 2006, 60 percent of the total worldwide art market.[31] In 2010, the sales figure has already reached 500 million RMB, although the main market is no longer in the West, but major Chinese cities such as Shanghai and Guangzhou. There were 652 art companies established in Dafen Village in 2006, among them 490 painting studios, 36 craft and embroidery studios, 63 traditional Chinese arts and calligraphy shops, and 63 art supply stores.[32] In 2008, the total number of art-related businesses operated in Dafen rose to 800. The incredible success of the village actually turned "Dafen" into one of the most lucrative labels in the world art market. Some of the studio owners also have begun to launch retail businesses in Shanghai and Beijing, selling "authentic" Dafen paintings.[33]

Ironically, in February 2006 the state declared Dafen Village a National Model Creative Industry Base (全國文化產業示範基地), alongside major cultural symbols such as the Shanghai Great Theater (上海大劇院), national high-technology centers such as Beijing's Zhongguancun (中關村), and prominent creative industries such as Shenzhen Yijing National Cartoon and Animation Industry Base (深圳怡景國家動漫產業基地). In December 2006 Dafen Village was named "The Best Creative Cluster in China" in the annual Chinese Creative Industry Awards. To fit the title of National Model Creative Industry Base, in 2006 the Longgang District Government of the City of Shenzhen financed and set up the Dafen Village Oil Painting Management Office (大芬油畫村管理辦公室) to coordinate different establishments to promote the general image of the village; the Management Office was also assigned the duty of settling IPR disputes and coordinating IPR enforcement.[34] In the beginning of 2007 Dafen established its own independent IPR office, which offers "originality" certificates to those companies seeking authorial endorsements.[35] However, encouraging original production is not the key duty of the office. Knowing too well the nature of Dafen, the Management Office does not intend to eliminate its knockoff industry but to reform it into an IPR-amenable one, so it encourages companies to take up commissioned works based on authorized originals provided by the clients (*laiyang jiagong* 來樣加工).[36] Dafen's studios still reproduce, but their reproductions must be "legal." Obviously this office is not functioning as expected—one can still easily find knockoffs of famous paintings throughout the village—but it demonstrates how pervasive the logic of IPR is in the age of the creative economy (figure 18).

The second layer of mimesis in *Made in Hong Kong* is revealed in the ways the paintings are installed, which demonstrates Leung's reflection on the nature of Dafen's creative industry. None of the paintings shown in the exhibition is singular; each has a duplicate, whether in a different size, in a different frame, or in a different set of collages. Leung displays a series of paintings that are painted either by her or by Dafen Village painters hired by her, but all the paintings bear Leung's signature. The installation also exhibits a video entitled *Made in Shenzhen*, directed by Leung herself, showing how she learned trade painting skills in Dafen Village and including discussions with her teacher about the art form (figure 19). *Made in Hong Kong* is a metapainting

18. Painting a "Yue Minjun" signature work in a Dafen Village store. Photo by author.

19. Leung practicing the trade painting skills in Dafen.
Photo by Joey Lam. Courtesy of Leung Mee Ping.

installation calling attention to the making and exhibition of the paintings. Recognizing the work's highly self-reflexive nature, we can read Leung's signature as a kind of self-mockery, calling attention not to her artistry but to the multiple and "inauthentic" authorship inscribed both in these paintings and in the Dafen Village enterprise. In fact Leung also sells these paintings, but her unspoken rule is that those interested in only a single painting will be charged a higher price than those who buy a pair of them; in effect, a single painting is a piece of fine art, while the paired paintings are knockoffs.[37] Both she and the paintings assume contradictory roles: the agent and the work of original art, and the facsimile.

A third layer of mimesis, as demonstrated in the titles of the exhibition and the video, resides in the Hong Kong and Shenzhen elements of the installation. Leung says her fascination with Dafen paintings can be traced back to her teenage memories of tourist paintings being sold on the streets of Hong Kong's tourist sites. As she explains, their crudeness gave her both a vague sense of art and the "mistaken identity" of Hong Kong; many of the components shown in those tourist paintings reflected the painters' imaginations

20. Paintings featured in *Made in Hong Kong*, among them fake film stills. Photo by Joey Lam. Courtesy of Leung Mee Ping.

or alterations and could not be found in the real Hong Kong. She wanted to know how Hong Kong was seen by tourists, and in the 1990s she started to learn the craft from an elderly Hong Kong painter; her studies later took her to Dafen Village.

The subjects of the works in this installation are not typical Dafen paintings, but were designed specifically by Leung. Reflecting on the original tourist paintings that made such a lasting impression on her, she commissioned the painters to reproduce how she imagines mainlanders understand Hong Kong. So in these paintings we can find the most popular tourist spots in Hong Kong, such as Lantau Island's Big Buddha. She also produces "fake" film stills by using Photoshop to extract elements from different scenes on a single frame (figure 20). Many of these stills come from commercial movies deemed too violent (such as the *Young and Dangerous* series) or too politically sensitive (such as *Her Fatal Ways*) to be distributed on the mainland, but they are enormously popular in the region thanks to pirated discs. These fake stills represent her vision of the mainland's imagination of Hong Kong. All in all, Leung's piece appropriates appropriations, and thus is necessarily invested with complex cultural and social references.

In both *Venice's Rent Collection Courtyard* and *Made in Hong Kong*, the authorial unity is caught in the technologies employed, and a careful comparison between the two works should help us rethink the political function of appropriation arts. In a recent article on *Venice's Rent Collection Courtyard*,

Kela Shang warns us not to apply the label "appropriation art" to the piece because "the work completely shifted focus from 'non-creativity' and 'slavish copying' typical of appropriation to the exploration of how artistic canons go through metamorphoses and turn into something else: from the socialist realist project on the nature of propaganda, to a piece of conceptual art."[38] I would argue just the opposite: that the creative energy of appropriation art is most vibrant when it is most consciously copying, which also demands that we rethink the value of Venice's *Rent Collection Courtyard*.

If most contemporary appropriation arts resort to the revealing capacity of new technologies such as photography, video, and digital media, Cai's *Venice's Rent Collection Courtyard* directs our attention to an extremely old but still important technology: the firing of clay. One of the main concerns in Western art history is preservation, ensuring that valuable artifacts are unchanged as long as possible. The use of unfired clay in Cai's work is probably not meant to take us back to a time before clay was used instrumentally—people are thought to have first begun to fire clay around 6000 B.C.—but the technological retreat can be seen as a comment on the style of social realism the original work adopted. Because the clay Cai used in Venice was not fired, it began to crack during the show. Whereas the original *Rent Collection Courtyard* was firmly rooted in the ideology of social realism and was meant to be an accurate and permanent reflection of China's feudal past, in Cai's version the figures were made at the Biennale and gradually disintegrated on site. In order to highlight the work as a piece in progress, a number of figures were never finished and remained skeletons standing alongside finished ones. Its creation and decay call attention to the work's independent trajectory, in contrast to the original work as a political instrument.

Realist sculpture is rooted in classical Greek culture and was revitalized during the Renaissance. Just as the form was being abandoned by mainstream artists in the West, it was taken up by the Soviet Union and Communist China in the twentieth century for political propaganda. So the new creation in Venice calls attention not only to the piece's disintegration but also to a sense of resurrection, or some kind of life cycle that runs on its own. As Cai said of his work, "You think of sculpture as dead, but there you saw it being reborn again."[39] By reflecting on the element and technology of clay, the Venice work implies many rebirths: of an old piece of artwork, of the medium of sculpture and figurative arts, and of the social realist style. However, what is important to me is not simply the act of resurrection, but whether these rebirths are free to continue on their own; Cai's work remains ambiguous in this sense. I believe the most interesting rebirth in this piece is realized in the subsequent accusation of plagiarism, which unintentionally calls the authorship function into question. Let me explain why.

While the manipulation of the technology of clay firing might help deconstruct the political meanings of the original piece, it does not imply self-reflection on the part of the author. Cai's authorship is imprinted precisely in the unfired clay, demarcating the old work and the new, as he calls his new work a performance and the original a traditional sculptural piece for permanent display. Some of the remaining Venice figures were actually shipped to the Italian town of Nove and fired there by local artists. Although this act was approved by Cai, he disavows the fired pieces and suggests the sculpture is authorless after firing.[40] Clearly the (anti)technique of unfiring is where Cai's authorship is embodied. Although *Venice's Rent Collection Courtyard* disintegrates on site, its authorship does not. The work helped Cai become one of the most important contemporary artists globally.

However, the piece became semiotically and politically rich when the Sichuan Fine Arts Institute threatened to sue Cai for copyright infringement, which ultimately ridicules both Cai's authorship of the new work and the Institute's authorship of the old work. Contemporary journalists now claim that the older work's historical reconstruction of the landlord Liu Wencai's oppression of his tenants was exaggerated for political purposes.[41] According to new research, Liu was actually a respectable businessman and philanthropist, and Phoenix TV recently made the "amended" version of Liu's life into a popular five-part television documentary, *Big Landowner Liu Wencai* (大地主 劉文彩). If the Sichuan Fine Arts collective wants to claim the work as its own, it is also expected to assume the political burden of defamation. The original work was produced during a time when individual authorship was unlawful, and the work itself is a perfect rendition of this rationale of mass politicization. Culture was nothing but reflections or components of class struggle, and without the Western modern legal framework the concept of the individual (fame) or the author (copyright) cannot be substantiated. In the copyright dispute, the original *Rent Collection Courtyard* is removed from its own social context and placed in an alien environment; the resulting distance inevitably calls our attention to, and therefore denaturalizes, both former and current legality.

Made in Hong Kong, on the other hand, shows more room in keeping the authorship of the work open and transient, and the piece is also more squarely about the relationship between technology and arts. Leung's technique, like Cai's, does not involve machines as such, but the most fundamental art form in the West: oil painting. Although oil painting, like sculpture, is a quintessential representative of Western fine arts, with the right kind of training one can also (re)produce it in a coarse and speedy manner. As Leung herself reflects, there are four key aspects to the technique of mass-reproduced paintings she learned in Dafen. First, it is important to emphasize the form—but not the details—of the object, so that viewers are provided merely an overall impression of the object, which calls to mind their vague recollections of classical art. Second, it is always good to use bright colors because they help sustain a decorative look. The third and probably most important key is speed; the painters are often encouraged to draw the same image on a number of canvases at the same time. The fourth aspect, which is directly related to the previous one, is collaboration, as a painter is generally responsible for one item or a section of the painting, and other parts are completed by other painters.[42] In general, there is no main author of any of these paintings; each work is the result of a collective, or industrial, collaboration, echoing the original *Rent Collection Courtyard* in an uncanny way. As Leung admits, the training she received in Dafen defies all the principles she learned in her academic training (she holds a MFA from California Institute of the Arts), which taught her to produce oil paintings slowly and meticulously. Her work demonstrates that the same Western oil painting technique can be used to produce both the highest art and the most conventional and lowbrow decoration.

Obviously, in the mass reproduction of trade painting, originality is simply not part of the training. But the irony is that precisely due to the emphasis on efficiency, these paintings also encourage painters to use their imagination and craftiness. Leung once asked a master Dafen painter to reproduce a photograph of fireworks (another symbol of Hong Kong), but he failed the task because he had never been taught how to paint fireworks. Technique and training are of vital importance. But these painters make imaginative use of the techniques they learn to paint many different kinds of flowers, which are as generic as they are unique. A Western commentator says, "Dafen's painters will produce whatever customers want. A few brushstrokes are enough to transform Gustav Klimt's famous portrait of Adele Bloch-Bauer into a likeness of the customer's sweetheart."[43] Isn't this exactly what the creative economy is all about? The ultimate author is also the consumer, whose pseudo-individualist taste and demands determine the final rendition of the work. Mass-produced trade oil painting is a rare genre and technique that involves both originality and mass reproduction; it retains a certain "aura" because every painting is handmade and therefore unique, but at the same time it is also factory-produced and panders to the masses' tastes.

The conundrum of authorship in *Made in Hong Kong* is also highlighted in the cultural tensions between China and Hong Kong, between Dafen and China, and between Dafen and Hong Kong. Although the name of the work suggests a strong sense of the city's identity, it is as much made in Dafen as in Hong Kong (remember that *Made in Shenzhen* is the name of the video work displayed in *Made in Hong Kong*). The pieces that Leung commissioned are meant to reveal a Hong Konger's fantasy of the mainland Chinese fantasy of Hong Kong, in such a way that neither the imagination of Hong Kong nor that of China is taken for granted, in contrast to the culturalist discourse implicit in the Sichuan Fine Arts Institute's copyright accusation. At the same time, in spite of its marginal position, Dafen has been appropriated as China's own "national" brand. The author function is bifurcated not only by the ambiguous relationship between Leung and the Dafen painters, but also by the intertwined but discrete cultural identities of Hong Kong, Dafen, and China.

In fact Hong Kong has played an important role in China's piracy culture, and also the other way around. The now widely circulated term *shanzhai*, which originally referred to barricaded mountain villages, was first employed in Hong Kong in the 1960s as *shanzhai chang* (山寨廠) to refer to small or family-owned factories sprouting up in the peripheral urban areas producing light industry products like watches, toys, and garments. These low-tech factories witnessed and participated in the economic growth of Hong Kong from an industrial city to a global financial center. Many of these factories were phased out, but some rapidly expanded and evolved into transnational corporations in the 1990s. In Hong Kong usage, *shanzhai* is primarily an industrial concept closely connected to a particular type of economy developed within a particular stage of modernization, and it can be seen as the symbol of a threshold connecting poverty and wealth, the underdeveloped world and the developed world.

While Hong Kong was a *shanzhai* city thirty or forty years ago, the term is now embraced by the mainland. In the past few years the term has been widely used in China to refer not only to copycat designs and knockoffs, as in "shanzhai cellular phone" and "shanzhai movie," but also to a uniquely grassroots culture which is adaptive, creative, and unashamed. The term has both negative and positive connotations: negative because of its illegal and low-quality status, but also positive precisely because of its implication of IPR offenses, as it implies a culture of rebellion, irony, and self-marginalization. A shanzhai product is usually not a perfect copy; there are flaws, and often there are adaptations suiting local needs. The term suggests a subtle tension, an ambiguous position between technological advancement and inferiority.

While this tension has made the shanzhai culture vibrant and attractive, the key question of the linear development model remains: Is shanzhai a threshold destined to be overcome, or will an alternative to the global development logic grow naturally out of this culture?

The development hierarchy continues to shape our global creative economy, whose postdevelopment rationale (and the celebration of shanzhai culture in this sense) is only a façade hiding fierce and often unfair international competition and division of labor. Dafen is definitely a shanzhai industry, and China, according to both industrial and creativity benchmarks, is still a shanzhai country. What is inspiring about *Made in Hong Kong* is the connection it makes between art and industry, demythologizing the creative economy's connection between creativity and wealth, and it also reminds us of the continuous development logic in Hong Kong, China, and all developing countries.

Creativity and Freedom

By way of concluding this book, I would like to link the authorship of Cai and Leung to the contemporary social situation in China. Referring back to the thesis in the first part of the book, that creativity is both a form of textuality and a form of social praxis, it is important for me to link creative agency to the general social conditions of contemporary times. Both Cai's and Leung's works reveal complex textures of social and historical embedding, and a careful contextual reading of their work necessarily involves the meanings of authorship, as well as the relationship between individuals who express and society which grounds these expressions. The copyright dispute associated with Cai's work is unintentional, while Leung's work endeavors to come to terms with precisely those issues related to copying. Looking at their differences from another perspective, Cai's work would more likely be granted copyright than Leung's. Although his technique of "clay unfiring" anticipates the work's disappearance, his artistic authorship is substantiated by the same technique because it marks his originality. In contrast, although Leung uses mass-production techniques to create hundreds of concrete paintings that can actually be sold, she probably cannot claim copyright to any of these works because the technique she uses deliberately defies the concepts of originality and authorship.

Many current IPR critics at heart support the principles of IPR, and their efforts are devoted to steering the right development of IPR from the manipulation of interested parties. In contrast to such liberal positions, I am critical of the fundamental rationale of IPR, that ideas and knowledge should be considered property, and this book challenges the social structure from which this understanding arises. It is true that IPR is not treated in the same way as property rights in current laws, as IPR is considered, in principle, a temporary state-created monopoly given to encourage further innovation. So IPR involves no entitlement, and none of the rights are permanent.[44] But the current understandings of IPR are clearly based on capitalist logics, which I think radically confine our understanding of culture and human relationships. I do not want to hail *Made in Hong Kong* as anti-IPR, as that was not its intention, but it does demonstrate that creativity, that of Dafen's and that of Leung's, can play with IPR control rather than be governed by it, and that culture can still flourish without equating author and owner. It is only by forgoing linear ownership that individual expressive selves can be connected back to the community.

In one of his fiercest criticisms of modernity, Heidegger argues that in the modern age the world (object) is a picture composed of the objectified knowledge that human beings (subject) use science (tool) to obtain. But, detrimentally, not only the world but also the subject himself is objectified, since the objective world is largely composed of humans. While he is representing the world, he is also representing himself to himself: "What is decisive is that man himself expressly takes up this position as one constituted by himself, that he intentionally maintains it as that taken up by himself, and that he makes it secure as the solid footing for a possible development of humanity."[45] By turning the world into knowledge, the subject turns himself into a piece of knowledge, so that the more objectively the object appears, the more subjectively the subject rises up.

I find this criticism pertinent to illustrate two main issues of the creative economy. First, Heidegger acutely points out the strong connection between instrumental thinking and humanity's arrogance toward the world and describes how the epistemological drive of Western modernity impels humans to use modern science and technology to subdue the world and themselves. So this world picture analogy suggests not only the modern subject's desire for control but also his insecurity, which can be appeased only by his turning himself into a knowable picture. Heidegger's insight helps us understand the creative economy's strong desire to subdue creativity, an essential but intractable part of humanity. In other words, the creative economy also has its metaphysical dimension, for by turning his creative ability into knowledge, the modern subject is made safe and secure. The creative economy therefore is a specific and extreme manifestation of this modernity project, so that one's potentially unfathomable creative ability is also turned into knowledge, thereby eluding the possibility of one's liberation through creative acts.

Second, following this logic, we can see a structural leap of the system of arts in recent years, in the sense that creativity is rendered not only as knowledge to be understood, but also as knowledge to be used and applied in an endless chain of commodification. Heidegger wrote "The Age of the World Picture" in 1949, long before the radical structural turn in this epistemological drive, in which knowledge and art must be fully absorbed into the global-capitalist machine. A key concept in the Heideggerian understanding of modernity is *techne*, which, according to Heidegger, should be understood along with *poiesis*, as both terms in the original Greek context concern revealing and bringing forth. So *techne* was actually a positive term germane to human creativity. But in modern times *techne* has been transformed into instrumental thinking, facilitating the human desire, through science and modern technology, to dominate the world.[46] The current creative economy, I believe, most dramatically represents the kind of Western epistemology dominated by this modern version of *techne*, which not only has turned away from its common roots with *poiesis*, but in fact has begun to subdue *poiesis* for its own purposes.

To Heidegger, *techne* in its original meaning could help human beings express themselves and develop a new relationship with the world. The most important feature differentiating ancient technology, which is abetting and nurturing, from modern technology, which is imposing and destroying, is precisely the relationship between the agent and the technology: ancient technology is characterized by a relationship between agent and tool of mutual bringing forth, while modern technology is simply the agent's control of the tool.[47] Heidegger believes that if we can use technology in a noninstrumental way, we can facilitate a process in which subject, tool, and final product are equally involved, equally brought forth, and equally revealed: "Unlocking, transforming, storing, distributing, and switching about are ways of revealing. But the revealing never simply comes to an end."[48] Technique and technology, if understood as *techne* in the original sense, need not put an end to human intercourse with the world; instead new forms of creativity can actually be realized, as evidenced by many Dafen painters who are subjected to painting techniques but continue to create a variety of works. By seriously engaging with the same techniques, Leung's self-reflection on her author role brings her a new connection with Dafen's cultural laborers, and also brings forth the multiple interactions between Hong Kong and the mainland. Differences and identities become mutually conditioning.

As such, we should not oppose Benjamin's political understanding of technology to Heidegger's, as at the heart of both criticisms is a yielding and a commitment to technology's unfolding, which then might achieve freedom—freedom not in the sense of radical differences that lead to the void, but as an ever renewing engagement with oneself and one's community. Benjamin and Heidegger represent two different approaches to counter the fascist and capitalist use of art. Benjamin believes that the technology of art can transfigure ordinary objects we have long taken for granted into agitating representations that arouse the political awareness of the artist and the audience. Heidegger wants us to keep culture open by allowing technology to unfold. To Benjamin, fascism imprisons intellectuals and masses alike in the iron cage of aestheticism; holding tightly onto the nonaesthetic nature of technology is therefore a sound strategy to break out of this cage. Heidegger's object of criticism is modernity's instrumentalism, and he argues that when we open ourselves expressly to the essence of technology, we find ourselves unexpectedly drawn into claims of freedom, which also offer us a way to cohabitate with nature, in contrast to a life alienated by industrial technology and bureaucratic control.[49] In light of Heidegger's ideas, Benjamin's political commitment in art does not necessarily lead to an instrumentalist use of technology. As Benjamin argues, the author's political commitment entails a critical sensitivity to social relations, which are determined by production relations. In this sense, a politically committed author would show a deep respect for technology's unfolding, instead of using it as a tool. Although Heidegger and Benjamin conceptualize the function of technology in two very different ways, and they were attracted to opposite political camps in their real life, both are firmly convinced that technology offers the greatest potential for emancipation.

This notion of freedom, however, is becoming increasingly utopian in this age of global capitalism, not only in the sense that we are distanced from creativity, but also because creativity has become a form of possession. I apply the criticisms of European theorists to contemporary China not because their claims are universal, but, thanks to colonialism and globalization, because the social background from which their criticisms arose has now spread all over the world, creating more contrived and devastating consequences. The creative economy, as the latest manifestation of Western modernity, engenders a global discursive environment that fiercely incorporates human productivity into capitalism. While the author's rights are celebrated, the author position is constantly usurped by any capable body of power, and such commercial appropriation of creativity destroys instead of promotes human creative power as a way to connect to other people and things.[50] A central concern of this book is precisely to probe the culture as induced by the related notion of authorship, which abducts individual ideas from the chain of creativity to become intellectual property, drastically limiting the prospect of cultural products to make connections, build community, and introduce changes.

A key area of concern in current studies of contemporary China is the fate of the individual: How can individual freedom be realized in the face of an all-embracing consumer culture, an omnipotent party-state, rampant global capitalism, and a desperate future?[51] There is a general sense of pessimism as the Chinese people are increasingly subject to a potent market economy and a politically conservative regime. We observe a dichotomized view of the individual–society relationship in contemporary China: the confrontation between the weak individual against the powerful system, or grief over a new generation of self-centered pleasure seekers in a sea of commodities.[52]

In fact the gloomy apprehension of the individual is not specific to China, but a focus of the questions asked by many contemporary critical scholars. Capitalism is believed to be capable of providing an "ever-more-comfortable life for an ever-growing number of people who, in a strict sense, cannot imagine a qualitatively different universe of discourse action."[53] As a result we see the growth of a specific form of individualism, in which individual rights and pleasures are privileged over social coherence and collective identity,[54] yet the individual is also increasingly silent. Meanwhile the gap between developed and developing countries continues to widen, and poverty prevails globally. Individual freedom can no longer be conceptualized outside of and as subversive to capitalism and globalization, because the present global order encompasses all. Mocking Kant, Slavoj Žižek describes the Enlightenment subject: "Think as much as you like, and as freely as you like, just obey!"[55] The situation is even more dire in the case of China and many other developing countries, as their neoliberal turns further remind much of the population of their vulnerability and alienation.

My exploration of IPR enforcement and offenses in the creative economy is driven largely by my critical stance toward the author function, which must be understood alongside this global discourse of market economy, in which the individual is both aggrandized and made powerless in the ocean of commodity. We also need to critically reexamine the pluralized relational social context to ground our being. Throughout the book I have tried to interrogate the author function from many different angles: the author as god, as creative laborer, as cultural heritage, as fan, as brand, as city, region, and nation, in order to explore how the creative agent is both discursively constructed and difficult to pin down. I emphasized the importance of dehumanizing creativity and connected such creativity to the serendipity of history, the production of space, text and sign, and technology. I believe that even in the age of creative industries, a careful examination of different kinds of cultural production is still capable of offering alternatives to the status quo.

But we must recognize that artistic transgression is itself extremely vulnerable to, and easily incorporated and overcome by, the IPR regime as well as the underlying capitalist ideology. It is precisely because of such vulnerability that we have to hold on to culture's unfolding instead of authorial will. Reiterating what I have emphasized in the previous chapters, the task of this book is a humble one: to call our attention to the potentiality of culture and the connections between one human and another as well as between humans and objects, which might offer us, as individuals, a more gentle position to occupy this world. I think Cai's and Leung's works give us some new insights into the complex relationship between the artist and technology, so that technology becomes a way of self-revealing as well as a way of revealing other people and things. In spite of the ambiguities associated with the authorship of their work, they are not simply dissipated in the process of art making. Personal memory still plays an important part in their work, which are initiated by the artists' own remote artistic reminiscences: tourist paintings for Leung, and the original *Rent Collection Courtyard* for Cai.[56] The Venice and Dafen works are as much about the "originals" as they are about the authors' memories of art. This subjective presence of the creative agent can be expanded into a complex web of self- and social reflexivity, which also disallows the fetishization of personal memory. This, again, is most clearly revealed in the case of *Made in Hong Kong*, as Leung both stresses and questions the agency of Hong Kong in her work. In a way, it is Leung's Hong Kong identity and sensibility which allow her to detect and personally experience a tangential part of China's painting history and creative economy. However, this Hong Kong agency, so heavily stressed in the title of the work, is caught in myriad Chinese factors, and the rich meanings of the paintings featured in Leung's installation come as much from Hong Kong's (post)colonial trajectory as from the city's own embeddedness in China.

To allow creativity to slide back into the chain of creation does not mean erasing the individual or the author; what we need to avoid is only the assertion of a commanding subject. In spite of the current all-encompassing rule of economics, there is yet room to imagine a creative engagement with the world that allows individuals to see themselves and one another in a less alienated fashion. In a way, the industrial operation of Dafen Village is a typical form of class exploitation, and there is nothing romantic about the mass reproduction of trade paintings, but Leung's sensitive rearticulation of the operation and technology helps reveal the conditions of both trade arts and fine arts; she takes neither one for granted but at the same time allows herself to be disclosed. In this sense, Leung has a profound engagement with this technology of mass reproduction. As Heidegger writes, "What has the essence of technology to do with revealing? The answer: everything. . . . Technology is therefore no mere means. Technology is a way of revealing. If we give heed to this, then another whole realm for the essence of technology will open itself up to us. It is the realm of revealing, i.e., truth."[57] We can substitute the term "technology" in this quote with "creativity," not the creativity commodified in the creative economy but creativity as textuality and as social praxis. Instead of dichotomizing the vulnerable individual against an overwhelming society, we need to reflect on the relationship between the two, which is perhaps the most valuable dimension of creativity. As Vico says, people's creativity is never other than that of being in the world.

Notes

Introduction

1 Bruce Nussbaum, "IDEO Makes the Top 25 Global Innovators: Here's Why," *Business Week*, April 17, 2006, online (accessed 15 September 2010).

2 "The Power of Design in Global Development," *International Trade Forum*, no. 3 (2009), online (accessed 4 September 2010).

3 Li Haiqiang, "Shanghai chuangyi chanye mishi Shanghai."

4 Taniguchi and Wu, "Shanzhai."

5 Su Xing, "IDEO Yataiqu zhixing zongcai Li Ruizhe."

6 See, for example, the special double issue of *Business Week* on "The Creative Economy," no. 3696 (21 August 2000).

7 Strong voices have been raised to protect these innovative methods from being copied. See Lyons, Chatman, and Joyce, "Innovation in Services."

8 Howkins, *The Creative Economy*, xi–xiv. Howkins, an English writer, educator, and businessman, is a well-known promoter of the creative economy in Asia, serving as consultant to both corporations and governments.

9 See, for example, Pike, *Virtual Monopoly*.

10 See, for example, Tapscott, *The Digital Economy*; Kelly, *New Rules for the New Economy*; Pine and Gilmore, *The Experience Economy*; Leadbeater, *Living on Thin Air*.

11 Chiodo, "Evolving from a 'Knowledge Economy' to a 'Creativity Economy.'"

12 Howkins, *The Creative Economy*, 119.

13 Some scholars explain that the lack of a precise academic definition of the term "creative industries" is due to the fact the discourse arises first in economic and regional policy rather than in academic analysis. See Hartley and Montgomery, "Creative Industries Come to China," 1.

14 Garnham, "From Cultural to Creative Industries."

15 See, for example, Keane, "Brave New World."

16 See Sawyer, *Group Genius*; Bilton and Leary, "What Can Managers Do for Creativity?"; Bekins and Williams, "Positioning Technical Communication for the Creative Economy"; Kong, Gibson, Khoo, and Semple, "Knowledges of the Creative Economy."

17   Richard Florida argues problematically that instead of working solely for wages, the creative class is motivated by passion, in *The Rise of the Creative Class*, 88.

18   See Boltanski and Chiapello, *The New Spirit of Capitalism*; Rossiter, *Organized Networks*.

19   See Ross, *No Collar*.

20   McRobbie, "Clubs to Companies."

21   Wayne, *Marxism and Media Studies*, 6–37.

22   Christopherson, "The Divergent Worlds of New Media"; Lovink and Gerritzen, *Everyone Is a Designer*.

23   For example, some social science researchers hypothesize that certain problem-solving instructions (heuristic instructions) spark creativity more than other kinds of instruction (algorithmic instructions). See Ruscio and Amabile, "Effects of Instructional Style on Problem-Solving Creativity."

24   See Bilton, *Management and Creativity*, 167.

25   Kleiman, "Towards Transformation."

26   Negus and Pickering, *Creativity, Communication and Cultural Value*, 24.

27   At least three journal special issues on related topics have been published in the past few years: Hartley and Keane, "Special Issue on Creative Industries and Innovation in China"; Carriço, de Muynck, and Rossiter, "Creative China: Counter-Mapping the Creative Industries"; Hartley and Montgomery, "Special Issue on China: Internationalizing the Creative Industries."

28   Keane, *Created in China*, 81–86.

29   In China the term "cultural industries" is used much more often than "creative industries," but in this book I choose to use the term "creative industries" consistently to emphasize the same global discourse influencing China. See chapter 4 for more historical details.

30   Andrew Baston and Piling Chiu, "China Loses Some Allure as World's Factory," *Wall Street Journal*, Eastern ed., 8 July 2006; See "The Problem with Made in China," *Economist*, U.S. ed., 13 January 2007, 68–70.

31   U.S.-China Business Council, "Foreign Direct Investment (FDI) in China."

32   Hu Jintao, "Nuli ba guanche luoshi kexue fazhanguan tigao dao xin shuiping."

33   Jing Wang, "The Global Reach of a New Discourse."

34   As Alan Liu aptly points out, our network society is characterized by decentralization and distributed centralization, in that the horizontal democratization of information demands ever more effective systematization and uniformity to ensure efficiency and control (*The Laws of Cool*, 141–73).

35   "Nike Sues Chinese Companies over Logo," *China Daily*, 2 April 2009, www.procedurallaw.cn (accessed 25 September 2009).

36   Qian and Hu, "Chuangyi chanye fazhan moshi jiejian yu tansuo," 47.

37   See Nye, *Soft Power*.

38   See Gill and Huang, "Sources and Limits of Chinese 'Soft Power.'"

39   Jing Wang, *Brand New China*, 134–43, 142.

40   Buckley, "China Design Now."

41   Dirlik, *Global Modernity*, 141–143.

42 The lecture was given by a Chinese Academy of Social Sciences researcher, Zhang Ximing (張西明), and a Tsinghua University professor, Xiong Chengyu (熊澄宇). Both are major government advisors on issues related to culture and the press.

43 Hu Jintao's speech of August 2003 can be found in "Zhonggong zhongyan zhengzhiju juxin diqici jiti xuexi" 中共中央政治局舉行第七次集體學習 (The Political Bureau of the Communist Party of China holds its seventh collective study), www.bjqx.org.cn (accessed 11 June 2009). My translation.

44 See Item 8.4 in the official document "Zhonggong zhongyang guanyu jiaqiang dang de zhizheng nengli jianshe de jueding" 中共中央關於加強黨的執政能力建設的決定 (The decision of the Chinese Central government to strengthen the Party's governing ability), 26 September 2004, http://cpc.people.com.cn (accessed 16 June 2009).

45 Hu Huilin, *Wenhua chanye fazhan*, 34–38, 10–14, 154–55, 185–214.

46 Rofel, *Desiring China*, 133.

47 See David Barboza, "For Chinese Filmmakers, Success Can Sting," *International Herald Tribune*, 1 July 2007.

48 Ling Yan discovers on the Internet heated discussions on *Zhongguo dapian/guochan dapian* (Chinese blockbusters) and over 5 million links related to the topic. Ling Yan, "Huayu kuajing dapian yu Zhongguo xiangxiang."

49 Žižek writes that ideology works best when it reminds its subjects that they are not subject to its control, so that self-reflection and conscious rationalization with the ideology make for the most successful interpellated subject ("Class Struggle or Postmodernism?," 100–101).

50 See Redding, *The Spirit of Chinese Capitalism*, 210.

51 Vijay Vaitheeswaran and Iain Carson, "A Dark Art No More," *Economist*, 13 October 2007, 10–12.

52 Branstetter, Fisman, and Foley, "Do Stronger Intellectual Property Rights Increase International Technology Transfer?"

53 This is happening not only in the commercial world, but also in academia. Many critics also use a modernity framework to comment on the widespread trend of academic plagiarism taking place in the PRC. For example, Lin Yusheng, emeritus professor at the University of Wisconsin, Madison, remarks that very few scholars teaching in Western universities would be charged with plagiarism because they respect themselves. He cites the tolerance of plagiarism on the mainland as evidence of China's failure to progress, and says that Chinese academia's boast of merging with the international academic community is only an empty slogan. Embedded in Lin's criticism is not only a moral condemnation of plagiarism, but also a common celebration of "creativity" as a modernity indicator across social sectors. See Zhang Chuanwen, "Lin Yusheng lun Wang Hui shijian."

54 See the epilogue to Pang, *The Distorting Mirror*.

55 See, for example, the research and reports collected in Ouyang and Ding, *Guoji wenhua fazhan baogao.*

56 Alford, *To Steal a Book Is an Elegant Offense*, 9–29; Keane, *Created in China*, 35–46.

57 Wang Hui, *Xiandai Zhongguo sixiang de xingqi*; see also Yongle Zhang, "The Future of the Past."

58 Puett, *The Ambivalence of Creation*, 3, 141–76.

59 As some scholars have pointed out, the Chinese conserve by copying. In traditional wooden architecture, for example, the original wood is made to be reproducible and perishable, so that rotten parts can simply be replaced as needed. The entire building might last forever, while the parts that compose the whole can be repeatedly renewed. See Stille, *The Future of the Past*, 40–42.

60 See, for example, Wang Hui, "Depoliticized Politics, from East to West."

61 *Chuangzao* (創造), the Chinese term used currently to refer to the concept of creation, did not originally denote creation from a void and does not connote "novelty" as such, but the original meaning of the word *chuang* (創) simply denotes the idea of production and beginning. Some of the earliest uses of the word *chuang* can be found in classic texts such as *Mencius* and the Confucian *Analects*.

62 Janice Hua Xu, "Brand-new Lifestyle," 367.

63 Caracostas and Mulder, "Long Cycles."

64 For a recent general introduction to the new economy, see, for example, Sennett, *The Culture of the New Capitalism*.

65 Commonwealth of Australia, *Creative Nation*, 7.

66 McLeay, "Investing Australia," 42.

67 See M. Leonard, *Britain* TM.

68 Driver and Martell, "New Labour." The U.K. Creative Economy Programme has released a number of reports on the development of the country's creative economy and the creative sector. See www.cep.culture.gov.uk (accessed 4 June 2007).

69 See New England Council, *The Creative Economy Initiative*.

70 Yue, "The Regional Culture of New Asia."

71 Klein, *No Logo*, 30–35.

72 This is also evidenced in our academic world. After presenting a survey of new R&D strategies in the sciences, Stuart Cunningham argues that humanities research should also take these strategies seriously: "Before we are recognized as contributing to the global knowledge economy and our national innovation systems, we must innovate through changing ourselves." Cunningham's criticism of the autonomous position of the humanities goes to extremes in its wholesale dismissal of the researcher's own critical position. Unfortunately, we are seeing more and more humanities research going in this direction; the rapid increase of knowledge and creative productions, ironically, provides far less room for us to critically engage with late capitalism. Cunningham, "The Humanities, Creative Arts, and International Innovation Agendas," 122.

73 Throsby, *Economics and Culture*, 3–5.

74 Major areas of studies include the economics of art, cultural policy, contractual behaviors and organization around the arts, and the IPR. For an array of examples, see Frey, *Arts and Economics*, 1–33; Heilbrun and Gray, *The Economics of Art and Culture*; Caves, *Creative Industries*; Landes and Posner, *The Economic Structure of Intellectual Property Law*.

75 Lury, *Brands*.

76 Thrift, "Capitalism's Cultural Turn."

77 Laclau and Mouffe, *Hegemony and Socialist Strategy*, 126–27.

78 Jameson, *Late Marxism*, 15–34, 28, 32.

79 Ibid., 33.

80 Žižek has used the fascist construction of the Jewish plot to remind us that ideology needs a constructed other to sustain itself (*The Sublime Object of Ideology*, 124–29).

81 Fisher, *Capitalist Realism*, 3.

82 Laclau and Mouffe, *Hegemony and Socialist Strategy*, 127–34.

83 Laclau, "Structure, History and the Political," 209–10.

Chapter One: Creativity as a Problem of Modernity

1 My project can be seen as connecting to Horkheimer's and Adorno's *Dialectic of Enlightenment*. While they focus on the dialectic manifestation of the Enlightenment, this book concerns a similar set of dialectics in our understanding and appropriation of creativity.

2 See Wigmans, "Contingent Governance and the Enabling City"; Castells, *The Rise of the Network Society*, 449.

3 My apologies for treating modernity in this chapter as if it were a singular, seamless project. We all know that modernity comes in different forms at different times and in different places, but it is strategic to assume some coherency of the project before any productive analysis can be reached. Here I choose to deconstruct Western modernity not by exposing its different manifestations, but by analyzing its internal repressions and stratifications.

4 R. Williams, *Keywords*, 82–83.

5 Williams's account has become a standard one in understanding the development of creativity in the West. See also Negus and Pickering, *Creativity, Communication and Cultural Value*, 1–21.

6 See Gibson's discussion of Weber's *The Protestant Ethic and the Spirit of Capitalism* in *Creating Selves*, 15–16.

7 Plato, *Timaeus*.

8 Boris DeWeil argues that the original conceptual model for "liberty as creativity," which so fundamentally informs the development of Western modernity, did not belong to classical Greek tradition but came from Judaism. See DeWeil, "Freedom as Creativity."

9 The Christian tradition, although it continues to struggle with the tensions between the doctrine of *creatio ex nihilo* and Plato's derivative model, remains peripheral to modernity. David T. Runia, among others, explains historically how the two different notions of creation, from the Platonic and the Judaic traditions, were painstakingly reconciled in early Christian thought—which at the same time also avoided the move to the Platonic derivative model of creation. See Runia, "Plato's *Timaeus*."

10 Cascardi, *The Subject of Modernity*, 128, 133–34.

11 Habermas, *The Theory of Communicative Action*, vol. 1.

12 See Habermas, "Modernity," 45.

13 Anthony Cascardi describes Kant's difficult task thus: "The ambition of the third *Critique* is to locate in aesthetic judgment a form of *knowledge* that does not subordinate

the affects (pleasure, pain) to the governance of universal laws but that begins from particulars and proceeds to find the concepts according to which they can be phrased with categorical validity" (*Consequences of Enlightenment*, 100, emphasis mine).

14   "This question of the existence of truths (that 'there be' truths) points to a coresponsibility of art, which produces truths, and philosophy, which, under the condition that there are truths, is duty-bound to make them manifest (a very difficult task indeed)." Badiou, *Handbook of Inaesthetics*, 15.

15   For an elaborate analysis of Badiou's theorization of the autonomy of art, see J. Roberts, "On the Limits of Negation in Badiou's Theory of Art."

16   Adorno, *Aesthetic Theory*, 175–225; Lukács, *The Historical Novel*, 251–350.

17   Benjamin, "Little History of Photography," 527.

18   Jameson, "Postmodernism and Consumer Culture."

19   Schelling, "Philosophical Investigations into the Essence of Human Freedom," 142, 146.

20   See Žižek, "The Abyss of Freedom." For related scholarship by Heidegger and Habermas, see Žižek's bibliographical note, 87–88.

21   Žižek, "The Abyss of Freedom," 14–16, 11, 17.

22   Deleuze and Guattari, *Anti-Oedipus*, 245–46.

23   Deleuze and Guattari, *A Thousand Plateaus*, 97–98.

24   Rancière, *Dissensus*, 170–81.

25   Hallward, *Out of This World*, 3, 79.

26   Žižek, "The Abyss of Freedom," 77.

27   Jameson, *A Singular Modernity*.

28   Ibid., 207, 206, 126–27.

29   Doane, *The Emergence of Cinematic Time*, 140–71.

30   See also, for example, related works by Tom Gunning: "The Cinema of Attractions" and "An Aesthetic of Astonishment."

31   Doane, *The Emergence of Cinematic Time*, 165–66.

32   Jameson, *A Singular Modernity*, 199.

33   Jameson, *Late Marxism*, 16–17.

34   Vattimo, *The End of Modernity*, 166.

35   Yúdice, *The Expediency of Culture*, 1–2.

36   Peter Osborne, "'Whoever Speaks of Culture Speaks of Administration as Well.'"

37   See, for example, Boltanski and Chiapello, *The New Spirit of Capitalism*, 217–72.

38   Vico, *The New Science of Giambattista Vico*, axioms 374–84.

39   Luft, *Vico's Uncanny Humanism*, 16–20, 8–10.

40   Ibid., 175, 195, 196.

41   Kaufman, *In Face of Mystery*, 264–80, 268, 275.

42   Bakhtin, "Response to a Question," 1–9.

43   Bakhtin, *The Dialogic Imagination*.

44   For further illustrations of Bakhtin's idea of "creative understanding," see Willemen, *Looks and Frictions*, 212–18; Gibson, *Creating Selves*, 129–31.

Chapter Two: Creativity as a Product of Labor

1   Lazzarato, "Immaterial Labor," 146–47.
2   This is shown, for example, in John Howkins's latest book, *Creative Ecology*, which privileges "ideas" as the basis of the creative economy.
3   Toffler, *Powershift*, 222–23.
4   Ibid.
5   Bjørn Asheim and Eric Clark argue that the "new economy" is characterized by competitions built on innovation and differentiation strategies, as opposed to previous competitions that were based on price competition. See "Creativity and Cost in Urban and Regional Development," 806. However, I believe that this "new economy" is composed of both components, and in fact their continual intensification.
6   See Reich, *The Work of Nations*, 208–24.
7   Dyer-Witheford, *Cyber-Marx*, 231.
8   For a historical analysis of the complex relationship between the stationer and the author in the earliest copyright laws, see Patterson, *Copyright in Historical Perspective*, 64–77. For the different emphases on the author's rights in European and American copyright cultures, see P. Goldstein, *Copyrights' Highway*, 137–42. For the authorial anxiety manifested in contemporary IPR laws in general, see Coombe, *The Cultural Life of Intellectual Properties*, 169–70.
9   Woodmansee, "The Genius and the Copyright."
10 For scholarship on the exploitative working conditions of contemporary creative workers, see related discussion in the introduction.
11 Marx, *Grundrisse*, 146.
12 The vigorous Dutch art market was originally more commodity market than art market; in the early seventeenth century people paid standard prices for pictures according to their subjects, rather than their artists. New marketing strategies were introduced toward the end of the century to respond to the saturation of the mass-produced portrait market, and there developed a new discourse of master artists. Discerning individuals also evolved a taste for finely crafted paintings. See North, *Art and Commerce in the Dutch Golden Age*, 82–105.
13 Marx, *Capital, Volume 1*, 284–85, 312, 289, 290.
14 Ibid., 579.
15 See, for example, Florida's description of "experiential life," in which the creative class gains creativity through leisure. *The Rise of the Creative Class*, 165–79.
16 Pratt, "Advertising and Creativity."
17 Ibid., 1892.
18 See Banks et al., "Risk and Trust in Cultural Industries."
19 Harney, "Unfinished Business."
20 McRobbie, "Clubs to Companies."
21 Such industrialization of creativity is elaborately discussed by Frankfurt school scholars, particularly in the culture industry model. See, for example, Adorno, *The Culture Industry*.

22 Marissa Ann Mayer, "Creativity Loves Constraints," *Business Week*, 13 February 2006, 102.

23 Martina Morris and Western, "Inequality in Earnings at the Close of the Twentieth Century."

24 Neff, Wissinger, and Zukin, "Entrepreneurial Labor among Cultural Producers," 331.

25 Here lies a major quandary of the current copyright debates: Should ideas be protected? A major principle of copyright discourse is the dichotomy of ideas and expressions: although expressions should be protected, ideas should not, because ideas belong to the entire human race. However, many recent cases demonstrate that ideas are now protected, although not entirely by copyright but by many other kinds of contract and business laws.

26 Klinger, "The Contemporary Cinephile."

27 Landes and Posner, *The Economic Structure of Intellectual Property Law*, 223–24.

28 Pierson, *Special Effects*, 149–58.

29 However, there are also strategic moments when IPR owners highlight the material conditions of the actual hierarchy of creative workers. Governmental and corporate antipiracy campaigns often exploit the notion and the interests of the creative worker to criminalize piracy. In television campaigns by the Motion Picture Association of America, movie trailers, and the Internet, the unauthorized reproduction and distribution of movies is portrayed as a threat to the livelihoods of people working in the film industry—not famous stars or directors but the actual workers. See Gates, "Will Work for Copyrights."

30 Yue, "Hawking in the Creative City"; Malanga, "The Curse of the Creative Class"; Mc-Cann, "Inequality and Politics in the Creative City-Region."

31 Florida, *The Rise of the Creative Class*, 67–82.

32 Florida, *Cities and the Creative Class*, 35, 5.

33 Seabrook, *Nobrow*, 72.

34 Gaines, *Contested Culture*, 63–64.

35 Fiske, "The Cultural Economy of Fandom," 30–49.

36 Wirtén, "Out of Sight and out of Mind."

37 Shorthose and Strange, "The New Cultural Economy," 50.

38 du Gay and Pryke, "Cultural Economy."

39 Benjamin, "Little History of Photography," 527, 526.

40 Marx, *Capital, Volume 1*, 133.

41 Arendt, *The Human Condition*, 105, 105–6, 111.

42 Fine and Saad-Filho, *Marx's Capital*, 10.

43 Rancière, *The Nights of Labor*, 15–23.

Chapter Three: Creativity as a Construct of Rights

1   This is made possible by the doctrine of "works made for hire." Many IPR critics appreciate the European IPR laws more than Anglo-Saxon laws, as the former support the creator's inalienable moral rights, so that creators retain their copyright even after the formal transfer of the title to new owners. For an elaborate discussion of the differences

between the European and the American logics of authors' rights, see Samuelson, "Economic and Constitutional Influences on Copyright Law in the U.S."; Warwick, "Is Copyright Ethical?" 272.

2   May and Sell, *Intellectual Property Rights*, 50–52, 52–55.

3   Patterson, *Copyright in Historical Perspective*, 4.

4   Robinson, "The Evolution of Copyright," 56.

5   Celia Lury provides a lucid historical account of the rise of commercial publishing in relation to the advent of mass printing technology in *Cultural Rights*, 97–120. I discuss copyrights in more details in chapter 9.

6   May and Sell, *Intellectual Property Rights*, 109.

7   Ibid., 117–22.

8   For the difficulties and concerns characterizing the transition between bilateral and multilateral copyright laws, see Sherman and Bently, *The Making of Modern Intellectual Property Law*, 111–14.

9   For the fierce copyright and patent controversies that took place in the early twentieth century that shaped the development of Hollywood, see Vaidhyanathan, *Copyrights and Copywrongs*, 87–105.

10 Smith, *Lectures on Jurisprudence*, 11, quoted in MacLeod, *Inventing the Industrial Revolution*, 198.

11 Recent IPR discussions echo debates and understandings of traditional property rights. For an elaboration of their relationships, see Vinciguerra, "The Dialectic Relationship between Different Concepts of Property Rights."

12 Locke, *Two Treatises of Government*, 111–12, 141.

13 Spooner, *A Letter to Scientists and Inventors*, 10. See May and Sell, *Intellectual Property Rights*, 18.

14 West, "Property Rights in the History of Economic Thought," 21.

15 MacPherson, *The Political Theory of Possessive Individualism*, 263–64.

16 Poulantzas, "Marxist Examination of the Contemporary State and Law," 25–46.

17 For an overview of the evolution of IPR from territorial to global, see Drahos, "Thinking Strategically about Intellectual Property Rights"; Maskus, *Intellectual Property Rights in the Global Economy*, 15–26.

18 In addition to the WTO, the World Intellectual Property Organization (WIPO) of the United Nations also plays a part in supervising global copyright issues, particularly in areas related to computers. For more discussions see chapter 5.

19 P. Goldstein, *Copyrights' Highway*, 160.

20 The WTO declares that all forms of artistic expression are services to be governed by GATS, and as such, WTO members should refrain from subsidizing the arts in any form. Allegedly, GATS has stripped national governments of their ability to protect their national markets from being totally monopolized by a narrow variety of mainstream cultural products.

21 Amin, *Obsolescent Capitalism*, 96.

22 Sell, *Private Power, Public Law*, 163.

23 Harvey, *The New Imperialism*, 148.

24   Fisher, *Capitalist Realism*, 6.

25   Collins, *Marxism and Law*, 87–88.

26   On the rampant media piracy situations in Myanmar, the Philippines, and Nigeria, as well as China, see Tosa, "Public Significance of Cultural Piracy," 39–46; Baumgärtel, "The Culture of Piracy in the Philippines"; Larkin, "Degraded Images, Distorted Sounds"; and Pang, *Cultural Control and Globalization in Asia*, 98–116.

27   May, "The Denial of History."

28   Gillespie, *Wired Shut*, 102.

29   I must emphasize that copyright and patent are concepts intimately related to natural rights, whereas trademarks and trade secrets have a greater basis in contract law. My focus here is mostly on the former two, but I will continue to use the general term IPR as I proceed, because it is this regime that conjures up the romantic notion of the creative agency whose rights must be protected at all costs.

30   For an introduction to concepts of copyright, see, for example, Julie Cohen et al., *Copyright in a Global Information Economy*.

31   Rønning, Thomas, Tomaseli, and Teer-Tomaseli, "Intellectual Property Rights and the Political Economy of Culture," 1.

32   See Boyle, *The Public Domain*, 24–25.

33   Marcuse, "Some Social Implications of Modern Technology."

34   Halbert, *Resisting Intellectual Property*, 1–2.

35   Among the most vocal and prominent critics in this regard is probably Lawrence Lessig and the Creative Commons project he represents. See http://creativecommons.org/ (accessed 13 August 2008).

36   See, for example, Boyle, *Shamans, Software and Spleens*, 25–34.

37   The Creative Commons license is a derivative of the copyleft license, which resulted from the earlier GNU Project, founded in 1983 by Richard Stallman with the goal of developing a complete UNIX-like operating system composed entirely of free software. Copyleft gives readers the right to copy, redistribute, and modify a work, but it requires all copies and derivatives to be available under the same license; Creative Commons does not stipulate that requirement. The largest project using the GNU license is Wikipedia.

38   Gibson, *Creating Selves*, 109–16.

39   Arendt, *The Origins of Totalitarianism*, 301. Many other recent philosophers have different perspectives, such as Singer and Dworkin, who question whether the notion of natural rights can be established at all. See Warwick, "Is Copyright Ethical?"

40   Having been a stateless refugee for eighteen years, Arendt realizes that the universal dimension of human rights is meaningless to a political refugee, who, without the protection of the state, has no property left other than the property of being human. Such subjects are mere "human beings" in the most abstract terms. See Arendt, *The Origins of Totalitarianism*, 290–302.

41   For elaborate discussions and intercultural comparisons of various pirate images and ideologies, see Pennell, *Bandits at Sea*.

42   Raymond, *The Cathedral and the Bazaar*.

43   Death, "Phrack Pro-Phile XXXIII," quoted in Thomas, *Hacker Culture*, 26.

44 Wirtén, "Out of Sight and out of Mind." Examples include *Hackers* (dir. Iain Softley, 1995), *The Net* (dir. Irwin Winkler, 1995), and *The Matrix* (dir. Andy Wachowski and Larry Wachowski, 1999).

45 Thomas, *Hacker Culture*, 117.

46 Kelty, *Two Bits*, 245.

47 Hu Yizhen, "Zhongguo zimuzu yu xinziyouzhuyi de gongzuo lunli."

48 Vann, "The Limits of Authenticity in Vietnamese Consumer Markets"; Luvaas, "Designer Vandalism."

49 Halstead, "Branding 'Perfection' Foreign as Self."

50 Barthes, "The Death of the Author," 146.

51 Lash and Urry, *Economies of Signs and Space*.

52 Dirlik, *Global Modernity*, 44–47.

53 Klein, "Reclaiming the Commons," 84.

54 Coombe, *The Cultural Life of Intellectual Properties*, 73–76.

55 Bick and Chiper, "Swoosh Identity."

56 Alan Liu, *The Laws of Cool*, 179.

57 Gillespie, *Wired Shut*, 1–6.

58 Kittler, *Literature, Media, Information Systems*, 166–67.

59 Philip, "What Is a Technological Author?"

60 Notable studies include Castells, *The Rise of the Network Society*; Sassen, *Cities in a World Economy*; Bauman, *Globalization*.

61 Lash, *Critique of Information*, 68.

62 See Aggarwal and Koo, "Beyond Network Power?"

63 Balibar, "(De)Constructing the Human as Human Institution," 733.

Chapter Four: Cultural Policy, Intellectual Property Rights

1 On the ways early capitalist economies were embedded in the current political environment, see Polanyi, *The Great Transformation*.

2 Gallagher, *Contagious Capitalism*, 100–102.

3 Miller and Yúdice, *Cultural Policy*, 5.

4 Bennett, *The Birth of the Museum*.

5 McGuigan, *Rethinking Cultural Policy*, 33–35.

6 Holm, *Art and Ideology in Revolutionary China*, 17–23.

7 Mao, "Talks at the Yan'an Forum on Literature and the Arts."

8 In the first years of the young nation, large-scale political programs condemning counterrevolutionary art and thinking include the nationwide criticism of the film *Wu Xun zhuan* (The story of Wu Xun) in 1951 and the movements against Yu Pingbo and Hu Shi in 1954 and against Hu Feng in 1955.

9 Jiang, "Jianguo yilai Zhonggong wenhua zhengce shuping (1949–1976)."

10 Model plays were the few heavily engineered propaganda theatrical pieces allowed to be performed in the country during the period. Clark elaborately discusses these plays in his book, *The Chinese Cultural Revolution: A History*.

11   Kraus, *The Party and the Arty in China*, 22.

12   Andreas, *Rise of the Red Engineers*, 1.

13   See Li Jun, *Kunrao yu zhuanji*, 54–58; Gao, *Wenhua yishu guanlilun*, 21–26.

14   See Pan, *Jiaru shijie mouyi zuzhi hou*, chapter 2.

15   McGrath, *Postsocialist Modernity*, 4.

16   Jing Wang, *Brand New China*, 352n43.

17   See, for example, Keane, "Bringing Culture Back In," 92.

18   Montgomery, "Space to Grow."

19   Potts, "Do Developing Economies Need Creative Industries?," 98–99.

20   Zhao Ming, "Jianguan bumen boyi."

21   Yang Jihua, "Lun Woguo wenhua chanye chanye de shishi jizhi," 72.

22   The Working Group is headed by the Central Propaganda Department. Its upper-level officials come from the National Bureau of Statistics; the Ministry of Culture; the State Administration of Radio, Film, and Television; the General Administration of Press and Publication; and the State Administration of Cultural Heritage.

23   Zhonggong zhongyang guowuyuan, "Guanyu shenhua wenhua tizhi gaige de ruogan yijian."

24   On the case of Shenzhen, see Zhu Zhe, "Zhiding wenhua zhengce fakuai, duidong Shenzhen wenhua chanye fazhen."

25   According to Hui, the term "creative industries" was not in use on the Chinese mainland until 2005, and "cultural industries" has been the official term in state policy ("From Cultural to Creative Industries," 318). In this chapter I use the term "creative industries" to describe the discourse, and "cultural industries" to refer to the term actually used in PRC policies.

26   Keane, "Brave New World," 267.

27   See Zhou Lin and Li, *Zhongguo banquan shi yanjiu wenxian*, 2–10; Kong Zhengyi, "Shilun gudai tushu de banquan baohu."

28   Wong, "An Overview of the Development of China's Patent System," 3.

29   See Alford, *To Steal a Book Is an Elegant Offense*, 13–14; Yang Yidong, "Zhongguo gudai banquan yishi."

30   Guo, "Zhongguo banquan wenti tanyuan."

31   Feng Nianhua, "Daoban dui Songdai banquan de yingxiang."

32   Berger, "Faith and Development," 73–74.

33   Liu Jianjun and Gan, "Zhuanli xingzhi de jiangli zhidu"; Yao Xiulan, "Zhidu goujian yu shehui bianqian."

34   Ganea and Pattloch, *Intellectual Property Law in China*, 2, 207.

35   Xin, *Banquan maoyi yu huawen chuban*, 22–23.

36   Yao and Zhang, "Jindai Zhongguo shangbiao lifalun." For a complete version of the Provisional Regulations, see Zuo Xuchu, *Zhongguo shangbiao falü shi: Jinxiandai bufen*, 94–103.

37   P. Feng, *Intellectual Property in China*, 3.

38   H. Zheng, "The Patent System of the People's Republic of China," 345.

39   Examples include the Interim Regulations concerning the Grant of Rights over Inventions and Patent Rights (enacted in 1950), Provisional Measures for the Registration of

Trademarks (also enacted in 1950), and the Decision on the Improvement and Development of Publication Activities (announced in 1951).

40 Ganea and Pattloch, *Intellectual Property Law in China*, 3.

41 Xin, *Banquan maoyi yu huawen chuban*, 22–23.

42 Zhonggong zhongyang guowuyuan, *Zhongguo zhishi chanquan baohu zhuangkuang*, 2–5.

43 Xue, "What Direction Is the Wind Blowing?" More discussions about DMCA follow in the next chapter.

44 Zhongguo chuban kexue yanjiu suo and Quanguo guomin yuedu yu goumai qingxiang chouyang diaocha keti zu, *Woguo guomin dui daoban chubanwu de renshi*, 178–84.

45 World Bank, "Fight Poverty: Findings and Lessons from China's Success," http://econ .worldbank.org (accessed 26 September 2007).

46 See Dimitrov, *Piracy and the State*; U.S. Department of Commerce, "Protecting Your Intellectual Property Rights (IPR) in China."

47 Jerome Cohen, "China's Reform Era Legal Odyssey."

48 See Zhang Zhiqiang, "Zhidu biangeng yu daoban fanlan."

49 A good reference is the film *Man yan* 蔓延 (pirated copy, 2004), directed by He Jianjun (何建軍).

50 J. L. Qiu, *Working-Class Network Society*, 171–73, 201–2.

51 Hong, "The Sustainable Development of Tourism in Lijiang."

52 See Mette Hansen, *Lessons in Being Chinese*.

53 See Blum, *Portraits of "Primitives*," 144–54.

54 Although Lijiang is still believed to be associated with the novel, it is Zhongdian that is now officially called China's Shangri-La, as the little town is now thought of as being the real inspiration for the novel. Foreign backpackers now favor Zhongdian, while Lijiang's tourists are now mostly Han.

55 Hong, "The Sustainable Development of Tourism in Lijiang."

56 Ayres, "Is Free Trade Selling Out the Arts?"

57 See Chan-Tibergien, "Cultural Diversity as Resistance to Neoliberal Globalization"; Coalition for Cultural Diversity (Ottawa), "UNESCO Stand Up," 23.

58 See, for example, Papandrea, "Trade and Cultural Diversity."

59 Hevia, "World Heritage," 224.

60 Announced at the third China Beijing International Cultural and Creative Industry Expo, 17 December 2008.

61 Beijing Office: World Heritage Guide Training, unesco.org (accessed 3 January 2009).

62 World Heritage Centre, UNESCO, "About World Heritage," http://whc.unesco.org (accessed 12 October 2007).

63 See Feltault, "Development Folklife."

64 Executive Committee of the Congress of the People of Yunnan Province, "Yunnan sheng Naxi zu Dongba wenhua baohu tiaoli," see specifically Regulations 11–17.

65 Lijiang Science and Technology Bureau, "Zhishi chanquan ke."

66 Liang Caiheng, "Cong zhishi chanquan de jiaodu guanzhu Lijiang de shengcun yu fazhen."

67 Long Yue, "Zhou Xun zhuyan dianying qinquan Naxi Yinyue Shijia yinyue."

68　Rees, *Echoes of History*, 6.

69　Ambasada Republicii Populare Chineze în Romania, "Protecting Biodiversity for the Sake of Cultural Diversity," 2005, www.chinaembassy.org.ro (accessed 12 October 2007).

70　Center for Biodiversity and Indigenous Knowledge, "Indigenous Papermaking in Yunnan," 2007, www.cbik.org (accessed 12 October 2007).

71　Dongba paper is made from two endemic stringbush plants, *Wikstroemia delavayi* and *W. Lichiangensis*, noted for their well-developed bast fiber. Zhonghua Renmin Gongheguo Guojia Zhishichanquanju, "Anli texie."

72　Ibid.

73　Gibson, *Creating Selves*, 96–97.

74　Comaroff and Comaroff, *Ethnicity, Inc.*, 46.

75　Li Dezhu, "Dan de disandai lingdao jiti dui Makesi zhuyi minzu lilun de xinfazhan xingongxian."

76　See, for example, Yale, *From Tourist Attraction to Heritage Tourism*; Poria, Butler, and Airey, "The Core of Heritage Tourism."

77　He Liming, "Shilun Dongba wenhua de chuancheng."

78　He Jinguang, "Naxi zu Dongba wenhua yanjiu fazhen qushi."

79　Yamamura, "Authenticity, Ethnicity and Social Transformation at World Heritage Sites," 185–200.

80　Yamamura, "Dongba Art in Lijiang, China."

81　The project is primarily the work of the Beijing-based producer Lola, and it received support from the Propaganda Department of the Yunnan provincial government to increase Yunnan's tourist business. The project is made up of ten stories that take place in Yunnan and features ten young Chinese female directors from Hong Kong, Taiwan, and mainland China. See www.cinecn.net (accessed 28 May 2009).

82　Mu Xiaowen, "Fei zhuanye shijing yanchu Yingxiang Lijiang yi pinpai zhilu cu fazhen."

83　Peralta, "A Call for Intellectual Property Rights," 287–89.

84　Coombe, "Protecting Traditional Environmental Knowledge."

85　As Chun Lin demonstrates, the PRC never completely adopted the Leninist model of the right of nations to self-determination, and separatism is prohibited in China. See *The Transformation of Chinese Socialism*, 100–101.

86　Fei Xiaotong et al., *Zhongguo minzu duoyuan yiti geju.*

87　Zhonghua Renmin Gongheguo Wenhuabu, "Guanyu jinyibu jiaqiang shaoshu minzu wenhua gongzuo de yijian."

88　Zhonghua Renmin Gongheguo Guojia Tongjiju, "Wenhua ji xiangguan chanye fenlei"; Li Fang, "Woguo chutai *Wenhua ji xiangguan chanye zhibiao tixi kuangjia.*"

89　On a Shanghai Xuhui regional follow-up on these two national documents, see Feng Yuhui et al., "Guanyu jianli Xuhui qu wenhua chanye tongji de shikao."

90　Fronville, "The International Creative Sector."

91　Ong, *Neoliberalism as Exception*, 109–13, 19.

92　Auerbach, "The Meanings of Neoliberalism."

93　Rofel, *Desiring China*, 17–21.

94　Wang Hui, *China's New Order*, 119.

95   Pierre Bourdieu, "The Essence of Neoliberalism," trans. Jeremy J. Shapiro, *Le monde diplomatique*, English ed., 8 December 1998, http://mondediplo.com (accessed 28 May 2009).

Chapter Five: Cinema as a Creative Industry

1   See, for example, Rennie, "Creative World"; Hartley, "Creative Industries."
2   The U.K. Department of Culture, Media and Sport defines creative industries as "those industries which have their origin in individual creativity, skill and talent and which have a potential for wealth and job creation through the generation and exploitation of intellectual property" ("Creative Industries," www.culture.gov.uk, accessed 9 September 2005).
3   The British government recently set up a cross-government body, the Creative Industries Forum on Intellectual Property, to prepare the creative industries to turn their creations into profitable intellectual properties. A major role of the forum is to deliver seminars and online and face-to-face advice to ensure creative workers understand how to exploit and protect their ideas under the IPR rubric. U.K. Department of Culture, Media and Sport, "Creative Industries Forum on Intellectual Property Launched," 2004, www.culture.gov.uk (accessed 9 September 2005).
4   Leadbeater and Oakley, *The Independents.*
5   Zhonghua Minguo Xingzhengyuan, *Tiaozhan 2008*, 46–63.
6   Iwabuchi, "Useful Culture, Useless Media and Cultural Studies."
7   Lily Kong, Gibson, Khoo, and Semple, "Knowledges of the Creative Economy."
8   Tung, *The 1998 Policy Address*, 13.
9   Tung, *Capitalising on Our Advantages*, 11; Tung, *Seizing Opportunities for Development*, 18; Tung, *Working Together for Economic Development and Social Harmony*, 32–34.
10   Donald Tsang, "Hong Kong Gears Up to Diversify Growth," *China Daily*, 17 August 2008.
11   Centre for Cultural Policy Research, *Baseline Study on Hong Kong's Creative Industries*, 23.
12   For the predicaments of cinema within the British creative industries discourse, see Hill, "UK Film Policy," 34.
13   See, for example, Guneratne, "Introduction," 8.
14   See Guback, "Government Financial Support to the Film Industry in the United States," 91.
15   See, for example, Rutherford, "Australian Animation Aesthetics."
16   Zion, "Creating a Successful Local Industry."
17   UK Film Council, "UK Film Council at a Glance."
18   Neumann, "German Federal Film Fund (DFFF)."
19   See Tuomi, "Organisational Shifts in the Feature Film Industry."
20   Centre for Cultural Policy Research, *Baseline Study on Hong Kong's Creative Industries*, 105.
21   Film Services Office webpage, www.fso-tela.gov.hk (accessed 16 January 2008).
22   Tsang, *Proactive, Pragmatic.*

23   See Pang, "Postcolonial Hong Kong Cinema."

24   *Mingpao*, 28 April 2005. The newsgroup is hosted by iAdvantage Limited and is arguably the most popular BT site in Hong Kong.

25   The alias is translated as "Big Crook" in some newspapers.

26   He was found guilty on 24 October, and sentencing was announced on 7 November. *South China Morning Post*, 25 October 2005, 8 November 2005.

27   Although online film piracy has not attracted much legal attention since then, a wave of lawsuits and criminal proceedings against file-sharers has been instigated by music industries across the world. In January 2006 the British court for the first time declared file-sharing unlawful and fined two sharers. However, at around the same time, a new Swedish political party was established with the aim of abolishing copyright laws. For relevant news, see "File-sharers in Europe Face a Wave of Lawsuits?," *International Herald Tribune*, 5 April 2006; Jonathan Brown, "Illegal File-Sharers Fined for First Time in Britain," *Independent*, 28 January 2006; Gwladys Fouche, "Pirates Pursue a Political Point: A New Swedish Party Aims to Abolish the Copyright Laws that Criminalise File Sharers," *Guardian* (London), 9 February 2006.

28   The first Hong Kong International Film and TV Market (FILMART) was held in June 2004. The second FILMART was quickly incorporated into the Entertainment Expo. FILMART, "FILMART 2004 Promotes Cross Media Collaboration," press release, 8 June 2004, www.hkfilmart.com (accessed 19 July 2005).

29   *South China Morning Post*, 8 November 2005.

30   According to the Hong Kong Motion Picture Industry Association, in 2004 the total box office receipts of foreign films in Hong Kong were HK$460 million, while that of local films were HK$383 million. In 2007 the annual box office of foreign languages films reached HK$784 million, and that for local films fell to HK$229 million.

31   My own observations at www.hk-pub.com/forum and bt.newsgroup.com.hk.

32   McDonald and Wasko, "Introduction," 5.

33   Anup Tikku argues that in spite of the relentless demand by developed countries for a rigid IPR framework in India, India's IPR laws have an insignificant effect on the actual flow of foreign investment into India. See Tikku, "Indian Inflow."

34   Crofts, "Reconceptualizing National Cinema/s."

35   See Teo, *Hong Kong Cinema*, 207–18; S. C. K. Chan, "Figures of Hope and the Filmic Imaginary of Jianghu"; Abbas, *Hong Kong*, 16–47.

36   See T. Williams, "Space, Place, and Spectacle"; Fu, *Between Shanghai and Hong Kong*, 51–92; Tan, "Chinese Diasporic Imaginations in Hong Kong Films."

37   See, for example, Landry, *The Creative City*.

38   See, for example, Dahlström and Hermelin, "Creative Industries, Spatiality and Flexibility."

39   See Mossig, "Global Networks of the Motion Picture Industry in Los Angeles/Hollywood."

40   Brenner, Marcuse, and Mayer, "Cities for People, Not for Profit"

41   I have discussed the relationship between Hong Kong cinema and the city's tourism in Pang, "Jackie Chan, Tourism, and the Performing Agency."

42   Graham Fuller, "Ziyi/Icon: Thrill of the Still: How an Image from Wong Kar-wai's Art-
      house Hit Keeps You Gazing," *Village Voice*, 16 September 2005.

43   See Meaghan Morris, "Transnational Imagination in Action Cinema." Singapore has
      a similar situation. In 2003 the Media Development Authority of Singapore began to
      promote the exportation of Made-in-Singapore media and film content, which features
      products backed by Singaporean money, so that many of those Made-in-Singapore films
      have nothing to do with the culture, location, and people of the country. Singapore Film
      Commission, "SFC Launches Two New Film Development Initiatives: $350,000 Boost for
      Local Filmmaking Talents," news release, 3 December 2003.

44   Curtin, *Playing to the World's Biggest Audience*, 39–41.

45   Zhong Baoxian, *Xianggang yingshiye bainian*, 398–431.

46   The data are not very helpful in demonstrating that reality. According to *Baseline Study*,
      there were 1,730 establishments in the film sector in 2002, employing about 8,620 per-
      sons (Centre for Cultural Policy Research, 105). According to the data provided by Hong
      Kong Census and Statistics Department, there were 20,436 people employed in motion
      pictures and other entertainment services as of June 2008, although exactly how the sec-
      tor is defined was not explained, and clearly not all those jobs are directly related to film
      production (http://bso.hktdc.com, accessed 22 January 2009).

47   I conducted in-depth interviews with eight new Hong Kong directors between June 2007
      and November 2008 to understand their working conditions and creative environment.
      Because many of the details are personal, I have kept them anonymous.

48   Customs and Excise Department, "Press Releases: SCIT Visits Customs and Excise De-
      partment."

49   Legislative Council, Hong Kong Special Administrative Region, LC Paper No. CB(1)863/
      04–05, www.legco.gov.hk (accessed 12 September 2005). Some claim that there was a
      95 percent drop in locally posted BT seeds, which I find highly doubtful. See also *South
      China Morning Post*, 25 October 2005.

50   Following the film industry's practice, in September 2005 Hong Kong's music industry
      also tracked down about one thousand netizens performing illegal music downloads, to
      whom warning letters were sent. But data show that the number of illegal music down-
      loads has not decreased at all. See *Mingpao*, 7 October 2005.

51   On the political effects of cinema's publicness, see Donald and Donald, "The Publicness
      of Cinema"; on its social effects, see Miriam Hansen, *Babel and Babylon*.

52   McCall, for example, says that he does not "see how the institution of cinema—which
      involves the social act of looking at moving images, and talking about them—is going to
      be threatened by new technology" (McCall, Turvey, Foster, Iles, Baker, and Buckingham,
      "Round Table," 74).

53   Scott Morrison, "Intel Backs Star's Internet Movie Plan Film Distribution," *Financial
      Times*, U.S. ed., 7 July 2005.

54   We can take Lucasfilm, the Hollywood company arguably most committed to digi-
      tal technologies, as an example. Among its seven current divisions, three of them—
      Industrial Light and Magic, Lucasfilm Animation, and Skywalker Sound—handle digi-
      tal effects, while a completely different division, Lucas Online, is in charge of the online

distribution of films. The division of labor and the matters of concern among the groups do not seem to overlap. Lucasfilm Ltd., "Lucasfilm: Divisions," www.lucasfilm.com (accessed 7 January 2006). For a general description of the major tasks of Lucasfilm's several digital effects divisions, see Rubin, *Droidmaker*, 467–87. This account, however, does not discuss the Lucas Online division.

55 Hozic, *Hollyworld*, 138. Sheigh Crabtree, "Lucas: Future in Asia, Video Games," *Hollywood Reporter.com*, 2 August 2005.

56 Lunenfeld, "The Myths of Interactive Cinema," 149–50. Mulvey, "Passing Time."

57 DeCSS allows customers to play discs on computer systems that are encrypted by CSS, including open-source code programs such as Linux.

58 Two representative cases are *Universal City Studios et al. v. Shawn Reimerdes et al.*, 82 F. Supp 2d 21, 111 F. Supp. 2d 346 (S.D.N.Y. 2000), and *Universal City Studios et al. v. Eric Corley*, 273 F.2d 429 (2001). See G. K. Roberts, "DeCSS Code on the Internet"; Declan McCullagh, "DVD Piracy Judge Tells All," *Wired*, 17 November 2000, online (accessed 23 December 2005).

59 For historical background leading to the treaty, see Nimmer, *Copyright*, 141–48. It was mostly a matter of timing that caused the UN, instead of the WTO, to take up these issues. It was around the finalization of the Agreement on TRIPs, between 1992 and 1993, that the world began to feel the spectacular impact of the Internet, and it was too late to reopen negotiations on copyright and related issues in the WTO. The WIPO was considered the logical alternative forum to respond to new copyright issues related to the use of digital technology in an expanding global information network. See Ficsor, *The Law of Copyright and the Internet*, 25.

60 Summary of the WIPO Copyright Treaty, 1996, www.wipo.int (accessed 22 December 2005).

61 As an international treaty, the WCT does not enter into force until thirty instruments of ratification or accession by states have been deposited with the director general of WIPO. The United States was among the first nations to ratify the WCT through DMCA. After extremely long discussions, the European Union, which had resorted to sui generis rights to deal with copyright issues related to computer files and databases, finally passed the European Union Copyright Directive in 2001. The WCT finally took effect in March 2002, after its ratification by Gabon four months earlier. While there might be variations in different national laws and regulations governing digital copyright protection, the effect of the WCT is now clearly global.

62 On the historical development of the Berne Convention, see P. Goldstein, *Copyrights' Highway*, 150–61. On the concept of "fair use" and its problems, see Pang, *Cultural Control and Globalization in Asia*, 31–34.

63 Ernesto, "DRM Killing BitTorrent.com Video Store," 7 March 2007, http://torrentfreak .com (accessed 20 January 2011).

64 Gillespie, *Wired Shut*, 256.

65 Pang, *Cultural Control and Globalization in Asia*, 31.

66 Gillespie, *Wired Shut*, 7.

67 Lazzarato, "Immaterial Labor."

68 Harney, "Unfinished Business."

69 Data obtained from Wu Guojun, "Dianyingyuan yu Xianggang shehui, jingji mailuo xia de jingying zhuankuang," 4. For a comparison of Hong Kong's film admission rates with other countries,' see Acland, *Screen Traffic*, 253.

70 Gibson, *Creating Selves*, 115.

Chapter Six: Branding the Creative City

1   On the branding campaign of the University of North Texas, see "Branding at UNT," www.unt.edu (accessed 23 October 2006). Fitch, the international design and branding consultancy firm, has helped brand the British Army by delivering a new modern image of bravery, emphasizing adventurous training, fear management, personal growth, and team spirit as benefits of army training. The overall purpose is to promote recruitment. See www.fitch.com (accessed 3 June, 2011). The branding battle is heated between Dasani and Aquafina, the bottled water brands of Coca-Cola and Pepsi-Cola, respectively. The branding of soil, or geography, has become an increasingly important category of the IPR regime; a classic example is the Mexican spirit tequila, which has acquired a geographic indication which ensures that no liquor made with alternative ingredients can be marketed as tequila.

2   See Comaroff and Comaroff, *Ethnicity, Inc.*, 122–38.

3   Wigmans, "Contingent Governance and the Enabling City," 203.

4   Ibid., 208.

5   For a more detailed analysis of the recent development of the tourist discourse in Hong Kong, see Pang, "Jackie Chan, Tourism, and the Performing Agency."

6   For a brief summary of Beijing's city planning from the 1920s to the 1990s, see Visser, "Spaces of Disappearance."

7   Braester, *Painting the City Red*, 281–309.

8   See Hui, "From Cultural to Creative Industries"; Keane, "The Capital Complex."

9   Jing Wang, "Culture as Leisure and Culture as Capital."

10 Keane, "The Capital Complex."

11 See Friedmann, *The World City Hypothesis*; Sassen, *Cities in a World Economy*.

12 Scholars have also begun to map the development of creative industries according to cities instead of nations. See, for example, Gilbert, "From Paris to Shanghai."

13 Wang Shaoguang, *Fenquan de dixian*, 42–62; Jing Vivian Zhang, "Decentralizing China."

14 M. Johnston and Hao, "China's Surge of Corruption," 84. A political storm raged in Shanghai in 2006, when the central government filed corruption charges against the most powerful local officials of the city. See Joseph Kahn, "Shanghai Party Boss Held for Corruption," *International Herald Tribune*, Asia-Pacific ed., 25 September 2006.

15 Nan Wang, "Shanghai Goes Creative over Eight Sectors."

16 Guangzhou shi zhengfu, "Yuexiu dazao guonei zhiming chuangyi zhongxin."

17 "Created and Made in China!," *Financial Times Information*, 30 May 2006.

18 "1000 New Museums Are Expected to Be Built in China over the Next Ten Years," *Space Daily*, 29 March 2006.

19 Ibid.

20 For the concept of cluster, see Porter, "Clusters and the New Economics of Competition."

21 Yi, "Is 798 a Cultural Petting Zoo?," 4.

22 Gaubatz, "China's Urban Transformation," 1497.

23 Luo, "Recollections on the History of 718," 13.

24 See Lloyd, *Neo-Bohemia*, 89–104. The classic and most studied example is the gentrification of New York's East Village. See Mele, *Selling the Lower East Side*.

25 It is reported that the first artistic use of the space can be traced back to 1995, when the Central Academy of Fine Arts rented a warehouse to produce a statue commissioned by the government to commemorate the Anti-Japanese War. Zuo Lin, "798."

26 Zhu Yan, *798*, 46–47.

27 Stenning, "Shaping the Economic Landscapes of Postsocialism?," 763.

28 Luo, "Recollections on the History of 718," 11–12.

29 Hui, "From Cultural to Creative Industries," 317–31.

30 Wang Shucheng, "Shangye dongle jiya yishu gongchang."

31 Zhou Hongyu, "Linggan, laizi '798.'"

32 I have not been able to find such a report in *Newsweek*, other than an article specifically on design culture, which cited Beijing, along with eleven other cities, as places where one could find vigorous design cultures. In spite of the wide references in China's media, there is no mention of Beijing being one of the world's top twelve cities, although the report does mention 798. Rana Foroohar et al., "Funky Towns: Where Would You Go to Discover the World's Top Hot Spots for Design?," *Newsweek International*, 27 October 2003, 48.

33 See the Bernard Tschumi Architects Company website, www.tschumi.com (accessed 30 December 2006).

34 The two reports are titled "Guangyu Beijingshi chengshi dingwei he fahui Beijing dute de wenhua canye youshi de jianyi" 關於北京市城市定位和發揮北京獨特的文化產業優勢的建議 (Suggestions for Beijing to position the city according to its best cultural industries) and "Guangyu yuan 718 lianhechang diqu jianzhu ji wenhua canye baohu de jianyi" 關於原 718 聯合廠地區建築及文化產業保護的建議 (Suggestions for the protection of the architecture and cultural industries at the original United Factory 718 Area). For a more detailed analysis of the two reports, see Cui Yongfu et al., "Dashanzhi 798 chang yishuqu diaoyan baogao."

35 Gaubatz, "China's Urban Transformation," 1516.

36 Chen Baohong, "Songzhuang de yishu 'jiaofu.'"

37 Ge, "Zhongguo yishupin gaiwai kuangbiao."

38 See the report by Changchang, "Baiwen renminbi yishujia."

39 "2010 diliujie Zhongguo—Songzhuang wenhua yishu jie" 2010 第六屆中國-宋莊文化藝術節 (2010 The sixth China—Songzhuang culture and arts festival), 23 July 2010, http://style.sina.com.cn (accessed 17 August 2010).

40 Yang Yufeng, "Songzhuang huajiacun." Artkey helped Taipei's National Palace Museum license the images of its famous collections to commercial enterprises, such as 7-Eleven, for mutual promotion.

41 Gu Weijie and Liu, "Songzhuang Xiaobaocun shuji Cui Dabo fangtan," 262.

42 Jansen, "Designer Nations," 122.

43 Donald, *Imagining the Modern City*, 1–11.

44 See, for example, Wu Wenguang's (吴文光) documentary film *Liulang Beijing* 流浪北京 (Bumming in Beijing: The last dreamers, 1989), and Qiu Huadong's popular novel *Chengshi zhanche*.

45 Sassen, *Cities in a World Economy*, 32.

46 See Benjamin, *Charles Baudelaire*; Simmel, "The Metropolis and Mental Life."

47 Appadurai, "Spectral Housing and Urban Cleansing," 649–50.

48 Studwell, *The China Dream*, 68–73.

49 Walker and Buck, "The Chinese Road."

50 Liu Liang, "Sun Jianjun 'zuoju.'"

51 Lefebvre, *The Urban Revolution*, 155–60; Harvey, *Social Justice and the City*, 313.

52 Ge, "Zhongguo yishupin gaiwai kuangbiao."

53 Xu Zhihao, "Zhongguo youhua."

54 Gu Lieming, "Wenzhou zijin yu 'chao' Beijing guoqi."

55 Liu Liang, "Sun Jianjun 'zuoju.'"

56 See Fang and Zhang, "Plan and Market Mismatch"; on the complexity of China's recent land reform, caught between socialism and capitalism, see Hin, *Urban Land Reform in China*, 129–50.

57 See Ching-Ching Ni, "Wave of Social Unrest Continues across China," *Los Angeles Times*, 10 August 2006; Minnie Chan, "A Rash of Conflicts Entangles Local Government, Firms and Residents," *South China Morning Post*, 1 May 2006.

58 Cary Huang and Bill Savadove, "Shanghai Scandal Spreads to Beijing," *South China Morning Post*, 20 October 2006.

59 Harvey, *The New Imperialism*, 137–61.

60 See Zhao Shufeng, Chen, and Zhang, *Beijing jiaoqu chengshihua tanshuo*, 89–90.

61 This is most clearly observed in a roundtable discussion among district leaders held on May 2006 on Beijing's overall creative industry plan, in which each raised grand plans for cultivating his own creative industries. The proceedings can be found in the editorial "Shoudu wenha chuangyi canye chengce quan jiexie."

62 Huang Xu, *Beijing chengxiang*, 149–50.

63 Interview with Li Xianting, Beijing, 15 September 2006.

64 Guangzhou daxuecheng Xiaoguwei yishucun bei biqian zhe, "Zhi Wen Jiabao zongli de gongkaixin."

65 Chen Jinfu and Liu, "Chengshi guihua xingzheng jiuji zhidu tantao," 23.

66 For the role of the university in the new knowledge economy, see Elizabeth George, "Positioning Higher Education for the Knowledge Based Economy," *Higher Education* 52, no. 4 (2006), 589–610.

67 "Songzhuang huajiacun chu liao 'taofang jingji ren.'"

68 Joey Liu, "Brush with the Law," *South China Morning Post*, 11 December 2007.

69 Antoaneta Bezlova, "Rights-China: New Property Law Ignores Farmers' Rights," IPS-Inter Press Service, 16 March 2007 (accessed through LexisNexis 31 January 2008).

70 "Zai Beijing Songzhuang mai xiaochanquanfang huajia."

71 Joey Liu, "Brush with the Law."

72 As K. W. Chan and Buckingham explain in "Is China Abolishing the *Hukou* System?," the *hukou* system in China has been operated along two sets of classification, agricultural and nonagricultural, as well as local and nonlocal. While the PRC is moving toward the abolition of the former type of segregation, the latter type of residence has only intensified in order to stop nonresidents from obtaining *hukou* in major cities.

73 Interview with two Beijing artists, Wang Yan (王燕) and Zhang Tingjun (張庭鈞), Beijing, 15 September 2006.

74 However, reflecting on the new cultural policy, starting in 2006 people in the creative industries are allowed to bid on special residences because creative practitioners are now heavily sought after in Beijing.

75 Interview with Beijing artist Li Feixue (里飛雪), Beijing, 16 September 2006. It was reported that in 1995 rent at 798 was thirty cents per square meter; by 2006 it rose to four dollars per square meter, close to the rate of the best office space in Beijing. Zuo Lin "798."

76 A similar situation has been observed in the Suzhou River area in Shanghai, another famous new art space in China, as rents in the neighborhood skyrocketed from less than 4,000 RMB per square meter to well over 10,000 RMB between 2000 and 2003. C. Lu, "From Underground to Public," 86.

77 See H. Wu, *Exhibiting Experimental Art in China.*

78 For a study of the importance of the body in contemporary Chinese art, see Berghuis, "Considering *Huanjing.*" For the specific performance piece of Zhu Yu's *Eating People*, see Cheng, "Violent Capital."

79 Interview with Li Xianting, Beijing, 15 September 2006.

80 Osborne, "Non-places and the Spaces of Art," 192.

81 Lefebvre, *The Production of Space*, 173, 171, 173, 18.

Chapter Seven: Animation and Transcultural Signification

1 Jenkins, *Textual Poachers*, 45–50.

2 Li Jianping, "Tashan zhi shi," 69.

3 Ge Hong, "Beijing, Shanghai qingshaonian donghua diaocha"; Zhao Hua and Xu, "'Sun Wukong' weihe doubuguo 'milaoshu'?"

4 *Silver-Haired Agito* (銀色の髪のアギト Gin'iro no kami no agito, dir. Sugiyama Keiichi 杉山慶一) was the first *anime* coproduced by Japanese and Chinese companies (Gonzo and Chinese Film Animation Ltd.). It was slated to be screened in China in March 2006, but, for unknown reasons, the theatrical release has still not happened. The DVD version was already available in Hong Kong in January 2007. See "Kaikyo!"

5 China began importing revenue-sharing foreign films in 1994, when the quota for foreign films was ten per year. After China joined the WTO, the quota increased gradually, and it reached twenty in 2005.

6 "'Anime' Subculture Exchange May Bridge Japan-China Gap," Jiji Press Ticker Service, 29 October 2005 (accessed through LexisNexis 2 March 2006).

7   "Riben dongman huobao weihe zhengqian nan?"

8   "'Made in Japan' Trademark to Fight Anime Piracy," *Mainichi Daily News*, 3 July 2004. Such figures are, of course, enormously misleading; Chinese consumers choose piracy partly because official products are so expensive.

9   Gaoge dianchenan, "Shei hai jide dangnian de Hainan shying meishu chubanshe?"

10   For example, one can find many examples of Japanese anime on the Chinese VERYCD website (accessed 27 February 2006). Some major Chinese websites featuring Japanese anime and manga include Comic-Anime Beat, www.cabeat.com (accessed 27 February 2006), and TotoroClub.net (accessed 27 February 2006).

11   Vivienne Chow, "Internet Piracy Nightmare for Anime Director," *South China Morning Post*, 9 January 2006.

12   Fei Yuxiao, *Chuangzhao mengxiang yu feixiang de laoren*. I bought the book at Idea Bookshop on 7 February 2006. It does not indicate the year of publication, but since *Howl's Moving Castle* was not released until 2004, the book was likely published around 2004 or 2005. This author has published similar items about Japanese manga and anime materials.

13   Chen Qijia and Song, "Zhongguo donghua fazhan wenti zhengyi."

14   For example, the Korean *Totoro* poster (p. 54) was likely copied from the Korean website Cincine.co.kr (accessed 27 February 2006); the many manga illustrations in *Nausicaa of the Valley of the Winds* (pp. 26–34) likely were copied directly from Miyazaki Hayao's original manga *Kaze no tani no naushika*; and many of the photos of the Ghibli museum (pp. 220–33) were copied from the Chinese book *The Hot Air of Ghibli* 《吉卜力的熱風》 (Beijing: Feitian dianzhi yinxiang chubanshe 飛天電子音像出版社, n.d.), which itself is a pirated book. The quality of the different images varies greatly; and those pictures with the lowest resolution are quite clearly television screen shots (e.g., pp. 91, 172).

15   Kanō Seiji, "*Kaze no tani no naushika* kara *Mononoke no hime* e."

16   Dan Martin, "Fakes a Real Fact of Life in China's Heated Economy," *The Standard*, 11 April 2007.

17   Kazuto Tsukamoto, "Shanghai Surprise: Animation on the Rise," *Asahi Shinbun*, 23 April 2005.

18   Kenji Kawase, "Hangzhou Aspires to Crown of Animation, 'Manga' Capital," *Nikkei Weekly*, 20 June 2005.

19   Siu-sin Chan, "Animation Industry Lacks Talent and Chinese Brands, says Official," *South China Morning Post*, 20 January 2006.

20   Yoon, "'In-between the Values of the Global and the National."

21   Tsukamoto, "Shanghai Surprise."

22   For a historical overview of South Korea's animation industry, see Kim, "Critique of the New Historical Landscape of South Korean Animation."

23   "Manga Course Attracts Lecturers," *Daily Yomiuri*, 9 June 2004.

24   Allison, *Millennial Monsters*, 13.

25   Quoted in Shen, "What Is 'Computer Animation'?"

26   P. Wells, *Understanding Animation*, 190–96.

27   Murakami, *Little Boy*, 152, quoted in Shen, "What Is 'Computer Animation'?"

28   O. Johnston and Thomas, *The Illusion of Life*.

29   Lamarre, "Platonic Sex."

30   See, for example, Napier, *Anime*, 172–77, 215–18. There are definitely scholarly efforts to understand Japanese cartoons from a culturalist perspective. Ito, for example, argues that the long history and popularity of manga in Japan is a result of the Japanese communication system, which relies more on contextual cues such as facial expressions, gestures, and eye glances, than direct expressions ("A History of Manga in the Context of Japanese Culture and Society"). I do not want to dispute such culturalist interpretations, but they do not, for example, explain the wide popularity of these Japanese cartoons in East Asia, and why the forms are imitated around the world.

31   P. Wells, *Understanding Animation*, 34–67.

32   Manovich, *The Language of New Media*, 298–307. The current game culture has benefited a lot from the logic of cartoon culture.

33   For example, *Steamboat Willie* (1928), the first animated feature film by Walt Disney, which made him and Mickey Mouse famous, was a spoof of a Buster Keaton film called *Steamboat Bill, Jr.*

34   Ito, "A History of Manga in the Context of Japanese Culture and Society."

35   Rifkin, *The Age of Access*, 140.

36   See Miller, Govil, McMurria, and Maxwell, *Global Hollywood*.

37   See "Going Hybrid: A Special Report on Business in Japan," *Economist*, 1 December 2007, 3–6.

38   Rowley, Dawson, Tashiro, and Moon, "The *Anime* Biz: Still an Adolescent," *Business Week*, 27 June 2005, 50–52.

39   Aoyagi, "What Does the Popularity of Japanese Trends across Asia Mean to the Japanese?"

40   Mehra, "Copyright and Comics in Japan."

41   Iwabuchi, *Recentering Globalization*, 38. See also S. Leonard, "Progress against the Law."

42   See A. F. K. Li, "Slash, Fandoms, and Pleasures."

43   For a sample of works in these projects, see www.caofei.com (accessed 26 January 2008).

44   Katyal, "Performance, Property, and the Slashing of Gender in Fan Fiction," 480.

45   Iwabuchi, *Recentering Globalization*, 23–35, 36.

46   See Mehra's analyses in "Copyright and Comics in Japan," and Condry's in "Cultures of Music Piracy."

47   Lessig, *Free Culture*, 25–28.

48   See, for example, the many negative responses from netizens collected by BBC Chinese, "Beijing Aoyun jixiangwu fuwa haokan ma?"

49   Lian Mian, "Sheji bopu yu mincui."

50   Ilan Greenberg, "Changing the Rules of the Games," *New York Times*, 30 March 2008.

51   As suggested at the forum Olympic Creative Industry and City Development, organized by the Department of Culture and Ceremonies of the Beijing Organizing Committee for the Games of the XXIX Olympiad, the Humanistic Olympic Studies Centre of Renmin University of China, and Beijing's Haidian District government, July 2006. For a summary of the forum, see "Opportunities Abound for Beijing," *Chinadaily.com.cn*, 24 July 2006 (accessed 26 January 2008).

52   Ibid.

53   Choo, "*Cool Japan* Nation."

54   "'Made in Japan' Trademark to Fight Anime Piracy."

55   Brian Bremner, "Raising Japan's Cool Quotient," *Business Week Online*, 8 May 2007.

56   Otmazgin, "Contesting Soft Power."

57   Condry, "Anime Creativity."

58   Japanese anime and manga are popular in many places; see Allison, *Millennial Monsters*, 234–70; Napier, *Anime*, 8; Fung, "Hong Kong as the Asian and Chinese Distributor of Pokemon." But such popularity can by no means be compared to large domestic reception.

59   Butler, *Theories in Subjection*, 28–30.

Chapter Eight: A Semiotics of the Counterfeit Product

1   Storper and Salais, *Worlds of Production*, 5.

2   Barthes, "Myth Today."

3   Pang, *Cultural Control and Globalization in Asia*, 63–79.

4   "Phony Ferrari," 28 April 2006, *South China Morning Post*.

5   Michael Fitzpatrick, "Frattini Finds Fake Ferrari," *Daily Telegraph*, 13 May 2006.

6   See Mertha, *The Politics of Piracy*, 1–17.

7   U.S. Congress, Congressional Budget Office, *China's Growing Demand for Oil and Its Impact on U.S. Petroleum Markets*, April 2006. www.cbo.gov (accessed 7 June 2011).

8   "Ferrari to Enhance Presence in China This Year," *SinoCast China Business Daily News*, 19 January 2006; "Ferrari Maserati Has Reached Sales of 100 in China," *SinoCast China Business Daily News*, 1 November 2005.

9   Bowerman, "Counterfeit Supply Chains in Asia."

10   K. Hu, "Made in China."

11   For example, the American Delphi Corporation supplies key systems for Ferrari's newest luxury vehicle, the 599 GTB, and most of them are produced in Delphi's Chinese plant. See Delphi's press release, www.delphi.com (accessed 3 June, 2010). On China's role in the global automobile supplies industry, see Xiaohua Yang, *Globalization of the Automobile Industry*.

12   Xianggang maoyi fazhanju yanjiubu, *Neidi qiche shichang*, 1.

13   Lance Winslow, "Will China Inherit the U.S. Auto Industry Market Share? Most Likely a Good Chunk of It," *EzineArticles.com*, 17 June 2009 (accessed 17 September 2009).

14   Liu Li and Yu Qiao, "IPR Disputes Fuelled by Auto Makers," *China Daily*, 6 September 2004.

15   Michael Dunne, "Chinese SUV Makers Smother the Cherokee," *Detroit News*, 15 April 2005.

16   Hanru Zou, "A Fake Story with Real Moral Value." *China Daily*, Hong Kong ed., 12 May 2006.

17   Angela Xu, "Court Told Singer Didn't Buy Fakes," *Shanghaidaily.com*, 11 April 2009.

18   T. L. Friedman, "China's Creativity Bubble," *New York Times*, 7 November 2005.

19   The database can be found at www.cnki.net (data retrieved 18 September 2009).

20   Baudrillard, *For a Critique of the Political Economy of the Sign*, 309–52.

21   C. Harding, "'*Hostis Humani Generis*,'" 34–35.

22   Vaidhyanathan, *Copyrights and Copywrongs*, 81–105.

23   The accusation was raised just before Mother's Day, 2006. Kirin also complained that Chinese farmers are not paying proper royalties to the company for planting carnations, whose patent it owns. See "Zhongguo shu Ri kangnaiqing she qingquang shoucha."

24   Bhabha, *The Location of Culture*, 92.

25   For an elaborate discussion of the historical development of mimesis as a Western concept, see Gebauer and Wulf, *Mimesis*.

26   See Benjamin, "The Work of Art in the Age of Mechanical Reproduction"; Girard, *To Double Business Bound*.

27   Benjamin, "The Work of Art in the Age of Mechanical Reproduction," 224.

28   Appadurai, "Introduction," 41–42.

29   Shujen Wang, *Framing Piracy*, 89–92.

30   Rutter and Bryce, "The Consumption of Counterfeit Goods."

31   See Liang Tingjia, *Mingpai tiantan*, 29. This Chinese "shopping" book provides tips for Hong Kong and Taiwan tourists about how and where to buy pirated name-brand bags in various Chinese cities.

32   Buck-Morss, *The Dialectics of Seeing*, 81–82.

33   "Brand Licensing in China," 2006, www.brandlicensing.sourcingchina.net (accessed 3 June, 2011).

34   Brian Milner, "More than Meets Eye in China's Advance," *Globe and Mail*, 16 August 2010.

35   Editorial, "Zhongguo pinpai guojihua zhi lü."

36   The application has been denied twice by China's National Patent Office, in 2004 and 2009, as it might create confusion among customers between food and medicine. "Shaolin Si zhuanggao shangbiao pingweihui." For China Mobil, see, "Top 10 Global Brands in 2011," *Economy Watch*, 9 May, 2011, www.economywatch.com/in-the-news/ (accessed 30 May 2011).

37   Ramo, "Brand China."

38   R. Williams, *Marxism and Literature*, 130.

39   Lury, *Brands*.

40   Ibid., 56.

41   Taussig, *Mimesis and Alterity*, 232.

42   Bhabha, *The Location of Culture*, 90.

43   John Frow also demonstrates the dialectic aspects of the commodity form, which he calls seriality and singularity. He believes that as a result of this duality the commodity form has the potential to be enabling and productive as well as limiting and destructive ("The Signature").

44   Fletcher, *Allegory*, 85–87.

45   Taussig, *Mimesis and Alterity*, 231.

46   "Nike Sues Adidas over Shoe Patent," BBC News, 17 February 2006, http://news.bbc .co.uk (accessed 25 January 2007).

47   Benjamin, "The Work of Art," 228–29. Judith Butler's famous theories of gender performance are also based on the mechanism of ritual and mimesis. I think it is interesting to

compare gender performative theories with Benjamin's notion of aura to further analyze the relation between aura and power. See Butler's *Gender Trouble* and *Bodies That Matter*.

48 Benjamin, "The Work of Art," 225.

49 Ouspensky, *Theology of the Icon*, 17.

50 Mondzain, *Image, Icon, Economy*, 70.

51 For example, in "Mapping Early Taoist Art," 87–88, Hung Wu demonstrates that Laozi, the deified man personifying Dao (the Way), cannot be represented by a figurative likeness in Daoist art, because Dao can only be formless.

52 De Man, "Thematic Criticism and the Theme of Faust," 87.

53 Yip, *Capitalism as Religion?*

54 The Mao badge contains an image of Mao's face or body; it was very popular during the Cultural Revolution and has now become a collectible item. According to some estimations, 2.5 billion to 5 billion Mao badges have been produced in China, with more than twenty thousand designs and made from twenty-seven different kinds of materials. Benewick, "Icons of Power," 131.

55 For a critical analysis of the Mao industry developed in China, see Dutton, "From Culture Industry to Mao Industry."

56 Rogerson, "Karl Polanyi," 136.

57 Both Wark and Himanen see the hacker as the exemplary challenge to recent capitalism. See Wark's *A Hacker Manifesto* and Himanen's *The Hacker Ethic and the Spirit of the Information Age*.

58 Mason, *The Pirate's Dilemma*, 36.

59 Klein, *No Logo*, 74.

60 Jia Zhangke, the famous independent Chinese filmmaker, self-reflexively commented on his film *Ren Xiaoyao* 任逍遙 (Unknown pleasures, 2002) on the importance of pirated movie discs to his generation of Chinese filmmakers. Another interesting example is Hu Ge's (胡戈) *Yige mantou yinfa de xuean* 個饅頭引發的血案 (A bloody crime caused by a bun), a mocking video reworking of Chen Kaige's blockbuster *Wuji* 無極 (The promise, 2005), which is very popular and widely circulated on the Internet in China. See http://ent.qq.com (accessed 20 April 2006). For the video works produced by fan filmmakers around the *Star Wars* saga, see Jenkins, *Convergence Culture*, 131–56.

61 Feng Jianhua, "Yancha 'haixin' shipin."

62 See "Killing Bogus Drug Maker Under Investigation," gov.cn, 15 May 2006; Kevin Huang, "Fake Drugs May Claim Two More," *South China Morning Post*, 24 May 2006.

63 Akunyili and Nnani, "Risk of Medicines." As the Nigerian activist Akunyili claims, "In Nigeria, there is hardly any family that does not have a history of somebody dying of fake drugs. My youngest sister died of diabetes in 1988. I'm a pharmacologist. I know it was fake insulin." Quoted in Aldhous, "Counterfeit Pharmaceuticals," 134. See also A. Harding, "Dora Akunyili."

64 Lu Shanbing, *Zhongguo guanggao chanye fazhan yanjiu*, 205–7; Yao Lin 姚林, "2009 Zhongguo baoye" 2009 中國報業 (China's newspaper industry in 2009), *Chuanmei* 傳媒 (Communication media), 23 December 2009, http://media.people.com.cn/BIG5/40628/10640468.html (accessed 30 May 2011).

65 In reality, Hong Kong is full of counterfeit products and is also a key site in the global

piracy network. See Shujen Wang, *Framing Piracy*, 167–86. But when placed in the hierarchy of the global imagination, Hong Kong the global city facilitates genuine commodity and capital flows, which are filtered down to other adjacent and minor networks.

66   "3 Charged with Stealing Coca-Cola Secrets," *New York Times*, 6 July 2006.

67   Barthes, "Myth Today," 156.

68   Such visual bias characterizes only the early works of Barthes. In his later works he no longer debases but asserts the affective power of "superficial" images, and he argues that image is most powerful when it is free from a knowledge background to define its meanings. See *Camera Lucida*. For an insightful analysis of the implications of Barthes's changing attitudes to image, see Rancière, *The Future of the Image*, 1–32.

69   Baudrillard, *For a Critique of the Political Economy of the Sign*, 149.

70   This news on forgery is also an effect of China's distorted freedom of the press. The media industry is flourishing in China, but it is not allowed to report on governmental errors; so much of the press's energy is directed at piracy, which supposedly does not relate to the government in any direct way, and therefore is a safe political topic.

71   The show was broadcast on 8 July 2007.

72   Jing Wang, *Brand New China*, 18.

73   I have demonstrated elsewhere more elaborately the sociopolitical background of movie piracy in China; see Pang, *Cultural Control and Globalization in Asia*, 98–116.

Chapter Nine: Imitation or Appropriation Arts?

1   Pang, *Cultural Control and Globalization in Asia*, 16–46.

2   See Rose, *Authors and Owners*; Woodmansee, "The Genius and Copyright."

3   Theoretically speaking, both the author and the laborer are primary owners of their creations. However, as James Boyle points out, laborers are not seen as having residual property rights in the goods they create for their employers, but artists, in general, do, because their creative input is considered more precious (*Shamans, Software, and Spleens*, 57).

4   The tangible–intangible paradox is inherent in all IPR categories: expressions are copyrightable only after they are embodied in concrete materials; patents are offered to novel ideas only when they are inscribed in actual utensils (hence, the controversies surrounding software patents); and trademark refers to an abstract image (or sound, pattern, or even a general "feel") tied to a concrete set of commodities.

5   See, for example, Fusco, "Who's Doin' the Twist?"

6   See chapter 8; Bhabha, "The Third Space," 216.

7   Drew, "Mixed Blessings."

8   Welchman, *Art after Appropriation*, 18.

9   Crimp, *On the Museum's Ruins*, 126.

10   Negativland, "Two Relationships to a Cultural Public Domain," 240.

11   On the case of Levi's, which frequently resorts to trademark infringement lawsuits to fend off competitors, see Michael Barbaro and Julie Creswell, "With Trademark in Its Pocket, Levi's Turns to Suing Its Rivals," *New York Times*, 29 January 2007.

12 Foucault, "What Is an Author?," 124–25.

13 Edelman, *Ownership of the Image*, 38, 51–52.

14 See, for example, L. Wells, "On and Beyond the White Walls."

15 One critic comments, "In Nam June Paik's work, the paradigmatic and multidimensional accumulation of signs and images far outweighs syntagmatic and linear integration. He piles up signs and images, takes accumulation to its most extreme point, and when it has reached a kaleidoscope climax, paradoxically, one becomes aware of a kind of void—a void full of images or the silence full of sounds." Asada, "Video," 126.

16 For the new creative possibilities digital sampling adds to appropriation arts, see, for example, Sæther, "Between the Hyperrepresentational and the Real."

17 Mulvey, "Visual Pleasure and Narrative Cinema."

18 Mulvey, "Passing the Time."

19 Benjamin, "The Author as Producer," 230, 237, 221.

20 Napack, "Chinese Artists May Sue Venice Biennale."

21 See Zaya, "Cai Guo-Qiang."

22 Sheng Wen, "Diaosu zuopin "Shouzuyuan" yinfa 10nian banquan zhengzhan."

23 For a more elaborate discussion of the incident, see He Wanli, *Yongyuan de qianwei*, 183–85.

24 Sichuan Fine Arts Institute, "Xueyuan gaikuang" 學院概況 (About the Institute), www .scfai.edu.cn/Survey.aspx (accessed 3 June 2011).

25 Erik Eckholm, "Expatriate Artist Updates Maoist Icon and Angers Old Guard." *New York Times*, 17 August 2000.

26 The piece was shown at the Manchester Urbis Art Center (January 2007), the Contemporary Art Museum in Shanghai (June 2007), and the Hexiangning Art Museum, Shenzhen (August 2008).

27 Interview with Hua'nü (華女), who worked as a painter in one of those studios in the late 1970s and early 1980s, 20 December 2007, Hong Kong.

28 "Zhongguo youhua diyicun, Shenzhen guanwai Dafencun de qishi" 中國油畫第一村, 深圳關外大芬村的啟示 (China's first painting village, implications for Dafencun, on the outskirts of Shenzhen), an episode of *Duihua*, 對話 (Dialogue), China Central Television, 23 November 2005.

29 Ibid.

30 UNESCO, "International Flows of Selected Cultural Goods and Services 1994–2003," 30–31, 57.

31 Guangzhou shi xinwen chuban he guangbo dianshi ju, "Shenzhen yi cujin chanye fazhan wei zhidao."

32 For 2010 sales figure, see Wen Jianmin 溫建敏, "Shengzhen Dafencun 30 nian chuanqi" 深圳大芬村30 年傳奇 (Thirty remarkable years of Shenzhen's Dafen Village), *Xinkuai bao* 新快報, 26 August 2010, online at big5.ycwb.com/news/2010-08/26/content_2627422_3 .htm (accessed 30 May 2011). Dafen youhuacun guanli bangongshi, "2006 nian gong-zuo zongjie."

33 For 2008 see Dafen Oil Painting Village 大芬油畫村, "Guanyu Dafen" 關於大芬 (About Dafen), cndafen.com/about.asp?Title=关于大芬 (accessed 30 May 2011). "Dafencun hua-

lang chaoshi guonei qiangtan." For a complete list of creative industries recognized in the PRC, see Zhongguo touzi zixunwang, *2007–2008 nian Zhongguo wenhua chanye jidi fenxi ji touzi zixun baogao.*

34 Dafen youhuacun guanli bangongshi, "2006 nian gongzuo zongjie."

35 Huang Rongqiang, "Dafencun chengli zhishichanquan gongzuo zhan." This, of course, is very unusual; such registrations would normally be carried out by national IPR offices.

36 Zhang Ke, "Guojia zhishichanquan jianchazu dao Dafen jiancha gongzuo."

37 Unless stated otherwise, all the information about the artist and the piece is based on my interview with Leung Mee Ping, 25 August 2007, Hong Kong.

38 Shang, "'Rent Collection Courtyard,'" 232.

39 Quoted in Eckholm, "Expatriate Artist Updates Maoist Icon and Angers Old Guard."

40 Shang, "'Rent Collection Courtyard,'" 225, 226.

41 See Xiao Shu, *Liu Wencai zhenxiang.*

42 Author's email communication with Leung Mee Ping, 25 October 2007.

43 Martin Paetsch, "China's Art Factories: Van Gogh from the Sweatshop," *Spiegel Online,* 23 August 2006, www.spiegel.de (accessed 24 October 2007).

44 Boyle, *The Public Domain,* 21.

45 Heidegger, "The Age of the World Picture," 132.

46 Heidegger, "The Question Concerning Technology."

47 See Rojcewicz, *The Gods and Technology,* 15–66.

48 Heidegger, "The Question Concerning Technology," 16.

49 Ibid., 25–26.

50 See, for example, the dichotomy Deleuze and Guattari set up between marketing and philosophy in reference to their different production of creativity, in *What Is Philosophy?,* 10–12.

51 See Rofel, *Desiring China*; Hook, *The Individual and the State in China*; Gallagher, *Contagious Capitalism*; Lee, *Against the Law.*

52 See O'Brien and Li, *Rightful Resistance in Rural China.* For a stereotypical portrayal of this materialistic and politically indifferent new generation of Chinese citizens, see Simon Elegant, "China's Me Generation: The New Middle Class Is Young, Rich and Happy. Just Don't Mention Politics," *Time,* 5 November 2007, 46–51.

53 Marcuse, *One Dimensional Man,* 23.

54 Bauman, *Liquid Modernity,* 22.

55 Žižek, *Welcome to the Desert of the Real,* 3.

56 Eckholm, "Expatriate Artist Updates Maoist Icon and Angers Old Guard."

57 Heidegger, "The Question Concerning Technology," 12.

Bibliography

English Materials

Abbas, Ackbar. *Hong Kong: Culture and the Politics of Disappearance*. Hong Kong: Hong Kong University Press.

Acland, Charles R. *Screen Traffic: Movies, Multiplexes, and Global Culture*. Durham: Duke University Press, 2003.

Adorno, Theodor W. *Aesthetic Theory*, trans. R. Hullot-Kentor. Minneapolis: University of Minnesota Press, 1997.

————. *The Culture Industry: Selected Essays on Mass Culture*, ed. J. M. Bernstein. London: Routledge, 1991.

Aggarwal, Vinod K., and Min Gyo Koo. "Beyond Network Power? The Dynamics of Formal Economic Integration in Northeast Asia." *Pacific Review* 18, no. 2 (2005), 189–216.

Akunyili, Dora Nkem, and Ijeoma P. C. Nnani. "Risk of Medicines: Counterfeit Drugs." *International Journal of Risk and Safety in Medicine* 16, no. 3 (2004), 181–90.

Aldhous, Peter. "Counterfeit Pharmaceuticals: In the Line of Fire." *Nature* 434 (10 March 2005), 134.

Alford, William P. *To Steal a Book Is an Elegant Offense: Intellectual Property Law in Chinese Civilization*. Stanford: Stanford University Press, 1995.

Allison, Anne. *Millennial Monsters: Japanese Toys and the Global Imagination*. Berkeley: University of California Press, 2006.

Amin, Samir. *Obsolescent Capitalism: Contemporary Politics and Global Disorder*, trans. Patrick Camiller. London: Zed, 2003.

Andreas, Joel. *Rise of the Red Engineers: The Cultural Revolution and the Origins of China's New Class*. Stanford: Stanford University Press, 2009.

Aoyagi, Hiroshi. "What Does the Popularity of Japanese Trends across Asia Mean to the Japanese?" Paper presented in the Ritsumeikan Asia Pacific Conference, "Asian Cultures: Confluence and Divergence," Beppu, Japan, 22 January 2008.

Appadurai, Arjun. "Introduction: Commodities and the Politics of Value." *The Social Life of Things: Commodities in Cultural Perspective*, ed. Arjun Appadurai, 3–63. Cambridge: Cambridge University Press, 1986.

———. "Spectral Housing and Urban Cleansing: Notes on Millennial Mumbai." *Public Culture* 12, no. 3 (2000), 627–51.

Arendt, Hannah. *The Human Condition*. Chicago: University of Chicago Press, 1958.

———. *The Origins of Totalitarianism*. London: André Deutsch, 1986.

Asada, Akira. "Video: Nam June Paik." *Nam June Paik: Video Time—Video Space*, ed. Toni Stooss and Thomas Kellein, 126. New York: Harry N. Abrams, 1993.

Asheim, Bjørn, and Eric Clark. "Creativity and Cost in Urban and Regional Development in the 'New Economy.'" *European Planning Studies* 9, no. 7 (2001), 805–11.

Auerbach, Nancy Neiman. "The Meanings of Neoliberalism." *Neoliberalism: National and Regional Experiments with Global Ideas*, ed. Ravi K. Roy, Arthur T. Denzau, and Thomas D. Willett, 26–50. London: Routledge, 2007.

Badiou, Alain. *Handbook of Inaesthetics*, trans. Alberto Toscano. Stanford: Stanford University Press, 2005.

Bakhtin, Mikhail. *The Dialogic Imagination*. Austin: University of Texas, 1981.

———. "Response to a Question from Novy Mir Editorial Staff." *Speech Genres and Other Late Essays*, ed. Caryl Emerson and Michael Holquist, 1–9. Austin: University of Texas Press, 1986.

Balibar, Étienne. "(De)Constructing the Human as Human Institution: A Reflection on the Coherence of Hannah Arendt's Practical Philosophy." *Social Research* 74, no. 3 (2007), 727–38.

Banks, Mark, et al. "Risk and Trust in Cultural Industries." *Geoforum* 31 (2000), 453–64.

Barthes, Roland. *Camera Lucida: Reflections on Photography*, trans. Richard Howard. New York: Noonday Press, 1981.

———. "The Death of the Author." *Image-Music-Text*, trans. Stephen Heath, 142–48. New York: Noonday Press, 1977.

———. "Myth Today." *Mythologies*, trans. Annette Lavers, 109–58. New York: Hill and Wang, 1984.

Baudrillard, Jean. *For a Critique of the Political Economy of the Sign*. St. Louis: Telos, 1981.

Bauman, Zygmunt. *Globalization: The Human Consequences*. New York: Columbia University Press, 1998.

———. *Liquid Modernity*. Cambridge: Polity, 2000.

Baumgärtel, Tilman. "The Culture of Piracy in the Philippines." Proceedings of the Conference on Media Piracy and Intellectual Property in South East Asia, November 24, 2006, www.asian-edition.org (accessed 10 April 2008).

Bekins Linn K., and Sean D. Williams. "Positioning Technical Communication for the Creative Economy." *Technical Communication* 53, no. 3 (2006), 287–97.

Benewick, Robert. "Icons of Power: Mao Zedong and the Cultural Revolution." *Picturing Power in the People's Republic of China: Posters of the Cultural Revolution*, ed. Harriet Evans and Stephanie Donald, 123–37. Lanham, Md.: Rowman and Littlefield, 1999.

Benjamin, Walter. "The Author as Producer." *Reflections*, ed. Peter Demetz, 220–38. New York: Schocken Books, 1978.

———. *Charles Baudelaire: A Lyric Poet in the Era of High Capitalism*. London: New Left Books, 1973.

———. "Little History of Photography." *Walter Benjamin: Selected Writings*, vol. 2, *1927–*

1934, ed. Michael W. Jennings, Howard Eiland, and Gary Smith, 507–30. Cambridge: Belknap Press of Harvard University Press, 1999.

———. "The Work of Art in the Age of Mechanical Reproduction." *Illuminations*, ed. Hannah Arendt, 217–51. New York: Schocken Books, 1986.

Bennett, Tony. *The Birth of the Museum: History, Theory, Politics*. London: Routledge, 1995.

Berger, Peter L. "Faith and Development." *Global Society* 46 (2009), 69–75.

Berghuis, Thomas J. "Considering *Huanjing*: Positioning Experimental Art in China." *positions* 12, no. 3 (2004), 711–31.

Bhabha, Homi. *The Location of Culture*. London: Routledge, 1994.

———. "The Third Space: Interview with Homi Bhabha." *Identity: Community, Culture, Difference*, ed. Jonathan Rutherford, 207–21. London: Lawrence and Wishart, 1990.

Bick, Paul B., and Sorina Chiper. "Swoosh Identity: Recontextualizations in Haiti and Romania." *Visual Communication* 6, no. 1 (2007), 5–18.

Bilton, Chris. *Management and Creativity: From Creative Industries to Creative Management*. Malden, Mass.: Blackwell, 2007.

Bilton, Chris, and Ruth Leary. "What Can Managers Do for Creativity? Brokering Creativity in the Creative Industries." *International Journal of Cultural Policy* 8, no. 1 (2002), 49–64.

Blum, Susan D. *Portraits of "Primitives": Ordering Human Kinds in the Chinese Nation*. Lanham, Md.: Rowman and Littlefield, 2001.

Boltanski, Luc, and Eve Chiapello. *The New Spirit of Capitalism*. London: Verso, 2005.

Bowerman, Gary, with Russel Beron. "Counterfeit Supply Chains in Asia." Global Supply Chain Council, 31 May 2009, www.supplychain.cn (accessed 25 September 2009).

Boyle, James. *The Public Domain, Enclosing the Commons of the Mind*. New Haven: Yale University Press, 2008.

———. *Shamans, Software, and Spleens: Law and the Construction of the Information Society*. Cambridge: Harvard University Press, 1996.

Braester, Yomi. *Painting the City Red: Chinese Cinema and the Urban Contract*. Durham: Duke University Press, 2010.

Branstetter, Lee G., Raymond Fisman, and C. Fritz Foley. "Do Stronger Intellectual Property Rights Increase International Technology Transfer? Empirical Evidence from U.S. Firm-Level Panel Data." *Quarterly Journal of Economics* 121, no. 1 (2006), 321–49.

Brenner, Neil, Peter Marcuse, and Margit Mayer. "Cities for People, Not for Profit." *City* 13, nos. 2–3 (2009), 177–78.

Buckley, Bernadette. "China Design Now." *Theory, Culture and Society* 25, nos. 7–8 (2008), 341–52.

Buck-Morss, Susan. *The Dialectics of Seeing: Walter Benjamin and the Arcades Project*. Cambridge: MIT Press, 1989.

Butler, Judith. *Bodies That Matter: On the Discursive Limits of "Sex."* New York: Routledge, 1993.

———. *Gender Trouble: Feminism and the Subversion of Identity*. New York: Routledge, 1990.

———. *Theories in Subjection: The Psychic Life of Power*. Stanford: Stanford University Press, 1997.

Caracostas, Paraskevas, and Ugur Mulder. "Long Cycles, Technology and Employment: Current Obstacles and Outlook." *STI Review* 15 (1995), 75–104.

Carriço, Mónica, Bert de Muynck, and Ned Rossiter, eds. "Creative China: Counter-Mapping the Creative Industries." Special issue of *Urban China* 33 (November 2008).

Cascardi, Anthony J. *Consequences of Enlightenment*. Cambridge: Cambridge University Press, 1999.

———. *The Subject of Modernity*. Cambridge: Cambridge University Press, 1992.

Castells, Manuel. *The Rise of the Network Society*. London: Blackwell, 2000.

Caves, Richard. *Creative Industries: Contracts between Art and Commerce*. Cambridge: Harvard University Press, 2000.

Centre for Cultural Policy Research, University of Hong Kong. *Baseline Study on Hong Kong's Creative Industries: For the Central Policy Unit, Hong Kong Special Administrative Region Government*. Hong Kong: Centre for Cultural Policy Research, University of Hong Kong, 2003.

Chan, Kam Wing, and Will Buckingham. "Is China Abolishing the *Hukou* System?" *China Quarterly* 195 (September 2008), 582–606.

Chan, Stephen C. K. "Figures of Hope and the Filmic Imaginary of Jianghu in Contemporary Hong Kong Cinema." *Cultural Studies* 15, nos. 3–4 (2001), 486–514.

Chan-Tibergien, Jennifer. "Cultural Diversity as Resistance to Neoliberal Globalization: The Emergence of a Global Movement and Convention." *International Review of Education* 52, nos. 1–2 (2006), 89–105.

Cheng, Meiling. "Violent Capital: Zhu Yu on File." *TDR: The Drama Review* 49, no. 3 (2005), 58–77.

Chiodo, Keri. "Evolving from a 'Knowledge Economy' to a 'Creativity Economy.'" *Observer* 23, no. 6 (2010), www.psychologicalscience.org (accessed 4 September 2010).

Choo, Kukhee. "*Cool Japan* Nation: Japanese Governmental Policy towards the Anime Industry." Paper presented in International Workshop on Popular Culture, Cultural Policy, and Cultural Discourse in East and Southeast Asia, Hebrew University of Jerusalem, June 2009.

Christopherson, Susan. "The Divergent Worlds of New Media: How Policy Shapes Work in the Creative Economy." *Review of Policy Research* 12, no. 4 (2004), 543–58.

Clark, Paul. *The Chinese Cultural Revolution: A History*. Cambridge: Cambridge University Press, 2008.

Coalition for Cultural Diversity (Ottawa). "UNESCO Stand Up." *New Internationalist* 382 (September 2005), 23.

Cohen, Jerome A. "China's Reform Era Legal Odyssey." *Far Eastern Economic Review*, 5 December 2008, 34–38.

Cohen, Julie E., et al. *Copyright in a Global Information Economy*. New York: Aspen Law and Business, 2002.

Collins, Hugh. *Marxism and Law*. Oxford: Oxford University Press, 1982.

Comaroff, John L., and Jean Comaroff. *Ethnicity, Inc.* Chicago: University of Chicago Press, 2009.

Commonwealth of Australia. *Creative Nation: Commonwealth Cultural Policy*. Canberra: Department of Communications and the Arts, 1994.

Condry, Ian. "Anime Creativity: Characters and Premises in the Quest for Cool Japan." *Theory, Culture and Society* 26 (March 2009), 139–63.

———. "Cultures of Music Piracy: An Ethnographic Comparison of the U.S. and Japan," *International Journal of Cultural Studies* 7 (2004), 343–63.

Coombe, Rosemary. *The Cultural Life of Intellectual Properties: Authorship, Appropriation, and the Law.* Durham: Duke University Press, 1998.

———. "Protecting Traditional Environmental Knowledge and New Social Movements in the Americas: Intellectual Property, Human Right, or Claims to an Alternative Form of Sustainable Development?" *Florida Journal of International Law*, March 2005, 115–35.

Crimp, Douglas. *On the Museum's Ruins.* Cambridge: MIT Press, 1993.

Crofts, Stephen. "Reconceptualizing National Cinema/s." *Quarterly Review of Film and Video* 14, no. 3 (1993), 55–56.

Cunningham, Stuart. "The Humanities, Creative Arts, and International Innovation Agendas." *Innovation and Tradition: The Arts, Humanities and the Knowledge Economy*, ed. Jane Kenway, Elizabeth Bullen, and Simon Robb, 113–24. New York: Peter Lane, 2004.

Curtin, Michael. *Playing to the World's Biggest Audience: The Globalization of Chinese Film and TV.* Berkeley: University of California Press, 2007.

Customs and Excise Department, Hong Kong Special Administrative Region Government. "Press Release: SCIT Visits Customs and Excise Department," 2006, www.info.gov.hk (accessed 2 June, 2011).

Dahlström, Margareta, and Brita Hermelin. "Creative Industries, Spatiality and Flexibility: The Example of Film Production." *Norsk Geografisk Tidsskrift: Norwegian Journal of Geography* 61 (2007), 111–21.

Death, Crimson. "Phrack Pro-Phile XXXIII." *Phrack* 3, no. 28 (1986), file 2.

Deleuze, Gilles, and Félix Guattari. *Anti-Oedipus: Capitalism and Schizophrenia.* Minneapolis: University of Minnesota Press, 1983.

———. *A Thousand Plateaus*, trans. Brian Massumi. London: Continuum, 2004.

———. *What Is Philosophy?*, trans. Hugh Tomlinson and Graham Burchell. New York: Columbia University Press, 1994.

de Man, Paul. "Thematic Criticism and the Theme of Faust (1957)." *Paul de Man, Critical Writings, 1953–1978*, ed. Lindsey Waters, 76–89. Minneapolis: University of Minnesota Press, 1989.

DeWeil, Boris. "Freedom as Creativity: On the Origin of the Positive Concept of Liberty." *Journal for the Studies of Religions and Ideologies*, no. 4 (2003), 42–57.

Dimitrov, Martin K. *Piracy and the State: The Politics of Intellectual Property Rights in China.* Cambridge: Cambridge University Press, 2009.

Dirlik, Arif. *Global Modernity: Modernity in the Age of Global Capitalism.* Boulder, Colo.: Paradigm, 2007.

Doane, Mary Ann. *The Emergence of Cinematic Time: Modernity, Contingency, the Archive.* Cambridge: Harvard University Press, 2002.

Donald, James. *Imagining the Modern City.* Minneapolis: University of Minnesota Press, 1999.

Donald, James, and Stephanie Hemelryk Donald. "The Publicness of Cinema." *Reinventing Film Studies*, ed. Christine Gledhill and Linda Williams, 114–29. London: Arnold, 2000.

Drahos, Peter. "Thinking Strategically about Intellectual Property Rights." *Telecommunications Policy* 21, no. 3 (1997), 202–4.

Drew, Rob. "Mixed Blessings: The Commercial Mix and the Future of Music Aggregation." *Popular Music and Society* 28, no. 4 (2005), 533–51.

Driver, Stephen, and Luke Martell. "New Labour: Culture and Economy." *Culture and Economy after the Cultural Turn*, ed. Larry Ray and Andrew Sayer, 246–69. London: Sage, 1999.

du Gay, Paul, and Michael Pryke. "Cultural Economy: An Introduction." *Cultural Economy: Cultural Analysis and Commercial Life*, ed. Paul du Gay and Michael Pryke, 1–20. London: Sage, 2002.

Dutton, Michael. "From Culture Industry to Mao Industry: A Greek Tragedy." *boundary 2* 32, no. 2 (2005), 151–67.

Dyer-Witheford, Nick. *Cyber-Marx: Cycles and Circuits of Struggle in High-Technology Capitalism*. Urbana: University of Illinois Press, 1999.

Edelman, Bernard. *Ownership of the Image: Elements for a Marxist Theory of Law*, trans. Elizabeth Kingdom. London: Routledge and Kegan Paul, 1979.

Fang, Ke, and Yan Zhang. "Plan and Market Mismatch: Urban Redevelopment in Beijing during a Period of Transition." *Asia Pacific Viewpoint* 44, no. 2 (2003), 159–62.

Feltault, Kelly. "Development Folklife: Human Security and Cultural Conservation." *Journal of American Folklore* 119, no. 471 (2006), 90–110.

Feng, Peter. *Intellectual Property in China*. Hong Kong: Sweet and Maxwell Asia, 2003.

Ficsor, Mihály. *The Law of Copyright and the Internet: The 1996 WIPO Treaties, Their Interpretation and Implementation*. Oxford: Oxford University Press, 2002.

Fine, Ben, and Alfredo Saad-Filho. *Marx's Capital*. London: Pluto, 2004.

Fisher, Mark. *Capitalist Realism: Is There No Alternative?* Winchester: Zero Books, 2009.

Fiske, John. "The Cultural Economy of Fandom." *The Adoring Audience: Fan Culture and Popular Media*, ed. L. S. Lewis, 30–49. London: Routledge, 1992.

Fletcher, Angus. *Allegory: The Theory of a Symbolic Mode*. Ithaca: Cornell University Press, 1964.

Florida, Richard. *Cities and the Creative Class*. New York: Routledge, 2005.

———. *The Rise of the Creative Class and How It's Transforming Work, Leisure, Community and Everyday Life*. New York: Basic Books, 2002.

Foucault, Michel. "What Is an Author?" *Language, Counter-Memory, Practice*, ed. Donald F. Bouchard, 113–38. Oxford: Blackwell, 1977.

Frey, Bruno. *Arts and Economics: Analysis and Cultural Policy*. Berlin: Springer, 2000.

Friedmann, John. *The World City Hypothesis*. Los Angeles: Graduate School of Architecture and Urban Planning, University of California, 1985.

Fronville, Clarie L. "The International Creative Sector: Its Dimensions, Dynamics, and Audience Development." Report to the Second UNESCO Meeting on International Creative Sector, June 2003, 4–5, www.culturalpolicy.org (accessed 2 October 2009).

Frow, John. "The Signature: Three Arguments about the Commodity Form." *Aesthesia and the Economy of the Senses*, ed. Helen Grace, 151–200. Nepean: University of Western Sydney, 1996.

Fu, Poshek. *Between Shanghai and Hong Kong: The Politics of Chinese Cinemas*. Stanford: Stanford University Press, 2003.

Fung, Anthony. "Hong Kong as the Asian and Chinese Distributor of Pokemon." *International Journal of Comic Art* 7, no. 1 (2005), 432–48.

Fusco, Coco. "Who's Doin' the Twist? Notes toward a Politics of Appropriation." *English Is Broken Here: Notes on Cultural Fusion in the Americas*, ed. Coco Fusco, 65–77. New York: New Press, 1995.

Gaines, Jane. *Contested Culture: The Image, the Voice, and the Law*. Chapel Hill: University of North Carolina Press, 1991.

Gallagher, Mary Elizabeth. *Contagious Capitalism: Globalization and the Politics of Labor in China*. Princeton: Princeton University Press, 2005.

Ganea, Peter, and Thomas Pattloch. *Intellectual Property Law in China*. The Hague: Kluwer Law International, 2005.

Garnham, Nicholas. "From Cultural to Creative Industries: An Analysis of the Implications of the 'Creative Industries' Approach to Arts and Media Policy Making in the United Kingdom." *International Journal of Cultural Policy* 11, no. 1 (2005), 15–29.

Gates, Kelly. "Will Work for Copyrights: The Cultural Policy of Anti-Piracy Campaigns." *Social Semiotics* 16, no. 1 (2006), 57–73.

Gaubatz, Piper. "China's Urban Transformation: Patterns and Processes of Morphological Change in Beijing, Shanghai and Guangzhou." *Urban Studies* 36, no. 9 (1999), 1495–521.

Gebauer, Gunter, and Christoph Wulf. *Mimesis: Culture-Art-Society*, trans. Don Reneau. Berkeley: University of California Press, 1995.

Gibson, Johanna. *Creating Selves: Intellectual Property and the Narration of Culture*. Aldershot: Ashgate, 2006.

Gilbert, David. "From Paris to Shanghai: The Changing Geographies of Fashion's World Cities." *Fashion's World Cities*, ed. Christopher Breward and David Gilbert, 3–32. Oxford: Berg, 2006.

Gill, Bates, and Yanzhong Huang. "Sources and Limits of Chinese 'Soft Power.'" *Survival* 48, no. 2 (2006), 17–36.

Gillespie, Tarleton. *Wired Shut: Copyright and the Shape of Digital Culture*. Cambridge: MIT Press, 2007.

Girard, René. *To Double Business Bound: Essays on Literature, Mimesis, and Anthropology*. Baltimore: Johns Hopkins University Press, 1978.

Goldstein, Joshua. "The Distorting Mirror: Visual Modernity in China." *American Anthropologist* 111, no. 4 (2009), 518–91.

Goldstein, Paul. *Copyrights' Highway: From Gutenberg to the Celestial Jukebox*. Rev. ed. Stanford: Stanford Law and Politics, 2003.

Guback, Thomas. "Government Financial Support to the Film Industry in the United States." *Current Research in Film: Audiences, Economics, and Law*, ed. Bruce A. Austin, 88–105. Norwood, N.J.: Ablex, 1987.

Guneratne, Anthony R. "Introduction: Rethinking Third Cinema." *Rethinking Third*

Cinema, ed. Anthony R. Guneratne and Wimal Dissanayake, 1–28. New York: Routledge, 2003.

Gunning, Tom. "An Aesthetic of Astonishment: Early Film and the (In)Credulous Spectators." *Art and Text* 34 (Spring 1989), 31–45.

———. "The Cinema of Attractions: Early Film, Its Spectator and the Avant-Garde." *Wide Angle* 8, nos. 3–4 (1986), 63–70.

Habermas, Jürgen. "Modernity: An Unfinished Project." *Habermas and the Unfinished Project of Modernity*, ed. Maurizio Passerin d'Entrèves and Seyla Benhabib, 38–55. Cambridge: MIT Press, 1997.

———. *The Theory of Communicative Action*. Vol. 1. Boston: Beacon Press, 1984.

Halbert, Debora J. *Resisting Intellectual Property*. London: Routledge, 2005.

Hallward, Peter. *Out of This World: Deleuze and the Philosophy of Creation*. London: Verso, 2006.

Halstead, Narmala. "Branding 'Perfection' Foreign as Self: Self as 'Foreign-Foreign.'" *Journal of Material Culture* 7, no. 3 (2002), 273–93.

Hansen, Mette Halskov. *Lessons in Being Chinese: Minority Education and Ethnic Identity in Southwest China*. Seattle: University of Washington Press, 1999.

Hansen, Miriam. *Babel and Babylon: Spectatorship in American Silent Film*. Cambridge: Harvard University Press, 1991.

Harding, Anne. "Dora Akunyili: Scourge of Nigerian Drug Counterfeiters." *Lancet* 367, no. 9521 (2006), 1479.

Harding, Chris. "'Hostis Humani Generis': The Pirate as Outlaw in the Early Modern Law of the Sea." *Pirates? The Politics of Plunder, 1550–1650*, ed. Claire Jowitt, 20–38. Basingstoke: Palgrave Macmillan, 2007.

Harney, Stefano. "Unfinished Business: The Cultural Commodity and Its Labour Process." Roundtable: Research Architecture, 12 May 2008, http://roundtable.kein.org (accessed 24 July 2008).

Hartley, John. "Creative Industries." *Creative Industries*, ed. John Hartley, 106–16. Malden, Mass.: Blackwell, 2005.

Hartley, John, and Michael Keane, eds. "Special Issue on Creative Industries and Innovation in China." *International Journal of Cultural Studies* 9, no. 3 (2006).

Hartley, John, and Lucy Montgomery. "Creative Industries Come to China." *Chinese Journal of Communication* 2, no. 1 (2009), 1–12.

Hartley, John, and Lucy Montgomery, eds. "Special Issue on China: Internationalizing the Creative Industries." *Chinese Journal of Communication* 2, no. 1 (2009).

Harvey, David. *The New Imperialism*. Oxford: Oxford University Press, 2003.

———. *Social Justice and the City*. London: Edward Arnold, 1973.

Heidegger, Martin. "The Age of the World Picture." *The Question Concerning Technology and Other Essays*, trans. William Lovitt, 115–54. New York: Harper and Row, 1977.

———. "The Question Concerning Technology." *The Question Concerning Technology and Other Essays*, trans. William Lovitt, 3–35. New York: Harper and Row, 1977.

Heilbrun, James, and Charles M. Gray. *The Economics of Art and Culture*. New York: Cambridge University Press, 2001.

Hevia, James Louis. "World Heritage, National Culture, and the Restoration of Chengde." *positions: East Asia Cultures Critique* 9, no. 1 (2001), 219–43.

Hill, John. "U.K. Film Policy, Cultural Capital and Social Exclusion." *Cultural Trends* 13, no. 2 (2004), 29–39.

Himanen, Pekka. *The Hacker Ethic and the Spirit of the Information Age.* London: Secker and Warburg, 2001.

Hin, Li Ling. *Urban Land Reform in China.* Basingstoke: Macmillan, 1999.

Holm, David. *Art and Ideology in Revolutionary China.* Oxford: Clarendon Press, 1991.

Hong, Zhang. "The Sustainable Development of Tourism in Lijiang," 2004, www.docstoc .com (accessed 2 June 2011).

Hook, Brian, ed. *The Individual and the State in China.* Oxford: Clarendon Press, 1996.

Horkheimer, Max, and Theodor W. Adorno. *Dialectic of Enlightenment: Philosophical Fragments,* trans. Edmund Jephcott. Stanford: Stanford University Press, 2002.

Howkins, John. *Creative Ecology: Where Thinking Is a Proper Job.* St Lucia, Queensland: University of Queensland Press, 2009.

———. *The Creative Economy: How People Make Money from Ideas.* London: Penguin Books, 2002.

Hozic, Aida. *Hollyworld: Space, Power, and Fantasy in the American Economy.* Ithaca: Cornell University, 2001.

Hu, Kelly. "Made in China: The Cultural Logic of OEMs and the Manufacture of Low-Cost Technology." *Inter-Asia Cultural Studies* 9, no. 1 (2008), 27–46.

Hui, Desmond. "From Cultural to Creative Industries: Strategies for Chaoyang District, Beijing." *International Journal of Cultural Studies* 9, no. 3 (2006), 317–31.

Ito, Kinko. "A History of Manga in the Context of Japanese Culture and Society." *Journal of Popular Culture* 38, no. 3 (2005), 456–75.

Iwabuchi, Koichi. *Recentering Globalization: Popular Culture and Japanese Transnationalism.* Durham: Duke University Press, 2002.

———. "Useful Culture, Useless Media and Cultural Studies." Paper presented at Cultural Studies and Institution Symposium, Lingnan University, Hong Kong, 27 May 2006.

Jameson, Fredric. *Late Marxism: Adorno or the Persistence of the Dialectic.* London: Verso, 1990.

———. "Postmodernism and Consumer Culture." *Movies and Mass Culture,* ed. John Belton, 185–202. London: Athlone, 1996.

———. *A Singular Modernity: Essay on the Ontology of the Present.* London: Verso, 2002.

Jansen, Curry. "Designer Nations: Neo-Liberal Nation Branding—Brand Estonia." *Social Identities* 14, no. 1 (2008), 121–42.

Jenkins, Henry. *Convergence Culture: Where Old and New Media Collide.* New York: New York University Press, 2006.

———. *Textual Poachers: Television Fans and Participatory Culture.* New York: Routledge, 1992.

Johnston, Michael, and Yufan Hao. "China's Surge of Corruption." *Journal of Democracy* 6, no. 4 (1995), 80–94.

Johnston, Ollie, and Frank Thomas. *The Illusion of Life: Disney Animation.* New York: Disney Editions, 1981.

Katyal, Sonia K. "Performance, Property, and the Slashing of Gender in Fan Fiction." *American University Journal of Gender, Social Policy and the Law* 14, no 3 (2006), 461–518.

Kaufman, Gordon D. *In Face of Mystery: A Constructive Theology.* Cambridge: Harvard University Press, 1993.

Keane, Michael. "Brave New World: Understanding China's Creative Vision." *International Journal of Cultural Policy* 10, no. 3 (2004), 265–79.

———. "Bringing Culture Back In." *Governance in China*, ed. Jude Howell, 77–96. Lanham, Md.: Rowman and Littlefield, 2003.

———. "The Capital Complex: Beijing's New Creative Clusters." *Creative Economies, Creative Cities: Asian European Perspectives*, ed. Lily Kong and Justin O'Conner, 77–95. Dordrecht: Springer Netherlands, 2009.

———. *Created in China: The Great New Leap Forward.* London: Routledge, 2007.

Kelly, Kevin. *New Rules for the New Economy.* London: Fourth Estate, 1998.

Kelty, Christopher M. *Two Bits: The Cultural Significance of Free Software.* Durham: Duke University Press, 2008.

Kim, Joon-Yang. "Critique of the New Historical Landscape of South Korean Animation." *Animation* 1, no. 1 (2006), 61–81.

Kittler, Friedrich A. *Literature, Media, Information Systems: Essays*, ed. John Johnston. Amsterdam: G and B Arts International, 1997.

Klein, Naomi. *No Logo.* New York: Picador, 2002.

———. "Reclaiming the Commons." *New Left Review* 9 (May–June 2001), 81–89.

Kleiman, Paul. "Towards Transformation: Conceptions of Creativity in Higher Education." *Innovations in Education and Teaching International* 45, no. 3 (2008), 209–17.

Klinger, Barbara. "The Contemporary Cinephile: Film Collecting in the Post-Video Era." *Hollywood Spectatorships: Changing Perceptions of Cinema Audiences*, ed. Melvyn Stokes and Richard Maltby, 132–51. London: BFI, 2001.

Kong, Lily, Chris Gibson, Louisa-May Khoo, and Anne-Louise Semple. "Knowledges of the Creative Economy: Towards a Relational Geography of Diffusion and Adaptation in Asia." *Asia Pacific Viewpoint* 47, no. 2 (2006), 173–94.

Kraus, Richard Curt. *The Party and the Arty in China: The New Politics of Culture.* Lanham, Md.: Rowman and Littlefield, 2004.

Laclau, Ernesto. "Structure, History and the Political." *Contingency, Hegemony, Universality: Contemporary Dialogues on the Left*, ed. Judith Butler, Ernesto Laclau, and Slavoj Žižek, 182–212. London: Verso, 2000.

Laclau, Ernesto, and Chantal Mouffe. *Hegemony and Socialist Strategy: Towards a Radical Democratic Politics.* London: Verso, 1985.

Lamarre, Thomas. "Platonic Sex: Perversion and Shojo Anime (Part One)." *Animation* 1, no. 1 (2006), 45–59.

Landes, William M., and Richard A. Posner. *The Economic Structure of Intellectual Property Law.* Cambridge: Belknap Press of Harvard University Press, 2003.

Landry, Charles. *The Creative City: A Toolkit for Urban Innovators.* London: Earthscan, 2000.

Larkin, Brian. "Degraded Images, Distorted Sounds: Nigerian Video and the Infrastructure of Piracy." *Public Culture* 16, no. 2 (2004), 289–314.

Lash, Scott. *Critique of Information*. London: Sage, 2002.

Lash, Scott, and John Urry. *Economies of Signs and Space*. London: Sage, 1994.

Lazzarato, Maurizio. "Immaterial Labor." *Radical Thought in Italy: A Potential Politics*, ed. Paolo Virno and Michael Hardt, 133–47. Minneapolis: University of Minnesota Press, 1996.

Leadbeater, Charles. *Living on Thin Air: The New Economy*. London: Penguin, 2000.

Leadbeater, Charles, and Kate Oakley. *The Independents: Britain's New Cultural Entrepreneurs*. London: Demos, 1999.

Lee, Ching Kwan. *Against the Law: Labor Protests in China's Rustbelt and Sunbelt*. Berkeley: University of California Press, 2007.

Lefebvre, Henri. *The Production of Space*, trans. Donald Nicholson-Smith. Oxford: Blackwell, 1991.

———. *The Urban Revolution*, trans. Robert Bononno. Minneapolis: University of Minnesota Press, 2003.

Leonard, Mark. *Britain TM: Renewing Our Identity*. London: Demos, 1997.

Leonard, Sean. "Progress against the Law: Anime and Fandom, with the Key to the Globalization of Culture." *International Journal of Cultural Studies* 8, no. 3 (2005), 281–305.

Lessig, Lawrence. *Free Culture: How Big Media Uses Technology and the Law to Lock Down Culture and Control Creativity*. New York: Penguin, 2004.

Li, Amy Fung Kwan. "Slash, Fandoms, and Pleasures." MPhil thesis, Chinese University of Hong Kong, 2006.

Lin, Chun. *The Transformation of Chinese Socialism*. Durham: Duke University Press, 2006.

Liu, Alan. *The Laws of Cool: Knowledge Work and the Culture of Information*. Chicago: University of Chicago Press, 2004.

Lloyd, Richard. *Neo-Bohemia: Art and Commerce in the Postindustrial City*. New York: Routledge, 2006.

Locke, John. *Two Treatises of Government and a Letter Concerning Toleration*, ed. Ian Shapiro. New Haven: Yale University Press, 2003.

Lovink, Geert, and Mieke Gerritzen, eds. *Everyone Is a Designer: Manifest for the Design Economy*. Amsterdam: Bis, 2001.

Lu, Carol. "From Underground to Public." *Beijing 798: Reflections on Art, Architecture and Society in China*, ed. Huang Rui, 84–87. Hong Kong: Timezone 8, 2004.

Luft, Sandra Rudnick. *Vico's Uncanny Humanism: Reading the* New Science *between Modern and Postmodern*. Ithaca: Cornell University Press, 2003.

Lukács, Georg. *The Historical Novel*. Lincoln: University of Nebraska Press, 1983.

Lunenfeld, Peter. "The Myths of Interactive Cinema." *The New Media Book*, ed. Dan Harries, 144–54. London: BFI, 2002.

Luo, Peilin, "Recollections on the History of 718." *Beijing 798: Reflections on Art, Architecture and Society in China*, ed. Huang Rui, 10–13. Hong Kong: Timezone 8, 2004.

Lury, Celia. *Brands: The Logos of the Global Economy*. London: Routledge, 2004.

———. *Cultural Rights: Technology, Legality and Personality*. London: Routledge, Chapman and Hall, 1993.

Luvaas, Brent. "Designer Vandalism: Indonesian Indie Fashion and Cultural Practice of Cut'n'Paste." *Visual Anthropology Review* 26, no. 1 (2010), 1–16.

Lyons, Richard K., Jennifer A. Chatman, and Caneel K. Joyce. "Innovation in Services: Corporate Culture and Investment Banking." *California Management Review* 50, no. 1 (2007), 174–91.

MacLeod, Christine. *Inventing the Industrial Revolution: The English Patent System, 1660–1800.* Rev. ed. Cambridge: Cambridge University Press, 2002.

MacPherson, C. B. *The Political Theory of Possessive Individualism: Hobbes to Locke.* Oxford: Oxford University Press, 1962.

Malanga, Steven. "The Curse of the Creative Class." *Opinion Journal*, 19 January 2004, www.opinionjournal.com (accessed 7 December 2006).

Manovich, Lev. *The Language of New Media.* Cambridge: MIT Press.

Mao Zedong. "Talks at the Yan'an Forum on Literature and the Arts." *Chinese Theories of Theater and Performance from Confucius to the Present*, ed. and trans. Faye Chunfang Fei, 129–41. Ann Arbor: University of Michigan Press, 1999.

Marcuse, Herbert. *One Dimensional Man.* Boston: Beacon Press, 1991.

———. "Some Social Implications of Modern Technology." *Technology, War and Fascism, Collected Papers of Herbert Marcuse*, ed. Douglas Kellner, 1:41–65. London: Routledge, 1998. Reprinted from *Studies in Philosophy and Social Science* 9, no. 3 (1941), 414–39.

Marx, Karl. *Capital, Volume 1*, trans. Ben Fowkes. London: Penguin, 1990.

———. *Grundrisse*, trans. Martin Nicolaus. London: Penguin, 1993.

Maskus, Keith E. *Intellectual Property Rights in the Global Economy.* Washington, D.C.: Institute for International Economics, 2000.

Mason, Matt. *The Pirate's Dilemma: How Youth Culture Is Reinventing Capitalism.* New York: Free Press, 2008.

May, Christopher. "The Denial of History: Reification, Intellectual Property Rights and the Lessons of the Past." *Capital and Class* 88 (Spring 2006), 33–56.

May, Christopher, and Susan K. Sell. *Intellectual Property Rights: A Critical History.* Boulder: Lynne Reinner, 2006.

McCall, Anthony, Malcolm Turvey, Hal Foster, Chrissie Iles, George Baker, and Matthew Buckingham. "Round Table: The Projected Image in Contemporary Art." *October*, no. 104 (Spring 2003), 71–96.

McCann, Eugene J. "Inequality and Politics in the Creative City-Region: Questions of Livability and State Strategy." *International Journal of Urban and Regional Research*, 31, no. 1 (2007), 188–96.

McDonald, Paul, and Janet Wasko. "Introduction: The New Contours of the Hollywood Film Industry." *The Contemporary Hollywood Film Industry*, ed. Paul McDonald and Janet Wasko, 1–9. Malden, Mass.: Blackwell, 2008.

McGrath, Jason. *Postsocialist Modernity: Chinese Cinema, Literature, and Criticism in the Market Age.* Stanford: Stanford University Press, 2009.

McGuigan, Jim. *Rethinking Cultural Policy.* Maidenhead: Open University Press, 2004.

McLeay, Colin. "Inventing Australia: A Critique of Recent Cultural Policy Rhetoric." *Australian Geographical Studies* 35, no. 1 (1997), 40–46.

McRobbie, Angela. "Clubs to Companies: Notes on the Decline of Political Culture in Speeded Up Creative Worlds." *Cultural Studies* 16, no. 4 (2002), 516–31.

———. "From Holloway to Hollywood: Happiness at Work in the New Cultural Economy?" *Cultural Economy: Cultural Analysis and Commercial Life*, ed. Paul du Gay and Michael Pryke, 97–114. London: Sage, 2002.

Mehra, Salil. "Copyright and Comics in Japan: Does Law Explain Why All the Cartoons My Kid Watches Are Japanese Imports?" *Rutgers Law Review* 55 (Fall 2002), 155–204.

Mele, Christopher. *Selling the Lower East Side: Culture, Real Estate, and Resistance in New York City*. Minneapolis: University of Minnesota Press, 2000.

Mertha, Andrew. *The Politics of Piracy: Intellectual Property in Contemporary China*. Ithaca: Cornell University Press.

Miller, Toby, Nitin Govil, John McMurria, and Richard Maxwell. *Global Hollywood*. London: BFI, 2001.

Miller, Toby, and George Yúdice. *Cultural Policy*. London: Sage, 2002.

Mondzain, Marie-José. *Image, Icon, Economy: The Byzantine Origins of the Contemporary Imaginary*, trans. Rico Franses. Stanford: Stanford University Press, 2005.

Montgomery, Lucy. "Space to Grow: Copyright, Cultural Policy and Commercially-focused Music in China." *Chinese Journal of Communication* 2, no. 1 (2009), 36–49.

Morris, Martina, and Bruce Western. "Inequality in Earnings at the Close of the Twentieth Century." *Annual Review of Sociology* 25, no. 1 (1999), 623–57.

Morris, Meaghan. "Transnational Imagination in Action Cinema: Hong Kong and the Making of a Global Popular Culture." *Inter-Asia Cultural Studies* 5, no. 2 (2004), 181–99.

Mossig, Ivo. "Global Networks of the Motion Picture Industry in Los Angeles/Hollywood Using the Example of Their Connections to the German Market." *European Planning Studies* 16, no. 1 (2008), 43–59.

Mulvey, Laura. "Passing Time: Reflections on Cinema from a New Technological Age." *Screen* 54, no. 2 (2004), 142–55.

———. "Visual Pleasure and Narrative Cinema." *Visual and Other Pleasures*. Bloomington: Indiana University Press, 1989, 14–26.

Murakami, Takashi. *Little Boy: The Art of Japan's Exploding Subculture*. New York: Japanese Society, 2005.

Napack, Jonathan. "Chinese Artists May Sue Venice Biennale: 1999 Appropriation of a 1965 Socialist Realist Work Causes Anger." *Art Newspaper* 11, no. 106 (2000), 3.

Napier, Susan J. *Anime: From* Akira *to* Princess Mononoke. New York: Palgrave, 2001.

Neff, Gina, Elizabeth Wissinger, and Sharon Zukin. "Entrepreneurial Labor among Cultural Producers: 'Cool' Jobs in 'Hot' Industries." *Social Semiotics* 15, no. 3 (2005), 307–34.

Negativland. "Two Relationships to a Cultural Public Domain." *Law and Contemporary Problems* 66 (Winter–Spring 2003), 239–62.

Negus, Keith, and Michael Pickering. *Creativity, Communication and Cultural Value*. London: Sage, 2004.

Neumann, Bernd. "German Federal Film Fund (DFFF): A Real Boost for the German Film Industry," 2009, www.ffa.de (accessed 12 September 2009).

New England Foundation for the Arts. *Strengthening the Creative Economy*, 2011, creative economy.org.

Nimmer, David. *Copyright: Sacred Text, Technology, and the DMCA*. The Hague: Kluwer Law International, 2003.

North, Michael. *Art and Commerce in the Dutch Golden Age*. New Haven: Yale University Press, 1997.

Nye, Joseph. *Soft Power: The Means to Success in World Politics*. New York: Public Affairs, 2004.

O'Brien, Kevin J., and Lianjiang Li. *Rightful Resistance in Rural China*. Cambridge: Cambridge University Press, 2006.

Ong, Aihwa. *Neoliberalism as Exception: Mutations in Citizenship and Sovereignty*. Durham: Duke University Press, 2006.

Osborne, Peter. "Non-places and the Spaces of Art." *Journal of Architecture* 6, no. 2 (2001), 183–94.

———. "'Whoever Speaks of Culture Speaks of Administration as Well': Disputing Pragmatism in Cultural Studies." *Cultural Studies* 20, no. 1 (2006), 33–47.

Otmazgin, Nissim. "Contesting Soft Power: Japanese Popular Culture in East and Southeast Asia." *International Relations of the Asia Pacific* 8, no. 1 (2008), 73–101.

Ouspensky, Leonid. *Theology of the Icon*, trans. Anthony Gythiel and Elizabeth Meyendorff. Crestwood, N.Y.: St. Vladimir's Seminary Press, 1992.

Pang, Laikwan. *Cultural Control and Globalization in Asia: Copyrights, Cinema, and Piracy*. London: Routledge, 2006.

———. *The Distorting Mirror: Visual Modernity in China*. Honolulu: University of Hawaii Press, 2007.

———. "Jackie Chan, Tourism, and the Performing Agency." *Hong Kong Film, Hollywood, and the New Global Cinema*, ed. Gina Marchetti and Tan See-Kam, 206–18. London: Routledge, 2007.

———. "Postcolonial Hong Kong Cinema: Utilitarianism and (Trans)Local." *Postcolonial Studies* 10, no. 4 (2007), 413–30.

Papandrea, Franco. "Trade and Cultural Diversity: An Australian Perspective." *Prometheus* 23, no. 2 (2005), 227–37.

Paquet, Darcy. "The Korean Film Industry: 1992 to the Present." *New Korean Cinema*, ed. Chi-Yun Shin and Julian Stringer, 32–50. New York: New York University Press, 2005.

Patterson, Lyman Ray. *Copyright in Historical Perspective*. Nashville: Vanderbilt University Press, 1968.

Pennell, C. R., ed. *Bandits at Sea: A Pirates Reader*. New York: New York University Press, 2001.

Peralta, Elias. "A Call for Intellectual Property Rights to Recognize Indigenous People's Knowledge of Genetic and Cultural Resources." *Widening Perspectives on Biodiversity*, ed. Anatole F. Krattiger et al., 287–89. Gland, Switzerland: IUCN, 1994.

Philip, Kavita. "What Is a Technological Author? The Pirate Function and Intellectual Property." *Postcolonial Studies* 8, no. 2 (2005), 199–218.

Pierson, Michele. *Special Effects: Still in Search of Wonders*. New York: Columbia University Press, 2002.

Pike, Christopher G. *Virtual Monopoly: Building an Intellectual Property Strategy in the Creative Economy*. Naperville, Ill.: Nicholas Brealey, 2001.

Pine, B. Joseph, II, and James Gilmore. *The Experience Economy*. Boston: Harvard Business School Press, 1999.

Plato. *Timaeus*, trans. Donald J. Zeyl. Indianapolis: Hackett, 2000.

Polanyi, Karl. *The Great Transformation: The Political and Economic Origins of Our Time*. Boston: Beacon, 1957.

Poria, Yaniv, Richard Butler, and David Airey. "The Core of Heritage Tourism." *Annals of Tourism Research* 30, no. 1 (2003), 238–54.

Porter, Michael E. "Clusters and the New Economics of Competition." *Harvard Business Review*, November–December 1998, 77–87.

Potts, Jason. "Do Developing Economies Require Creative Industries? Some Old Theory about New China." *Chinese Journal of Communication* 2, no. 1 (2009), 92–108.

Poulantzas, Nicos. "Marxist Examination of the Contemporary State and Law and the Question of the 'Alternative.'" *The Poulantzas Reader: Marxism, Law, and the State*, ed. James Martin, 25–46. London: Verso, 2008.

Pratt, Andy C. "Advertising and Creativity, a Governance Approach: A Case Study of Creative Agencies in London." *Environment and Planning A* 38 (2006), 1883–99.

Puett, Michael. *The Ambivalence of Creation: Debates Concerning Innovation and Artifice in Early China*. Stanford: Stanford University Press, 2001.

Qiu, Jack Linchuan. *Working-Class Network Society: Communication Technology and the Information Have-Less in Urban China*. Cambridge: MIT Press, 2009.

Ramo, Joshua Cooper. "Brand China." Report submitted to The Foreign Policy Centre, 2007, http://fpc.org.uk (accessed 16 August 2010).

Rancière, Jacques. *Dissensus: On Politics and Aesthetics*, ed. and trans. Steven Corcoran. London: Continuum, 2010.

———. *The Future of the Image*, trans. Gregory Elliott. London: Verso, 2007.

———. *The Nights of Labor: The Workers' Dream in Nineteenth-Century France*, trans. John Drury. Philadelphia: Temple University Press, 1989.

Raymond, Eric S. *The Cathedral and the Bazaar: Musings on Linux and Open Source by an Accidental Revolutionary*. Sebastopol, Calif.: O'Reilly, 1999.

Redding, S. Gordon. *The Spirit of Chinese Capitalism*. Berlin: Walter de Gruyter, 1990.

Rees, Helen. *Echoes of History: Naxi Music in Modern China*. Oxford: Oxford University Press, 2000.

Reich, Robert B. *The Work of Nations: Preparing Ourselves for 21st Century Capitalism*. New York: Alfred A. Knopf, 1991.

Rennie, Ellie. "Creative World." *Creative Industries*, ed. John Hartley, 42–54. Malden, Mass.: Blackwell, 2005.

Rifkin, Jeremy. *The Age of Access: The New Culture of Hypercapitalism, Where All of Life Is a Paid-for Experience*. New York: Jeremy P. Tarcher, Putnam, 2000.

Roberts, G. Keith. "DeCSS Code on the Internet: Is It Protected Speech?" *Computer and Internet Lawyer* 21, no. 12 (2004), 1–4.

Roberts, John. "On the Limits of Negation in Badiou's Theory of Art." *Journal of Visual Arts Practice* 7, no. 3 (2008), 271–82.

Robinson, A. J. K. "The Evolution of Copyright, 1476–1776." *Cambrian Law Review* 22 (1991), 1476–776.

Rofel, Lisa. *Desiring China: Experiments in Neoliberalism, Sexuality, and Public Culture.* Durham: Duke University Press, 2007.

Rogerson, Kenneth S. "Karl Polanyi." *Key Thinkers for the Information Society*, ed. Christopher May, 135–53. London: Routledge, 2003.

Rojcewicz, Richard. *The Gods and Technology: A Reading of Heidegger.* Albany: State University of New York Press, 2006.

Rønning, Helge, Pradip Thomas, Keylan G. Tomaseli, and Ruth Teer-Tomaseli. "Intellectual Property Rights and the Political Economy of Culture." *Critical Arts: A South-North Journal of Cultural and Media Studies* 20, no. 1 (2006), 1–19.

Rose, Mark. *Authors and Owners.* Cambridge: Harvard University Press, 1993.

Ross, Andrew. *No Collar: The Humane Workplace and Its Hidden Costs. Behind the Myth of the New Office Utopia.* New York: Basic Books, 2003.

Rossiter, Ned. *Organized Networks: Media Theory, Creative Labour, New Institution.* Rotterdam: NAi, 2006.

Rubin, Michael. *Droidmaker: George Lucas and the Digital Revolution.* Gainesville: Triad, 2006.

Runia, David T. "Plato's *Timaeus*, First Principle(s), and Creation in Philo and Early Christian Thought." *Plato's Timaeus as Cultural Icon*, ed. Gretchen J. Reydams-Schils, 133–51. Notre Dame, Ind.: University of Notre Dame Press, 2003.

Ruscio, Ayelet Meron, and Teresa Amabile. "Effects of Instructional Style on Problem-Solving Creativity." *Creativity Research Journal* 12, no. 4 (1999), 251–66.

Rutherford, Leonie. "Australian Animation Aesthetics." *The Lion and the Unicorn*, 27, no. 2 (2003), 251–67.

Rutter, Jason, and Jo Bryce. "The Consumption of Counterfeit Goods: 'Here Be Pirates?'" *Sociology* 42 (2008), 1146–64.

Sæther, Susanne Østby. "Between the Hyperrepresentational and the Real: A Sampling Sensibility." *The State of the Real: Aesthetics in the Digital Age*, ed. Damian Sutton, Susan Brind, and Ray McKenzie, 48–61. London: I. B. Tauris, 2007.

Samuelson, Pamela. "Economic and Constitutional Influences on Copyright Law in the U.S." *U.S. Intellectual Property Law and Policy*, ed. Hugh Hansen, 164–203. Cheltenham: Edward Elgar, 2006.

Sassen, Saskia. *Cities in a World Economy.* Thousand Oaks, Calif.: Pine Forge Press, 1994.

Sawyer, Keith. *Group Genius: The Creative Power of Collaboration.* New York: Basic Books, 2007.

Schelling, F. W. J. "Philosophical Investigations into the Essence of Human Freedom." *German Idealism: An Anthology and Guide*, ed. Brian O'Connor and Georg Mohr, 138–48. Edinburgh: Edinburgh University Press, 2006.

Seabrook, John. *Nobrow: The Culture of Marketing, the Marketing of Culture.* New York: Alfred A. Knopf, 2000.

Sell, Susan K. *Private Power, Public Law: The Globalization of Intellectual Property Rights.* Cambridge: Cambridge University Press, 2003.

Sennett, Richard. *The Culture of the New Capitalism.* New Haven: Yale University Press, 2006.

Shang, Kela. "'Rent Collection Courtyard': Fair Use Doctrine Revisited in the Context of Postmodern Visuality." *Perspectives* 7, no. 4 (2006), 223–47.

Shen, Lien Fan. "What Is 'Computer Animation'? Examining Technological Advancements and Cultural Aesthetics of Japanese Animation." 2007, http://delivery.acm.org (accessed 17 September 2009).

Sherman, Brad, and Lionel Bently. *The Making of Modern Intellectual Property Law.* Cambridge: Cambridge University Press, 1999.

Shorthose, Jim, and Gerard Strange. "The New Cultural Economy, the Artist and the Social Configuration of Autonomy." *Capital and Class*, no. 84 (Winter 2004), 43–59.

Simmel, Georg. "The Metropolis and Mental Life." *Simmel on Culture: Selected Writings*, ed. David Frisby and Mike Featherstone, 174–85. London: Sage, 1997.

Smith, Adam. *Lectures on Jurisprudence*, ed. R. L. Meek, D. D. Raphael, and P. G. Stein. Oxford: Clarendon Press, 1978.

Spooner, Lysander. *A Letter to Scientists and Inventors, on the Science of Justice, and Their Right of Perpetual Property in Their Discoveries and Inventions* (1884). *The Collected Works of Lysander Spooner*, ed. Charles Shively. Weston, Mass.: M and S Press, 1971.

Stenning, Alison. "Shaping the Economic Landscapes of Postsocialism? Labour, Workplace and Community in Nowa Huta, Poland." *Antipode* 35, no. 4 (2003), 761–80.

Stille, Alexander. *The Future of the Past.* New York: Farrar, Straus and Giroux, 2002.

Storper, Michael, and Robert Salais. *Worlds of Production: The Action Frameworks of the Economy.* Cambridge: Harvard University Press, 1997.

Studwell, Joe. *The China Dream: The Quest for the Last Great Untapped Market on Earth.* New York: Grove Press, 2003.

Tan, See-Kam. "Chinese Diasporic Imaginations in Hong Kong Films: Sinicist Belligerence and Melancholia." *Screen* 42, no. 1 (2001), 1–20.

Taniguchi, Makiko, and Eddie Wu. "Shanzhai." *Patterns: Design Insights Emerging and Converging*, no. 27, January 2010, http://patterns.ideo.com (accessed 15 September 2010).

Tapscott, Don. *The Digital Economy: Promise and Peril in the Age of Networked Intelligence.* New York: McGraw-Hill, 1996.

Taussig, Michael. *Mimesis and Alterity: A Particular History of the Senses.* New York: Routledge, 1993.

Teo, Stephen. *Hong Kong Cinema: The Extra Dimensions.* London: BFI, 1997.

Thomas, Douglas. *Hacker Culture.* Minneapolis: University of Minnesota Press, 2002.

Thrift, Nigel. "Capitalism's Cultural Turn." *Culture and Economy after the Cultural Turn*, ed. Larry Ray and Andrew Sayer, 135–61. London: Sage, 1999.

Throsby, David. *Economics and Culture.* Cambridge: Cambridge University Press, 2001.

Tikku, Anup. "Indian Inflow: The Interplay of Foreign Investment and Intellectual Property." *Third World Quarterly* 19, no. 1 (1998), 81–113.

Toffler, Alvin. *Powershift: Knowledge, Wealth, and Violence at the Edge of the 21st Century.* New York: Bantam Books, 1991.

Tosa, Masaki. "Public Significance of Cultural Piracy in the Global Flow of Popular Culture." *Asia Japan Journal* 3 (March 2008), 39–46.

Tsang, Donald. *Proactive, Pragmatic, Always People First: The 2006–07 Policy Address.* Hong Kong: Government Logistics Department, 2006.

Tung, Chee Hwa. *Capitalising on Our Advantages, Revitalising Our Economy: The 2003 Policy Address*. Hong Kong: Government Logistics Department, 2003.

——. *The 1998 Policy Address*. Hong Kong: Government Logistics Department, 1998.

——. *Seizing Opportunities for Development, Promoting People-based Governance: The 2004 Policy Address*. Hong Kong: Government Logistics Department, 2004.

——. *Working Together for Economic Development and Social Harmony: The 2005 Policy Address*. Hong Kong: Government Logistics Department, 2005.

Tuomi, Krista. "Organisational Shifts in the Feature Film Industry: Implications for South Africa." *Transformation* 62 (2007), 68–91.

U.K. Film Council. "U.K. Film Council at a Glance," 2009, www.ukfilmcouncil.org.uk (accessed 12 September 2009).

UNESCO. "International Flows of Selected Cultural Goods and Services 1994–2003." 2005, www.uis.unesco.org (accessed 8 October 2009).

U.S.-China Business Council. "Foreign Direct Investment (FDI) in China," 2009, www .uschina.org (accessed 5 November 2009).

U.S. Department of Commerce, International Trade Administration. "Protecting Your Intellectual Property Rights (IPR) in China: A Practical Guide for U.S. Companies," 2003, www.mac.doc.gov (accessed 21 September 2007).

Vaidhyanathan, Siva. *Copyrights and Copywrongs: The Rise of Intellectual Property and How It Threatens Creativity*. New York: New York University Press, 2001.

Vann, Elizabeth F. "The Limits of Authenticity in Vietnamese Consumer Markets." *American Anthropologies* 108, no. 2 (2006), 186–96.

Vattimo, Gianni. *The End of Modernity*, trans. Jon R. Snyder. Baltimore: Johns Hopkins University Press, 1988.

Vico, Giambattista. *The New Science of Giambattista Vico*, trans. Thomas Goddard Bergin and Max Harold Fisch. Ithaca: Cornell University Press, 1968.

Vinciguerra, Vincenzo. "The Dialectic Relationship between Different Concepts of Property Rights and Its Significance on Intellectual Property Rights." *Journal of Technology Law and Policy* 155 (June 2005), 156–71.

Visser, Robin. "Spaces of Disappearance: Aesthetic Responses to Contemporary Beijing City Planning." *Journal of Contemporary China* 13, no. 39 (2004), 282–85.

Walker, Richard, and Daniel Buck. "The Chinese Road." *New Left Review* 46 (July 2007), 39–66.

Wang, Hui. *China's New Order: Society, Politics, and Economy in Transition*. Cambridge: Harvard University Press, 2003.

——. "Depoliticized Politics, from East to West." *New Left Review* 41 (September 2006), 29–45.

Wang, Jing. *Brand New China: Advertising, Media, and Commercial Culture*. Cambridge: Harvard University Press, 2008.

——. "Culture as Leisure and Culture as Capital." *positions: East Asia Cultures Critique* 9, no. 1 (2001), 87–88.

——. "The Global Reach of a New Discourse: How Far Can 'Creative Industries' Travel?" *International Journal of Cultural Studies* 7, no. 1 (2004), 9–19.

Wang, Nan. "Shanghai Goes Creative over Eight Sectors." Hong Kong Trade Development Council, 7 February 2006, www.tdctrade.com (accessed 30 January 2007).

Wang, Shujen. *Framing Piracy: Globalization and Film Distribution in Greater China.* Lanham, Md.: Rowman and Littlefield, 2003.

Wark, McKenzie. *A Hacker Manifesto.* Cambridge: Harvard University Press, 2004.

Warwick, Shelly. "Is Copyright Ethical? An Examination of the Theories, Laws, and Practices Regarding the Private Ownership of Intellectual Work in the United States." *Readings in CyberEthics*, ed. Richard A. Spinello and Herman T. Tavani, 305–21. Sudbury, Mass.: Jones and Bartlett, 2001.

Wayne, Mike. *Marxism and Media Studies: Key Concepts and Contemporary Trends.* London: Pluto, 2003.

Welchman, John C. *Art after Appropriation: Essays on Art in the 1990s.* Amsterdam: G and B Arts International, 2001.

Wells, Liz. "On and Beyond the White Walls: Photography as Art." *Photography: A Critical Introduction*, ed. Liz Wells, 273–80. London: Routledge, 1996.

Wells, Paul. *Understanding Animation.* London: Routledge, 1998.

West, Edwin G. "Property Rights in the History of Economic Thought: From Locke to J. S. Mill." *Property Rights: Cooperation, Conflict and Law*, ed. Terry L. Anderson and Fred S. McChesne, 20–42. Princeton: Princeton University Press, 2003.

Wigmans, Gerard. "Contingent Governance and the Enabling City: The Case of Rotterdam." *City* 5, no. 2 (2001), 203–23.

Willemen, Paul. *Looks and Frictions: Essays in Cultural Studies and Film Theory.* Bloomington: Indiana University Press, 1994.

Williams, Raymond. *Keywords: A Vocabulary of Culture and Society.* Rev. ed. Oxford: Oxford University Press, 1985.

———. *Marxism and Literature.* Oxford: Oxford University Press, 1977.

Williams, Tony. "Space, Place, and Spectacle: The Crisis Cinema of John Woo." *Cinema Journal* 36, no. 2 (1997), 73–77.

Wirtén, Eva Hemmungs. "Out of Sight and out of Mind: On the Cultural Hegemony of Intellectual Property (Critique)." *Cultural Studies* 20, nos. 2–3 (2006), 284–87.

Wong, Flora. "An Overview of the Development of China's Patent System." *Chinese Intellectual Property and Practice*, ed. Mark A. Cohen, A. Elizabeth Bang, and Stephanie J. Mitchell, 3–24. The Hague: Kluwer Law International, 1999.

Woodmansee, Martha. "The Genius and the Copyright: Economic and Legal Conditions of the Emergence of the 'Author.'" *Eighteenth Century Studies* 17 (1984), 425–48.

Wu, Hung. *Exhibiting Experimental Art in China.* Chicago: David and Alfred Smart Museum of Art, University of Chicago, 2000.

———. "Mapping Early Taoist Art: The Visual Culture of Wudoumi Dao." *Taoism and the Arts of China*, ed. Stephen Little, 77–93. Chicago: Art Institute of Chicago, and Berkeley: University of California Press, 2000.

Xu, Janice Hua. "Brand-new Lifestyle: Consumer-oriented Programmes on Chinese Television." *Media, Culture and Society* 29, no. 3 (2007), 363–76.

Xue, Hong. "What Direction Is the Wind Blowing? Protection of DRM in China." *The De-*

velopment Agenda: Global Intellectual Property and Developing Countries, ed. Neil Wein-
stock Netanel, 177–89. Oxford: Oxford University Press, 2009.

Yale, Pat. From Tourist Attraction to Heritage Tourism. Huntingdon, Calif.: ELM Publications, 1997.

Yamamura, Takayoshi. "Authenticity, Ethnicity and Social Transformation at World
Heritage Sites: Tourism, Retailing and Cultural Change in Lijiang, China." Tourism and
Transition: Governance, Transformation and Development, ed. Derek R. Hall, 185–200.
Oxford: CABI, 2004.

———. "Dongba Art in Lijiang, China: Indigenous Culture, Local Community and
Tourism." Indigenous Tourism: The Commodification and Management of Culture,
ed. Chris Ryan and Michelle Aicken, 181–99. Amsterdam: Elsevier, 2005.

Yang, Xiaohua. Globalization of the Automobile Industry: The United States, Japan, and the
People's Republic of China. Westport, Conn.: Praeger, 1995.

Yi, Jinan. "Is 798 a Cultural Petting Zoo?" 798: A Photographic Journal, ed. Zhu Yan, 3–11.
Hong Kong: Timezone 8, 2004.

Yip, Frances. Capitalism as Religion? A Study of Paul Tillich's Interpretation of Modernity.
Cambridge: Harvard Theological Studies, Harvard Divinity School, 2010.

Yoon, Ae-Ri. "In-between the Values of the Global and the National: The Korean Animation Industry." Cultural Studies and Cultural Industries in Northeast Asia: What a Difference a Region Makes, ed. Chris Berry, Nicola Liscutin, and Jonathan D. Mackintosh,
103–15. Hong Kong: Hong Kong University Press, 2009.

Yúdice, George. The Expediency of Culture: Uses of Culture in the Global Era. Durham:
Duke University Press, 2003.

Yue, Audrey. "Hawking in the Creative City." Feminist Media Studies 7, no. 4 (2007),
365–80.

———. "The Regional Culture of New Asia: Cultural Governance and Creative Industries
in Singapore." International Journal of Cultural Policy 12, no. 1 (2006), 17–33.

Zaya, Octavio. "Cai Guo-Qiang." pressPLAY: Contemporary Artists in Conversation, 65–66.
London: Phaidon Press, 2005.

Zhang, Jing Vivian. "Decentralizing China: Analysis of Central Strategies in China's Fiscal
Reforms." Journal of Contemporary China 18, no. 60 (2009), 445–62.

Zhang, Yongle. "The Future of the Past: On Wang Hui's Rise of Modern Chinese Thought."
New Left Review 62 (March–April 2010), 47–83.

Zheng, Henry R. "The Patent System of the People's Republic of China." University of San
Francisco Law Review 23, nos. 2–3 (1987), 345–92.

Zhu Yan, ed. 798: A Photographic Journal. Hong Kong: Time Zone 8, 2004.

Zion, Lawrie. "Creating a Successful Local Industry." www.afc.gov.au (accessed 9 September 2005).

Žižek, Slavoj. "The Abyss of Freedom." The Abyss of Freedom/Ages of the Word, by Slavoj
Žižek and F. W. J. Von Schelling, 3–89. Ann Arbor: University of Michigan Press, 1997.

———. "Class Struggle or Postmodernism? Yes, Please!" Contingency, Hegemony, Universality: Contemporary Dialogues on the Left, ed. Judith Butler, Ernesto Laclau, and Slavoj
Žižek, 90–135. London: Verso, 2000.

———. *The Sublime Object of Ideology*. London: Verso, 1989.

———. *Welcome to the Desert of the Real*. London: Verso, 2002.

Chinese Materials

"Beijing Aoyun jixiangwu fuwa haokan ma?" 北京奧運吉祥物福娃好看嗎? (Is Beijing's Olympic mascot Fuwa beautiful?), 14 November 2005, http://news.bbc.co.uk (accessed 30 November 2006).

Bi Guoxue 畢國學, "Dafencun hualang chaoshi guonei qiangtan" 大芬村畫廊超市國內搶灘 (Dafencun painting supermarket taking hold of the national market). *Dafen youhua xiaoshou wang* 大芬油畫銷售網 (Dafen oil painting sales network), http://news.sznews .com/content/2007-10/16/content_1578945.htm (accessed 18 October 2007).

Changchang 萇萇. "Baiwen renminbi yishujia" 百萬人民幣藝術家 (Million Renminbi artists). *Shenghuo zhoukan* 生活週刊 (Lifeweek) 392 (17 July 2006), 44-45.

Chen Baohong 陳寶宏. "Songzhuang de yishu 'jiaofu'" 宋莊的藝術「教父」 (The art "god-father" of Songzhuang). *Zhongguo xinwen zhoukan* 中國新聞週刊 (Chinese Newsweek), 30 October 2006, http://magazine.sina.com/chinanewsweek/20061030/2006-11-05/ 195222918.shtml (accessed 23 November 2006).

Chen Jinfu 陳錦富 and Liu Jia'ning 劉佳寧. "Chengshi guihua xingzheng jiuji zhidu tantao" 城市規劃行政救濟制度探討 (Urban planning administrative relief system). *Chengshi guihua* 城市規劃 (Urban planning) 10 (2005), 19-23, 64.

Chen Qijia 陳奇佳 and Song Hui 宋暉. "Zhongguo donghua fazhan wenti zhengyi" 中國動畫發展問題爭議 (On the issue of the development of Chinese animation). *Jiangxi shifan daxue xuebao* 江西師範大學學報 (Journal of Jiangxi Normal University) 38, no. 6 (2005), 72-78.

Cui Yongfu 崔永福 et al. "Dashanzi 798 chang yishuqu diaoyan baogao" 大山子 798 廠藝術區調研報告 (Research report on the art area at Dashanzi 798 Factory). *Meishu yanjiu* 美術研究 (Fine arts research), 2006, www.sznews.com/art/content/2006-08/18/ content_266758_2.htm (accessed 29 December 2006).

Dafen youhuacun guanli bangongshi 大芬油畫村管理辦公室 (Dafen Village Oil Painting Management Office). "2006 nian gongzuo zongjie" 2006 年工作總結 (Annual report, 2006), 14 December 2006, http://bbs.sznews.com/redirect.php?fid=1023&tid=247448 &goto=nextoldset&sflag= (accessed 22 October 2007).

Editorial. "Shoudu wenhua chuangyi chanye zhengce quan jiexi" 首都文化創意產業政策 全解析 (A complete analysis of the capital's creative industry). *Reference to Creative Industry*, inaugural issue, August 2006, 6-8.

Editorial. "Zhongguo pinpai guojihua zhi lü" 中國品牌國際化之旅 (The journey of the internationalization of Chinese brand names). Guowuyuan fazhan yanjiu zhongxin zixun wang 國務院發展研究中心資訊網 (Development Research Centre of the State Council Net), http://218.246.21.135:81/gate/big5/www.drcnet.com.cn (accessed 23 May 2006).

Executive Committee of the Congress of the People of Yunnan Province. "Yunnan sheng Naxi zu Dongba wenhua baohu tiaoli" 雲南省納西族東巴文化保護條例 (Regulations on the Protection of the Culture of Dongba, Naxi, Yunnan), 5 December 2005, www.lijiang.gov.cn (accessed 14 October 2007).

Fei Xiaotong 費孝通 et al. *Zhongguo minzu duoyuan yiti geju* 中華民族多元一體格局 (The unifying structure of the pluralist Chinese people). Beijing: Zhongyang minzu xueyuan chubanshe, 1989.

Fei Yuxiao 緋雨宵. *Chuangzao mengxiang yu feixiang de laoren: Gong Qijun* 創造夢想與飛翔的老人: 宮崎駿 (The world of Miyazaki Hayao). Dongfang yinxiang dianzi chubanshe 東方音像電子出版社 and Kuilü wenhua 葵綠文化. (Publication city and year unknown.)

Feng Jianhua 馮建華. "Yancha 'heixin' shipin" 嚴查 '黑心' 食品 (Harsh inspection for food with "black heart"), 2004, *Beijingreview.com* (accessed 21 May 2006).

Feng Nianhua 馮念華. "Daoban dui Songdai banquan de yingxiang" 盜版對宋代版權的影響 (The impact of piracy on the protection of copyright in the Song dynasty). *Tushuguan gongzuo yu yanjiu* 圖書館工作與研究 (Library work and research) 133, no. 3 (2006), 63–65.

Feng Yuhui 馮玉惠 et al. "Guanyu jianli Xuhui qu wenhua chanye tongji de sikao" 關於建立徐匯區文化產業統計的思考 (Thoughts on compiling cultural industry statistics for the Xuhui region). 11 December, 2006 http://tjj.xh.sh.cn (accessed 16 April 2007).

Gao Zhanxiang 高占祥. *Wenhua yishu guanlilun* 文化藝術管理論 (Theories of culture and art management). Beijing: Beijing daxue chubanshe, 1994.

Gaoge dianchenan 高個電車男. "Shui hai jide dangnian de Hainan sheying meishu chubanshe?" 誰還記得當年的海南攝影美術出版社? (Who still remembers Hainan Press of Photography and Arts?). 12 April 2007, http://www.tianya.cn/publicforum/content/3d/1/30187.shtml (accessed 25 November 2007).

Ge Hong 郭虹. "Beijing, Shanghai qingshaonian donghua diaocha" 北京、上海青少年動畫調查 (Survey of the reception of animation among Beijing and Shanghai youths). 2 July 2004, www.chinanim.com (accessed 13 March 2006).

Ge Qing 葛清. "Zhongguo yishupin haiwai kuangbiao" 中國藝術品海外狂飆 (The rapidly rising status of Chinese art in foreign markets). *Nanfang zhoumo* 南方周末 (Nanfang weekend), 10 August 2006.

Gu Lieming 顧列銘. "Wenzhou zijin yu 'chao' Beijing guoqi" 溫州資金欲 "炒" 北京國企 (Wenzhou capital aimed at Beijing's national enterprise). *Xin jingji zazhi* 新經濟雜志 (New economic magazine), no. 3 (2006), 28–29.

Gu Weijie 顧維潔, and Liu Hui 劉輝. "Songzhuang Xiaobaocun shuji Cui Dabo fangtan" 宋莊小堡村書記崔大柏訪談 (Interviewing Cui Dabo, Xiaobaocun's party secretary). *Jintian* 今天 (Today), no. 76 (Spring 2007), 258–63.

Guangzhou daxuecheng Xiaoguwei yishucun bei biqian zhe 廣州大學城小谷圍藝術村被逼遷者 (Those forced to leave Xiaoguwei Art Village at Guangzhou's University City). "Zhi Wen Jiabao zongli de gongkaixin" 致溫家寶總理的公開信 (Open letter to Premier Wen Jiabao). *Boxun.com*, 11 July 2004 www.peacehall.com (accessed 5 December 2006).

Guangzhou shi xinwen chuban he guangbo dianshi ju 廣州市新聞出版和廣播電視局 (Guangzhou City Office of Press, Publication, Broadcasting and Television). "Shenzhen yi cujin chanye fazhan wei zhidao, kaichuang banquan gongzuo xinjumian" 深圳以促進產業發展為指導, 開創版權工作新局面 (Industrial growth is Shenzhen's direction, new prospects for copyright development), 12 October 2007, www.xwgd.gov.cn (accessed 23 October 2007).

Guangzhou shi zhengfu 廣州市政府 (Guangzhou City Government). "Yuexiu dazao guonei zhiming chuangyi zhongxin" 越秀打造國內知名創意中心 (Building Yuexiu into a nationally famous creativity center), 11 January 2007, http://www.gz.gov.cn/vfs/content/newcontent.jsp?contentId=437168 (accessed 23 January 2007).

Guo Mengliang 郭孟良. "Zhongguo banquan wenti tanyuan" 中國版權問題探源 (Searching for the historical roots of Chinese copyright issues). *Qilu xuekan* 齊魯學刊 (Qilu journal) 159, no. 6 (2006), 30–35.

He Jinguang 和金光. "Naxi zu Dongba wenhua yanjiu fazhan qushi" 納西族東巴文化研究發展趨勢 (Recent developments in research on the Dongba culture of the Naxi people). *Yunnan minzu daxue xuebao* 雲南民族大學學報 (Journal of Yunnan Nationalities University) 24, no. 1 (2007), 81–84.

He Liming 和力民. "Shilun Dongba wenhua de chuancheng" 試論東巴文化的傳承 (On the transition of Dongba culture). *Yunnan shehui kexue* 雲南社會科學 (Social sciences in Yunnan), no. 1 (2004), 83–87.

He Wanli 賀萬里. *Yongyuan de qianwei: Zhongguo xiandai yishu de fansi yu pipan* 永遠的前衛: 中國現代藝術的反思與批判 (Everlasting avant-garde: Rethinking and criticizing modern Chinese art). Zhengzhou: Zhengzhou daxue chubanshe, 2003.

Hu Huilin 胡惠林. *Wenhua chanye fazhan yu guojia wenhua anquan* 文化產業發展與國家文化安全 (The development of cultural industries and national cultural security). Guangzhou: Guangdong renmin chubanshe, 2005.

Hu Jintao 胡錦濤. "Nuli ba guanche luoshi kexue fazhanguan tigao dao xin shuiping" 努力把貫徹落實科學發展觀提高到新水平 (Work hard to put scientific development into practice and elevate it to a new level), 18 September 2008, http://news.xinhuanet.com/politics/2009-01/01/content_10588218.htm (accessed 10 June 2009).

Hu Yizhen 胡綺珍 (Kelly Hu). "Zhongguo zimuzu yu xinziyouzhuyi de gongzuo lunli" 中國字幕組與新自由主義的工作倫理 (Chinese subtitling groups and the neoliberal work ethic). *Xinwenxue yanjiu* 新聞學研究 (Mass communication research) 101 (October 2009), 177–214.

Huang Rongqiang 黃榮強. "Dafen youhuacun zhishichanquan gongzuo zhan guopai chengli" 大芬油畫村知識產權工作站掛牌成立 (The establishment of an IPR office in Dafen Village), http://www.sznews.com/epaper/szwb/content/2007-01/18/content_787125.htm (accessed 23 October 2007).

Huang Xu 黃序, ed. *Beijing chengxiang: Tongchou xietiao fazhen yanjiu* 北京城鄉: 統籌協調發展研究 (Beijing's city and countryside: Research on structured and balanced development). Beijing: Zhongguo jiancai gongye chubanshe, 2004.

Jiang Jiwei 蔣積偉. "Jianguo yilai Zhonggong wenhua zhengce shuping (1949–1976)" 建國以來中共文化政策述評 (1949–1976) (Commentary on Chinese cultural policies since the establishment of the PRC [1949–1976]). *Dangshi yanjiu yu jiaoxue* 黨史研究與教學 (Party history research and teaching) 194, no. 1 (2007), 51–56.

Kong Zhengyi 孔正毅. "Shilun gudai tushu de banquan baohu" 試論古代圖書的版權保護 (An attempt to discuss the copyright protection of ancient books). *Chuban faxing yanjiu* 出版發行研究 (Publication and distribution research), no. 6 (2003), 77–80.

Li Dezhu 李德洙. "Dang de disandai lingdao jiti dui Makesi zhuyi minzu lilun de xinfa-zhan xingongxian" 黨的第三代領導集體對馬克思主義民族理論的新發展新貢獻 (The Party's third-generation leaders' new contribution to the development of Marxist ethnic theory). *Zhongguo minzu* 中國民族 (China's nationalities) 7 (2002), 4–6.

Li Fang 李舫. "Woguo chutai *Wenhua ji xiangguan chanye zhibiao tixi kuangjia*" 我國出台 《文化及相關產業指標體系框架》 (Our country releasing *Framework of the indexical structure of cultural and related industries*), 2 March, 2005, www.china.com.cn (accessed 3 June, 2011).

Li Haiqiang 李海強. "Shanghai chuangyi chanye mishi Shanghai" 上海創意產業迷失上海 (Shanghai's creative industries lost in Shanghai). *Huanqiu qiyejia* 環球企業家 (Global entrepreneurs), 23 September 2006, www.ccmedu.com (accessed 15 September 2010).

Li Jianping 李劍平. "Tashan zhi shi—Riben donghuapian daigei women de sikao" 他山之石—日本動畫片帶給我們的思考 (How we could learn from Japanese animation). *Dianshi yanjiu* 電視研究 (Television studies), no. 9 (2000), 69–71.

Li Jun 李軍. *Kunrao yu zhuanji—wenhua yishu guanlixue chutan* 困擾與轉機—文化藝術管理初探 (Anxiety and change: A preliminary investigation of culture and art management). Hunan: Hubei renmin chubanshe, 1987.

Lian Mian 連冕. "Sheji bopu yu mincui: ping aoyun fuwa zuowei gonggong sheji yishu" 設計波普與民粹—評奧運福娃作為公共設計藝術 (Design pop and populism: The Olympic Fuwa as public design art). *Meishu guancha* 美術觀察 (Observation), no. 2 (2006), 25–26.

Liang Caiheng 梁彩恆. "Cong zhishi chanquan de jiaodu guanzhu Lijiang de shengcun yu fazhan" 從知識產權的角度關注麗江的生存與發展 (Concerning the survival and the development of Lijiang from an intellectual property rights perspective), 6 September 2005, http://legal.people.com.cn (accessed 12 October 2007).

Liang Tingjia 梁庭嘉. *Mingpai tiantang—Beijing, Shanghai, Shenzhe heishi youji* 名牌天堂—北京, 上海, 深圳黑市游記 (Brand paradise: A travelogue of the black market in Beijing, Shanghai, and Shenzhen). Taipei: Shangzhou Liang, 2006.

Lijiang Science and Technology Bureau. "Zhishi chanquan ke" 知識產權科 (The Department of Intellectual Property Rights), December 2006, www.ljkj.cn (accessed 16 October 2007).

Ling Yan 凌燕. "Huayu kuajing dapian yu Zhongguo xiangxiang" 華語跨境大片與中國想像 (Chinese-language transborder blockbusters and the imagination of China). Paper presented at Transborder Activities of Chinese-language Commercial Cinema workshop, Chinese University of Hong Kong, 19 January 2008.

Liu Jianjun 劉建軍 and Gan Xiangyang 甘向陽. "Zhuanli xingzhi de jiangli zhidu" 專利性質的獎勵制度 (The award system of patents). *Kexue jishu yu bianzhenfa* 科學技術與辯證法 (Science, technology, and dialectics) 21, no. 1 (2004), 84–87.

Liu Liang 劉亮. "Sun Jianjun 'zuoju' Beijing wenhua chanye" 孫健君"做局"北京文化產業 (Sun Jianjun pleading with Beijing's cultural industries). *Ziben shichang* 資本市場 (Capital markets), no. 4 (2006), 79–81.

Long Yue 龍樂. "Zhou Xun zhuyan dianying qinquan Naxi Yinyue Shijia yinyue—Huayi bei qisu" 周迅主演電影侵權納西音樂世家音樂 華誼被起訴 (The film featuring Zhou Xun

infringes the copyright of Naxi Music's music—Huayi is sued), 27 August 2009, www
.cmusic.com.cn (accessed 11 September 2009).

Lu Shanbing 廬山冰. *Zhongguo guanggao chanye fazhan yanjiu: yige guanyu guanggaoye de
jingji fenxi kuangjia* 中國廣告產業發展研究: 一個關于廣告業的經濟分析框架 (A study of
the development of China's advertising industry: An economic-oriented analytic framework for the advertising industry). Xi'an: Shanxi renmin chubanshe, 2005.

Mu Xiaowen 木曉雯. "Fei zhuanye shijing yanchu Yingxiang Lijiang yi pinpai zhilu cu
fazhen" 非專業實景演出《印象麗江》以品牌之路促發展 (Nonprofessional live perfor-
mance *Yingxiang Lijiang* finds its development through branding), 21 August 2009,
http://yn.people.com.cn (accessed 28 November 2009).

Ouyang Jian 歐陽堅 and Ding Wei 丁偉, eds. *Guoji wenhua fazhan baogao* 國際文化發展報告
(Report on the development of international culture). Beijing: Commercial Press, 2005.

Pan Jiawei 潘嘉瑋. *Jiaru shijie maoyi zuzhi hou Zhongguo wenhua chanye zhengce yu lifa
yanjiu* 加入世界貿易組織後中國文化產業政策與立法研究 (China's cultural industries
policy and legislation after joining the WTO). Beijing: Renmin Chubanshe: 2006.

Qian Jing 錢競 and Hu Bo 胡波. "Chuangyi chanye fazhan moshi jiejian yu tansuo—yi
Shanghai wei li" 創意產業發展模式借鑒與探索: 以上海為例 (Modeling and exploring
the development of creative industries: Using Shanghai as an example). *Jingji luntan*
經濟論壇 (Economic tribune), April 2006, 47-48.

Qiu Huadong 邱華棟. *Chengshi zhanche* 城市戰車 (City chariot). Beijing: Zuojia chubanshe,
1997.

"Riben dongman huobao weihe zhengqian nan?" 日本動漫火爆為何掙錢難? (Why is the
highly popular Japanese anime and manga so unprofitable?). *Chuanmei Ribao* 傳媒日報
(Mass media daily), 5 April 2007, static.chinavisual.com (accessed 31 December 2007).

"Shaolin Si zhuanggao shangbiao pingweihui" 少林寺狀告商標評委會 (Shaolin Temple
suing Patent Office), *Mingpao* 明報, 1 December 2009, news.sina.com.hk (accessed
1 December 2009).

Sheng Wen 盛文. "Diaosu zuopin 'Shouzuyuan' yinfa 10nian banquan zhengzhan" 雕塑
作品《收租院》引發 10 年版權爭戰 (Ten years of copyright battle of the sculpture work
"Rent Collection Courtyard"), 28 December, 2009, www.sina.com.cn (accessed 3 June,
2011).

"Songzhuang huajiacun chule 'taofang jingji ren'" 宋莊畫家村出了 "討房經紀人" ("House
reoccupation agent" appears in Songzhuang painter village). *Beijing qingnian bao* 北京
青年報 (Beijing youth), 25 July 2007.

Su Xing 蘇醒. "IDEO Yataiqu zhixing zongcai Li Ruizhe: Peiyu sheji jiyin" IDEO 亞太區執行
總裁李睿哲：培育設計基因 (Cultivating genes of design). *Ershiyi shiji shangye pinglun* 21
世紀商業評論 (Twenty-first century business review), no. 57 (May 2009), finance.sina
.com.cn (accessed 3 June, 2011).

Wang Hui 汪暉. *Xiandai Zhongguo sixiang de xingqi* 現代中國思想的興起 (The rise of
modern Chinese thought). Beijing: Sanlian shudian, 2004.

Wang Shaoguang 王紹光. *Fenquan de dixian* 分權的底限 (The bottom line of decentralization). Beijing: Zhongguo jihua chubanshe, 1997.

Wang Shucheng 王樹成. "Shangye dongli jiya yishu gongchang" 商業動力擠壓藝術工廠

(Commercial forces pressing on the art factory). *Jingji cankao bao* 經濟參考報 (Economic information daily), 3 January 2005, finance.sina.com.cn (accessed 3 June, 2011).

Wu Guojun / Ng Kwok Kwan 吳國鈞. "Dianyingyuan yu Xianggang shehui, jingji mailuo xia de jingying zhuangkuang" 電影院於香港社會、經濟脈絡下的經營狀況 (Operation of cinemas under the social and economic contexts of Hong Kong). MPhil thesis, Chinese University of Hong Kong, 2009.

Xianggang maoyi fazhanju yanjiubu 香港貿易發展局研究部 (Research Department of Hong Kong Trade Development Council). *Neidi qiche shichang: lingbujianye de jiyu* 內地汽車市場: 零部件業的機遇 (Mainland's automobile market: Opportunities in automobile supplies). Hong Kong: Hong Kong Trade Development Council, 2005.

Xiao Shu 笑蜀. *Liu Wencai zhenxiang* 劉文彩眞相 (The truths of Liu Wencai). Xi'an: Shanxi shifandaxue chubanshe, 1999.

Xin Guangwei 辛廣偉. *Banquan maoyi yu huawen chuban* 版權貿易與華文出版 (Copyright trading and Chinese language publication). Chongqing: Chongqing chubanshe, 2003.

Xu Zhihao 許志浩. "Zhongguo youhua: 'zuihou de fengkuang'" 中國油畫: "最後的瘋狂" (Chinese paintings: "The ultimate madness"). *Shanghai yishujia* 上海藝術家 (Shanghai artists), no. 1 (2006), 23.

Yang Jihua 楊吉華. "Lun Woguo wenhua chanye zhengce de shishi jizhi" 論我國文化產業政策的實施機制 (On the implementation of cultural industrial policy in our country). *Zhengzhou Hangkong gongye guanli xuexue xuebao* 鄭州航空工業管理學院學報 (Journal of the Zhengzhou Institute of Aeronautic Industrial Management) 24, no. 5 (2006), 77–80.

Yang Yidong 楊屹東. "Zhongguo gudai banquan yishi yu xiandai banquan zhidu bianxi" 中國古代版權意識與現代版權制度辨析 (An analysis of China's ancient copyright concepts and its modern copyright institutions). *Tushuguan xue yanjiu* 圖書館學研究 (Research in library science), no. 1 (2006), 97–99.

Yang Yufeng 楊玉峰. "Songzhuang huajiacun: xiexshou guoji zhuming yishu jigou" 宋莊畫家村: 携手國際著名藝術機構 (Songzhuang painter village: Collaborating with internationally renowned art institution). *Chenbao* 晨報 (Morning post), 11 June 2006.

Yao Xiulan 姚秀蘭. "Zhidu jiangou yu shehui bianqian—jindai Zhongguo zhuanli lifanlun" 制度構建於社會變遷—近代中國專利立法論 (Institutional construction and social change: A discussion of patent legislation in modern China). *Falü luntan* 法律論壇 (Rule of law forum) 21, no. 4 (2006), 118–23.

Yao Xiulan 姚秀蘭and Zhang Honglin 張洪林. "Jindai Zhongguo shangbiao lifalun" 近代中國商標立法論 (The legislation of trademarks in modern China). *Fazhi luntan* 法治論壇 (Rule of law forum) 21, no. 2 (2006), 85–89.

"Zai Beijing Songzhuang mai xiaochanquanfang huajia yaoqiu cunmin peichang sunshi" 在北京宋莊買小產權房畫家要求村民賠償損失 (Painter purchasing a minor-property house in Beijing Songzhuang now seeks compensation from villager). Sina Net, 5 January 2008, http://news.sina.com.cn (accessed 31 January 2008).

Zhang Chuanwen 張傳文. "Lin Yusheng lun Wang Hui shijian: Qinghua ying fuqi zhengzhi yu daode zeren" 林毓生論汪暉事件: 清華應負起政治與道德責任 (Lin Yusheng's comments on the Wang Hui incident: Qinghua should bear political and moral responsibilities). *Nanfang dushi bao* 南方都市報 (Southern Metropolis Daily), 6 June 2010, http://big5.ifeng.com (accessed 11 June 2010).

Zhang Ke 張可. "Guojia zhishichanquan jianchazu dao Dafen jiancha gongzuo" 國家知識產權檢查組到大芬檢查工作 (State Intellectual Property Office arrives in Dafen), 2008, news.artxun.com (accessed 3 June 2011).

Zhang Zhiqiang 張志強. "Zhidu biangeng yu daoban fanlan: zhuanxingqi dalu daoban wenti yanjiu zhi yi" 制度變更與盜版氾濫—轉型期大陸盜版問題研究之一 (Institutional change and widespread piracy: Studies of the mainland's piracy problems in the time of transition, no. 1). *Jiaoyu ziliao yu tushuguan xue* 教育資料與圖書館學 (Educational information and library studies) 42, no. 2 (2004), 257–73.

Zhao Hua 趙華and Xu Yang 徐揚. "'Sun Wukong' weihe doubuguo 'milaoshu'?" "孫悟空" 為何鬥不過" 米老鼠"？(Why is the Monkey King defeated by Mickey Mouse?). *Xinhuanet.com*, 12 August 2004 (accessed 8 March 2006).

Zhao Ming 趙明. "Jianguan bumen boyi: *Moshou Shijie* qiantu buming" 監管部門博弈《魔獸世界》前途不明 (The tug-of-war between censoring departments: The future of *World of Warcraft* remains unclear). *Zhongguo jingji shibao* 中國經濟時報 (China's economic times), 5 November 2009, http://edu.cyol.com (accessed 5 November 2009).

Zhao Shufeng 趙樹楓, Chen Guangting 陳光庭, and Zhang Qiang 張強. *Beijing jiaoqu cheng-shihua tansuo* 北京郊區城市化探索 (A reading of the urbanization of Beijing's provincial areas). Beijing: Shoudu shifan daxue chubanshe, 2001.

Zhong Baoxian 鍾寶賢. *Xianggang yingshiye bainian* 香港影視業百年 (One hundred years of Hong Kong's film and television industries). Hong Kong: Sanlian shudian, 2004.

Zhonggong zhongyang guowuyuan 中共中央國務院 (State Council of the PRC). *Zhongguo zhishi chanquan baohu zhuangkuang* 中國知識產權保護狀況 (The status of the protection of China's intellectual property rights). Beijing: Wuzhou chuanbo chubanshe, 1994.

———. "Guanyu shenhua wenhua tizhi gaige de ruogan yijian" 關於深化文化體制改革的若干意見 (Opinions on deepening the reform of cultural institutions). *Remin ribao* 人民日報 (People's daily), 13 January 2006, http://politics.people.com.cn (accessed 12 May 2007).

Zhongguo chuban kexue yanjiu suo 中國出版科學研究所 (China's Publication Science Research Centre) and Quanguo guomin yuedu yu goumai qingxiang chouyang diaocha keti zu 全國國民閱讀與購買傾向抽樣調查課題組 (Committee on surveying nationwide citizens' reading and purchasing trends). *Woguo guomin dui daoban chubanwu de renshi* 我國國民對盜版出版物的認識 (Our citizens' understanding of pirated publications). Beijing: Zhongguo chuban kexue yanjiusuo, 1999.

"Zhongguo shu Ri kangnaixin she qinquan shoucha" 中國輸日康乃馨涉侵權受查 (The Chinese carnations exported to Japan are under IPR inspection). *Mingpao* 明報, 14 May 2006.

Zhongguo touzi zixunwang 中國投資諮詢網 (China Investment Consulting Web), ed. *2007–2008 nian Zhongguo wenhua chanye jidi fenxi ji touzi zixun baogao (shang xia juan)* 2007–2008 年中國文化產業基地分析及投資諮詢報告（上下卷）(Analysis and investment report of China's creative industry base 2007–2008, 2 vols.). Beijing: Zhongguo touzi zixunwang, 2007.

Zhonghua Minguo Xingzhengyuan 中華民國行政院 (Council for Economic Planning and

Development, Executive Yuan, Republic of China). *Tiaozhan 2008: Guojia fazhan zhong-dian jihua* (2002–7) 挑戰2008: 國家發展重點計畫 (2002–7) (Challenge 2008: National development focus plan [2002–7]), 2003, www.edu.tw (accessed 3 June 2011).

Zhonghua Renmin Gongheguo Guojia Tongjiju 中華人民共和國國家統計局 (National Bureau of Statistics of China). "Wenhua ji xiangguan chanye fenlei" 文化及相關產業分類 (Classification of culture and related industries). 2004, www.stats.gov.cn (accessed 16 April 2007).

Zhonghua Renmin Gongheguo Guojia Zhishichanquanju 中華人民共和國國家知識產權局 (State Intellectual Property Offices, PRC). "Anli texie: Dongba zaozhi yiren zaoyu zhuanli ganga" 案例特寫: 東巴造紙藝人遭遇專利尷尬 (Case in focus: The patent embarrassment of Dongba paper-making artisans). 11 November 2005, www.sipo.gov.cn (accessed 10 November 2007).

Zhonghua Renmin Gongheguo Wenhuabu 中華人民共和國文化部 (Ministry of Culture, PRC). "Guanyu jinyibu jiaqiang shaoshu minzu wenhua gongzuo de yijian" 關於進一步加强少數民族文化工作的意見 (Opinions on further strengthening the cultures of racial minorities). 13 February 2000, law.lawtime.cn (accessed 3 June, 2011).

Zhou Hongyu 周紅玉. "Linggan, laizi '798'" 靈感，來自"798" (Inspiration, from "798"). *Xin Jingji daokan* 新經濟導刊 (New economic journal), 2 June 2006.

Zhou Lin 周林 and Li Mingshan 李明山. *Zhongguo banquan shi yanjiu wenxian* 中國版權史研究文献 (Collection of historical documents on China's copyright history). Beijing: Zhongguo fangzheng chubanshe, 1999.

Zhu Zhe 朱喆. "Zhiding wenhua zhengce fagui, tuidong Shenzhen wenhua chanye fazhen" 制定文化政策法規, 推動深圳文化產業發展 (Establishing the legislature of cultural policy, promoting the development of Shenzhen's cultural industries). *Tequ jingji* 特區經濟 (Economics of the special zone), no. 9 (2005), 322–23.

Zuo Lin 左林. "'798,' Beijing 'chengshi mingpian' de weilai" "798" 北京 "城市名片" 的未来 ("798": The future of Beijing's "city identity"). *Zhongguo xinwen zhoukan* 中國新聞週刊 (*Chinese Newsweek*), 6 March 2006.

Zuo Xuchu 左旭初. *Zhongguo shangbiao falü shi: Jinxiandai bufen* 中國商標法律史：近現代部分 (The legal history of trademarks in China: Late Qing and modern periods). Beijing: Zhishi chanquan chubanshe, 2005.

Japanese Materials

"Kaikyo! Nihon anime-shijō hatsu no Chūgoku kōkai kettei!! *Gin'iro no kami no agito*" 快挙! 日本アニメ史上初の中国公開決定! ! 『銀色の髪のアギト』, (Fierce! The first Japanese anime publicly screened in China: *Silver-haired Agito*), 2006, www.gin-iro.jp (accessed 20 February 2006).

Kanō Seiji 叶精二. "*Kaze no tani no naushika* kara *Mononoke no hime* e—Miyazaki Hayao to Sutajio Jiburi no 13 nen" 「風の谷のナウシカ」から「もののけ姫」へ—宮崎駿とスタジオジブリの13 年 (From *Nausicaa of the Valley of the Winds* to Princess Mononoke: 13 years of Studio Ghibli), 1997, www.yk.rim.or.jp (accessed 25 February 2006).

Miyazaki Hayao 宮崎駿. *Kaze no tani no naushika* 風の谷のナウシカ (*Nausicaa of the Valley of the Winds*), vols. 1–6. Tokyo: Tokuma Shoten, 1987.

Index

Laikwan Pang is professor of cultural studies at
The Chinese University of Hong Kong. She is the
author of *The Distorting Mirror: Visual Modernity in
China* (2007) and *Cultural Control and Globalization
in Asia: Copyright, Piracy, and Cinema* (2006).

Library of Congress Cataloging-in-Publication Data
Pang, Laikwan.
Creativity and its discontents : China's creative industries
and intellectual property rights offenses / Laikwan Pang.
p. cm.
Includes bibliographical references and index.
ISBN 978-0-8223-5065-1 (cloth : alk. paper)
ISBN 978-0-8223-5082-8 (pbk. : alk. paper)
1. Cultural industries—China. 2. Creative ability—
Economic aspects—China. 3. Intellectual property—
China. 4. Intellectual property infringement—China.
5. Law and economic development. I. Title.
HD9999.C9473C455524 2012
338.4'7700951—dc23
2011027537